Roman Philosophy and the Good Life

Roman Philosophy and the Good Life

RAYMOND ANGELO BELLIOTTI

LEXINGTON BOOKS
A division of
ROWMAN & LITTLEFIELD PUBLISHERS, INC.
Lanham • Boulder • New York • Toronto • Plymouth, UK

Published by Lexington Books
A division of Rowman & Littlefield Publishers, Inc.
A wholly owned subsidiary of The Rowman & Littlefield Publishing Group, Inc.
4501 Forbes Boulevard, Suite 200, Lanham, Maryland 20706
http://www.lexingtonbooks.com

Estover Road, Plymouth PL6 7PY, United Kingdom

British Library Cataloguing in Publication Information Available

Library of Congress Cataloging-in-Publication Data

Belliotti, Raymond A., 1948-
    Roman philosophy and the good life / Raymond Angelo Belliotti.
        p. cm.
    Includes bibliographical references and index.
    ISBN 978-0-7391-3969-1 (cloth : alk. paper) -- ISBN 978-0-7391-3970-7 (pbk. :
alk. paper) -- ISBN 978-0-7391-3971-4 (electronic)
    1. Philosophy, Ancient. 2. Epicureans (Greek philosophy) 3. Stoics. I. Title.
    B505.B45 2009
    180.937--dc22   2009015282

To Marcia, Angelo, and Vittoria

Nella città dell'insuccesso le strade

sono fatte di scuse

Contents

Preface

This is a book for those who are drawn to Roman history and politics, and, especially, for those who enjoy viewing philosophy in action. The Romans were practical people not lured to philosophical abstraction for its own sake. Instead, the most thoughtful among them looked to philosophy for guidance on how to live. Lacking a religion that provided a thick book of do's and don'ts for everyday existence, Romans celebrated moral and political exemplars from their own tradition; they were instinctively drawn to sentimentalizing and mythologizing their illustrious past; and they were convinced that the world was a battleground for military and political glory.

Honoring relentless competition and championing a merciless class-divided society often coalesced unsteadily with venerating the rule of law and advancing the common good. Romans steeped in their own traditions and intoxicated by their military and political successes cast wary eyes on foreign influences such as Greek philosophy. Yet they would come to see the need for philosophies such as Stoicism, Epicureanism, Platonism, and Aristotelianism to point the way to leading the good life.

Influential Romans in the final days of the republic such as Caesar, Pompey, Cicero, Cato, Brutus, and Cassius were saturated with Roman traditions, customs, and expectations. They struggled valiantly with the often conflicting demands of seeking personal salvation, honoring philosophical conviction, and fulfilling patriotic duty. Later, during the building of the Roman empire, icons such as Seneca, Musonius Rufus, and Marcus Aurelius confronted the same conflicts but in different political contexts. Each of these men, whether operating in the republic or in the empire, arrived at different tentative resolutions to those conflicts. This book chronicles their stories.

The conflicts and struggles of the Romans discussed in this work mirror enduring concerns that are part of the human condition. Who am I? How should I live my life? What, if anything, is my destiny? These questions were theirs, they are now ours, and they will soon belong to our children. I conclude each chapter by providing a glimpse of the contemporary relevance of the issues and challenges that vexed these honorable Romans. The quest to attain robustly meaningful and valuable human lives is timeless.

Chapter 1 briefly describes the life and times of Cicero, the man most responsible for the spread of philosophy in Rome. An adherent of the Skeptical Academy, Cicero also had deep appreciation for Stoic ethics. I explain and analyze the highlights of his thinking, and stress the five competing dimensions of his character and convictions that animated his philosophical vision. Although he was not a participant in the assassination of Caesar, Cicero later celebrated and sketched a justification of the deed. I use that sketch to develop a general analysis of when, if ever, citizens are morally justified in assassinating their political leaders.

Chapter 2 introduces the fundamental methods and beliefs of Stoicism through the life and thought of Cato the Younger. Although Cicero exaggerated when he called Cato "The Perfect Stoic," that Cato's reputation for moral rectitude and his courageous battle against perceived tyranny inspired future generations is beyond dispute. I subject basic Stoicism to critical scrutiny and conclude by introducing the image of the joyful transcender, a portrait drawn from the work of Friedrich Nietzsche and Robert Nozick. The joyful transcender shares several crucial Stoic convictions, but offers a much different picture of the good life for human beings.

Chapter 3 explores Epicureanism through the words and acts of Lucretius, Caesar, and Cassius. A brief history of the rise of hedonism and the bedrock beliefs of Epicurus is followed by an explanation of the poetic refinements to Epicureanism offered by Lucretius. The relationship between philosophy and political action is then discussed in the contexts of Caesar and Cassius. Finally, I take up the Epicurean challenge to explain how death can be bad for human beings even though when we are alive, death is not with us and when we are dead we are no longer. In so doing, I also advance and defend a view of how posthumous events can harm or benefit human beings.

Chapter 4 takes a close look at the events of the Ides of March. The assassination of Caesar marks the intersection of politics and philosophy. The major players rationalized and justified their plot by appeal to philosophical doctrine; they selected some of their fellow travelers only after examining the answers candidates offered to philosophical questions; and their motives were partially fueled by adherence to the doctrines of particular philosophical schools. After revisiting the lives and thoughts of Caesar, Brutus, and Cassius, I apply the analysis of assassination developed in chapter 1 to draw conclusions about the murder of Caesar.

Chapter 5 deepens the discussion of Stoicism by probing Roman refinements to doctrine offered by Seneca, Musonius Rufus, Epictetus, and Marcus Aurelius. Several of these thinkers also held political positions and their struggles with the conflicting demands of conscience, of the expectations of their offices, and of philosophical principles are illustrative. I underscore the Stoic cognitive theory of the emotions and why Stoics were convinced that deep emotional reactions were nearly always generated by epistemological errors. Finally, I offer a contemporary version of the cognitive theory of the emotions that concludes, against the Stoics, that human emotions are the ballast of a robustly meaningful, valuable life.

The purposes of this book, then, are multiple: First, to provide an accessible picture of the major philosophical influences in Rome, especially Stoicism and Epicureanism. Second, to show the role philosophy played during these times of major political upheaval. Third, to illustrate the contemporary relevance of some of the philosophical issues that beset the Romans.

Fourth, to learn from the past—drawing strength from Roman insights and correcting Roman excesses where appropriate—as we face our own struggle to sculpt meaningful, valuable lives.

Acknowledgments

I owe debts of gratitude to Joanne Foeller for her exceptional word processing, editing, and indexing skills, and unvarying good cheer; to Bill Wallace, an old and dear friend, whose love of competitive sports vivified my youth and whose discussions with me, spanning almost fifty years, about Roman history inspired me to write this book; to Bill Jacobs, an expert in Greek philosophy, who generously and effectively read and critiqued the manuscript prior to publication. His comments led to numerous improvements in the work; and to my family— Marcia, Angelo, and Vittoria—for nourishing my soul and animating my spirit.

I deeply appreciate the editors of the following journals and publishers for granting me permission to adapt, reprint, or revise my previously published work: *Happiness is Overrated* (Lanham, MD: Rowman & Littlefield Publishers, 2004); *What is the Meaning of Human Life?* (Amsterdam: Rodopi, 2001); *Good Sex: Perspectives on Sexual Ethics* (Lawrence, KS: University Press of Kansas, 1993); *Seeking Identity: Individualism versus Community in an Ethnic Context* (Lawrence, KS: University Press of Kansas, 1995); *Justifying Law* (Philadelphia: Temple University Press, 1992); *Watching Baseball, Seeing Philosophy: The Great Thinkers at Play on the Diamond* © 2008 Raymond Angelo Belliotti by permission of McFarland & Company, Inc., Box 611, Jefferson, NC 28640 www.mcfarlandpub.com; and "Do Dead Human Beings Have Rights?" *Personalist* 60 (1979): 201–10.

Introduction

The Philosophical Schools

At first blush, the plan was ingenious. Rome was about to levy a tax on Athens in 155 BC that Athenians found onerous and misconceived. How might the Athenians sway the Romans and preserve their resources? Well, they would play to their strength and summon their big guns: Athens would run out its greatest philosophers! The Athenians sent Rome a coterie of their highest-powered theorists, an unequalled dream team of intellectuals: Diogenes of Seleucia, leader of the Stoics; Critolaus the Peripatetic; and Carneades the Skeptical Academic. Surely, this trio, unsurpassed in persuasive power, would win the day and compel the Romans to recant their error.

Rarely has one country misunderstood another so wildly. Philosophical wisdom, as it often has, was met with stern reprisals. Carneades notoriously presented two orations on political philosophy. The first was a brilliant ode to the natural virtue of Roman justice. The second was an equally brilliant refutation of his first oration that concluded that justice was merely a conventional expedient. Marcus Porcius Cato (237–149 BC), known historically as Cato the Elder or Cato the Censor, shocked at the malleability of Carneades's methods, convinced the senate to send Carneades and his cronies packing. Cato was convinced that studying philosophy would seduce the youth into reassessing and possibly repudiating Roman traditions and customs. Cato insisted that the future leaders of Rome would better spend their time venerating law and established social conventions. Sweet talking philosophers were as dangerous to the Roman republic as lascivious poets, innovative theologians, and radical politicians. The oratorical legerdemain of the Skeptical Academy was squandered on hostile ears.

However, philosophy, much like prodigal children and destitute in-laws, was fated to return. The gods of the Greco-Roman world did not provide clear rules of behavior for everyday life. Human beings living during those periods observed natural phenomena and their own personal qualities. Lacking a refined science to provide explanations, they mythologized their observations into a pantheon of deities—fertility, love, pestilence, famine, thunder, rain, power, anger, and the like, were all represented. Stories were conjured that accounted for the occurrence of, say, famine—the governing deity in this area must have been offended by human conduct. Elaborate ceremonies intended to please the gods were established, as well as rituals of atonement after the gods had been insulted and had retaliated. Beyond the felt need to curry favor with the gods and avoid divine retribution, few specific principles of behavior followed. Philosophy was the discipline that was destined to fill this void and address the fundamental questions of human existence: What is the good life? Why am I here?

What, if anything, is my destiny? How should I live my life?

For centuries in Greece, four major philosophical schools competed for advocates: Socratic-Platonism, Aristotelianism, Stoicism, and Epicureanism. These schools would also set the terms for Roman philosophy.

The Academy

Around 387 BC, Plato (428–347 BC) founded a philosophical school, located about one mile from the Dipylon Gate in Athens. At that time, no system of organized higher education was available to young men who had completed basic schooling. Those who sought advanced training became apprentices to doctors, architects, and tradesmen, or employed the services of traveling teachers, the Sophists. Teaching the art of persuasion—a skill crucial for a successful public life in the Athenian courts and assembly—the Sophists wandered from town to town putting on rhetoric displays and hiring out to the scions of the upper class. Plato stigmatized the Sophists for charging fees for their services; for shilling glib rhetoric techniques instead of searching for objective truths; and for embracing a flaccid system of moral relativism. Plato's academy featured a rich curriculum staffed by several instructors, and provided a counterweight to Sophistic teachings. The academy underwent changes, but endured until the Eastern Roman Emperor Justinian banned the pagan schools of philosophy in AD 529. Historians cite five distinct phases of Plato's academy.

The Old Academy, also called the First Academy, centered on Platonic questions and their refinements. Upon Plato's death, his nephew, Speusippus became head of the academy. The third head was Xenocrates of Chalcedon. The nature of Being, the implications of Platonic dualism, the relationship of the Forms to mathematics, and the nature of the ethical life were paramount concerns. Human happiness, the school argued, flows from moral virtue alone, but moral virtue is not the only human good. The Old Academy sought certainty as the foundation of the knowledge required to lead the good life. Polemon of Athens and Crantor of Cilicia were the last two heads of the Old Academy. Throughout this work, *I will refer to the Old Academy as the Platonic Academy.*

The Middle Academy, also called the Second Academy, is identified with Arcesilaus of Pitane (316–241 BC) who assumed leadership around 268 BC. Arcesilaus rejected dogmatic Platonic metaphysics and, instead, stressed the skeptical side of Socratic-Platonism: the bromide that Socrates's wisdom was grounded in a negative dialectical—he knew with certainty only that he did not know; the structure of the early Platonic dialogues that ended not with final answers, but only more nuanced questions; and the assault on dogmatism that underwrote Socrates's interrogations in the marketplace. Arcesilaus even emulated Socrates's aversion to committing his views to writing. Arcesilaus centered his critical analysis on the inconsistencies infecting Stoic epistemology and argued for a suspension of judgment while both sides of an issue were debated openly and thoroughly. Stoics argued that certain sense perceptions were so distinct and clear that we could entertain no reasonable doubt about them. Wise men used such perceptions to ground firm conclusions. Arcesilaus countered that the senses are an unreliable guide to truth and inflexible philosophical systems must be shunned. The ongoing search for truth, whether finally and firmly attainable or not, was frustrated by premature and self-defeating dogmatism. Where suspension of judgment was impossible, such as the domain of morality where choice and action under conditions of uncertainty were required, the standard of reasonableness should apply. In any case, wise men do not pontificate. The proper result of philosophical inquiry is the elimination of poorly grounded beliefs.

The New Academy, also called the Third Academy, was inaugurated by Carneades of Cyrene (214–129 BC). His skepticism went far beyond Stoic epistemology and gleefully scourged all dogmatism. He invoked a standard of probabilism as a guide for action. Carneades insisted that wise men could still render opinions and act resolutely in the face of epistemological uncertainty. Human beings pursue more than moral virtue and the guidance of probabilistic reasoning is enough to fulfill our reasonable desires. Stoic absolute certainty and correctness are unnecessary and unattainable. For Carneades, our sense perceptions are not stamped on the blank slates of our minds. Instead, our subjectivities influence our perceptions. Accordingly, sense perceptions cannot ground objective certainty. Carneades also defended human free will and argued against several Epicurean and Stoic claims about the gods. Of course, he did not embrace the existence of a transcendent world of Forms. For Carneades, the dominant epistemological theories failed to establish anything about knowledge. In sum, Carneades extended his skeptical arguments regarding ethics and epistemology to cover every possible philosophical theory, but retained a probabilistic account that permitted conviction and action in practical matters. Carneades could not conclude definitively that knowledge is impossible, only that it appeared to be thus.

The Fourth Academy is identified with Philo of Larissa (160–80 BC). He argued that truth and falsity are metaphysically different, but human reason and judgment cannot access and discern that difference. Wise men make choices and act on a provisional certainty, but should suspend judgment on theoretical matters. True sensations often mix with false sensations so tightly and the two types sometimes resemble each other so closely that certain judgments are unavailable. Philo, although a skeptic, moderated the methods of Carneades and built bridges to advocates of the Old Academy. He resided in Rome around 88 BC, lectured on rhetoric and philosophy, while greatly impressing Cicero. Throughout this work, *I will refer to the Second, Third, and Fourth Academies as The Skeptical Academies.*

The Fifth Academy was energized by Antiochus of Ascalon (130–68 BC). Antiochus was concerned that the skeptical academies had destroyed proper criteria for truth and falsity. Without such criteria, social and moral action became problematic. His remedy was to insist that the senses could ground truth claims that could be grasped by the mind as self-evident. Antiochus strove to minimize the differences between the academic school, Stoicism, and the Peripatetics: they quibbled merely on terminology not in substance: "The content of Antiochus's view was a combination of the Stoic belief in certain knowledge on reliable sense-perception with the ethical theory of Aristotle and his followers the Peripatetics, which laid down that virtue, though the highest good, was not the only good: such things as health, wealth, and a certain length of days were also necessary components of the absolutely good or perfect life for man."[1]

Thus, for Antiochus, happiness, the final human good, was possible through virtue alone; but the highest happiness requires external goods such as health and a measure of material prosperity. While the highest part of human nature is the soul, human perfection required that all parts of our nature be fulfilled. Embracing a form of eclecticism, Antiochus reserved the right to change allegiance as he saw fit. Antiochus studied under Philo but deviated from his teacher's convictions. Cicero studied with Antiochus in Athens around 79 BC and lauded him as the sharpest philosopher of his time. Antiochus claimed to be restoring the doctrines of the Old Academy and argued, against Philo and Carneades, that the human intellect could distinguish truth from falsity. Against the skeptics, Antiochus argued that if no certain assumptions are available then skeptical conclusions themselves are dubious. Skepticism, then, falls prey to the self-referential paradox: its own assertions undermine its philosophical conclusions. In sum, Antiochus sought to resurrect the Old Academy by uniting the doctrines of other philosophical schools, particularly the Stoics and Peripatetics. However, his unifying aspiration often coalesced uneasily with the historical facts and the doctrines of the competing philosophical schools. Throughout this work, *I will refer to the Fifth Academy as The Eclectic Academy.*

The Peripatetics

Aristotle (384–322 BC) founded the Peripatetic school in 335 BC at the Lyceum. The name of the school derived from the Greek word for covered walking place. Aristotle may also have taught while walking with his students. Aristotle laid the foundation for the Peripatetic conviction that human flourishing requires more than moral virtue. The good life must also embrace a host of external goods: friendship, congenial family relations, a measure of material accumulation, honorable reputation, and the like. Theophrastus (371–286 BC) became head of the school in 323 BC. He was most responsible for preserving and disseminating Aristotle's work for future generations, although Theophrastus refined several of Aristotle's major ideas in logic and metaphysics. The focus of the Peripatetics was the study of worldly phenomena energized by empirical methods. Strato of Lampsacus succeeded Theophrastus around 286 BC and remained head of the Peripatetics until his death around 269 BC. He was most interested in scientific and natural philosophy, with a keen influence from the pre-Socratic cosmologists. He argued against Aristotelian teleology and in favor of a non-mechanical necessity. Strato rejected personal immortality, divine providence, and the possibility of disembodied souls. After Strato's death, the Peripatetics stressed examination of the proper way to attain the good life and issues underlying rhetoric. Gradually losing much of its distinctively Aristotelian motivation, the Peripatetics were eventually revitalized by Andronicus of Rhodes who became head of the Peripatetic school around 58 BC. Cratippus of Pergamum succeeded Andronicus as head of the Lyceum in 44 BC. Cicero called Cratippus—who tutored Cicero, his son, and Marcus Junius Brutus at different times—the most distinguished of the Peripatetics. Cratippus rejected most appeals to divination, although he retained faith in dreams and supernatural inspiration. Direct action of the divine mind on the human soul allegedly generated such inspiration. The Peripatetics, resurrecting their earlier emphasis on rhetoric, gained renown for their ability to debate both sides of an issue, a crucial oratorical skill. Peripatetics generally believed that anger, if moderate and justly directed, was appropriate and virtuous. In fact, passivity where anger is justified is inappropriate.

Stoicism

Following the law of nature was the major imperative of the Stoics. Founded by Zeno of Citium (336–264 BC) on a *stoa* (porch), the Stoic school gained early momentum under the leadership of Cleanthes of Assos (303–233 BC) and Chrysippus of Soli (280–206 BC). As mentioned earlier, around 155 BC, Diogenes of Seleucia, leader of the Stoic school, arrived with Carneades the Skeptical Academic and Critolaus the Peripatetic on an ill-fated mission to persuade the Romans to refrain from levying a fine on Athens.

Zeno set the foundation for Stoic theory: follow nature instead of social convention and custom. Chrysippus, though, was the early thinker most responsible for developing Stoic philosophy. He was a versatile logician and theorist, who purportedly composed over seven hundred books. Chrysippus was also well known for his replies to Skeptical Academics such as Arcesilaus.

Basic Stoic doctrine included the following: Human wisdom, founded on moral virtue, is the key to the good life; the world is orderly and purposive, and guided by reason and natural laws; the divine is not located in a single place, but, instead, permeates all of nature; the divine, as the reason that controls and structures nature, determines events; thoughts are generated from sense perceptions furnished by physical objects; everything in the universe is a form of dynamic, changing, ordered matter; matter behaves in accordance with the principle of reason that permeates it; divine providence generates events; human beings also embody a spark of the divine as each person's soul is part of divinity; human wisdom arises from distinguishing what is within our control from that which is outside of our control; human beings should recognize and accept the specific roles they have been assigned by the divine in the drama that is life; happiness grounded in serenity is the mark of wise people; navigating the flow of events artfully distinguishes the good life; freedom is best understood as the absence of emotional turmoil; all human beings are members of the same community; suicide is appropriate when an honorable or qualitatively meaningful life is no longer possible; the emotions of love, sorrow, pity, hate, and anger all threaten our prospects of attaining the good life; and human beings share a moral duty to promote social structures that reflect the rationally ordered physical cosmos.

Panaetius of Rhodes (185–110 BC) introduced Stoicism to Rome around 140 BC. He moderated Stoic asceticism, found a place for external goods in a revised Stoic understanding of the good life, and stressed degrees of progress in meeting the Stoic ideal of the sage. Posidonius of Apamea (135–51 BC) refined the Stoic conviction in the basic unity of the cosmos and concocted a purportedly ideal age of history in which human beings flourished by following nature. Later Stoics, such as Seneca (4 BC–AD 65), Musonius Rufus (30–100), Epictetus (55–135), and Marcus Aurelius (121–180), placed decidedly Roman twists on basic Stoic doctrines.

Epicureanism

Founded by Epicurus (341–270 BC), an Epicurean community, called the Garden, emerged in Athens around 307 BC. The members aimed at a pleasurable life grounded in friendship, tranquility, and moderation. After the death of Epicurus, the school was headed by Hermarchus of Mytilene. The most renowned Roman Epicurean was the poet Lucretius (95–50 BC).

Basic Epicurean doctrines include the following: the sensations of pleasure and pain are the criteria of value and disvalue, respectively; pleasure is the greatest good and the foundation of a happy life; some pleasures are natural and necessary, such as food; other pleasures are natural but unnecessary such as sex; still other pleasures are neither natural nor necessary, such as material luxury and fame; wisdom and self-control are required to sustain pleasure; the good life is defined by the absence of bodily pain and serenity of the mind; desires should be pared, fears overcome, and mental calm nurtured; sexuality and love typically produce frustration and disappointment; friendships are crucial to the good life; pleasures of the mind are more valuable than bodily pleasures; the state is required to establish adequate conditions for human life, but it cannot create the good life for individuals; wise people will withdraw from robust political and social projects; the gods do not interfere with human affairs; neither the gods or death are to be feared; human destiny includes neither personal immortality nor divine judgment; the good life is within the reach of everyone and requires no technical or deeply theoretical training; physical objects are purely material and composed of atoms; atoms have no beginning and were thus not created by gods; atoms fell freely and independently in space until one underwent a lateral swerve that energized a host of collisions; human beings, the gods, celestial bodies, and physical objects in the world are the product of these accidental collisions; no cosmic purpose, order, or design underwrites human life; human conventions, not natural laws, justify social arrangements; and moral virtue is merely an instrumental good that leads to happiness.

The Romans were tough, practical people weaned by a military culture and honed by relentless competition. Philosophy, with its unbridled joy in critically analyzing fundamental beliefs, threatened the traditions and convictions that had solidified into Roman common sense. Worse, philosophy was imported from Greece, a country Rome viewed as inferior in all important dimensions. Yes, Greece surpassed Rome in literature and learning, but Rome prevailed in the crucial domains of regulating social life: family, household efficiency, social institutions, and practices. Romans lagged behind in music, poetry, and geometry only because they did not highly value those disciplines. Surely, where both Romans and Greeks invested a comparable interest, Roman products were superior. Preeminent in war, in construction, in government, in rhetoric, and in law, Romans were gravely suspicious of foreign ideologies and social practices. Could any sane person doubt that Roman military, political, and moral *practices* were vastly superior to Greek *theories*? Worse, excessive study of philosophy could too easily diminish a citizen's contributions to the state: he might be lured away from public life by the seductions of the idleness of philosophical contemplation; he might be seduced by impractical doctrines which distorted social reality; or he could become uppity and reluctant to subscribe to the authority of established legal, political, and social norms. The politically subversive dimensions of Greek philosophy were numerous and striking.

Still, with the brief appearances of the Athenian representatives of three philosophical schools in 155 BC and the increasingly pressing need to understand crucial matters of human existence and destiny, opening the gate to Greek philosophy was inevitable. Marcus Tullius Cicero oiled the hinges of the gate.

Note

1. A. E. Douglas, "Cicero the Philosopher," in T. A. Dorey, ed., *Cicero* (New York: Basic Books, 1965), 145.

Chapter One
The Skeptical Academy: Cicero

This chapter briefly describes the life and times of Cicero, the man most responsible for the spread of philosophy in Rome. An adherent of the Skeptical Academy, Cicero also had deep appreciation for Stoic ethics. I explain and analyze
the highlights of his thinking, and stress the five competing dimensions of his
character and convictions that animated his philosophical vision. Although he
was not a participant in the assassination of Caesar, Cicero later celebrated and
sketched a justification of the deed. I use that sketch to develop a general analysis of when, if ever, citizens are morally justified in assassinating their political
leaders.

Life and Times

Marcus Tullius Cicero (106–43 BC) was a Renaissance man centuries before
that phrase had been coined. Lawyer, orator, politician, poet, and philosopher,
Cicero was the most versatile intellectual of his time. He was born in Arpinum, a
hill town about seventy miles south of Rome. Cicero's family was prosperous
but lacked genetic ties to the Roman senatorial class. Cicero's father was a
member of the equestrian class ("knights" who were landowners or business-
men). Impaired by ill-health, he set a paternal example for Marcus Tullius by
studying relentlessly. He moved the family to Rome around 91 BC to advance
the education and social prospects of his two sons.[1]

As a young man, Cicero met and absorbed the teachings of Phaedrus the
Epicurean, Philo of Larissa, head of the Skeptical Academy, and Diodotus the
Stoic. The world of the mind and the contemplation of enduring questions attracted Cicero as strongly and inexorably as a floodlight draws a moth. More
important, philosophical study was crucial to Cicero's quest to fashion himself
into the ideal orator. Cicero understood his scholarly gifts and simmered with
ambition. The Roman path to enduring glory was sharply bordered: military and
political excellence was the required vehicle for the journey. Oratory might well
serve as Cicero's chauffeur.

Although temperamentally and physically unsuited for military life, Cicero
was prepared to pay the entry fee for his trip to immortality. At the age of sixteen, he began a two-year military hitch under Gnaeus Pompeius Strabo (father
of "Pompey the Great") and Lucius Cornelius Sulla in the Social War, in which
Rome tussled with an alliance of Italian communities seeking greater accommodations.

In 81 BC, Cicero made his first splash as an attorney defending Sextus
Roscius, who was accused of parricide. Cicero demonstrated that the accusation

was false and concocted by a disreputable lackey of Sulla, who was hurling terror as the dictator of Rome. Cicero's strategy would later define textbook legal
defense: he argued that Roscius did not and could not commit the murder; he
offered other suspects with motive, opportunity, and means to commit the crime;
and he impugned the henchman of Sulla who inspired the allegation. Cicero's
impassioned advocacy won the moment and Roscius was acquitted. Given the
gravity of the charge and the viciousness of the man who inspired it, every other
lawyer in the city demurred when asked to assist Roscius. Cicero gained an immediate following and reputation. He was heralded by some citizens as a virtuous counterweight to Sulla's regime; he was denounced by others as a stone cold
fool. Understanding Sulla's typical response to those brazen enough to oppose
his designs, Cicero scurried out of Italy. For the next several years he studied
philosophy, rhetoric, and oratory in Athens and Rhodes, including a stint with
Antiochus, founder of the Eclectic Academy.

After Sulla died, Cicero returned to Rome. He became a quaestor in 75 BC.
Quaestors, who were elected annually, managed financial matters in Rome or
assisted the financial administration of the Roman provinces by serving as governors (proconsuls). Cicero shone as quaestor of Western Sicily. Sicily was the
breadbasket of Rome and Cicero was in charge of hustling grain from Sicily to
the city. At first blush, the Sicilians resented serving as the agricultural resource
for the mainland. But Cicero's administrative qualities of justice, clemency,
honesty, and compassion were unprecedented on the island. The Sicilians were
grateful for his overall influence and regretted his return to Rome at the end of
his service.

Cicero and the Sicilians, though, would soon be reunited in cause. In 70 BC,
the Sicilians were outraged by the excesses of Gaius Verres, the evil governor
Rome had sent to rule the island. They turned to Cicero to prosecute the case.
Verres, understanding the magnitude of the situation, hired the most honored
barrister and orator in Rome, Quintus Hortensius, to defend him. The adage reminds us that "to be the best you must defeat the best." Cicero prevailed. Verres
was convicted and fled into exile. Cicero was henceforth considered the ablest
lawyer and orator in Rome.

Cicero married Terentia. Determined and politically ambitious, she was
spawned from an influential Roman family. He rose up the *cursus honorum*—the
"course of honors" that comprised the sequence of Roman political offices—
with alacrity. A quaestor in 75 BC, curule aedile in 69 BC, and praetor in 66 BC,
Cicero held each office at the youngest age of eligibility. When Cicero became
an aedile, his friends, the Sicilians, honored the occasion with an avalanche of
presents. Instead of padding his own bank account, Cicero used their largesse to
reduce the public price of food and goods. In general, Cicero spurned two roads
to political success: lavish spending on entertainments and spectacles—which
would serve Gaius Julius Caesar (100–44 BC) well—and self-righteous austerity
which considered such spending ostentatious extravagance. Cicero, as always,
preferred moderate allocations to serve the public to the bread and circuses so
appreciated by the masses.

Throughout his life and despite enormous success, Cicero was plagued with doubts and insecurities. In Rome, he was a *novus homo* ("new man"), unconnected genetically to the patronage of the established nobility. A *novus homo* had not been elected consul since 94 BC.

Cicero was approaching age forty-three, the youngest age of eligibility. The big score remained. Cicero lusted to be elected a consul during his first year of eligibility. But the Roman nobility enjoyed its stranglehold on this highest political post. Their family honor required that consular families hold power in every generation. Only two consuls were elected each year. Little room existed for a *novus homo*, with neither pedigree nor Roman birth, to squirm through. Cicero needed a larger-than-life ally to realize his political dreams. Only one man qualified: Gnaeus Pompeius Magnus (Pompey the Great) (106–48 BC). Cicero curried favor by supporting the law that gave Pompey supreme command against the forces of Mithridates in Asia Minor. That and other speeches rendered on Pompey's behalf secured the influence that helped rocket Cicero to the position of consul. In 63 BC, the *novus homo* had scampered up the highest mountain and peered down on Rome. Cicero was on top of the world.

The most noteworthy event during Cicero's year as consul was his role in extinguishing the Catilinian conspiracy. Lucius Sergius Catilina (Catiline) (108–62 BC), unsuccessful candidate for consul and profligate noble, plotted to seize power through force. In a series of orations, Cicero unmasked the plot and exposed Catiline, who fled from Rome to Etruria to regroup his forces. Several of Catiline's co-conspirators, though, were arrested. After they were forced to confess their crimes in front of the senate, deliberations began about their proper punishment. Julius Caesar, struggling mightily to quell the growing sentiment for execution, argued that the prisoners should have their estates confiscated then be imprisoned for life in various Italian towns. After all, executions of Roman citizens without trial were illegal and would set a pernicious precedent. But Marcus Porcius Cato (95–46 BC), the moral compass of the senate, advocated forcefully for the death penalty. Cato, impudent and accusatory as ever, levied his firm suspicion that Caesar, given his fervent compassion for the evil-doers, was also a member of the conspiracy.

Moreover, the senate passed a *senatus consultum ultimum* ("the senate's ultimate decree") that suspended constitutional protections and granted consuls emergency powers. In effect, such a decree gave senatorial endorsement to whatever actions consuls devised to protect the republic during extraordinarily dangerous times. Still, although it was clear that Catiline had taken up arms against the republic, the co-conspirators had not been nabbed in the act of rebellion. A type of *res ipsa loquitor* notion prevailed: their storehouse of arms, connections to Catiline, and coerced confessions spoke for themselves. The senate, swayed by Cato and Cicero, soon passed a decree for the execution of the conspirators. Cicero, accordingly, escorted the prisoners to the most notorious prison in Rome where they were strangled. For him, the conspirators, as enemies of the state, had forfeited their rights as citizens. Lacking support in Rome, Catiline mounted a revolutionary offensive and was slain at the battle of Pistoia.

The Catilinian conspiracy had met its deserved end.[2]

Although Caesar and his cohorts remained dissatisfied, Cato, who was a tribune at the time, extolled Cicero's consulship. Cicero was lavished with public honors typically reserved for military heroes. With Cato's urging, Cicero was honored with the title *Pater Patriae* (Father of the Country): "Brave and determined as he had been, the praise unfortunately went to Cicero's head. Always susceptible to flattery, he was never slow to remind others of his achievement."[3] However, as time passed and the felt danger of revolution evaporated, Cicero's role in the Catilinian conspiracy would bring more than just unambiguous praise. His political enemies would be quick to remind the public that Cicero wholeheartedly transgressed a sacred Roman law that prohibited political executions of citizens without trial.

During his consulship, Cicero also presented three stirring orations that helped defeat an agrarian law advanced by the tribune Publius Servilius Rullus. This proposal united important agriculture reform with the creation of a commission that would have nurtured the political ambitions of Caesar and Marcus Licinius Crassus (115–53 BC). By the conclusion of the Catilinian conspiracy, Cicero was politically aligned with the *optimates*, the conservative, aristocratic faction in Rome committed to limiting the power of the popular assemblies and the plebeian tribunes; to extending the influence of the senate; to curtailing the extension of Roman citizenship; to preserving traditional ways; and, ironically in Cicero's case, to restricting the ascension to political power of new men (*novi homines*). Cicero was thereafter a staunch political conservative, who defended the ruling aristocrats with unparalleled zeal and philosophical argument.

Caesar and Crassus were politically aligned with the *populares*, the reformist, aristocratic-military faction in Rome committed to strengthening the power of the plebeians; to mitigating the influence of the senate; to distributing food and land to the poor; to relocating some Roman citizens to the provinces; to expanding Roman citizenship; to lavishing generous economic rewards for victorious military forces; and to nurturing greater concentration of executive authority as the most effective, efficient means to progressive change. Unsurprisingly, the *optimates* were replete with senators obsessed with retaining their own prerogatives and privileges, under cover of venerating Roman tradition and established glory, while the *populares* harbored no shortage of green-eyed power-hounds, lusting after their own political preeminence cloaked in the slogan "power to the people."

On the first day of 62 BC, Cicero mustered out of the consulship and became a private citizen. The new consuls awarded him a position of honor as leader of the senate. In the summer of 60 BC, Caesar returned from a successful military campaign and ran successfully for the consulship. After his term, the senate refused to assign him an important governorship. Thereafter, Caesar entered into the covenant known as the first triumvirate with Crassus, the wealthiest man in Rome, and Pompey, who, with Caesar, was fast tiring of the senate's opposition. Pompey also married Caesar's daughter, Julia. Cicero was asked to join these merry swashbucklers, considered the offer carefully, but his loyalty to the republican constitution won out over his personal ambition. Cicero had been linked with Pompey; he thrived on Caesar's cunning flattery; and was never completely accepted by the Roman aristocracy. He was tempted, but the better angels of his nature prevailed.

A major enemy emerged for Cicero: the wild, vengeful, violent, Publius Clodius Pulcher (92–52 BC). While a quaestor in 61 BC, Clodius, apparently armed with the motive of seducing Caesar's wife, tried to crash an all-female religious rite held at Caesar's home. Shades of Alcibiades! His ploy to impersonate a female musician, unsurprisingly, crumbled. Clodius escaped, but was tried for blasphemy. Cicero demolished Clodius's alibi. But the first lesson of Roman history is that the republic could not keep an enterprising thug down forever. Through the timeless intrigues of force and fraud—in this case, intimidation and bribery of the jurors—Clodius escaped. The second lesson of Roman history is that in the republic today's villain was tomorrow's man of the year. Clodius sought the office of tribune in 58 BC. Unfortunately, that office was open only to plebeians, while Clodius's blood was bluer than Frank Sinatra's eyes. Clodius, never a stickler for rigid rules, solicited his adoption into a plebeian house, this accomplished with the blessing of the members of the first triumvirate. Yes, one of whom was the same Caesar who was targeted by Clodius to be cuckolded three years earlier.

Once he attained office, Clodius, as would any successful hellcat, began to hurl righteous vengeance on his enemies. He charged Cicero with executing Roman citizens without a trial. Cicero, the moniker of Father of the Country weaving unsteadily, argued that the *senatus consultum ultimum* provided him legal authority for his deed. He tried to consolidate support from politicians, especially the members of the first triumvirate. Caesar offered Cicero a position on his staff in Gaul as a way of evading Clodius's design, but Cicero thought that escape mechanism dishonorable. That was the first triumvirate's first, final, and best offer. Thereafter, the silence was stunning. Cicero, sensing the force of the gale that was gathering, fled in exile. Clodius proposed a bill prohibiting everyone within 500 miles of Italy from permitting Cicero into their home. This bill was modified by Cicero's allies and roundly ignored by the people. Clodius then razed Cicero's home, and dedicated the ground to the goddess *Libertas*. Ever the grateful scion, Clodius also passed a law bestowing free grain upon the plebeians.

Cicero spiraled into mental depression. Stumbling from the top of the world to Palookaville in about five years often has that effect: "During the period of his exile, Cicero appears in a poor light; he did not endure his adversity with fortitude, and showed an unattractive (but very human) inclination to blame other people for his predicament, even suggesting that some of the advice that did not turn out well had been given treacherously."[4] All of Cicero's deepest insecurities were amplified: "His desire for public recognition was increased by his exile, after which he seems to have felt that only the voting of a Triumph for him could heal that wound to his vanity and his sense of justice. But it would be a hopeless task to try to palliate every instance of his touchiness."[5]

His exile also strained relations with his wife, who apparently mismanaged financial affairs in his absence. The third lesson of Roman history, though, is that in the republic the authority of cutthroats and desperados had a brief shelf life: gangsters always overreached. The influence of Clodius and his posse of heavily armed thugs was dependent on the support, or at least benign neglect, of the members of the first triumvirate. Clodius, never one to be cautious where rashness was an option, rallied the senate against Pompey the Great. After being threatened by one of Clodius's sword-brandishing hooligans, Pompey retreated to the safety of his home. Clodius's reign of terror, though, was doomed. The members of the first triumvirate supported the tribune Titus Annius Milo as a political adversary, a type of counter-thug, to Clodius.

Do you remember the second lesson of Roman history? After sixteen months in exile, Cicero was recalled to Rome, amid cheering crowds and considerable pomp. Yes, at least sometimes, absence does make hearts grow fonder. Cicero soon thereafter retaliated against Clodius, charging that Clodius, an unrepentant patrician, had attained the office of tribune illegally. Accordingly, Cicero insisted that all of Clodius's actions while a tribune should be invalidated. Cato, although no fan of Clodius or his methods, opposed Cicero. Cato feared the violence such a widespread policy would have on the rule of law. Less loftily, Cato understood that many of Cato's own decrees while serving as governor of Cyprus and Byzantium during that period might be invalidated. This disagreement would weaken, although not destroy, the friendship between Cato and Cicero.

In April, 56 BC, Cicero dropped the political ball. Still fantasizing a republic, guided by Pompey and under the senate, he hatched a scheme. He attacked Caesar's land bill in an effort to sever Pompey, who was fast distancing himself from Crassus, from Caesar: a classically bad read. Pompey also supported the land bill, which benefited his former soldiers. The first triumvirate closed ranks at a conference at Lucca: Caesar's command in Gaul was renewed for five more years; Pompey and Crassus were to be consuls in 55, with Pompey overseeing Rome and Spain while Crassus sought military glory by invading Parthia. Cicero had to back off from his opposition as his senate colleagues deserted him. He had been thoroughly outflanked by the first triumvirate.

The fourth lesson of Roman history is that in the republic those who lived violently would die violently. Clodius, whose strong suit was intimidation and bribery at the hands of his armed gangs, was whacked by Milo and his gladiators when the two groups met on the Via Appia in 52 BC. Clodius's relatives accused Milo of murder. Cicero, who had supported Milo since his own return from exile, was asked to defend the accused. Cicero, perhaps unnerved by the vehemence and vitriol of Clodius's supporters, rendered a less than stirring performance. Milo, who did not aid his cause by his haughty demeanor, was found guilty and fled into exile. Cicero, whether from guilt or to fix the record, composed a glorious speech, *Pro Milone,* a rewritten version of his defense of Milo, which eloquently chronicled the case for the defense.

The members of the first triumvirate kept Cicero on a short leash, compelling him to defend their sycophants in court and casting suspicious eyes on his political initiatives. He turned to philosophy for consolation and therapy. Cicero was, though, elected to the elite priesthood of Augurs, assuming the spot of Crassus's son, who had died in his father's disastrous military expedition in Parthia. In 51 BC, Cicero was appointed governor of Cilicia. As always, he administered frugally, justly, and compassionately. After his forces defeated pesky bandits terrorizing Mount Amanus, Cicero was saluted as *Imperatore* by his forces. Cicero, ever the glory-hound, sought a triumph in Rome to commemorate his military victory. A triumph (*triumphus*) was often awarded Roman commanders after a significant, victorious campaign. An ornate procession, feasts, games and spectacles, and the bestowal of special privileges upon the honored commander highlighted the event. To soften pretensions and repel the jealousy of sensitive gods, soldiers of the amplified general would later congregate and subject him to ribald teasing.

But the stormy clouds of civil war raged on the horizon. No time remained for pomp and circuses. After Crassus's defeat and death, the relentless rioting between Clodius's and Milo's rival gangs, and the marginalization of Cicero, Pompey was sole consul while Caesar campaigned in Gaul. Sharing power was not on the agenda of either man. Each began jockeying for the political edge. Caesar wanted to run in 49 for the consulship in 48. In 51, the senate, with a wink and a nod from Pompey, refused a request from Caesar for a short prolongation of his command in Gaul. The schism between Caesar and Pompey expanded into an abyss by 50 BC. The senate, fearing that a Caesarian consulship would spell the death of the republic, plotted to indict Caesar during his brief period as a private citizen between the termination of his command in Gaul and his becoming consul-elect for 48 at the voting in 49.

In August, 50 BC, Cicero received a letter from a friend:

> Whereas Pompey is determined not to allow Caesar to become consul unless he gives up his army and provinces, Caesar is convinced that he cannot be safe once he has parted with his army. Caesar does, however, propose this compromise, that both should give up their armies. (Ltr 58: 8/8/50 BC)

Cicero had periodically written letters to both Caesar and Pompey to smooth out their differences. He had a longstanding alliance with Pompey and a friendship with Caesar, yet he distrusted the long term motives of both military leaders. The *amicitia* (friendship) between Caesar and Cicero was asymmetrical: Caesar, through his largesse, wanted Cicero to be politically dependent upon and obliged to him, while Cicero preferred to keep their *amicitia* personal.

Cicero, who returned to Rome after his one-year term in Cilicia, understood unequivocally that he must soon take a side, but he wavered: Pompey seemed to have the more noble cause, but Caesar was more decisive and the more able administrator of military and political affairs. Most important, Cicero's *amicitia* with Pompey was both political and personal (or so Cicero thought), whereas his *amicitia* with Caesar was only personal (at least from Cicero's perspective). The

Roman network of *amicitiae* and *clientelae*—family and political connections bound by traditional, financial, or mutually advantageous considerations—played a dominant role in the machinations of the time. Moreover, Cicero was not the keenest evaluator of men and their motives. He did sense, correctly, that both Caesar and Pompey were more concerned about their individual *dignitas* (worth, merit, reputation) than about the common good. This, though, was the stock in trade of most Roman politicians during this period. As T. A. Dorey attests:

> In the Ciceronian age, the main objective of a Roman Senator was not the upholding of some political principle but the maintenance of his own *dignitas*. To change sides, to join the stronger party, in order to enhance one's *dignitas*, was quite in accordance with the normal and accepted code of political ethics. . . . Never was there an age in the history of the Roman Republic when unscrupulous opportunism and the uninhibited pursuit of self-interest could reap a richer reward.[6]

On December 1, 50 BC, the senate voted by a margin of 370 votes to 22 that both Caesar and Pompey should resign their commands in order to avoid civil war. A few days later, rumors circulated that Caesar had crossed the Alps and was marching on Rome. The *optimates* argued that Caesar should be declared a public enemy and two legions should be dispatched to oppose him. A tribune of the plebeians, Gaius Scribonius Curio (90 BC–49 BC), who was loyal to Caesar, vetoed the motion and insisted, accurately, that the rumors were false. Curio was forced to leave Rome and hustled to Ravenna, where Caesar was quartered. He encouraged Caesar to amass his army and proceed to Rome. Caesar, determined not to be the instigator of civil war, refused. Instead, he sent a messenger to urge his supporters in Rome to propose that he be allowed to retain two legions and his provinces in Cisalpine Gaul and Illyricum until he assumed his consulship. He was willing to immediately relinquish Gaul and the legions stationed there.

Pompey was willing to accept this compromise. The consuls and the *optimates*, though, rejected Caesar's petition. When he learned of this, Caesar sent Curio to Rome with another message: Caesar would surrender his command at the same time as Pompey. But should Pompey refuse, Caesar would retain his command and move quickly to avenge the wrongs committed against him and his country. Curio arrived in Rome on December 31. He delivered Caesar's ultimatum to the newly elected consuls, Lucius Cornelius Lentulus and Gaius Claudius Marcellus. They refused to bring the proposal before the senate. Caesar, with keen foresight, had anticipated their recalcitrance. When Curio's tribuneship had expired on December 10, Caesar had maneuvered his cronies, Marcus Antonius ("Marc Antony") (83–30 BC) and Quintus Cassius Longinus, into position as tribunes of the plebeians. They argued forcefully that Caesar's proposal should be taken before the senate. The consuls demurred.

On the next day, the senate endorsed a resolution advanced by Quintus Caecilius Metellus Pius Scipio, Pompey's father-in-law, that Caesar should disband his army prior to March 1, 49 BC, or be considered a treasonous enemy of the state. The senate passed the decree with only two dissenting votes. Antony and Cassius vetoed the measure. The tribunes of the people were shortly thereafter forced out of the city. The senate then passed a *senatus consultum ultimum* empowering state officials to take all necessary measures to protect the republic.

The *optimates* in the senate, careless observers of the general whose enmity they courted, assumed obtusely that Caesar would await the arrival of his eighth and twelfth legions in Gaul prior to marching on Rome. Caesar, whose trademarks were speed and boldness, assembled his fabled thirteenth legion, about 5,000 infantry and 300 cavalry, and moved resolutely. At daybreak on January 10, 49 BC, he shouted "Let the dice fly," and crossed the Rubicon River, which divided Cisalpine Gaul from Roman Italy. The Roman Civil War had begun. The republic so cherished by the *optimates* would never be the same.

Cicero decided not to commit himself until he had spoken to Caesar. Caesar desired Cicero's backing. After all, Cicero was an outspoken, respected, republican senator whose allegiance could provide strong legitimacy to Caesar's cause. When they met, in March, Cicero insisted that he be permitted to address the senate freely and to propose that Caesar not extend the war to Spain and Greece, and that he be allowed to speak sympathetically about Pompey. Caesar expressed his misgivings. Cicero demanded either free speech or the right to absent himself from senate deliberations. Caesar coldly concluded that if he could not convince Cicero to join him, he would use the advice of those he could convince. In any case, Caesar was clear that he would stop at nothing. Negotiations broke down (Ltr. 75: 3/28/49 BC).

Cicero, finally, judged that duty and loyalty weighed more heavily in favor of Pompey. Moreover, Caesar was more likely to harbor monarchial designs on Rome than Pompey, who was less interested in political matters. Pompey may have desired to be the leading figure in Rome, but Caesar lusted for complete political control of the world. A victory by Caesar meant tyranny: redistribution of private property, cancellation of debts, the return of political scoundrels from exile, and honors, authority, and prestige to the undeserving. Cicero's aristocratic heart ached.

Caesar's aspirations were nourished by the corruption and selfishness rife in the republic. Bribery, violence, plundering of the provinces, and the quest for material bounty overwhelmed the common good and civic virtue.

> The Ciceronian age was marked by decay and disintegration leading to the final collapse. Even more than before, senators and equestrians had embarked on a frenzied course of self-aggrandizement, each for himself in an insatiable quest for property and riches, and a bloody lust of power after power. . . . "No administration in history has ever devoted itself so whole-heartedly to fleecing its subjects for the private benefit of its ruling class as Rome of the last age of the Republic."[7]

Soon after Caesar crossed the Rubicon, Pompey unwisely abandoned Italy and withdrew to Greece. Convinced that his greatest strength lay in the East, especially in Greece and Syria, Pompey reasoned that Caesar's supply lines would be strained as he struggled in lands hostile to him. The fifth lesson of Roman history is that in the republic fleeing from the homeland did not amplify one's political or military legitimacy. Caesar was able to traipse through Italy virtually unopposed. As already noted, he had urged Cicero to join his cause, but after negotiations between the men broke down, Cicero skipped out of Italy and joined Pompey.

Cicero's welcome in Pompey's camp was underwhelming. Cato scolded him for yielding his role as peacemaker, Pompey had no clear use for a man lacking honed military skills, and the military officers talked mostly about the vengeance they would exact once Caesar was defeated and they returned to Rome. Worse, Cicero was stunningly unimpressed by Pompey's preparations and war strategies, or the lack thereof. Cicero wrote his friend Titus Pomponius Atticus (110–32 BC), a wealthy, cultured, Epicurean, who avoided direct participation in politics but intensely followed events:

> Both [Pompey and Caesar] have aimed at personal domination, not the happiness and fair fame of the community. Pompey did not abandon Rome because he could not have defended her, nor Italy because he was driven from her shores. His plan from the first has been to ransack every land and sea, to stir up foreign kings, to bring savage races in arms to Italy, to raise enormous armies. . . . Neither sees our happiness as his mark. Both want to reign.[8]

Caesar destroyed Pompey's supporters in Spain. He followed Pompey to Greece and, as predicted, his supply lines were slim to zero and slim was suffocating from lack of space. Nevertheless, aided by Pompey's curious timidity, Caesar's forces, although badly outnumbered, won the decisive battle at Pharsalus in 48 BC. As the battle neared completion, Caesar demanded that his men not slay Roman citizens unnecessarily. Caesar's seemingly boundless mercy for vanquished enemies extended to the senate's leaders who had opposed him. Thoughts of subsequent purges and proscriptions, the standard fare of victorious generals, never entered his mind. Caesar followed Pompey to Egypt, where Pompey had been murdered by his ungracious hosts while transferring from his ship to a vessel to transport him to shore. Caesar was by then the absolute ruler of Rome, holding the posts of consul in 48 and 46 BC, annual dictatorships during that period, and, finally, dictator for life in 44 BC.

Cato tried to convince Cicero to assume command of the remainder of Pompey's forces after Pharsalus. After all, Cicero was the senior ex-consul among Pompey's supporters. Cicero refused. He would return to Italy and make his peace with Caesar. Cicero was almost murdered by Pompey's sons for this decision. Cato's intervention was crucial in preventing the assassination. In late summer of 48 BC, Cicero returned to Italy. He waited for Caesar for over a year in Brundisium.

Once Caesar arrived, predictably, reconciliation flowed. Caesar, magnanimous and merciful in victory, was pleased to forge a peace with Cicero. He publicly demonstrated his esteem for Cicero as the two men strolled arm in arm. Cicero, not exactly bargaining from strength, was relieved to escape retribution.

Caesar thought he could make fine use of Cicero in healing the wounds in the Roman polity. Cicero fantasized that Caesar would restore the republic or, at least, that he would not install a monarchy. Marcus Tullius Cicero was almost sixty years old. His future was radically uncertain.

Cicero increasingly committed himself to philosophy, while Caesar engaged the vestiges of Pompey's forces in Africa. In April, 46 BC, the climactic battle was won by Caesar's men at Thapsus. Caesar, conciliatory as always in victory over fellow Roman citizens, offered to pardon Cato. However, the unrepentant Stoic committed suicide rather than owe his life to his most despised enemy: death before dishonor. Cicero wrote a eulogy to Cato, being careful to avoid directly disparaging Caesar and his allies: "Cicero was greatly moved by Cato's death. He had found him an unbearable nuisance who bore no little responsibility for the slide into civil war. But his suicide burned away the inessentials of his character, leaving him as the symbol of pure principles and of a lost time for which he mourned."[9] Caesar, in an uncharacteristic strategic blunder bereft of grace and class, wrote an Anti-Cato response, in which he hurled every imaginable accusation against the deceased conscience of the senate, while generously lauding the life and work of Cicero. Cicero also struggled to gain the pardon and recall of his numerous friends still in exile. He could endure Roman politics only when Caesar was present. Caesar's allies were not as forgiving as their leader.

Early in 46 BC, Cicero divorced Terentia, from whom he had grown increasingly estranged over the years. He thought she had betrayed him, perhaps cheating out of some money, and was generally repelled by her financial instincts. Cicero's political failures, Terentia's poor choice of a husband for their daughter, and Terentia's disinterest in the intellectual matters that animated Cicero also contributed to the dissolution of the marriage. In late 46 BC, he married a young girl, Publilia, who had been his ward. Virtually all Roman marriages had a political, social, or financial genesis; so, too, the coupling of Cicero and Publilia. He needed her money, in part to repay the dowry of Terentia. Cicero's second marriage was ill-fated. Early in 45 BC, shortly after the wedding, Tullia, Cicero's daughter, died after childbirth. Cicero was inconsolable and driven into his deepest depression. Publilia, young and undiplomatic, was insufficiently sympathetic, probably because she was jealous of Cicero's unbridled affection for his daughter. Later that year, when Cicero received a significant legacy from a banker in Puteoli, he divorced Publilia.

The death of his beloved daughter was too much for Cicero to bear. He withdrew into his philosophy books, especially those addressing the expiation of grief. Friends such as Marcus Junius Brutus (85–42 BC), Caesar, and Servius Sulpicius Rufus (106–43 BC), governor of Greece, wrote him consoling letters. For several months, Cicero composed philosophy prolifically.

Time and the therapy of philosophy drew Cicero back into politics. But Caesar ruled supreme, having been named dictator for life in 44 BC. Cicero longed for the return of the republic—which would coincidentally increase his political influence—but appreciated the personal attributes of Caesar: "Cicero did not hate Caesar the man; whenever he met him he came under the spell of his personal magnetism, but he did hate what Caesar had done to the political life of the free Republic which he loved. This does not mean that Cicero wanted him killed; he probably agreed with Caesar himself that his death would only provoke a new civil war."[10]

The conspirators who assassinated Caesar on March 15, 44 BC, made no effort to include Cicero in their design. Although Cicero and Brutus were confidants, the architects of Caesar's slaying understood keenly that Cicero labored under too much political and personal baggage to aid their plot. First, Cicero was garrulous and might unwittingly jeopardize the secrecy of their intrigue. Second, Cicero was indecisive and this was a time for action, not a moment for carefully weighing the reasons for and against the scheme. Third, Cicero was naturally timid and cautious, and the plot demanded physical courage. Fourth, Cicero was manifestly drawn to Caesar on a personal level.

Despite such misgivings, Brutus allegedly called out Cicero's name, invoking him to restore the republic, as he removed his bloody dagger after the assassination. A year later, Cicero wrote to one of the conspirators expressing regrets that he was not included in the plan and that the assassins did not also execute Antony: "How I wish you had invited me to that splendid banquet on the Ides of March. There would have been no leavings! As it is they [Antony and other Caesarian loyalists] are causing us such trouble that we feel your immortal service to your country left something to be desired" (Ltr. 142: 2/2/43 BC). He also wrote to Brutus: "You had banished a great plague, wiped out a great stain on the Roman people, and won immortal glory for your own names" (Ltr. 147: 7/15/43 BC).

Later, in his *De Officiis*, Cicero argued along Stoic lines that Caesar's murder was morally just: human beings are obligated to preserve the well-being of other human beings; tyranny destroys, generally, the welfare of society; Caesar's reign was a growing tyranny; under such circumstances, slaying the tyrant is a moral duty even where the tyrant is a personal friend to whom greater concern is otherwise owed than to people generally (O 3.19, 3.32).

> If a man murders a tyrant, even if he is a friend, has he thereby implicated himself in a criminal act? The Roman people in fact do not think so, for they regard this as the most noble of illustrious deeds. . . . We do not share fellowship with tyrants. On the contrary, there is the widest cleavage between them and us, and should it lie within your power, nature does not forbid you to rob the person whom it is honorable to kill. Indeed, the whole of that noxious, sacrilegious breed should be banished from human society. Just as certain parts of the body are amputated once they begin to be drained of blood . . . so once the savagery and brutality of the beast takes human shape, it must be excised, so to say, from the body of humanity which we all share. (O 3.19, 3.32)

This attempt at justification, though, seems more an after-the-fact examination of the deed. If Cicero was thoroughly convinced of the argument prior to the Ides of March, why did he not discharge his alleged moral duty and hatch his own assassination plot? In Cicero's post-assassination evaluation, Caesar deserved death because he aspired to kingship. Cicero also claimed—either disingenuously or delusionally—that the assassination of Caesar had wide popular support.

> All good men, so far as their own power went, slew Caesar; some lacked a plan, others courage, others opportunity: will no man lacked . . . in [the senate's and even Marc Antony's] judgment [the slayers of Caesar] are saviors . . . they have been absolved by [the senate and Marc Antony] from crime, by [the senate and Marc Antony] they are adjudged most worthy of the fullest rewards. (P 2.12, 2.13)

Cicero assumed a leading role during the political and social instability that ensued. Although he had never appreciated Marc Antony, Cicero labored mightily as a peacemaker to avoid civil war. Once the terms of Caesar's will were read and his largesse undeniable—he left every citizen a sum of money and his land as a public domain—a mob joined Caesar's military veterans in riots. Cicero's amnesty efforts brought mixed results. Soon thereafter, Cicero, responding to Antony's personal attack, delivered the first of fourteen *Philippic Orations*, biting invectives against the tyranny of Antony. He also cultivated Caesar's heir, the young Gaius Octavian (later, Augustus Caesar) (63 BC–14 AD). Cicero strategized that he could cultivate Octavian, exploit his standing as Caesar's chosen one, and then discard him when propitious. Octavian needed Cicero to supply a patina of legality upon his actions.

Antony was driven from Rome and defeated in battle. *Optimates* cheerfully anticipated that their polity would be restored. But Octavian, sensing Cicero's design for him from one of Cicero's speeches in the senate, set in motion with Marcus Aemilius Lepidus plans for a second triumvirate, which would include Antony. Antony was pleased to sign on but only after the trio composed a proscription roll. A proscription was a recurrent Roman technique of politically purging dissenters. The reigning state authorities composed a hit list of, typically prominent, people who were declared public enemies. The rulers seized their property and placed a contract on their life. The murderers of those listed were generously rewarded for their service to the state.

Antony insisted that Cicero head that list. Octavian allegedly resisted for two days, and then relented. Whether this is true is highly contestable. The members of the second triumvirate were also confiscating the lands of eighteen Italian towns to reward their military forces. The specific towns and the particular proscription victims were negotiated during those two days. Given Antony's unwavering obsession to whack Cicero, that Octavian would even provisionally jeopardize his chance for autocratic power to rescue Cicero is difficult to accept.

The proscriptions violated every element of the rule of law. They were directed at specific citizens who were condemned without trial, and required not merely death but decapitation. Assassins were well rewarded; slaves who rendered service would gain their freedom; and anyone who aided victims would themselves be proscribed. Rumors of the hit list circulated throughout Rome.

Cicero moved to his villa in Tusculum. When official word of the proscriptions filtered through Italy, Cicero was unsure whether to flee to Greece. He started once, but then returned. Assassins captured him at a villa at Formiae. Cicero, never perceived as physically courageous, faced doom with poise and grace. He stared steadfastly into the eyes of his murderers, stuck his neck out of the carriage in which he was being transported, and awaited his decapitation. By Antony's command, Cicero's hands and head were impaled on the rostrum, where the orators spoke, in the Roman forum. Antony's wife, Fulvia, former widow of (Who could make this up?) Clodius, allegedly stuck pins in Cicero's tongue. Treachery and desecration ended the life of Rome's most learned citizen on December 7, 43 BC.

Cicero's Temperament and Philosophical Allegiance

Critics have maligned Cicero for his vanity, indecisiveness, and single-minded quest for honor.

> He was always excessively pleased with his own praise, and continued to the very last to be passionately fond of glory; which often interfered with the prosecution of his wisest resolutions . . . he also filled his books and writings with his own praises, to such an excess as to render a style, in itself most pleasant and delightful, nauseous and irksome to his hearers; this ungrateful humor like a disease, always cleaving to him . . . he was intemperately fond of his own glory.[11]

These annoying personal traits flowed not from arrogance, but from insecurity. The *novus homo* competed in a culture that prized social standing, military prowess, pedigree, and political excellence. Cicero's only weapons were his nimble mind, rhetorical style, and educational advantage.

> One must make up one's mind to be amused rather than exasperated by [Cicero's] constant itch for applause and appreciation. It is only one symptom of . . . the determining element in Cicero's character—his dependence for his peace of mind on the good opinion of others. . . . As a "new man" with ambitions he had felt that his only chance of success and happiness was to adapt himself to the ways of the aristocracy to which his talents had obtained him entry. . . . Another result of this dependence on others was a tendency to hero-worship.[12]

He was not physically tough; he lacked antecedent connections to political power and social status; and he was never convinced that his hard-won successes would endure. Caesar, ever crafty, understood instinctively how to curry Cicero's support even when their interests conflicted: he played to Cicero's insecurities and patriotism, while offering vague promises of enduring glory. The overachieving Cicero, ever fearful that his merit would be washed away, was obsessed with external validation and struggled mightily to court it. His boundless self-satisfaction at being named Father of the Country in the aftermath of the Catilinian conspiracy, his quest for a triumph after his military forces prevailed in a minor battle, the self-promotion that infected too much of his writing, and his irresistible attraction to the limelight flowed from the pernicious currents that tormented his soul: doubt, inadequacy, vulnerability, and anxiety. Moreover, the avid pursuit of glory, Stoicism and Epicureanism notwithstanding, was underwritten by Roman values and Peripatetic philosophy. Deserved, enduring glory was perhaps the only way to strike back at the Grim Reaper.

However, Cicero's love of country, acute intellect, oratorical panache, and commitment to public service were undeniable. Cicero internalized the Roman veneration of high energy and disdain for idle relaxation. He pursued his political, philosophical, and literary labors with an almost deranged avidity. Moreover, despite his reputation for queasiness under pressure, Cicero acted courageously and resolutely on several occasions: his defense of Sextus Roscius; his determination during the Catilinian conspiracy; his rejection of the offer to join the first triumvirate; his refusal, prior to his exile, to be bought off by Caesar's offer of a post in Gaul; his decisiveness during his failed negotiations with Caesar just prior to civil war; his actions after Caesar's assassination, particularly with his *Philippic* orations against Antony; and his aplomb at the moment of his death.

T. A. Dorey provides a balanced view of Cicero's personality:

[Cicero] was out of place in a world where political power ultimately rested on the power of the sword. . . . He was not a man to offer resistance when resistance was clearly futile; if he had to make up his mind as to which was the lesser evil of two possible courses, he often showed hesitation and irresolution; but whenever he was faced with a choice between two practicable alternatives, he usually chose the one that was the more honorable and the more dangerous.[13]

Contemporary philosophers are enthralled by the self-deceit that their temperaments are irrelevant to their work. We pretend that only the dispassionate search for truth is paramount and our philosophical conclusions are unaffected by our interests, purposes, and aspirations. This self-understanding is critical to a discipline that prides itself on logical rigor and a quasi-scientific method. My view is that this self-understanding is seriously flawed. However hard we may try, philosophers, their temperaments, and their work are inextricably bound. My defense of this view, though, must be left for another day.

I introduce it here, though, to begin the discussion of Cicero's philosophy. Cicero's philosophical allegiance is unsurprising given his basic disposition. The Skeptical Academy suited Cicero perfectly. Although he had a strong appreciation for all of the Greek philosophical schools—Epicureanism finished far up the track—Cicero was most strongly attracted to the notions of suspending judgment on theoretical matters where appropriate; acting on the most reasonable, most probable, evidence where decisions were required; examining carefully all sides of a question; and rejecting dogmatism wholeheartedly. This approach, after all, most carefully tracked his personality and his profession. The Skeptical Academy was most suited to people, such as Cicero, who were lawyers by trade and intellectual adventurers by character (A 2.46–63; 2.99–105).

Cicero might be viewed as adopting a flaccid eclecticism. Such an indictment is unfair. The Skeptical Academy provides a philosophical approach that does not of itself establish substantive conclusions. The imperatives to follow the most probable and reasonable course of action; to suspend judgment where appropriate; to examine carefully all sides of a question undogmatically; to join rhetoric with philosophy, and the like, do not automatically generate answers to specific philosophical questions. Instead, they establish only a mindset from which to proceed. Philosophical answers, founded on probability and reasonableness, may be supplied or created from various sources or schools. We should hope that the resulting body of conclusions would form as cohesive a whole as practicable, bearing in mind that Cicero might well suspend judgment on crucial theoretical matters where inconclusiveness persists. Moreover, Cicero can be expected to adopt substantive philosophical positions more frequently during hopeful political and personal times than during periods of crisis. Doubts, anxiety, and political upheaval tend to fuel skeptical inclinations. Social and personal contexts always greatly affect philosophy.

Cicero had great respect, particularly, for Stoic ethics and the Platonism of the Old Academy. He was less enamored of Stoic rigidity and lack of human compassion. Epicureanism, at least at first reading, coalesced uncomfortably with basic Roman beliefs. First, that pleasure was the greatest good struck Romans as indolent and unmanly. Even though Epicureanism grounded that pursuit in the intellectual and moral virtues, the doctrine was so easily misinterpreted, in theory and practice, as the unrestrained quest for luxury and leisure. Moreover, Epicureans oscillate unconvincingly between defining pleasure as the absence of pain and as positive fulfillment. If absence of pain is the chief good, then why do we allegedly desire pleasure (DF 2.6–10; 2.28–39)? Second, that wise men refrained from political activity and social entanglements struck at the core of Roman civic virtue. Although some avowed Epicureans, such as Gaius Cassius Longinus (85–42 BC), senator and one of the primary architects of the assassination of Caesar, participated in politics, they did so by ignoring the counsel of Epicurus or through a strained reading of doctrine or by an appeal to emergency conditions. Epicureanism, to many Romans, championed selfishness and withdrawal during social crisis, when political participation was most required.

Thus, Cicero rejected the Epicurean belief that pleasure was the greatest human good, in part because it did not reside comfortably with traditional Roman values. Cicero also disparaged Epicurean physics: the atomic swerve, the denial of the infinite divisibility of matter, and the conviction that the sun is only as large as it appears were unconvincing.

> The political struggle [in Rome] was mirrored in an ideological struggle . . . between Epicureans, who believed all the world is composed of atoms in constant flux, that nothing is permanent, including human institutions; and Stoics, who

believed that the world was a divine creation, perfect and immutable, including all the institutions supported by [repressive oligarchs]. To Cicero and Cato and their faction, the Epicureans were as subversive as the Communists and fellow travelers to Joe McCarthy. The great bulk of Cicero's writings are devoted to unmasking Epicureanism as ungodly, unRoman, and destructive of all the ancestral values.[14]

Stoic doctrines of natural law, an orderly, rational universe and divine providence, though, resounded patriotically with Roman practices. For Cicero, Roman traditions and the *mores maiorum* (customs of fathers and ancestors) were the adjudicators of philosophical convictions, at least those related to social action. The Epicurean belief that pleasure was the supreme good was incompatible with traditional Roman values (DF 2.67–68), whereas the Stoic precepts of divine providence, natural law, and abstemious living glittered with the wisdom of Roman folklore (ND 3.95; D 2.148; L 1.39). Combined with his allegiance to the Skeptical Academy's guideline of acting on what was probable, even if unprovable, Cicero often adjusted his philosophical beliefs to accommodate the *mores maiorum*.

However, to insist that Cicero invariably demanded that coherence with Roman traditions was a requirement of acceptable philosophical conclusions is too strong. But such coherence offered a sterling recommendation. Moreover, the doctrines of the philosophical schools were more elastic than commonly supposed. For example, Stoicism, while generally favoring political participation, advised withdrawal in the face of certain obstacles such as a thoroughly corrupt regime, ill health, or suppression of free speech. Epicureanism, which generally championed withdrawal from robust social life, allowed political participation in emergency situations. What constituted the requisite Stoic obstacle and Epicurean emergency was invariably contestable.

In general, understanding the place philosophy would assume in relation to the imperatives of Roman tradition and political exigencies is critical. Cicero also interpreted, at times, the *mores maiorum* in ways compatible with his philosophical beliefs. For example, in March of 49, when Cicero was deciding whether to join Pompey in the East, he weighed the competing claims of *utile* (expediency) and *honestum* (right action). Cicero concluded that the Stoics were correct: nothing could be *utile* which was not *honestum*.

Perhaps we should look more to the language of decision and justification when we are trying to understand the role that philosophy played in the thought and conduct of Roman statesmen. . . . Philosophy provided the moral vocabulary and the concepts with which to analyze moral problems. But it was Cicero who had to decide what the *honestum* [morally right action] was in [the case of deciding whether to join Pompey in the East in 49 BC], as in any other, particular case.[15]

Some thinkers have argued that Cicero was first affiliated with the Skeptical Academy as represented by Philo, and then drawn to the Eclectic Academy (which purported to revive the Old Academy) represented by Antiochus, only to return to the Skeptical Academy represented by Carneades around 45 BC.[16] Others argue that what first appears as a shift in philosophical allegiance is otherwise explainable:

> There was always an antagonism in Cicero. He strongly wished to believe in certain doctrines: Immortality of the soul, existence of God, self-sufficiency of virtue, etc. But from youth on, he was a skeptic, knowing well that none of this could ever be proved. In his early and middle years, up to 46/45 BC, the dogmatic side often prevailed. . . . But there are skeptical provisos. . . . [In the later period] skepticism as a method is in the foreground, presumably from [March 45 BC] on. The dialectical procedure to "elicit the probable" shapes the very structure of the great dialogues: it is constitutive and ubiquitous. . . . In all periods of his life, Cicero experienced inner conflict, sometimes painfully felt, between scrupulous reason and edifying ideals, between doubt and belief. In this sense, he was a skeptic continuously and incessantly.[17]

However, what are undeniable are "Cicero's constant and recurring statements of allegiance to the Skeptical Academy in his later philosophical works."[18] As legal and political work occupied most of his life, Cicero's liveliest philosophical period was the two-year period of Caesar's dictatorship, 46–44 BC, during which he wrote over thirty books. Accordingly, the prevalent tone in most of these works mirrors the methods of the Skeptical Academy.

What is most probable is a temporal judgment, one subject to change in the light of new arguments, evidence, and findings. Cicero uses his idealized image of the Roman republic, typically during the age of Scipio Aemilianus (184–129 BC), as part of the equation. Fusing theory with practice, Cicero takes compatibility with Roman values and traditions as critical in assessing philosophical conclusions.

In any case, Cicero did not aspire to advance a new philosophical system. His primary motivations are clear: to introduce a Latin vocabulary to philosophy; to use contemporary Roman examples to animate Greek philosophy; to evaluate Roman customs and traditions in light of philosophical insight; to unite philosophy with rhetoric; to aid fellow citizens in living fulfilling lives; to provide a moral guide, especially to youth, in an increasingly corrupt society; to seek the good of the whole community; and to rescue Rome from the political abyss into which it had leaped (D 1.6–7; ND 1.9). Moreover, he had personal goals: to cope with the death of Tullia; to remain active despite social and political unrest in Rome; to develop his early political, ethical, and speculative ideas. Indeed, Cicero is credited with producing a new literary genre.[19] Cicero made himself a source "of an enlightened and humane outlook, the Roman spirit at its best."[20]

Following Plato, much of Cicero's philosophical work is written in dialogue form. Cicero's contemporaries and friends, aligned to the philosophical schools they favored, serve as speakers in his writings. Cato and Balbus represent Stoicism; Atticus and Velleius champion Epicureanism; Brutus, Varro, and Piso advocate for the Platonic Academy; and Cicero and Cotta speak for the Skeptical Academies. Most strikingly, Cicero was firmly convinced that the contemplative life, so celebrated by the classical Greek philosophers, placed a poor second to the practical life of statesmen inclined toward the common good and social justice.

In sum, five vectors animate Cicero's philosophy: (1) *The epistemological presuppositions of the Skeptical Academies:* renounce dogmatism and absolute certitudes; accept the standard of probabilism as a guide for action; insist that wise men could still render opinions and act resolutely in the face of epistemological uncertainty; pursue moral virtue and the guidance of probabilistic reasoning in service of reasonable human desires. (2) *The basic tenets of Stoic ethics:* accept human wisdom, founded on moral virtue, as the key to the good life; understand the world as orderly and purposive, and guided by reason and natural laws; conceive of the divine as not located in a single place, but, instead, as permeating all of nature; fashion human wisdom as arising from distinguishing what is within our control from that which is outside of our control; and be suspicious of raging emotions. (3) *The demonstrable superiority of republicanism in politics:* celebrate the doctrine of proportionate, not absolute, equality; preserve the entitlement to private property; establish a mixed constitution with a robust appreciation for aristocratic authority; honor the rule of law; avoid economic redistribution schemes; and inculcate civic virtue among citizens and a sense of the common good. (4) *The practical tests of Roman history:* illustrate proper moral and political actions through historical examples, mostly from the glory days of the republic; strengthen commitment to those Roman traditions, customs, religious practices, and social convictions that have proved politically salutary; and relish the connections between the excellence of statesmen, the industriousness of citizens, and the health of the state. (5) *Cicero's own pre-philosophical aspirations:* hope for the glorious union of moral virtue and human fulfillment; imagine moral virtue as the only true human good; refuse to see conflicts between what is morally right and what appears to be expedient; and strive for a self-sufficiency that marginalizes the effects of luck and circumstances.

These five vectors frequently intermingle awkwardly. For Cicero, whether he explicitly recognizes it, they always remain in the forefront of his philosophy. As such, those who find Cicero's philosophy maddeningly inconsistent or flabbily eclectic or irritatingly indecisive have a basis for their criticisms. But a sharper realization of the five dimensions of his thought provides the reader a greater opportunity for understanding than do a closed mind and an unsympathetic heart.

The Good Life and Moral Virtue

Romans were practical people with an affinity for Stoic self-sufficiency, stripped of its penchant for logical paradoxes and occasional impractical abstractness. Depending only on one's own character and excellence, freeing one-self from fortuities and circumstances, and perfecting the spirit by understanding and nurturing its essential qualities, stoked the pre-Christian outlook. Disdain for enduring emotional ties, material goods, and esteem from others were essential ingredients for individual emancipation. This Stoic plank, though, did not fit comfortably with the Roman traditions of pursuing military excellence, exalted social status, political and social rank, and abiding personal glory. We could expect antecedently that Roman adherence to Stoicism would be less than doc-trinaire. Cicero did not appreciate Stoicism's dogmatism and technical leanings, but endorsed its values of rationality, social duty, and moral rectitude. Cicero, though, could never viscerally accept Stoicism's rejection of the pursuit of po-litical achievements and enduring glory. In general, Cicero's political convic-tions and metaphysical commitments were also not compatible with Epicurean-ism.

Cicero's four prime virtues are wisdom, justice, courage, and temperance. These are pursued entirely for their own sake. More complex motivations—which seek glory, status, influence, and friendship—are sought both for their intrinsic value and for practical advantage (O 2.159–169; DF 2.45). Cicero in-sists that any conjuring of advantage when pursuing the four prime virtues sul-lies the ideal of *honestas*. The evil of disgrace is worse than all others. Disgrace, the loss of honor, is far worse than suffering pain: pain can lead to virtue and its torments grow softer by act of will as long as honor and nobility of spirit persist (TD 2.31). Cicero crafts courage as having two main functions: the scorn of death and the scorn of pain (TD 2.43).

Much of Cicero's moral musings is summarized in *De Officiis*, an essay to his son on the behavior, dispositions, and duties that vivify the exemplary Ro-man citizen. As his son had given few indications of interests beyond the pursuit of *la dolce vita*, Cicero felt obliged to record his expectations. Cicero includes examples from his own career, attacks on those, such as Caesar, who have un-dermined the republic, and his usual menu of Roman historical allusions. For Cicero, morality is grounded in human nature. Given that we are certain types of creatures, morality is a necessary condition of our fulfillment. Our natural curi-osity inclines us toward the pursuit of wisdom; our natural sociability and need of others fuels our sense of justice; our anxieties and insecurities drive us to de-velop courage; our yearning for pleasures, not all of which are salutary, impels us toward temperance. (Whether morality is a sufficient condition of human fulfillment is a question Cicero pondered at length.)

Cicero issues four guiding principles: (1) Wisdom is the paramount *virtue,* but justice is the most important *duty*; (2) social action is more valuable than contemplation; (3) human beings are innately social and justice, which benefits society, is more valuable than courage; and (4) justice must be moderated by decorum, which prohibits the repulsive and shocking (O 1.152–159): "Our pri-mary duties are owed to the immortal gods; secondly, to our country; thirdly, to our parents; and then the rest in descending order of priority" (O 1.60).

Nature decrees four different human roles: shared human nature; our individual aptitudes and limitations; fortune and circumstance; and our choices and acts. The weight of the moral duties accompanying these roles tracks the same order. Duties imposed by human nature are, thus, crucial. Convinced that human beings have a natural inclination toward the good and that appreciation of moral duty flows from proper training and effort, Cicero subscribes to free will (F 26–38): "Broad control by fate, and the gods' benevolent providence can be conceded, as long as divine intervention *in detail* is denied. . . . Assent [in major decisions and choices] is a matter of ethics, but it also involves logic, since it does not follow *necessarily* upon sense-perceptions; if it did we would be automata."[21] Cicero anticipates the philosophical distinction between compelled actions and caused actions.

> A free act can be determined and predictable (it has external causes) but it need not be *necessary*: the human actor has spontaneity. If assent is fated, and not voluntary, just judgment is impossible: this endangers society . . . if assent results from auxiliary [as contrasted with principal] causes, then assent is in our power, i.e., we are self-determined, and "captains of our soul." Our will is free, and we are responsible for our actions.[22]

If we extend the chain of causality for human actions back infinitely, free will seems extinguished; but human beings do make choices, we do exert free will, and not everything flows from fate. The auxiliary causes of our actions are not compelled.

Cicero has deep appreciation for the role of religion in molding public opinion and reinforcing traditional values. Religion helps sustain what came later to be called the directive function of law: conferring the state with a halo of rightful authority; commanding obedience to the law because it is perceived as natural and moral; and convincing the masses to internalize the imperatives of the state. For the Romans, religion was less a matter of spiritual piety and more an issue of venerating established customs and traditions.

> Religion was not so much a set of personal beliefs as precisely laid-down ways of living in harmony with the expectations of the gods. In fact, by the end of the Republic educated men believed less in the literal truth of the apparatus of religious doctrine than in a vaguer notion of the validity of tradition.[23]

The Natural Law

Crucial here is the understanding that philosophers do not conjure moral rules *ex nihilo*, but instead establish the justificatory grounds for social traditions, customs, and practices devised by wider communal groups. Moral reasoning and social understandings involve an ongoing process of matching theory to practice (O 1.147–148). This understanding of morality—which involves social conventions and their empirical and theoretical testing—rests uneasily with Cicero's general reliance on natural law as the timeless ballast of morality and politics:

True law is right reason in agreement with nature; it is of universal application, unchanging, and everlasting. . . . We cannot be freed from its obligations by senate or people, and we need not look outside ourselves for an expounder or interpreter of it. . . . One eternal and unchangeable law will be valid for all nations and all times, and there will be one master and ruler. That is, god, over us all, for he is the author of this law, its promulgator, and its enforcing judge. . . . Whoever is disobedient [to the dictates of natural law] is fleeing from himself and denying his human nature. (R 3.22; 3.33)

Natural law, for Cicero, provides a secure foundation for moral and political judgments. Moreover, once a judgment is grounded in natural law that conclusion solidifies and is invulnerable from attack. The banner of natural law, then, fits comfortably with Cicero's aristocratic resistance to innovation. But declaring that natural law reigns supreme and determining precisely which moral and political judgments are underwritten by natural law are two different matters. Cicero's appeal to social traditions, customs, and practices—adjusted by theoretical insight—is a way to discover which moral and political judgments are grounded in natural law. The process is not intended to conflict with or undermine the authority of natural law. Accordingly, the justificatory grounds philosophers seek for normative judgments do not replace the sanctions of natural law with merely conventional understandings. Instead, Cicero offers a path for discovering which normative judgments flow from natural law.

Still, reliance upon natural law as the supreme authority for normative judgments is spectacularly problematic. Reliance upon the existence and ultimate dominion of a supreme being; an unchanging human essence or nature; and objective standards of morality which are allegedly part of the structure of the universe seems mysterious and dubious to critics of natural law: Either such entities have been proved not to exist, or they are in principle and practice impossible to prove or disprove.

Natural law has traditionally aspired to translate physical and biological generalities into normative propositions. Natural law theorists hope to discover moral laws comparable to scientific findings. Unfortunately, most modern versions of this theory are wedded too closely with specific theologies, which even if correct may alienate those of different persuasions and thus fail to provide much common ground for normative reasoning. Moreover, even if there exists an eternal human essence, how should we select which of its features reflect "natural law"? Neither the nature of the universe nor human nature sends us an unambiguous message about the world and our place within it. We must translate the universal descriptive elements, if any, that we perceive into prescriptions for human conduct; but if nature transmits contradictory messages then the advice "Follow Nature" is itself logically incoherent. The journey out of this quagmire has included reliance on a unique human *telos*. But it is precisely this maneuver that forces natural law theorists to embrace specific theologies and additional metaphysical suppositions which expose them to further criticism.

Finally, the anthropological evidence is quite ambiguous as to the existence of a timeless human nature: numerous variations in norms and customs are pervasive. Furthermore, it is difficult to separate the innate inclinations of humans (our nature) from environmental influences (our nurture). Only by heightening the level of abstraction and generality to triviality and definitional truths can natural law theorists persuasively demonstrate the human commonality they allege.

At times, natural law theorists invoke the notion of "self-evidence." But this maneuver is disturbing. What is self-evident may be only what the community has agreed to accept. Can natural law theorists truly identify the universal elements of morality? Is it not possible for equally rational humans, who are in good faith trying to apprehend natural law, to arrive at different, even contradictory discoveries? Should not we be uncommonly suspicious of claims of "self-evidence" and "nondemonstrable truth"? Are not such claims the first refuge of charlatans and scoundrels who pretend to unveil timeless truths while they are in fact merely holding a mirror to their own projections, aspirations and interests? In any event, are claims of self-evidence the best starting point when those claims result either in merely definitional (and thus trivial) truths or in radically contestable axioms?

In the face of all this, critics press the following questions: Even if there exists a code of natural law how do we discover it? More important, how do we know when we have discovered it? Because of its controversial and slippery character, and the high generality of its alleged prescriptions (e.g., "Do good, avoid evil"), natural law may be of limited use to human beings. Those searching for answers to concrete moral and legal questions will not find their purposes served by the abstract definitional truths of natural law. Even if "universal practical principles" and "universal forms of good" exist they do not provide by themselves, or in concert with methodological principles of reason, any clear answers to the normative questions human beings ask. Natural law seems too much like an apology for those who aspire to place moral reasoning on a plane similar to scientific reasoning—as searching for and discovering truths which presumably exist antecedently—and too little like a method for arriving at specific right answers to questions of value.

Despite, or maybe because of, its indeterminacy and malleability, natural law theory has had great historical significance. Among other things, natural law theory vivified Christian moral doctrine, inspired numerous political theorists during the Enlightenment, provided the philosophical underpinnings of the American Revolution, and influenced later arguments about the social emancipation of slaves and women.

However, contemporary political discussions about natural law exploit its indeterminacy. Indeed, both ends of the political spectrum whipsaw the theory. Radical leftists allege that natural law theory is an apology for the political status quo. By mystifying and legitimating the present social order as fundamentally in accord with universal and timeless morality, natural law theory elevates and transforms the contingent present into the transcendent eternal. This transformation process is dangerous because it results in a societal perception that the status quo is beyond reimagination and re-creation. Too often, it seems to such leftists, natural law theorists identify the natural and the prescriptive with that which is familiar, habitual, and established.

Political conservatives, on the other hand, charge that natural law is too unsettling to the received order. By seeming to allow all citizens to judge for themselves whether the propositions commonly thought to be conventional are truly "law," and by permitting all citizens to act effectively as judges, natural law encourages individuals to destabilize the collective judgment of rightful authority and the community as a whole. Moreover, such an open invitation for civil disobedience jeopardizes the very possibility of nurturing the type of directive power of law that natural law theorists claim to prize.

Cicero and the Schools

In his *Paradoxa Stoicorum* *(Stoic Paradoxes),* Cicero manifests his classic connection of using Roman history as part of his evaluation of moral problems. Roman history is crucial because it illustrates the success of certain approaches to the good life and the poverty of other strategies. Reflecting relentless Roman practicality, Cicero is not content to judge moral questions only through abstractions. The value of philosophical abstractions is filtered through history, experience, and results. Throughout this work, Cicero extols the virtues of ancient Rome, while sketching the excesses of the Rome of his day. He also explicitly lays out his appreciation of basic Stoic ethics and his disdain for Epicurean hedonism.

More important, Cicero insists that the Epicurean pleasure principle is an unworthy human end. We are made for a higher calling. Bodily strength, health, beauty, generosity, gratitude, and other physical and mental excellences are all preferable to the accumulation of pleasure (DF 2.113–116). The pleasure principle leads only to self-regarding quietude and withdrawal. Is it not clear that such a life is inferior to the heroism of, say, Hercules (DF 2.117–119)? Courage, justice, self-sacrifice for higher causes, and the like are all values superior to the pursuit of pleasure. Epicurus, says Cicero, separates pleasure from the greatest good, virtue. He wrongly defines pleasure sensually, in terms of taste buds, sex, entertainments, music, and the like. Although Epicurus praises virtue, Cicero reminds readers that the lavish-spending Gaius Gracchus praised frugality. The Epicurean emphasis on materialism, utility, and self-interest are unworthy (TD 3.46–51).

Cicero sometimes ignores that Epicureanism rejects pleasure as wine, women/men, and song; instead, Epicureans exalt the pleasures of the mind, friendship, and the simple life. He may be responding to how Epicureanism, and any explicitly hedonist doctrine, can be so easily perverted in practice by those antecedently yearning for *la dolce vita.*

Cicero invokes the penitent's paradox to illustrate a possible limitation of Stoicism's theory of the emotions. At times, negative emotions are appropriate as a deserved reaction to our recognition of our shortcomings: "When Alcibiades was overcome with tears [after Socrates had convinced him of his moral failings] and begged Socrates to give him virtue and take way his depravity, what shall we say? . . . Surely not that there was nothing bad in what caused him such sorrow!" (DF 3.77)

The Peripatetics argued that moderate emotions are useful: anger and competitiveness for the soldier and orator; greed for philosophers pursuing wisdom; annoyance to remedy one's personal faults; guilt feelings to cure people from wrongdoing; fear to deter people from lawlessness; and the like (TD 4.43–46). Cicero rejects this view and concludes that the emotions at stake are unnecessary for the desired behavior sketched (TD 4.47–56). Living in a culture in which marrying for love was scorned, Cicero derides love as the most trivial and unworthy emotion. Worse, love is accompanied by longing, anxiety, insecurity, bad judgment, and fruitless intrigue (TD 4.68–76). Regarding the hopelessness that typically accompanies suicide, Cicero notes that suicide may well have been a duty in Cato's case, but under the same circumstances, no such duty could be levied on people of less obdurate constitution (Cicero?) (O 1.112).

Cicero's understanding of the emotions is inadequate, but I will address the critical issues in my analysis of the Stoics.

Friendship

Friendship was a vexing problem for philosophy during Cicero's time, except for Peripatetics and some Academics. Peripatetics, after all, could invoke Aristotle's argument that external goods, including friendships, were necessary for the good life. For Stoics, though, emphasizing friendship was reneging on the sage's ideal of self-sufficiency and the doctrine that virtue was a guarantee of happiness. For Epicureans, the problem was describing the nature of friendship. Was friendship of only instrumental value—a way of attaining a tranquil, pleasurable life? Epicureans, says Cicero, advanced three false or inconsistent theories of friendship: attaining pleasure is the prime and proper motive of friendship; intimacy gives rise to friendship valuable for its own sake, which suggests that moral action independent of pleasure is possible; and friendship as mutual agreement, which suggests friendship aims at mutual advantage. Cicero intuits, but does not carefully distinguish, the possibility that different types of friendship, with differing degrees of intensity, commitment, and genesis, are possible. The natural human instinct of self-love impels us to seek others like ourselves for friendship (O 1.47; AM 74). For Cicero, we are not generally permitted to prefer a friend's interests over that of the common good. Clearly, we must not follow a friend who undermines his own republic. More strikingly, political differences justify ending a friendship (AM 36–43).

Cicero's sketch of friendship is redolent with Roman aristocratic goals of mutual benefit, political aid, and peer attraction. But such goals are subordinate to choosing a friend who is another self, equally committed to moral goodness (F 80–82, 83–85). Genuine friendships can exist only among morally good people (F 18). Friends are alter egos who make pleasures more enjoyable and burdens more bearable (F 22–24). Profit and personal advantage in friendship are ancillary to the good will produced by mutual admiration grounded in the love of virtue (F 29–32).

Still, some nuances of friendship elude Cicero. Genuine friendship of the highest quality is uncommon for at least two reasons. First, relatively few people embody the requisite moral quality. Second, the enterprise of friendship requires considerable time, shared commitments, and joint activities. Friendship, like erotic love, is an inherently discriminatory notion. I cannot be a friend, in the deepest sense, to everyone even if I was so inclined and even if everyone was morally good. I would still not have enough time and I could not expend enough effort to pursue the common commitments and joint activities that genuine friendship demands.

While I may perceive, accurately, that a stranger possesses a higher degree of moral virtue than my friend, my past connection and mutually satisfying relationship exudes currency. My friend and I are not *lontananza* (at a distance), but forge a shared identity. Our relationship, if profound enough, entails that my interests are not experienced as fully apart from my friend's interests and vice versa. Relationships, of course, vary in intensity and depth, but all genuine friendships share this element. Accordingly, I would not trade-up easily because my current friend and I share a relationship that has valuable ramifications for who I am. I would recognize the transition costs—time, energy, uncertainty, changes to my self-image—of substituting the stranger for my current friend. I would also understand that even if the stranger bears more goodness than my friend, the stranger cannot exemplify that goodness in the same way as my friend. The moral virtue of my friend and that of the stranger will differ qualitatively in the particular ways they are manifested. Just as the stranger may be more physically beautiful than my friend, the stranger does not have more of *my friend's* beauty. The unique way my friend embodies and expresses beauty may be more appealing to me than the way the stranger expresses his or her admittedly greater physical beauty. Finally, the historical relationship friends have shared has special significance that should not be dismissed. Friends form a union or federation that is not defined merely by adding the interests of the parties together. In friendship, like in well-functioning marriages, the whole is greater than the sum of the parts. The bond or union or federation that friends nurture transforms the parties. The historical relationship that chronicles that development bears independent value in a way similar to the value produced by positive family relationships. Shared memories, gratitude, reciprocal self-making, and a sense of belonging make trading-up in friendship problematic. Where trading-up does seem to happen easily we can legitimately call into question whether a salutary, deep friendship was present.

I do not suggest that we should nurture only one friendship. Clearly, most of us have several friends of varying closeness and contact. We have even more acquaintances that provide a host of mutually beneficial interactions. Often, instead of facing a choice of trading-up—dumping our current friend for another person—we can simply add to our list in a way that is precluded in romantic love. Still, practicalities limit the number of close friends with whom we can share deep relationships.

Even so, our choice of friends is limited by circumstances of geography, time, economics, culture, and the like. Our social context profoundly affects whom we meet and what activities we undertake. But the same can be said about our choices of spouse, career, and almost all else. Few of our most important choices are limitless.

The joint identity principle I am urging will trouble some philosophers. They will screech that my standard of friendship is too high as it requires a loss of individual autonomy. Once we talk of extended or shared identity, we seem to infringe on an individual's freedom of choice and independence. My choices, projects, and actions are no longer *mine*, they are *ours*. Does this not demand concessions of the individual's will?

The short answer is "yes, but why the surprise?" Every intimate relationship has that consequence. Can we coherently conjure, say, romantic love where each spouse retains full, individual autonomy? Living together, sharing a life, pooling material resources, planning for the future require shared decision-making, reciprocity, and mutuality. To believe that full independence can be retained is fatuous. Granted, friendships come in more shadings and forms than Cicero catalogued. But the deepest versions of friendship—the ones that are most transforming to our characters—are akin to loves. Why should we shrink back in horror when we find that our independence is no longer sacrosanct? A world of strangers may be a world of complete independence for individuals; a community of friends is not.

We care about our friends, at least in part, because we perceive that they bear excellences or admirable qualities. We could be mistaken in that assessment, of course. Our evaluations are not infallible, our perceptions are not flawless. Once we realize our error, the incipient friendship may end. But the ground of our initial attraction is the value we think the other possesses.

However, a critic would rejoin that making the perceived value of the other the ground of friendship is troubling. First, our real focus seems to be on that value, wherever it may reside, and not on a particular person. Human beings are not merely repositories of value, nor does value alone define who we are. We have other qualities—beyond our glorious value—that are neutral in terms of value or that are imperfections or disvalues. To focus only on the other's value is to befriend her only for a part of her personhood. Second, to ground friendship in only the other's current perceived value is to freeze the other in time. We all change, grow, and regress. To rivet a friendship in the current image of the other is to deny inevitable change. Again, such a friendship is not directed at a whole person but at certain value which we now think we have found in the other.

These criticisms are difficult, but not impossible, to answer. To establish a friendship of whole persons, our critic is correct: we must appreciate more than the current perceived value of each other. Each of us is a compendium of qualities, not all admirable, wrapped together by our unique way of embodying and expressing those qualities, seasoned by hosts of possibilities (potential qualities that we can develop into actualities). By considering the other person's qualities beyond their perceived value, we parry the charge that we are drawn only to value not whole people. By attending to the other idealized possibilities, we block the charge that friendship wrongly freezes the other in the present. Friends affect each other's choices, actions, and personal development. They do not simply take the other as a fixed, permanent character.

Friendships are intimate relationships of varying degrees, typically less so than romantic loves and more so than polite acquaintanceships. One of the functions of friendship is to control access to ourselves and to regulate our privacy. Intimacy is mutually nurtured in several ways: through privileged self-disclosure, participation in shared projects, discerning and advancing each other's best interests, and having a roughly similar system of values. Bonds of trust, far beyond the level we enjoy with strangers, flow from the heightened mutual vulnerability distinguishing deep friendships.

I disclose information about myself to my friends that I keep shrouded from the general public. In so doing, I regulate my privacy—permitting more access to those whom I choose—and both acknowledge and reinforce the bonds of trust between my friends and me. By participating in shared projects, friends reveal and sustain the projects of their most profound concern. Friends share activities at least partly for the sake of sharing them. Friends often strive to advance each other's interests. I can advance my friend's interests only after appraising what my friend's best interests are. Throughout all these processes, the values of the parties are paramount. Sometimes friends come to their relationship with roughly similar values. Sometimes they develop roughly similar values as a consequence of their relationship and shared activities. In any case, friends mutually influence each other's values in proportion to the closeness of the relationship.

I may be drawn to or try out a new value or project simply because my friend already embodies the value or pursues the project. But my initial attraction need not translate into final acceptance of the value or project into my life scheme. We should recognize a distinction between what motivates my desire to try out a new project or examine a new value—I pursue them just because they rivet my friend's concern—and the grounds upon which I will decide whether to adopt the value or project as my own. My friend's values and projects never fully define mine. I must make a relatively independent assessment of the new value or project at some point.

Friendship is also an exercise in self-making in proportion to the closeness of the relationship. Cicero, following Aristotle, insisted that human beings are social animals. A person alone in a desert island might be a beast or a god, but not a human being. We need others to help understand and define ourselves. Those closest to us play a disproportionately strong role.

The annoying parental warning—"Be careful who your friends are, don't associate with the wrong crowd"—hits the mark squarely. Friends influence the people we are becoming.

Friendship is, accordingly, a process, not a fixed condition. It begins in lack and is grounded in power. But the grandeur of friendship is that it is not a commodity: it cannot be bought or sold, yet it isn't costless. Friendship struggles to overcome its internal paradoxes of consolation and growth, dependency and freedom. The uniqueness and specialness of the friends—understood not wholly in terms of their facility in guiding the mutual quest for individual perfection—forms the core of the relationship. Friendship is a mysterious mixture of choice and discovery that changes our perception of the world without actually changing the world. Friendship is transformative but not redemptive. But, mostly, it is an acknowledgment of bonds not fully chosen.

Friendship cannot be an arm's-length, mutual aid exercise in individualism. Friends cannot be creators in *lontananza*. No, friendship widens our subjectivity and creates a new identity that immediately embodies its own unrealized ideals. And the unrealized ideal possibilities of friends-bound are never merely the sum of the unrealized ideal possibilities embodied by the two individuals. The friendship is not two minds thinking or valuing as one. Even the closest of friends, like the most committed lovers, must keep a salutary amount of independence.

Friendship is also dangerous. Other than our spouse or a blood relative, no one can betray us more hurtfully or thoroughly than a close friend. Any time we heighten our vulnerability through revealing special information about ourselves, sharing intimate activities, forging bonds of trust, and relying upon the good will of others, we not only enjoy the fruits of positive self-making but also risk treachery. My friends know more about me, have shared and helped to shape my values, and benefit from my trust. They are in a better position than the general public to advance my best interests but also to extinguish my deepest aspirations.

Are the risks worth the value of friendship? Friendships increase our flow experiences by energizing our efforts in the projects at hand. Shared activities and commitments are also necessary for moral and intellectual growth. Friends help us accurately evaluate the quality and meaningfulness of our lives. The sense of belonging and intimate validation friendships produce soften our fears that we are alone and powerless. Because we are social animals, friendships are valuable for their own sake, not just for benefits directly derived from the relationships.

Cicero does not adequately capture how friendships amplify our identities; he tends to minimize the moral conflicts generated by duties of friendship and obligations to wider communities; he, in my judgment, is willing to discard friends too easily because of political disagreements; he fails to address how friendships might develop between those not thoroughly committed to moral goodness; and he downplays the role of intimacy.

Is Moral Virtue Sufficient for Human Happiness?

The role of *virtus* (moral goodness) in the quest for *beata vita* (the good life) invigorates Cicero's ethical writings. Socrates and the Stoics presumably argued that a morally virtuous person could not be harmed. Sure, he could be physically injured or killed, but harm is more fundamentally impairment of the soul. The virtuous person could be fulfilled and happy even while being tortured insofar as he understood that no one could harm him without his (typically unwitting) collaboration: he would be connected to human excellence; would die nobly in the face of extreme adversity; and would not himself commit any wrongs. Under this view, the happy life, understood as the life defined by the proper objective condition of the human soul, and the virtuous life were identical.

Aristotle found such a view preposterous and argued that being morally virtuous was a necessary but not sufficient condition of fulfillment and happiness. Human beings also required external goods—a measure of material goods, friendships, congenial home life, health, an acceptable physical appearance, and the like—in order to attain happiness. Aristotle's conclusions meshed much better with common sense, but they rendered human beings less self-sufficient: good fortune and circumstances—matters not fully in our control—played a greater role in human well-being. Antiochus, founder of the Eclectic School that aspired to revive the Platonic Academy, characteristically tried to mediate the dispute by judging both sides correct: virtue is both necessary and sufficient for human happiness, but the happiest life includes the enjoyment of some conventional goods.

Cicero, wisely, refused the bait. Under Antiochus's view the happiest life, not the merely happy life, is the most complete; hence, the Socratic-Stoic goal of uniting moral virtue to greatest human fulfillment remains unreconciled. If Antiochus's school admits external goods such as health, friends, children, wealth, and power, then it must also allow for evils, too, in which case moral virtue does not guarantee happiness (DF 5.76–79). Whereas the Eclectic School judges a life by what it has most of—a life with a preponderance of moral good is happy—Cicero, following Stoicism, insists that a life containing even a touch of evil cannot be happy (DF 5.86–90). For Cicero, happiness does not admit degrees (TD 5.21–23). Virtue is sufficient for happiness, even under torture (TD 5.12). Virtuous people are always happy; happiness is the possession of all good and no evil; but if people regard external matters—such as bodily or material misfortune, loneliness, exile, enslavement, loss of loved ones, and the like—as evils then virtue alone may not bring them happiness. Having the proper disposition and understanding, then, are critical to human happiness (TD 5.28–31).

Cicero, although never completely convinced, accepts, probabilistically, the Stoic doctrine that the only human good is moral worth. External goods such as money, luxurious homes, power, and pleasures merely inspire greed and fear of their loss. The founding fathers of Rome regarded such external goods as transitory and unworthy. Romulus was honored for his virtue and heroism; Lucius Junius Brutus, who spearheaded the expulsion of the tyrannical Tarquin the Proud, acted from duty not concern for pleasure or wealth; and the same could be said for other legendary figures such as Scaevola, Horatius, Fabricius, and the Scipios (SP 6–12). The Epicurean celebration of pleasure undermines the importance of human intellect; pleasure does not improve its possessors—it does not bring honor or righteousness (SP 14–15).

Virtue is sufficient for human happiness. M. Atilius Regulus retained his happiness although tortured by Carthaginians. Steadfastness of purpose, moral virtue, and personal integrity sustain the good person. Marius said and showed that heroism in the face of adversity is our highest glory. The self-sufficient person, invulnerable to misfortune, is the happiest. Death cannot devastate those whose glory endures. Exile cannot destroy those whose perspective is cosmopolitan (SP 16–18).

Human happiness does not arise from luck, but from contemplating, understanding, and subscribing to the natural order. Philosophy is required for this project (H 63–87). Happiness is not living licentiously and as one pleases; instead, it requires wanting what one ought to want. Internalizing the requirements of natural law is crucial to human flourishing (H 57–62).

The Eclectic Academy, founded by Antiochus and presumably reviving the Platonic Academy, held that the greatest happiness required bodily and external goods (A 1.22). Cicero, at times, entertains positions critical of the Stoic bromide that virtue is sufficient for human happiness (TD 5.12–121). Even a disembodied mind would desire health, freedom from pain, self-preservation, external goods, and the like, all of which are in accord with nature (DF 4.24–26). Virtue is choosing things according to nature, including the whole range of desires that are inseparable from human nature (DF 4.40–42). The greatest good is inseparable from our natural motives for action. We must distinguish health from disease, absence of pain from suffering, warmth from cold, satiation from hunger, and the like in order to conduct our lives. What the Stoics call preferences are simply what other philosophers and common sense call external goods (DF 4.68–72). Moreover, human nature is partially physical. To live in accordance with nature must include desiring things good for the body.

But ultimately, as already noted, Cicero, in his *Tusculan Disputations*, concludes that philosophy's most vivid message is that virtue is sufficient for human happiness (TD 5.1–4). Cicero refuses to admit degrees of happiness. The virtuous are always happy, even if tortured; happiness is the possession of all good and no evil; virtue is the sole good; people should not regard external, physical, or political maladies as evil. The thoroughly philosophical sage will seek internal happiness and view external benefits indifferently (TD 5.28–31). The virtuous person has a free will, nobility, security, independence, and is invulnerable to the vicissitudes of the world (TD 5.80–82).

Cicero, following Socrates, Plato, Stoics, and Cynics, trumpets an unyielding, unusual position: moral and intellectual virtues are necessary and sufficient for happiness. At first blush, the position is preposterous. Are we *guaranteed* happiness through moral and intellectual virtues? Are moral and intellectual virtues *required* for happiness? If we take a positive, subjective psychological state—extended joy, contentment, exuberance, or peace—as necessary for happiness, Cicero's account is unpersuasive. Imagine a moral and intellectual paragon who suffers greatly from debilitating illness, the slings and arrows of outrageous fortune, disastrous relationships, and extreme maliciousness of peers.

Draw this picture as bleakly and starkly as you are able. (Voltaire's *Candide* may help.) How can such a beleaguered soul be happy? Do we not reach a point where the moral and intellectual virtues are insufficient ballast for happiness?

Analyzed from another angle, that moral and intellectual virtues are necessary for happiness is also doubtful. Imagine someone who falls far short of a moral and intellectual paragon, but who enjoys robust health, uncommon good luck, satisfying relationships, and lavish honors from peers. Draw this picture as vividly and extravagantly as you are able. Must such a fortunate pilgrim be unhappy? Does he or she not reach a point where extremely good fortune, adaptation to one's environment, and personal success carry the day and produce happiness regardless of moral and intellectual deficiencies?

Achieving the Ciceronian conception of happiness, then, does not guarantee that a person will be predominantly joyful, peaceful, or exuberant; nor is attaining a balanced, harmonious soul required to attain those states of mind.

However, Cicero has a rejoinder. First, he could argue that my objections miss the mark. I am explicitly taking a positive, subjective psychological state—extended joy, contentment, exuberance, or peace—as at least necessary for happiness. He understands happiness, in accord with the Platonic Academy and Stoicism, as an objective condition of the inner person. Why should we be surprised that Cicero's account does not fulfill criteria appropriate to a different understanding of happiness? Viewed in this light, my objections are irrelevant to his account.

This response gives Cicero a fighting chance, but invites further questions. Has Cicero ruled critics out of order by definitional fiat only? Has he conjured an account of happiness that is unpersuasive to contemporary users of the term? Even if happiness is an objective condition of a person, cannot that condition be undermined by extremely adverse states of affairs? Finally, if all Cicero means by happiness is "moral and intellectual virtues," then why even use the term? Why not simply proselytize for more and better moral and intellectual virtues among people? What is added by calling this happiness? Is not Cicero tacitly smuggling in the praiseworthy and highly desired qualities of happiness—those flowing from enduring, positive psychological states—while simultaneously denying the need for those subjective qualities in the definition of happiness? Either Cicero's thesis is true but trivial—"happiness" simply means "possessing the moral and intellectual virtues"—or it is interesting but stunningly false.

Cicero could challenge my suggestion that people falling far short of moral and intellectual paragons can be happy. He was firmly convinced that such people are slaves to their appetites and desires. The unjust soul is unhealthy due to internal disharmony. Unjust people are not happy regardless of external appearances that suggest otherwise. In the same way that physically unhealthy people may seem healthy to their acquaintances, unhealthy souls cannot always be detected by the naked eye. Injustice, nevertheless, manifests an illness that is never in the interests of the perpetrator. Justice is always in our interests because it manifests and nurtures the health of our psyches. A person's health, whether physical or spiritual, is an objective condition not subject to popular plebiscite.

Cicero is probably correct if we are assessing a thoroughly, morally depraved, intellectually bankrupt tyrant. Most such people are unlikely to be happy. Their excesses are themselves often attributable to their unhappiness and inability to adapt to their social environments. Even their episodic satisfactions evaporate quickly. Cicero is less convincing if we are assessing the vast majority of human beings who are neither moral paragons nor unrepentant tyrants. That people can be reasonably happy while falling far short of being moral and intellectual paragons remains plausible. Consult your own lives and those of your peers.

Accordingly, that relentless commitment to moral and intellectual virtues is necessary and sufficient for happiness that requires an enduring, positive, subjective psychological state, such as extended joy, contentment, exuberance, or peace, is highly doubtful. Yet, Cicero highlights numerous features of the relationship of happiness to value: Happiness is desired for its own sake, not for the sake of anything else; the direct pursuit of pleasure, the project of Epicurean hedonism, cannot be the greatest good; happiness must be connected to moral and intellectual virtues if it is to embody maximum value; happiness that embodies maximum value must be more than merely an enduring, positive, subjective psychological state, such as extended joy, contentment, exuberance, or peace; and although passions for justice, knowledge, truth, and virtues have no excess, moderating the passions is often a reliable path to happiness.

Cicero, following a long Greek tradition, identifies human happiness with human fulfillment and as an objective condition of the inner person. He was aware of the powerful Peripatetic critique of his position. But the needs of the republic and his own sense of loss fueled his aspiration to shield himself and other seekers of the good from the outrageous assaults of ill fortune and evil doers. If only we attend, in upright Stoic fashion, to that matter under our control—namely our personal rectitude—our fulfillment is assured. Although the pursuit of numerous external goods had energized his political life, he was now resigned to accommodating his fate. He would brush off, at least in his writing, the undeserved suffering he had borne and underscore the consolations of a good man whose inner psyche remained undaunted, at least on paper. Cicero had peered into the abyss and confronted the emptiness of the human condition, but his character would prevent him from jumping.

[The *Tusculan Disputations* is] a book which has been aptly described as "a manual of enlightened resignation": it is Cicero's living word about life's problems; he is trying in Existentialist fashion to teach his fellow man to accept the Human Condition. It is a pessimistic book: more men are unlucky than lucky; to fear is more sensible than to hope; there is emphasis on suicide. . . . [Cicero] in this book tried manfully to assuage his grief for Tullia; it also reflects his disappointment and that of the *optimates* after their final defeat at Munda in Spain. (March 17, 45 BC)[24]

Does Moral Virtue Conflict with Expediency?

Cicero argued unconvincingly that the benefits of expediency, when severed from honorable action, are only apparent. No genuine conflict between the honorable and the useful exists because all human beings form a common fellowship. Actions must be evaluated by their effects on everyone involved, not just on the individual moral agent. Benefits cadged by wrongfully ignoring the interests of others are wholly illusory (O 2.9–10, 3.26–27).

What is *honestas* (morally right) and what is *utile* (useful and expedient), happily, coincide. Utilitarian calculations cannot rightfully occur outside the framework of the moral virtues and duties required for human fulfillment. The conflict between the virtuous and the expedient is real only to those, such as Epicureans, who measure virtue by the standard of personal gain. In fact, all virtuous action is expedient and nothing can be accurately called expedient that is not virtuous (O 3.11–34). By refusing to adopt a narrowly personal perspective, by identifying virtue as the only good, and by conceiving the good as necessarily social, Cicero is able to affirm the Stoic union of the good and the useful. For Cicero, *honestas* is more than what is morally right; it connotes a rectitude grounded in respect for the traditions of a social group backed by sanctions devised by that group.

Cicero understands the good as the social welfare and the expedient in terms of individual advantage (O 2.18). The genuine interests of the individual and society are identical. Cicero posits a happy but unrealistic marriage between the common good and the individual good. Immorality is contrary to nature, which connotes harmony and rectitude. If *honestas* is the only or chief good then it must also be expedient: the notion of "expedient vice" is contradictory (O 3.34–36). Any apparent conflicts among the interests of individuals within a community are trumped by the common good (O 3.26). When the individual's interests seem to be advantaged by expediency which conflicts with morality, expediency must retreat. Throughout these lessons, Cicero—like the authors of the Bible who understood that a finely crafted parable is worth pages of logical proofs—spices his ideas with Roman historical examples.

Cicero's assumptions recall the Socratic bromide that being morally virtuous is always in our interests while vice is always to our disadvantage. Socrates appealed to the condition of our souls to press this case: Even if our wrongdoing remains undetected the harmony of our souls is unsettled by our deed; likewise, even if we suffer physical harm or loss of reputation from performing morally righteous actions the harmony of our souls persists; the harmony, balance, and overall health of our souls define our well-being; accordingly, virtue is always in our interests and vice always sets back our interests, regardless of the assessments of others or ourselves. Socrates's argument rests on a highly contestable metaphysics: a dualism that contends a human being consists of a body and a soul, with personal identity vesting only in the soul; a human soul divided into three parts—the rational, spiritive, and appetitive; the health of the soul (and person) defined in terms of the dominance of rationality; a dismissal of physical harms and the loss of external goods as irrelevant to human well-being; and the health of the soul (and person) fashioned on mathematical and musical analogues such as harmony, balance, equilibrium, and attunement.

Cicero does not explicitly invoke Socratic metaphysics. Instead he separates personal gain, as measured by so-called external goods, from virtuous action and the common good. The genuine interests of the individual and the common good are aligned, once we understand the poverty of pursuing external goods and recognize the way we are bound to wider society for our deepest well-being. As social animals, individuals need a well-functioning society to flourish. Such a society requires robust *honestas*.

If only matters dovetailed so neatly. Conflicts between the interests of some individuals and society occur frequently. Conflicts between the competing interests of individuals are prevalent. Only if *honestas* can resolve such conflicts objectively and fairly, and only if *honestas* is genuinely the only human good can Cicero's thesis succeed. But I have already cast suspicion on the view that virtue is sufficient for human happiness and flourishing. As long as moral virtue is not the only human good some tension between *honestas* and expediency will endure. Cicero's pre-philosophical aspirations may have skewed his analysis on this issue.

What Is the Proper Role of Glory?

Cicero, whose entire political life was spurred by his dependence on external validation, warned against the quest for fame and glory. True honor rests in honorable deeds, not reputation. He grants that heroic men generally expect enduring glory as their merited reward. But that expectation is dangerous as it nurtures the thirst for war as a means of attaining fame. Those who care little for glory, on the other hand, should not use their muted ambition as a disgraceful excuse to retreat from public life (O 1.65, 1.71).

That Roman traditions and practices celebrated the pursuit of fine reputation and enduring glory is beyond dispute. Tom Holland captures the Roman mindset well:

> Ruthless competition was regarded as the basis of all civic virtue. . . . Hardness was a Roman ideal. The steel required to hunt out glory or endure disaster was a defining mark of a citizen. It was instilled in him from the moment of his birth. . . . To raise heirs successfully, to instill in them due pride in their bloodline and hankering after glory, these were achievements worthy of a man. . . . "Gain cannot be made without loss to someone else." So every Roman took for granted.[25]

How can one reconcile (a) Cicero's own persistent glory-seeking actions, which were in accord with Roman traditions and practices with (b) his apparently Stoical critique of glory in parts of *De Officiis*? The easiest, but inaccurate, conclusion is to cite the paradox as evidence of Cicero's inconsistency or nagging ambivalence or flaccid eclecticism. A more careful and charitable reading of Cicero reveals two renderings of glory: descriptive and normative. The descriptive notion is merely factual—a person may gain fame, honor, and reputation. But such celebrity is worthless and dangerous unless it is linked to just, morally appropriate deeds. The normative notion adds that evaluative element—a person should gain fame, honor, and reputation only for those actions that exude moral merit. Cicero's own quest for enduring glory was allegedly fueled by his commitment to the common good. Actions pursuant to that end should be publicly acknowledged, both to encourage future normatively glorious deeds and as a deserved reward for political achievements.

> The Romans recognized no difference between moral excellence and reputation, having the same word, *honestas*, for both. . . . Praise was what every citizen most desired. . . . To place personal honor above the interests of the entire community was the behavior of a barbarian . . . citizens were schooled to temper their competitive instincts for the common good . . . in their relations with other states, however, no such inhibitions cramped them.[26]

Cicero's critique of glory, then, is not Stoical in the least: he does not caution against the pursuit of honor and reputation because he suspects such external goods, depending so much on luck and social circumstances, should be matters of indifference to the sage. Instead, his critique centers on the pursuit of glory severed from its normative moorings. For Cicero, the Julius Caesars of the world gain undeserved glory because their efforts undermine the common good and eviscerate the moral fabric of the republic (O 1.26). The most ambitious men in Cicero's time had lost sight of the distinction between descriptive and normative glory. Personal advantage, expediency writ small, was jeopardizing the common good. Material aggrandizement, military and political success loosened from republican values, and personal gains as such were overrunning Cicero's vision of the free republic (O 1.25). The passion for glory had been disconnected from its traditional Roman meaning.

A. A. Long sums the matter up well:

> In his earlier speeches, Cicero had no hesitation in identifying himself as intensely ambitious for glory and in regarding the survival of glory beyond one's lifetime as the only spur to patriotic achievement. . . . As the years passed, however, his comments on glory become more qualified and equivocal. . . . [The reason for the difference] is Cicero's recognition that passion for glory was degenerating into a euphemism for personal ambition at the expense of the health and stability of society.[27]

Genuine, enduring glory is won by the love, admiration, and respect of the people (O 2.31, 2.38). Such popularity is properly attained only through just actions. The pursuit of glory, when normatively sound, remained for Cicero a crucial and required aspiration for noble statesmen. Justified attributions of glory advance the common good and vivify the healthy republic.

Still, the normative rendering of glory may conflict with Cicero's view that virtue is sufficient for human happiness and flourishing. If glory is not merely a Stoical preferred indifferent—not simply an externality that human beings prefer but which does not add or subtract from their good—then who receives such recognition should be a concern of sound social policy. Cicero is infuriated that external validation in his time has been disconnected from normative analysis. That is, the unworthy, particularly that usurper of proper authority Caesar, were lavished with glory, while some who were worthy (Cicero himself?) went unrewarded. Cicero is implicitly granting that human beings have an interest in being recognized in accord with the quality of their deeds, and society has an interest in recognizing individuals accordingly. Again, meritorious actions should be publicly acknowledged, both to encourage future normatively glorious deeds and as a deserved reward for political achievements. When the deserving are not so recognized their interests have been set back: they have been harmed to that extent. When undeserving people are wrongly recognized their interests have been falsely amplified: they have been undeservedly advantaged.

One might take a Stoical *personal* outlook: Yes, I deserved recognition and I preferred to attain it, but I know my deeds were meritorious and that is all that counts; my good is in no way impaired by the failure of others to recognize and reward these truths; so I am not harmed by the inadequate acknowledgement of others. But *honestas* has a striking *social* component for Cicero: erroneous notions of glory are corrupting the republic. The health of society depends in part on proper (translated: normative) understandings of glory which mold the ambitions of powerful men. Even if one takes a Stoical personal outlook on this, the objective common good is enhanced by a proper understanding of glory and undermined by an improper understanding. If the individual's well-being is ultimately connected to the well-being of the republic, as Cicero often alleges, then the meting out of glory must be more than a preferred indifferent—at least from the standpoint of sound social policy.

The tension here is between picturing people as abstracted from their social context, where they can take purely Stoical personal points of view and minimize glory as a preferred indifferent, and visualizing citizens as embedded in their republics, where they must take a normative understanding of glory as critical to the common, and thus their own, good. Accordingly, on this issue, Cicero's penchant for Stoic ethics coalesces uncomfortably with his prephilosophical aspirations and the practical tests of Roman history.

Divine Providence

In sum, Stoics were firmly committed to it, Epicureans rejected it, and Academics raised suspicions and doubts about it. In an age when omens, augury, and celestial movements were commonly taken as signs of divine providence, permitting human beings to predict the future and divination was an important Roman religious practice, that Cicero is inclined toward the Stoic view should not surprise (ND 3.94). More important, Roman religion was instrumental: the worship of traditional gods underwrote the political ends of the state and served the common good. Also, Cicero accepted a version of the design argument for the existence of god: the beauty of our world suggests a grand architect. Observing a sun-dial, we understand immediately that it tells time by design and not by chance. As the universe encompasses everything—including products and their creators—how can it be devoid of purpose and a guiding intelligence? (ND 2.34). Stoicism, though, also curried the excesses of soothsaying, astrology, prophecy by celestial movement, and prediction by omens.

As to the existence of the gods, Cicero finds the universal assent argument most probable.

> Cicero retained the demonstration of the existence of God from the universal consent of mankind, in spite [of entertaining the Skeptical Academy's] refutation of the use which the Stoics and Epicureans made of it. There is no race so uncivilized and no man so barbarous as to be wholly without a belief in gods. . . It is by nature that we believe the gods exist; we learn their nature by reason. Belief in the immortality of the soul is likewise established by the agreement of all races of mankind, but reason is required to learn the nature of the soul and the manner of its survival.[28]

The Roman religion assumed a contractual relationship between human beings, currying divine favor by performing rituals, and gods granting favors to the fortunate. The gods, contra the teachings of Epicureanism, monitored human actions (ND 1.123). Religious officials were elected in Rome, by the usual means of connections, bribes, and deals. During Cicero's consulship, Julius Caesar, who was possibly an Epicurean and certainly often impious, was elected *ponifex maximus*. Roman religion was taken, in any case, to be critical for political ends: for controlling the potentially revolutionary fervor of masses; curtailing progressive legislation; reinforcing traditions and customs; and distracting people through rites and ceremonies from observing political chicanery. Cicero insists that

> I will defend [views about the immortal gods that I have inherited] always, and I have always defended them, nor will any speech of anyone . . . move me from the views about the worship of the immortal gods that I have inherited from my ancestors. . . . Romulus, by taking the auspices, and Numa, by establishing religious rituals, laid the foundations of our state, which never could have grown so great without the gaining of the complete favor of the immortal gods. (ND 3.5–6)

The Skeptical Academy argued that the beauty and design of the universe may well flow from impersonal, natural forces, not divine agency; that the beauty of the world does not demonstrate its justice or rationality; and that the assent of mankind to the existence of gods is less than universal and what assent persists may be ungrounded (ND 1.61–64). The Skeptical Academy also argued that human beings are mortal because they are corporeal, sentient, and subject to change (ND 3.29–37).

Cicero was drawn to Platonic imagery and believed in an immortal soul striving for freedom from the body and destined to enjoy everlasting benefit. The Epicurean belief in annihilation and the Stoic belief in temporary survival after death for the worthy were insufficient. The soul, for Cicero, is not material; its primary powers of memory, reflection, and foresight are divine and eternal. Such powers mirror the incorporeality, freedom, and self-movement of god (TD 3.76; H 111–115; OA 77–85).

Cicero concludes that on any plausible theory death should not be feared. If the soul perishes and death for a human being is annihilation, the deceased will not be unhappy because nonexistence means no subjects are present. The process of dying is either brief or nonexistent, also. While death severs us from everything desirable in life it also relieves us from evil, and in this life bad luck outweighs good fortune (TD 1.82–86). The more probable theory is that the soul is immortal. We have a naturally implanted conviction in personal immortality which manifests itself in the care we take about burial rites; the manner we deify glorious people such as Romulus and Hercules; the universal agreement on immortality evidenced by all people; and the concern we have for future generations (TD 1.26–35). Cicero follows much of Plato's speculations in the *Phaedo:* the soul is self-moving; indivisible; simple; with a divine nature given to wisdom, discovery, and memory; and death is most probably entrance to eternal life with the gods (TD 1.53–81). However, Cicero is far from dogmatic. He antecedently desired to believe in the consolations of religion, the link between Roman greatness and divine providence, and the prospect of personal immortality. Cicero was also an augur with a defined stake in the state religion. He strove diligently to distinguish superstition from the political use of augury (D 2.28–30). The highest political value is the welfare of the republic and the means required to secure the common good. Accordingly, he found conventional religious conventions of his day probable and reasonable.

Such judgments reflect Cicero's pre-philosophical aspirations and commitments to Roman traditions. The alleged universal assent to the existence of gods need not be a truth implanted by nature. Surely, explanations other than the reality of gods can be offered for the prevalence of religious commitment. For example, widespread religious belief may have its genesis in political, psychological, and sociological hopes and fears, not necessarily in a truth implanted by nature.

In the nineteenth century, the masters of suspicion undermined theism with relish. Karl Marx (1818–1883) called religion "opium for the masses," a way to divert the pain of proletariat life by focusing on a better world after death.[29] Part of the ideological superstructure that serves the interests of the dominant classes, religion distracts the disenfranchised from the misery of their social condition, forestalls revolutionary fervor, and reinforces prevailing economic systems. Marx, himself pursuing a quasi-religious grand redemption of the human race, argued that the functions religion serves will wither away once the communist paradise on earth is realized.

Sigmund Freud (1856–1939), although far from original on this issue, argued that we create gods; they do not create us.[30] We project our own deepest yearnings and fears on an indifferent universe, conjuring up various theisms to soften the human condition. Religion is thus an illusion that makes life palatable. Many people accept a theistic assumption: either God exists as the creator of meaning embedded in the universe or there is only chaos and meaninglessness. Fearing cosmic meaninglessness and yearning for the consolations of an objective foundation for morality, politics, and human destiny, human beings imagine divinities.

Friedrich Nietzsche (1844–1900) viewed the creation of the major Western religions as the revenge of the herd.[31] The masses of human beings, resentful and fearful of those more noble and excellent, devise religion as a way of humbling their betters. Slogans such as "the meek will inherit the earth" and "the wealthy are as likely to pass through the gates of heaven as a camel is of passing through the eye of a needle" warm the cockles of the resentful masses and tame the haughtiness of the powerful. Religion, under this view, is a method born of ill motives to install and reinforce a particular system of values that glorifies equality, mediocrity, and social domesticity. Fueled by a lowest-common-denominator mentality, religion honors herd values to the detriment of potentially noble types. To ensure general compliance with these values, religion invents an all-powerful Supreme Being with strong retributive leanings: to fall out of line is to risk eternal suffering. Such an enforcer, who knows everything and can do anything, gives pause to even the most powerful on earth. Nietzsche concluded that the rise of science and the disaggregation of passionate religious conviction, the kind that truly animates everyday social life, showed that belief in God was no longer worthy. Human beings have created social conditions, including technological achievements that undermine intense religious commitment. Priests, ministers, and rabbis now preside over the "death of God" as they orchestrate rituals that lack the power to energize daily life.

Cicero's argument from design, to be made famous in the eighteenth century by William Paley (1743–1805), is also fraught with difficulties, many of which were first pointed out by David Hume (1711–1776). Any universe will have the appearance of being designed, as the parts will be mutually adapted to a significant degree. That this design was the result of deliberate, conscious planning does not follow. Natural physical processes that are not conjured by anthropomorphic designers—say, the forces of evolution and naturalistic adaptation—may be the sources of apparent order. Also, any analogy between human artifacts and natural objects is contestable. Even if both types of objects share some similar properties, they may have them for different reasons. That only intelligent, deliberate designers can produce orderly systems remains doubtful. Moreover, natural objects that are alive and self-sustaining bear numerous striking dissimilarities from human artifacts which are material and inert. How are we to independently select the relevant similarities and dismiss the irrelevant differences? The discontinuity in the natural world—tornadoes, hurricanes, floods, plagues, pestilences, and the like—suggest that if a grand designer was fashioning our world then he/she/it was thoroughly fallible, perhaps inept. Or perhaps our world was produced by a shoddy committee.[32]

Contemporary philosopher George Smith adds:

> Consider the idea that nature itself is the product of design. How could this be demonstrated? Nature . . . provides the basis of comparison by which we distinguish between designed objects and natural objects. We are able to infer the presence of design only to the extent that the characteristics of an object differ from natural characteristics. Therefore, to claim that nature as a whole was designed is to destroy the basis by which we differentiate between [human] artifacts and natural objects. Evidences of design are those characteristics *not* found in nature, so it is impossible to produce evidence of design *within* the context of nature itself. Only if we first step beyond nature, and establish the existence of a supernatural designer, can we conclude that nature is the result of conscious planning.[33]

Objections of equal or greater power can be raised against Cicero's acceptance of the existence of human souls, personal immortality, and an afterlife.[34] But fairness requires that readers note that Cicero did not offer his musings on the gods, divine providence, personal immortality, the afterlife, and the nature of religion as deductive *proofs* that conclusively establish truths. Instead, they provide Cicero probabilistic support for his antecedent convictions.

The Place of Rhetoric

For the most part, Cicero concludes that oratory and philosophy have developed as two fractured disciplines: Philosophers have failed to teach, or be taught by orators; thus philosophy is not as persuasive as it might be and oratory is not as grounded in principles as sound as it might be (OR 11–13). For Cicero, great philosophy and powerful rhetoric must be joined (I 2.8).

At least three senses of "rhetoric" are prevalent. The first is morally neutral: effective and persuasive speech. The second is morally disreputable: deceitful speech designed to sway people to certain views without regard for their truth content. The third sense is morally ambiguous: performative or entertaining speech designed to show the elasticity of language or the skill of the artist in conjuring seemingly strong reasons for intuitively weak positions. This need not be morally tainted, at least when everyone participating understands the drill.

Plato, in his death battle with the Sophists, thoroughly lambasted rhetoric as subversive to the pursuit of truth. Rhetoric in the second and third senses led listeners to become skeptics, cynics, and, horror of horrors, relativists. Although Plato was a stunning exemplar of rhetoric in the first sense, he never carefully distinguished the three senses of the term and, accordingly, history records him, too simplistically, as the archenemy of rhetoric as such.

Cicero identified great orators with grand statesmen. Moreover, grand statesmen, who fulfill the highest human function, are always more valuable than great philosophers. Rhetoric, which combines style and content, is a critical skill for both statesmen and philosophers. The ideal man will combine philosophy with grand rhetoric (in the first sense). The ideal orator will enjoy a broad education which provides the ballast for his skills and a safeguard against the dangers of rhetoric in the second sense. The ideal orator must practice arguing hypothetical court cases; practice writing speeches; undergo voice and memory training; critically analyze historians, theorists, and poets; learn Roman laws and history thoroughly; understand the traditions of the senate and the rights of allies contained in treaties; and study political philosophy (OO 1.134–159).

Style matters for Cicero, in philosophy, statesmanship, and everyday life. This view, unsurprisingly, influenced the way he wrote philosophy. Cicero eschewed the quasi-scientific philosophical prose so common today—passionless, technical, and often excruciating—in favor of explicitly rhetorical, lively advocacy that was particularly suited to the ethical, political, practical subjects he most appreciated. He found Epicurean compositions stylistically inadequate, and Stoic writings even worse. Cicero sums up his view:

> It is possible for someone to have a correct opinion and not to be able to express it with style. But to assign one's reflections to literature without the ability to organize or clarify them or do anything to captivate the reader is a mark of a man who squanders leisure and literature. . . . I have always judged that philosophy to be perfect which can discuss the biggest questions fully and elegantly. (TD 1.6–7)

Cicero advised that oratorical and literary styles must be appropriate to their audience and subject. In contrast to the grand and florid styles matched to other disciplines and purposes, philosophy requires a simple mode of speaking and writing characteristic of passionate, intelligent, refined conversations. Accordingly, much of his work is written in dialogue form. For Cicero, the marriage of rhetoric and philosophy is a humanistic ideal that nourishes a free, republican society.

Contemporary philosophers would do well to heed Cicero's advice about rhetoric and oratory. Persuasion does not automatically mean deceiving arguments, disregard for truth, and fraudulent manipulation. Our greatest stylist, Plato, was also the philosopher most opposed to rhetoric and oratory in those senses.

The Grand Republic

The state, for Cicero, is the property of a people united by justice and a common good: "a people [in the requisite sense] are a union of a large number of men in agreement in respect to what is right and just and associated in the common interest" (R 1.39). A constitution earns the honorific title *res publica* if and only if the people form a society grounded on their agreements about justice and on their common good, and the agents conducting public affairs systematically consult and advance those agreements about justice and the common good. Natural law grounds all moral and political judgments. That law is eternal, unchanging, and universal. Altering, restricting, or abolishing judgments based on natural law are wrongful acts. Human beings do not need an external interpreter of natural law because we share reason, basic human biological nature, and an implanted sense of justice. Thus, natural law requires that all citizens share a moral equality before the law (L 2.10–2.14). Accordingly, a state that systematically transgresses the principles of natural law relinquishes its legitimacy; it no longer merits the honorific title "state." So, too, laws that transgress the moral substance of natural law are not truly "laws." A systematically unjust polity is a tyranny, not a state. Accordingly, Rome under Caesar was a state in form but a tyranny in substance (O 2.23–29; O 3.83–85). The people, then, are logically and empirically prior to the state; they are a greater unity, part of which is the state, whose laws, practices, and institutions are subordinate to and derive their authority from the people. The common good, as a precondition of the state, is also prior to the state.

Borrowing freely from Plato, Aristotle, and Polybius, Cicero classified the three just states as monarchy, aristocracy, and democracy; the three comparable unjust politics that did not merit the term "state" were tyranny, oligarchy, and mob rule. Another, more complex state is that of the mixed constitution, which combines, in a moderate and balanced fashion, the elements of the three just states. Sparta, Carthage, and Rome were the best exemplars of the mixed constitution (R 1.69; R 2.41–42). For Cicero, the delicate balance between the value of the individual and the imperative of the common good defines justice: "justice is a disposition of mind which accords to each his *dignitas* [worth, merit, reputation] while preserving the common interest" (I 2.160). Any state that erases social distinctions or that aspires to a classless society automatically violates the natural law: "A gentlemen and *novus homo* like Cicero is exceedingly sensitive to the differences, both acquired and inherited, among human beings, to the uniqueness of each, and consequently to the question of station, rank, and privilege."[35] Caesar's alleged tyranny had stripped Cicero of his *dignitas* by restricting his freedom to speak about and enact political judgments.

Accordingly, Cicero, a staunchly conservative aristocrat, was not a fan of popular rule, or social equality, or economic redistribution from wealthy to destitute. The state exists primarily to preserve private property, not as an engine of soul-crafting. Cicero championed the relatively small aristocratic class who enjoyed predominate control of the agricultural lands in Italy and political power in the senate. Although firmly convinced of the presence of natural law, Cicero is vague as to its specific content. He advises that natural law covers the right of property ownership, revenge, religion, duty, gratitude, reverence, justice, and truth (T 90; I 2.65–66, 161). The reference to natural justice contrasts with the Epicurean position that justice is purely conventional and flows from human fears and self-interest. Cicero insists that human society, instead, arises from

human reason. The natural sociability of human beings, arising from shared reason and speech, is the origin of all human relationships. The state is also natural,
not merely conventional, because it facilitates basic human needs such as survival, security, and the development of virtue (R 1.1–2).

Cicero's libertarian leanings on private property reflect and reinforce Roman practices of his day: "The acute competition and struggle of members of the
ruling class for power and riches, the unbridled exploitation of the provinces, the
resort to violence and the proscription of great families, and the rapid rise and
fall of family fortunes are all manifestations of an increasing social atomism."[36]
Cicero does not raise issues of fair distribution of private property or whether an
allocation advances the common good. On the contrary, he consistently rages
against agrarian laws, redistribution schemes, and forgiveness of debt (O 2.78;
2.84). Unsurprisingly, he opposes property taxes and all intervention of government in the domain of private ownership (O 2.84). Clearly, Cicero holds sacred
the entitlement of a person to retain whatever they possess. The only exception
he mentions is transfer of property in the interest of the survival of a person who
would greatly benefit the state and the wider community (O 3.29; 3.30). Rendering assistance to others based on their need is generally a function of private
charity not the state's distributive justice (O 1.49). The roots of economic con-
servatism and libertarian principles of just entitlement, then, may well be
planted in Cicero's philosophical soil.

Populist historians, such as Michael Parenti, lambaste Cicero's sense of
aristocratic privilege:

> During his tenure in office, Cicero lifted not a finger on behalf of the [common]
> people, and vigorously opposed all reform proposals. He and his Senate col-
> laborators quashed motions designed to cancel debts, effect land distribution,
> and allow the offspring of those exiled by Sulla to occupy public office. . . . He
> regarded the people as worthless groundlings, akin to criminals and degener-
> ates, "the common herd," the "masses and worst elements . . . many of them
> simply out for revolution." . . . To [Cicero], their restiveness was an outgrowth
> of their own personal malevolence rather than a response to unforgiving mate-
> rial circumstances.[37]

Cicero advocates the protection of private property and the preservation of the
class structure as the essential functions of the state for several reasons: the distinction between rulers and ruled is natural and eradicable; class differences between the working but propertyless and the non-working but propertied are also
natural and timeless; and both of these convictions assume the need for a social
division of labor. As the non-working but propertied—the ruling class—are
fewer in number than the working class, the state's protection of property rights
serves to safeguard the relatively few against the many. A cheerful reading
might even interpret this as Cicero's keen appreciation for minority rights!

A mixed constitution is the best form of government. The simple, just states
are too vulnerable to degeneration into tyrannies. Mixed constitutions, the best
example of which is the Roman republic in the age of Scipio Aemilianus, em-

body *potestas* (power) for the ruling magistrates, *auctoritas* (authority) for the meritorious aristocrats, and *libertas* (freedom) for the masses (R 1.69; R 2.57). Equitable balance, keen appreciation for social rank, and institutional constraints on instability generate a harmonious state and serene social order (R II 69). Although voting would be open to all citizens, ballots would be examined by the traditional leaders of the state (translated: aristocratic senators) to ensure that secret voting would not deprive the aristocrats of all influence (L 3.15; L 3.33–34). Viewed more skeptically, the mixed constitution is

> entirely compatible with an authoritarian, elitist, inegalitarian political society. It represents a partnership of landlord and peasant, in which the latter is a very junior partner. The mixed constitution is a masterful device for stabilizing and conserving lordly domination, while at the same time pacifying the peasantry and maintaining the solidarity of the state as a whole. . . . In the name of natural justice and moral equality he persists in a policy . . . of preservation of the · propertied status quo, regeneration of time-honored gentlemanly values, restoration of the ancestral constitution, and economic prescriptions to the advantage of the rich and the detriment of the poor. At the same time, he fails utterly to grasp the futility and bankruptcy of his recommendations.[38]

Cicero's unbridled patriotism and admiration for Roman history convinced him that the long development of Roman institutions achieved a united polity far better than could the efforts of any one strong man:

> In Rome [Cicero] finds a perfect state which is the creation not of the genius of one man but of the experience of generations and he discovers and tests political institutions by tracing the history and examining the operation of Roman institutions. Moreover, the entire universe is conceived on the analogy of the associations of men; and the vast order of celestial motions . . . is translated into the vast order of political relations shared by the gods and men in the Roman *mundus* (world).[39]

Lured by the consolations of retrospective falsification, Cicero peered back to the days of Scipio Aemilianus, consul in 147 and 134 BC, as the golden age. Scipio, grandson of the conqueror of Hannibal, demolished two hostile cities—Carthage and Numantia in Spain—was a master diplomat in dealing with the Roman senate, and shone as a man of culture. He spoke fluent Greek and his social circle included intellectuals such as the great historian Polybius and the Stoic philosopher Panaetius. Scipio combined military valor, a commitment to remedy the political corruption growing in Rome, and a calm, poised demeanor. He accepted Polybius's view that Rome must remain a republic balanced by its monarchical (consuls), aristocratic (senate), and democratic (tribunes) elements.

Cicero's patriotism was not parochial. As the Stoics had instructed, for Cicero all human beings are bonded to each other and to the divine by their common humanity and by their duties to universal, natural laws (R 3.33). *De Re Publica* concludes with "the dream of Scipio"—modeled on Plato's *Timaeus* and *Phaedo*—which chronicles the cosmology of the times, but also includes a decidedly religious theme. Accepting the reasonableness of Plato's proofs for immortality, Cicero cautions against suicide, underscores the need to care for one's country, but insists we should not neglect matters of eternal life. Those who do will remain earthbound after death. For Cicero, the existence of an afterlife and personal immortality is reasonable and probable, not the fantasies of deluded philosophers as suggested by the Epicureans (R 6.3–16). As always, for Cicero, diligent public service is the highest vocation and earns the greatest prizes. The reward for a virtuous life of political service is enduring glory and reunion with the souls of other virtuous statesmen after death:

> For all who have saved, defended or increased their fatherland, a special place in heaven has been assigned, where they may enjoy an eternal life of happiness. For nothing that is done on earth is more pleasing to that supreme god . . . than the councils and assemblies of men who have joined in just communities, which are called states. Those who govern and defend them come from this place, and to this place they return. (R 6.13)

Rejecting Plato's utopianism in *The Republic*, Scipio, Cicero's mouthpiece, sanctions a mixed constitution, with an elected aristocracy, and a judicial system that stresses the rule of law. Instead of conjuring an ideal state, Cicero extols the theory, if not the practice, underlying the Roman constitution. Incremental development, checks and balances, learning from successful experimentation, and insight into universal, natural law prevail. Throughout his work, Cicero unabashedly highlights his principles with Roman historical examples. This was required for his self-understanding as the path maker of Roman philosophy.

Moreover, Cicero tried to codify existing law in his *De Legibus*:

> Laws were scattered among the Twelve Tables, decrees of the Senate, records of court verdicts, opinions of jurisconsults, and praetors edicts. Rome had never had a lawgiver. Cicero aimed to take law away from the experts and give it to the people. By placing Natural Law above man-made statutes, he tries, innovatively, to put the hodge-podge in order. . . . Though his conservative bias is obvious, the freedom of the *populus* and the humanity of the law are important to him.[40]

The use of violence as a political instrument, though, was well known to Cicero. After all, such use was the stock in trade of Roman politics during his lifetime. Cicero justifies the use of violence only when it is required for self-defense and survival when law and order has disintegrated; when employing it will possibly be successful; when greater evil will not result; and when doing so enhances the preservation or security of the state.

Cicero cautions, though, that we may not harm others unless provoked by injustice (O 1.20; 3.76). In fact, to fail to avenge an unjust injury is itself wrong (O 3.74). He is especially harsh on Caesar:

> In the foolhardiness of depraved ambition Caesar has turned all the laws of god and men upside down. His confiscations of property were as unjust as Sulla's.

He was such a tyrant that Cato preferred to die rather than to look upon his face. He dominated everything, like master over slaves. He ruled by armed force, and by inspiring fear—the act of a madman. He is to be compared with the most notorious tyrants of all time. . . . He turned the subjects of the Republic Empire into slaves. . . . He was a co-conspirator with Catiline and positively exulted in doing wrong. He was a tyrant and so deserved death: to kill a tyrant is salutary surgery.[41]

Cicero's invective contrasts with his words in the *Second Philippic*, in which he contrasts Antony unfavorably with Caesar:

> Caesar was a man of genius, intellect and memory, literate and careful, with the ability to plan and the industry to execute. His military achievements, though disastrous to the state, were immense. He planned a monarchy for many years and labored through immense dangers to effect his plan. By his gifts, public works, distributions of food, and public hospitality he reconciled the uneducated masses to his rule. He attached his supporters to him by rewards, his enemies by an exhibition of mercy. (P 2.45)

Cicero explicitly endorses tyrannicide. No rightful society can be led by a tyrant. Those able to do so have a duty to slay such usurpers of power even though they are friends to whom one would typically have greater obligations than to strangers and acquaintances (O 3.19; 3.32). Tyrants destroy states and the common good that underlies states. Caesar's dictatorship, unlike those assumed during the history of the Roman republic, was unlimited in duration and not directed specifically in defense of a republic in crisis. For Cicero and his fellow *optimates*, Caesar's reign struck at the core of the constitutional system. Caesar demonstrated clearly that he regarded the Roman republic as obsolete. He consolidated and wielded all genuine political power. Murdering a tyrant is an act in the common interest, not private wrongdoing motivated by selfishness, and advances the security of the state. The termination of a tyrant ends systematic injustice and thereby rescues the state and redeems the common good. Those who systematically transgress natural law and the common good automatically place themselves in conflict with the rest of the people and should be regarded as public enemies. As always, preserving the state and supporting the common good, defined in his particularly aristocratic fashion, are paramount for Cicero (O 3.32).

For Cicero, the primary duties of natural justice include a negative duty not to physically harm others unjustifiably; a negative duty to respect private and socially-held property; negative and positive duties to fulfill promises and contracts; and positive duties to care for others in proportion to their worth and in accordance with our resources (O 1.15, 20, 23, 42–45). Cicero advocates not absolute, but proportionate, equality: people differ in value according to their station in society—defined by birth, wealth, and political and social status—and we owe more to those of greater value than we do to common folks. Cicero's unabashed aristocratic cheerleading underscores his commitment to property, wealth, trade, and social inequality as the cornerstones of republicanism. His notion of proportionate equality decrees that we should treat equals equally, but unequals unequally. The masses are inferior and should not be treated on a par with their social superiors. Accordingly, Cicero broke out in hives at the mere mention of land reform or redistribution during his political career.

> Cicero and his peers rarely, if ever, feel any pressing moral duty or humanitarian impulse to be generous to the poor. If money is to be given to the destitute, they must be worthy. Generosity has little to do with pity. In fact, the two are quite conveniently separated. Generosity is, rather, thought of as an investment in friendship or a method of winning friends for the future.[42]

Although he is drawn to Stoic cosmopolitanism and subscribes to the shared rationality and moral nature of all human beings, Cicero's life and deepest instincts led him to a thoroughly aristocratic ideal: an essentially leisured, wealthy elite should rule over the vast majority of working poor. Vast inequalities in privilege, material resources, and political power are justified by the factual superiority of the few over the many. Class division between social superiors and social inferiors is critical to every flourishing state, and the former are entitled to rule while the latter are obligated to obey. Cicero reconciles the two strains of his thought—beliefs in natural moral equality and factual inequality—by pointing out that although all humans share equally rational potentials, we do not equally actualize our rational and moral natures.

In that vein, Cicero divides occupations into three categories. Vulgar careers include shop keeping, retail trade, tax-collecting, and money-lending. The most vulgar careers pander to sensual delights: fishermen, butchers, cooks, dancers, and entertainers. Respectable careers such as medicine, architecture, and teaching are acceptable for those who must labor for a living. Gentlemanly careers, the highest callings, include the military, politics, philosophy, oratory, farming, and large-scale commerce (O 1.150–151, 115–116; TD 2.35).

The ballast for these distinctions is Cicero's disdain for salaried employees who labor for a living, thereby underscoring their economic dependence. True gentlemen are economically independent, having amassed sufficient private property to engage in lofty pursuits. Although earlier thinkers, particularly Aristotle and Polybius, discussed the important of private property, Cicero, anticipating Locke, was the first political theorist to make it the foundation of his political philosophy. As stated earlier, Cicero was not alarmed by vast disparities of property and wealth. He consistently denounced redistribution efforts, convinced that they arose from populist politicians bent on securing political power by soaking the wealthy to placate the poor: "Guardians of the republic will avoid the type of gift-giving by which things are taken away from one group and given to another. Above all, they will work to see that each person keeps what is his by means of the fairness of justice and the law courts" (O 2.72–85). In a classic question-begging exercise, Cicero took a person's accumulated property as a demonstration of his superior industry, skill, rationality, and desert (R 1.27–28;

O 1.106). Nature, itself, decrees that the superior man will amass more than common folks, who should be content with their less gaudy holdings.

In sum, Cicero addressed a political structure hugely more complicated and larger than the Greek city-state model that had obsessed earlier theorists. He placed the protection of private property at the forefront of political theory; refined the notion of natural law and the definitions of the state and law, which provided a criterion of legitimacy for the states and their laws; sketched a justification of assassination; advocated a mixed constitution where moral equality before the law and political inequality coalesced uneasily; and enthusiastically accepted class society. Freedom is defined by law which acknowledges class distinctions and proportionate equality: some are owed more commensurate with their social station; the masses are designed only for labor, while a minority benefit more from those labors and manage the state; and such class division is part of the natural order. All citizens have a political voice—they may deliberate and vote—but only the propertied aristocrats hold critical political power. Cicero is an unrepentant champion for supreme control of the Roman republic by his own class.[43]

> Cicero's weakness as a politician was that his principles rested on a mistaken analysis. He failed to understand the reasons for the crisis that tore apart the Roman Republic. Julius Caesar, with the pitiless insight of genius, understood that the constitution with its endless checks and balances prevented effective government, but like so many of his contemporaries Cicero regarded politics in personal rather than structural terms. For Caesar the solution lay in a completely new system of government; for Cicero it lay in finding better men to run the government and better laws to keep them in order. . . . [Cicero] needed continuity and stability to thrive and it was his misfortune to live in an age of change; he was a temperamental conservative caught in the nets of a revolution.[44]

Cicero did not grasp the stark divergence between ideas developed in a different time and the exigencies of contemporary Roman circumstances. That, and his unwavering aristocratic outlook, cast his gaze backward rather than forward. Cicero prescriptions ignore the realities of Roman life at the time he wrote: If only events and attitudes can revert to an idealized past will present social maladies be cured. He turns a myopic eye to the presence of vast economic disparities, the problem of the relationship between Rome and its provinces, the deep political chasms within the ruling class, the increasing use of violence and fraud as a means to political success, the growing slave-labor force, the stentorian demands of the professionalized military, and the legitimate grievances of those pesky peasants. As with most obdurate *optimates,* Cicero stood steadfastly opposed to social reform. Refusing to consider the ineradicable effects of the historical events interspersed between the supposed golden age of Scipio and his own time, Cicero yearned to scamper back in time.

If only political ills were so easily cured. Imagine an American curmudgeon in the early twenty-first century wistfully recalling the Eisenhower era—

preferably before the wholesale introduction of rock and roll. Surely, the civility, serenity, and firmer understandings of social expectations and the common good of that era would be a welcome relief to the fractious individualism, social coarseness, and technological hegemony of our own. (At least for those who benefited from the class structure of that era.) Reimagining the world through the prism of retrospective falsification can be a consoling exercise, but ultimately it squanders time. Given the massive social, political, scientific, and technological changes of the past two score and ten, reverting to the dominant mentality of the 1950s would require an incomprehensible collective amnesia. This, all of it, is stone cold obvious.

Yet Cicero, floundering in devastatingly perilous, political times, could offer little more than dusting off past certitudes as the remedy for present ills. Coincidentally, his idealized images of the supposed golden age of Rome invigorated his own privileges, prerogatives, and authority, as well as those of his social class. But, after all, the doctrine of proportionate equality would demand nothing less.

Cicero's motives, though, were not cynical. His veneration of *mores maiorum* was a challenge to his contemporary aristocrats to measure up to past ideals. He pleaded with his peers to reward only the deserving with enduring glory; to reclaim a moral basis for the republic; to celebrate the common good and to denigrate petty, personal ambition; to abrogate fraud and force as political weapons and to replace them with Roman valor and free speech; and to cherish the founding principles of the republic as the cornerstones of noble conduct. Perhaps many of his political conclusions were naïve or unimaginative, and a few sprung from mixed motives and were self-serving. But to deny Cicero his appropriate honor as a zealous patriot and virtuous statesman would be uncharitable and mean-spirited. The *novus homo* struggled mightily to carve his place alongside Romulus, Lucius Junius Brutus, and the Scipios. Through his political, philosophical, and oratorical labors he merited enduring glory in its normative sense; so let us now praise yet again this deservedly famous Roman.

When, If Ever, Is Assassination Morally Justified?

After Caesar's assassination, Cicero sketched a justification for tyrannicide: human beings are obligated to preserve the well-being of other human beings; tyranny destroys, generally, the welfare of society; Caesar's reign was a growing tyranny; under such circumstances, slaying the tyrant is a moral duty even where the tyrant is a personal friend to whom greater concern is otherwise owed than to people generally (O 3.19; 3.32). Tyrants destroy states and the common good that underlies states. Murdering a tyrant is an act in the common interest, not private wrongdoing motivated by selfishness, and advances the security of the state. The termination of a tyrant ends systematic injustice and thereby rescues the state and redeems the common good. Those who systematically transgress natural law and the common good automatically place themselves in conflict with the rest of the people and should be regarded as public enemies (O 3.32).

Cicero's account is incomplete and unrigorous, but it captures well numerous moral intuitions that retain currency today. I will now use Cicero's outline as a springboard to constructing a general theory of assassination that I will later implement to assess the events of March 15, 44 BC.

Political assassinations, those energized by the slayers' concern to seize power or significantly affect public policy, arouse citizens' sentiments of national identity and political affiliation. Such killings affect society as a whole, not merely the victims and those closest to them. Unless almost all citizens are thoroughly repelled by the structure and processes of government, the social relation a country's leader has to his or her constituents must be taken into account when trying to justify the murder.

The perpetrators justified the assassination of Caesar by appeal to traditional values rooted in the *mores maiorum*. The object was to destroy Caesar's political innovations and restore republican values. Modern tyrannicides, in contrast, are typically justified by appeal to revolutionary ends: changing the world, or at least one's nation, by clearing the way for new social organizations vivified by an enlightened minority.

The analysis I provide applies only to assassinations of political leaders by their constituents. Tyrannicides undertaken by foreign interveners will require additional criteria.

Assassination is morally justified if and only if the following conditions pertain:

1. *The Tyrant Has Evilly and Systematically Transgressed against the Common Good: The existing state practices, policies, institutions, or laws must be gravely incompatible with the common good and the target of the assassination must be morally responsible for that situation or for its prolongation.*

Some state rulers are tyrants because they gained power illegitimately; others are tyrants because they rule for their own aggrandizement and not for the common good. An enormously unrepentant tyrant gains power illegitimately only to sacrifice the common good to his own interests. Rulers who gain power illegitimately but exercise their power in service to the common good typically discard their initial stigma of tyranny.

To assassinate a political leader merely to enhance an already decently functioning society is morally wrong. The political atmosphere must be so corrupt that appeals to the common good are empty rhetoric. The political atmosphere is below the standard of a minimally decent society. If the target of the assassination also seized power illegitimately, that would add to the overall incompatibility of the regime to the common good, but illegal seizure of power is not a necessary condition of morally justified assassination.

Cicero highlighted this criterion in his work. Caesar had allegedly destroyed republican institutions; corroded the common good that underwrote them; and by systematically transgressing against natural law, Caesar had positioned himself as a public enemy. The state, under Caesar, was seriously incompatible with the common good and Caesar was responsible for the sorry transformation of the state from republic to tyranny. All human beings have a moral duty to preserve the well-being of others; that duty requires the elimination of systematic state injustice and those responsible for perpetrating it.

2. *The Assassination Will Advance the Common Good:* The beneficial changes to state practices, policies, institutions, or laws that the assassins seek would in fact facilitate the common good.

The assassination must have a positive effect on the common good and the perpetrators must be able to articulate the reasonable probability that those salutary consequences will ensue. If the assassination is followed by a comparable or worse tyrant coming to power, or the absence of political changes compatible with the common good, the assassination has produced no positive advance. Also, if few citizens desire political change it is highly unlikely that the assassination of the political leader will have the desired effects.

Assassins must also bear in mind that successful tyrannicides guarantee one person will die and open possibilities that several others will perish or be seriously harmed during the process. Will the elimination of the tyrant dramatically increase prospects for liberty? Or will the assassination invite intensified repression, worse tyranny, and civil war? Those are the questions. A reasonable, good faith belief that tyrannicide will accomplish its long-range aims is required to justify the act. But what standard for such belief should be imposed?

Surely, requiring potential assassins to demonstrate their case beyond a reasonable doubt is too onerous. We can rarely prove antecedently, to a moral certainty, that our future actions will produce only welcome results. But requiring potential assassins to demonstrate their case by preponderance of the evidence seems too weak and would justify too many murders. Tyrannicide is enormously risky and tears at the fabric of government. Allowing plotters to justify their actions by a showing that their murder of a leader of state is, say, only 51 percent likely to attain the good ends they seek is morally irresponsible. Accordingly, the standard imposed for justification of contemplated tyrannicide should be clear and convincing evidence. The standard of knowledge required to draw conclusions from the various criteria of justification listed here approaches, but need not meet, "to a moral certainty." The problem is that great uncertainty typically pervades the actual consequences of political assassination. This obstacle, though, also attaches to political revolutions and modern warfare, both of which are sometimes judged morally permissible.

Cicero assumes that by rightfully eliminating the tyrant, the common good and beneficial political institutions would automatically rise up or be invigorated. This assumption is rash. Eliminating an evil-doer does not necessarily establish or restore a healthy polity. In that vein, to conclude accurately that a tyrant, by his systematic misdeeds, has forfeited his right to life (or may have his right to life overridden) does not automatically imply that others should slay the tyrant. Several other prudential and moral considerations must be examined prior to asserting that implication.

> *3. Assassination Is a Last Resort: From a practical standpoint, the assassination is a last resort.*

Conditions must be such that (a) it is highly probable that the salutary changes cannot be produced in a reasonable time through a means less evil than murder; and (b) all other reasonable means of securing the desired political modifications, short of murder, have been explored and have failed.

Theoretically, the "last resort" criterion is almost impossible to satisfy. Always, it seems, some actions short of murder can still be attempted. That is why I add the "from a practical standpoint," "reasonable time," and "reasonable means" modifiers. Although such notions are contestable, they permit action without requiring an impossibly lofty epistemological standard.

> *4. Assassination Produces the Greatest Balance of Good over Evil: Of all available practical alternatives under the circumstances, assassination must result in the greatest overall balance of good over evil.*

The beneficial changes to state practices, policies, institutions, or laws that the assassins seek must have a high probability of facilitating the common good significantly more than other beneficial modifications that can be achieved within a reasonable length of time but which do not require assassination. Conditions must be such that (a) not only will the assassination nurture political modifications that will advance the common good, but (b) no other method, short of assassination, will achieve comparable salutary political changes within a reasonable time.

This standard is slightly different from the last resort criterion. The last resort criterion addresses only the *specific* beneficial political changes brought on by the assassination and asks if *those* changes can be brought about by less violent means. The instant standard addresses beneficial political changes *generally* and asks if other comparably beneficial modifications can be brought about by less violent means.

Moreover, the good brought about by the assassination must outweigh the evil involved in murder. If the salutary modifications brought about by political assassination clearly but only marginally advance the common good then the assassination is unjustified because the benefits do not outweigh the evil of murder. For example, if a citizen of Iran assassinates his leader in order to secure only a change in the laws on curfew the murder is unjustified.

Finally, straightforward utilitarian moral calculations force potential assassins to revisit the alternatives to murder to ensure that no less violent means of securing salutary political modifications are available. For example, if a significantly less violent alternative to political assassination would generate modifications to state practices that were only slightly less beneficial than those changes produced by political assassination then the less violent alternative is morally prescribed. If a contemplated assassination would foreseeably result in, say, fifty units of social good with a cost of, say, thirty units of social evil, the net social advance would be twenty units. If a less violent means of social change would produce forty units of social good at a cost of fifteen units of social evil, the net social advance would be twenty-five units. Under such circumstances, assassination is unjustified. Also, even if the net social advance were the same—if both assassination and the less violent means of social change would both produce, say, twenty-five net units of social good—assassination is not morally justified.

> **5. *The Assassination Must Flow from Morally Acceptable Motives:*** *The motives of the assassins must be morally appropriate and grounded in the realities of the situation insofar as they are discoverable.*

Even where standards (1)–(4) pertain, assassination is not morally justified if the perpetrators bear wrongful motives for their actions. If their reason for acting is to advance the common good after a good faith analysis of the moral nuances of the realities of the situation then they pass this test. If they are using the slogan of the common good merely as a cover for their own perceived interests and dispositions—personal revenge, lust for political power, hatred of the victim, and the like—then they fail this test. Granted, motives for dramatic actions are typically mixed and difficult to unravel. Nevertheless, an overall assessment must be made because wrongful motives morally contaminate our deeds.

Cicero noted that murdering a tyrant is an act in the common interest—it advances state security—not private wrongdoing motivated by selfishness. He understood that motives are relevant in assessing behavior. While it may be argued generally that moral agents can sometimes do the right action for the wrong reasons—for example, saving the life of a drowning child is morally righteous even though the rescuer acted only to secure a reward—cases of political assassination are especially delicate and merit strict scrutiny of the agent's motives. An ill-motivated conspirator is also more likely not to assess the other requirements for justified political assassination, or to assess them in bad faith.

> **6. *The Assassins Must Employ the Least Wicked Means:*** *The assassins must strive to minimize the evil of the method of execution.*

Even where all other standards have been met, if the assassins do not minimize the pain and suffering of their victim, then the act is morally flawed. The infliction of gratuitous pain and suffering is morally wrong even though the assassination is otherwise justified. To needlessly torture the victim or employ methods designed to increase the victim's pain and suffering is unjustified.

The victim of political assassination is forcibly abducted or detained, against his or her will, without due process of law and without opportunity to mount a defense, and the assassins deem themselves judge, jury, and executioners. Especially under such circumstances, the moral requirement to refrain from the infliction of needless pain and suffering must be underscored.

7. The Assassins Should Subject Their Actions to Legal Processes, If Practical: *Should the assassins submit voluntarily to the due processes of law after their deed?*

Even assassins who do not *regret* their decision—who lack all desire to have acted otherwise given the situation—may appropriately feel *remorse* about having to murder a state ruler in the name of the common good. Although the action was required for higher ends, the fact that it was necessary to terminate a person's life is horrifying. The assassins understand that events would have been much better had the political situation been different. Although they purportedly acted in defense of liberty, in service to the common good, and as representatives of those citizens unable to defend themselves, the assassins would have preferred that murdering the tyrant was unnecessary.

Perhaps the most controversial issue surrounding political assassination is whether the perpetrators should submit voluntarily to the due processes of law after slaying their target. The case in favor of including this requirement: The murderers have substituted their personal judgments for the laws and processes of their state; murder is universally denounced as a legal wrong; in order to show their ongoing commitment to the rule of law and to underscore the purity of their motives, the assassins should submit voluntarily to legal processes; pristine motives for political assassination should not translate into immunity from prosecution for a serious violation of law; if the assassins' cause is genuinely noble they should be willing be die for it, if deemed necessary, just as they were willing to murder another person in its name; doing so also decreases the risk that this act of political assassination might wrongly inspire other, unjustified political murders. Moreover, submitting to legal processes after their deed subjects the assassins to the judgment of their fellow citizens—it gives them an opportunity to justify their murder in open court to their peers who will impartially assess their case.

The case against including this requirement: The freedom fighters have merely held the state accountable to its own professed beliefs, at least in a democracy or republic; if the common good is central to the polity, doing that which is required to reinstate it is not a substitution of judgment, but a recommitment to shared, fundamental values; yes, murder is a legal wrong, but under emergency situations (review the criteria above) it is sometimes morally permissible; even though the tyrant has been slain, many of his minions and bobos will remain in high political office and will skew any legal process to which the freedom fighters voluntarily submit; the court procedure, accordingly, will not be a dispassionate, objective examination of the defense offered by the freedom fighters; instead, the legal process will be thoroughly and irredeemably contaminated by an emotionally charged, prejudiced atmosphere—determinations of guilt will depend entirely on the prior political commitments of the jury and/or judge. What possible forum in the nation would actually result in impartial deliberations and judgments? Accordingly, how would voluntarily submitting to an arbitrary process make peace with the rule of law?

Judged from abstract, moral theory, the assassins should submit voluntarily to due process after murdering their target, at least under a democracy or republic underwritten by the rule of law. In practice, though, political assassinations that would pass the justificatory muster of criteria (1)–(6), occur in social contexts that fall well below the standards of a decently functioning society. The immediate aftermath of political assassination is typically chaos. The assassins should be subjected to due process of law if and only if decently functioning political and legal institutions have been established or resuscitated. Thus, the assassins' day in court may occur well after their murderous deed. But in such cases, justice delayed is justice affirmed.

Notes

1. I used the following sources for my account of Cicero's life and times: Philip Matyszak, *Chronicle of the Roman Republic* (London: Thames & Hudson, Ltd., 2003); Marcus Tullius Cicero, *Letters of Cicero*, ed. and trans. by L. P. Wilkinson (Bristol, GB: Bristol Classical Press, 1982); Plutarch, *The Lives of Noble Grecians and Romans*, vol. II, trans. by John Dryden, ed. and rev. by Arthur Hugh Clough (New York: The Modern Library, 1979); Cassius Dio, *The History of Rome*, vol. 1–6. (Middlesex: The Echo Library, 2007); Sallust, *Catiline's War, The Jugurthine War, Histories*, trans. by A. J. Woodman (London: Penguin Books, 2007); W. K. Lacey, *Cicero and the End of the Roman Republic* (London: Hodder and Stoughton, 1978); Anthony Everitt, *Cicero: The Life and Times of Rome's Greatest Politician* (New York: Random House, 2001); T. A. Dorey, ed., *Cicero* (New York: Basic Books, 1965); A. E. Douglas, *Cicero* (Oxford: Clarendon Press, 1968); Marcus Tullius Cicero, *Philippics*, trans. by Walter C. A. Ker (Cambridge, MA: Harvard University Press, 1926); Mary T. Boatwright, Daniel J. Gargola, and Richard J. A. Talbert, *The Romans: From Village to Empire* (New York: Oxford University Press, 2004).

2. Historians critical of Cicero's role in the Catiline conspiracy are less sanguine: "Modern and ancient interpretations have been heavily influenced by Cicero's own versions of events, which sought first to demonize and exaggerate the threat, then to sing his own praises and sometimes to justify the summary executions which later returned to haunt him and even drove him briefly into exile." Greg Woolf, *Et tu, Brute?* (London: Profile Books, Ltd., 2006), 28. See also, Michael Parenti, *The Assassination of Julius Caesar* (New York: The New Press, 2003), 85–111.

3. Matyszak, *Chronicle of Roman Republic*, 214.

4. Lacey, *Cicero and the End*, 66.

5. Wilkinson, *Letters of Cicero*, 18.

6. T. A. Dorey, "Honesty in Roman Politics," in Dorey, *Cicero*, 41, 42.

7. Neal Wood, *Cicero's Social & Political Thought* (Berkeley: University of California Press, 1988), 31–32.

8. Quoted in Wood, ibid., 179.

9. Everitt, *Cicero*, 232.

10. Lacey, *Cicero and the End*, 138.

11. Plutarch, *Lives*, 412, 424.

12. Wilkinson, *Letters of Cicero*, 18–19.

13. Dorey, "Honesty in Roman Politics," in Dorey, *Cicero*, 44.

14. Arthur D. Kahn, "Was There No Superstructure in Ancient Rome?" *Monthly Review* 41 (February 1990): 36.

15. Miriam Griffin, "Philosophy for Statesmen: Cicero and Seneca," in H. W. Schmidt and R. Wulfing, eds., *Antikes Denken* (Heidelberg: Gymnasium Beihefte 9, 1987): 146.

16. John Glucker, "Cicero's Philosophical Affiliations," in John Dillon and A. A. Long, eds., *The Question of "Eclecticism"* (Berkeley, CA: University of California Press, 1988), 34–69; John Glucker, "Cicero's Philosophical Affiliations Again," *LCM* 17 (1992): 134–38.

17. Woldemar Gorler, "Silencing the Troublemaker," in J. G. F. Powell, *Cicero: The Philosopher* (Oxford: Clarendon Press, 1999), 111–12.

18. Glucker, "Cicero's Affiliations," 61.

19. J. G. Davies, "The Originality of Cicero's Philosophical Works," *Latomus* 30 (1971): 119.

20. A. E. Douglas, "Cicero the Philosopher," in Dorey, *Cicero*, 140.

21. Paul MacKendrick, *The Philosophical Books of Cicero* (New York: St. Martin's Press, 1989), 201

22. Ibid., 202.

23. Everitt, *Cicero*, 55.

24. MacKendrick, *Philosophical Books*, 163–164.

25. Tom Holland, *Rubicon: The Last Years of the Roman Republic* (New York: Doubleday, 2003), 33, 109, 113, 143.

26. Ibid., 5.

27. A. A. Long, *From Epicurus to Epictetus* (Oxford: Clarendon Press, 2006), 310.

28. Richard McKeon, "Introduction to the Philosophy of Cicero," in Marcus Tullius Cicero, *Selected Works*, trans. by Hubert M. Poteat (Chicago: University of Chicago Press, 1950), 44.

29. Karl Marx, *Karl Marx: Selected Writings*, ed. by David McLellan (Oxford: Oxford University Press, 1977).

30. Sigmund Freud, *The Future of an Illusion*, trans. by James Strachey (New York: W.W. Norton & Co., 1961).

31. Friedrich Nietzsche, *Beyond Good and Evil*, trans. by Walter Kaufmann (New York: Vintage Books, 1966); *On The Genealogy of Morals*, trans. by Walter Kaufmann and R. J. Hollingdale (New York: Vintage Books, 1967).

32. John Hick, *Philosophy of Religion* (Englewood Cliffs, NJ: Prentice-Hall, Inc., 1963), 25- 27.

33. George H. Smith, *Atheism: The Case Against God* (Amherst, NY: Prometheus Books, 1980), 268.

34. See, for example, Hick, *Philosophy of Religion*; Smith, *Atheism*; Richard Dawkins, *The God Delusion* (New York: Houghton Mifflin, 2006)

35. Wood, *Cicero's Thought*, 149.

36. Ibid., 115.
37. Parenti, *Assassination of Caesar*, 92, 87, 88.
38. Wood, *Cicero's Thought*, 175, 204–5.
39. McKeon, *Introduction*, 9–10.
40. MacKendrick, *Philosophical Books*, 77.
41. Ibid., 250.
42. Wood, *Cicero's Thought*, 101.
43. Ibid., 206–8.
44. Everitt, *Cicero*, 321–22.

Texts and Their Abbreviations

As is common practice, where I have cited from Cicero's writings the references in all cases have been given immediately in the text and not in the notes. All references are to Book numbers and/or sections, not page numbers, unless otherwise stated.

For example:

O 1.25= *De Officiis*, Book 1, section 25.

I have used the following abbreviations:

A =	*Academica*
AM =	*Laelius de Amicitia*
B =	*Brutus*
C =	*Consolatio*
D =	*De Divinatione*
DF =	*De Finibus Bonorum et Malorum*
F =	*De Fato*
H =	*Hortensius*
I =	*De Inventione*
L =	*De Legibus*
ND =	*De Natura Deorum*
O =	*De Officiis*
OA =	*Cato Maior de Senectute*
OO =	*De Oratore*
OR =	*Orator*
P =	*Philippics*
R =	*De Republica*
SP =	*Paradoxa Stoicorum*
T =	*Topica*
TD =	*Tusculanae Disputationes*

Parenthetical references to the correspondence of Cicero include the letter number and date as compiled in Marcus Tullius Cicero, *Letters of Cicero*, ed.

and trans. by L. P. Wilkinson (Bristol, GB: Bristol Classical Press, 1982). Thus, "Ltr. 147: 7/15/43 BC" is letter number 147, dated July 15, 43 BC.

Chapter Two
Stoicism I: Cato

This chapter introduces the fundamental methods and beliefs of Stoicism through the life and thought of Cato the Younger. Although Cicero exaggerated when he called Cato "The Perfect Stoic," that Cato's reputation for moral rectitude and his courageous battle against perceived tyranny inspired future generations is beyond dispute. I subject basic Stoicism to critical scrutiny and conclude by introducing the image of the joyful transcender, a portrait drawn from the work of Friedrich Nietzsche and Robert Nozick. The joyful transcender shares several crucial Stoic convictions, but offers a much different picture of the good life for human beings.

The Roots of Stoicism

Founded by Zeno of Citium (336–264 BC), Stoicism's most famous early disciples were Cleanthes of Assos (331–232 BC) and Chrysippus of Soli (280–207 BC).[1] Stoics were monotheists and adhered to natural law, a universal code of morality. Everything happens as it must happen, according to fate. The world-soul or Zeus or Nature directs everything for the best. Happiness flows from reasonableness, from understanding the natural law, and from judging and acting compatibly with natural law. Although external events are fated, our attitudes toward and judgments about those events are in our control. Unlike Platonists who believed that our world is a shadowy imitation of a higher reality, Stoics were materialists. Only bodies exist; but time, void, place, and the meanings of utterances subsist (exist as abstractions). Some entities, then, may not exist, but still be something. Platonic Forms or Universals, though, neither exist nor subsist; they are mere imaginings.

Basic Stoic beliefs included the following: the gods exist and act providentially; the human soul is divine and immortal; the human will can earn freedom; the proper path to the good life is to follow nature; the universe is governed by natural law; the virtuous and the rational are united; the virtuous person is self-sufficient and happy; and moral duty requires human beings to live honorably. Most interesting is the view that human beings are not antecedently free, but the Stoic sage wins freedom by aligning his desires with natural law in accordance with god's overall plan. Fate, then, is a continuous series of causes flowing from that plan and embodied in natural law. Stoics assumed that innate human tendencies—our natural dispositions—should be retained in any adequate rendering of human wisdom. They looked to the tendencies already present in newborn babies as strong evidence of what is innate in us. This approach is now known as the cradle argument: the fundamental drive of all living creatures is self-love, which is reflected in the tendency of babies to desire what supports health and to reject what does not. That which flows from nature and produces consequences in accord with nature is worthy.

> The first duty is to preserve one's self in one's natural condition; the second is to retain those things which are in accordance with nature and to repel those which are not; the third is choice conditioned by duty, once the principle of choice and rejection has been discovered; and the fourth is choice which is constant and in accordance with nature, at which final stage the good, properly so called, emerges and is understood in its true nature.[2]

Stoics took happiness to be freedom from passion and the realization of inner peace. We should be indifferent to joy and grief, and flexible when facing life's changes. Virtue and right attitude are enough for happiness. By living according to nature, elevating reason over the passions, nurturing good habits, freeing ourselves from the desire to change the unalterable, and being indifferent to pleasure and pain, we can achieve the inner peace that defines happiness. The cardinal virtues are wisdom, courage, self-control, and justice. Distinguishing things within our control from things beyond our control is paramount. Our judgments, attitudes, and evaluations are the only things solely under our control. By controlling these we can attain right will and virtue. The usual litany of desirables—love, honor, wealth, good health, worldly success, avoiding maltreatment from others, the well-being of friends and relatives, congenial family life, personal freedom—depend too much on external circumstances beyond our control, including the actions of others. Stoics refer to external things that are ordinarily desired as preferred indifferents. Once we accept the slings, arrows, and seductions of life without rebellion or discontent, we are in control of our lives and happiness is attainable.

Stoicism differed from Epicureanism in several ways. First, Stoics regarded pleasure, along with sorrow, desire, and fear, as an evil. We must be indifferent to both pain and pleasure if passion is to be purged. Second, Stoics advocated social engagement. They recognized a brotherhood and sisterhood of human beings, and denied the currency of class distinctions and social hierarchies. We have a duty to promote a world that mirrors the rationality embedded in the universe. Third, Stoics thought marriage and family facilitated inner peace. Fourth, Stoics were monotheists who believed in one supreme, universal Deity as creator and sustainer of the universe. They accepted the Roman deities as media for the worship of Zeus. Fifth, Stoics believed our fate to be determined by the mechanistic laws governing all natural phenomena.

For Stoics, the connections between divinity, nature, and living a good human life are crucial. The Stoic god, Zeus, is a conscious being that orders the cosmos, but is not external to nature. God is nature understood as a living entity. The order, movement, and cosmic design are independent of any entity outside the cosmos. Nature organizes, regulates, and moves itself. At the moment of the great fire, the cosmos will dissolve, only to be reborn. This process continues endlessly. Each cosmic cycle is identical to its predecessor and successor. The

Stoics assumed that nature was governed by reason, so the one best possible cosmic organization eternally recurs.[3]

Stoics oscillate between a strong notion of fate—seeing the cosmos as an ongoing causal chain that connects and orders events—and recognition of divine providence. If Stoics insist that fate is pervasive then god's providence is either limited or an illusion. If god's providence determines the causal chain that is fate then the cosmic order is contingent in that it is the product of divine will. The typical Stoic resolution was that divine providence and fate are merely two different names for the same phenomenon. The cosmic order of necessary causes and the divine will are one. As god is perfectly rational and perfectly good, only one course of action is genuinely open to god: the morally best and most rational. Fate, then, is necessary and unalterable, but god providentially selects the morally best and most rational possible cosmic arrangement.[4]

Shades of Leibniz and Voltaire! If this is the best of all possible worlds, what about the problem of evil? Do not natural disasters, wrongful exercises of human free will, and cosmic injustice pervade everyday life? Stoics, of course, are better placed to answer such questions than are contemporary theists. For Stoics all external events are morally indifferent. At worst, they are non-preferred indifferents, but no external event is evil as such.

This response may work if and only if we embrace the Stoic understanding of human beings as essentially rational beings whose good is connected with the condition of their souls and not with their physical well-being. But what of the grave physical injuries that natural disasters inflict on nonhuman animals? Animals are not essentially rational beings and their good must be connected primarily to their physical connection. Are not some external events harmful to animals? Are not the natures of god and the best possible world called into question by the existence of such events? Although Stoics did not ponder such questions, they might insist that how seemingly gratuitous injuries to animals fit into the cosmic picture is unclear but we can rest assured that the inclusion of such events is part of the best possible world. The discussion probably ends, as do most philosophical disputes, with a question-begging primitive conviction.

The rehabilitation of the fate-providence matter, though, opens another concern. Within the Stoic system of fate, providence, the best of all possible worlds, and the strict cosmic order, where lies a place for human free will? Stoicism confronted this problem from its own inception. The standard response, attributed to Chrysippus, relies on two sets of distinctions. Stoics separate simple from complex fated events. Simple fated events are necessary and flow from the nature of things: I will die because mortality is part of my nature as a human being. Complex fated events implicate a second distinction between internal and external causes. Both types of causes constitute complex fated events: that I will die at some point is an internal cause because it is part of my nature as a human being; that I will die on Saturday depends on external causes such as the type of disease I have contracted, the level of medical care, if any, I receive, and the like. Human free will cannot alter simple fated events or internal causes, but it can influence complex fated events and external causes.

Chrysippus uses this distinction between simple fated and [complex] fated
things to argue that human actions can in fact make a contribution to the outcome of events in a deterministic cosmos. It *will* make a difference [in whether
I die on Saturday] whether we call a doctor out or not, but the final outcome
will nevertheless be completely determined, shaped by a range of both internal
and external causes.[5]

The Stoics defined happiness as inner peace. Their recipe for attaining happiness
included minimizing desire, controlling our own judgments and attitudes, and
acting in accord with natural law. Stoics explained how and why following this
recipe makes us happy by analyzing human desire and our relationship to the
world. To judge external events as good is as misguided as judging them bad.
Such judgments are erroneous because for Stoics all external events are indifferent: only moral virtue is good. Moreover, such judgments cultivate improper
emotions.

Stoicism invented the happiness quotient: divide what you have by what
you want, the higher the figure, the happier you will be. The best recipe for happiness is limiting what you want. The happiness quotient is still unveiled breath-
lessly, without attribution to the Stoics, in popular self-help books today: Divide
your satisfactions by your desires; the higher the figure the greater the happiness; limiting your desires is the surest road to success.

Stoics draw a distinction between preferences and goods. The good is that
which is by nature perfect; what is useful is in accord with the good; value is our
estimation of the good and involves our preferences. Stoics divided preferred
things into three categories: per se (for example, acceptable physical appearance), instrumental (for example, material goods), and both (for example
health). Although it is natural and rational to prefer such things to their opposites, either result is irrelevant to human goodness and happiness. They would
understand that we would prefer one scenario, a warm lunch with a loved one,
over another, the brutal murder of that loved one. They would deny that one
scenario is better than the other. They would understand that we would prefer,
say, a gourmet Italian dinner to hunger. They would deny that the Italian dinner
is better than hunger. Nothing is inherently good or evil other than moral virtue.
Human beings label events as such. Eliminate the labels and we remove much
needless anxiety and suffering. Stoics can thereby account for our preferences—
we are not antecedently indifferent to numerous events—but retain their view
that outcomes are inherently neutral. By focusing on the inherent neutrality of
events, Stoics aspire to mute our reactions to and judgments of them.

The human good, our fulfillment or happiness, depends entirely on virtue.
The virtuous person is happy and fulfilled regardless of circumstance and fortune. Thus, the citadel of the self is invulnerable. Once we understand that the
good life is fully under our control, regardless of our station and the outrages of
others, we are liberated. Our judgments, attitudes, choices, actions, and affective
responses are internal to us and under our control. They can be evaluated with
the coherent pattern that defines our biographical lives. They are good or bad

insofar as they facilitate or impair, respectively, our fulfillment as human beings. So-called external goods—health, material goods, fame, glory, and the like—are in truth neither good nor bad; they are indifferent in that they do not affect our prospects for attaining the human good. Human beings will, of course, prefer good health, material resources, high reputation, and the well-being of family and friends over their opposites. But attaining these preferences is not completely under our control—luck and the responses of others are critical elements to success. Thus, realizing my preferences is not part of my good, which consists of my character, beliefs, and actions. If I am a teacher, for example, I will want my students to learn and prosper. This motivation should spur me to do everything in my control to nurture those goals. But whether my students learn and prosper is not fully under my control and not, strictly speaking, part of my good. That I do all in my power to nurture those goals is under my control and is part of my good. In sum, pursuing robust health, material well-being, favorable reputation, and the like is appropriate for human beings, but achieving those goals is not truly good for us and failing in our quest is not genuinely bad for us.

Unfortunately, human beings typically assume that attaining external goods is not merely a goal appropriate to pursue, but that realizing that goal is part of our good. Accordingly, we bemoan and mourn ill health, financial loss, loss of reputation, and the like because we wrongly conclude that our good has been set back. From a Stoic perspective, our false judgment makes us unwitting collaborators in needless misery. We also invite and cheer robust health, financial gain, favorable reputation, and the like because we wrongly conclude that our good has been amplified. From a Stoic perspective, this false judgment distorts our vision and distracts us from what truly constitutes our good. Ultimately, our false beliefs generate emotional distress; correct epistemology is the remedy for better living. Stoics advise us to pursue our preferences as long as we do so with the understanding that our success in achieving external goods is not part of our genuine good and our failure to amass external goods is not a genuine setback.

For the Stoics, emotional responses are not merely unreflective instincts or drives; they are judgments. Accordingly, human beings are responsible for their emotions because emotions are voluntary actions. Although our emotional responses are not under our conscious control at every specific instant, they flow from our beliefs and our evaluations of those beliefs. Even when we feel we are carried off by, say, anger or jealously to act against our self-interest, our emotional response follows our rational assent to the truth of certain beliefs and to an evaluation that reacting angrily is appropriate to the situation. As such, our emotions are within our control. Human beings committed to actualizing their best potentials should eliminate most, if not all, emotional responses. Our emotional responses are rational in a *descriptive* sense: they originate cognitively in our beliefs and judgments. But our emotional responses are not rational in a *normative* sense: they depend on wrong attributions of value to events outside our control; and they mistakenly assume certain events and the realization of external goals are part of the human good. The Stoics insist that what is grounded in false beliefs should not be part of a wise person's life plan. Hence, those aspiring to the best human life should eliminate emotional responses as much as possible. The Stoic condemnation of emotions, then, is grounded on the connection between sound epistemology and the human good. If our strong emotions and feelings originate from correct judgments about value such reactions are valid. If I react strongly to, say, my accurate realization that I did not respond appropriately to an event that was completely within my control, my strong feelings are warranted. Although the initial strong feelings can serve a corrective function, we should also recognize that persistent self-flagellation and lingering self-recriminations serve no purpose.

Physical calamities cannot impair our souls unless we wrongly assent to some beliefs about them. Epistemological errors corrode our judgments, some of which solidify into wrongful emotions. For Stoics, forming judgments involves perception, evaluation, and understanding. Impressions, whether sense perceptions caused by observations or products of reasoning flowing from the mind, imprint themselves on the soul. We turn the impression into a proposition and then we either accept or reject the proposition. For example, we look in a certain direction and gain sense perceptions. We turn the sense perceptions into the proposition that "there is a dog relieving itself against a tree." We then either accept or reject the proposition depending on, in this case, how certain we are that there truly is a dog relieving itself against a tree. Sometimes the propositions we form may contain a value judgment such as "that a dog is relieving itself against a tree is a good (or bad) event."

The impressions we get, the sense perceptions, are beyond our control. They imprint themselves on us. However, whether we accept or reject the propositions accompanying those impressions is within our control. Even Stoics may fall prey to "first movements"—being overwhelmed by the force of a first impression. If someone suddenly cracks me over the head with a club, I garner immediate impressions of pain. Instantaneously, I form the propositions, "I have been smacked upside the head; my head hurts; and this event is awful, unwarranted, unjust, and, in general, not conducive to my good." (In truth, at least in my case, the propositions would be richly spiced with expletives and embraced with overflowing anger.) I will not, though, at this point have wrongly concluded, from a Stoic perspective, that the physical injury is evil. I have succumbed only to a first movement, which is not a judgment but only an immediate reaction. I have not yet assented to the proposition that the physical injury is evil. I still have time to suck it up and affirm Stoic wisdom that only corrosions of my soul are genuinely evil and physical injury is merely a non-preferred indifferent.

Accordingly, Stoics dismiss my spontaneous reaction to a first movement as essentially involuntary and even natural. For, aside from the Marquis de Sade and his fellow travelers, who enjoys being smacked across the head? The proposition I formed consisted of both the sense perception (sensations of pain) forced upon me and the involuntary initial value judgment. But my final assent to or rejection of the value judgment marks me as a Stoic. For Stoics, external events are neither good nor evil. When I assent to a proposition containing in part a value judgment describing an external event, I stumble into epistemological error. In this manner, my emotional response to giving assent—"I am angry at the injustice of this evil assault"—is wrong, based on a mistaken judgment, and fully under my control.[6]

Impressions, themselves, can be true or false. I look in a certain direction and impressions of a youthful Sophia Loren imprint themselves on my mind. Upon further review, these impressions are false. My eyes clear and genuine impressions of an aging Roseanne Barr materialize. How might we distinguish true from false impressions? Stoics claimed that some impressions are self-certifying: "they require no further proof or justification beyond"[7] themselves. Epictetus says that at noon time a person cannot assent to the proposition that it is evening (DS 1.28.2–3). Over time, human beings develop a strong ability to recognize such self-certifying impressions. Although critics will object that we are sometimes mistaken even about self-certifying impressions—imagine an eclipse of the sun—Stoics need not concede that we can never be certain about such impressions. As always, the trick is to distinguish the few illusions from the many veridical perceptions.

When we assent to self-certifying impressions we have an instance of cognition. Knowledge, though, requires more: "It is an organized and structured system of assents to adequate [self-certifying] impressions, something close to what we would today call systematic scientific knowledge. Not surprisingly, this fully comprehensive and consistent sort of systematic knowledge is reserved only for the sage."[8]

The cognitive and normative connections between beliefs and passions are straightforward: If I believe (a) that an event has occurred or is occurring; (b) that the event is bad or evil; and (c) that responding to it passionately is appropriate; then my emotions will flow. My emotions should cease when any of the three links are no longer accepted. Suppose I believe that Jones had spread lies about me. I also believe that my favorable reputation has been well-earned and is part of my good. I further believe that anger is an appropriate response to an undeserved wrong. In all probability, I will become angry. The intensity of my anger will be greatly influenced by how bad I believe the event to be and how appropriate I think an emotional response would be. Over time, as my beliefs cease to be fresh, my anger will typically, although not automatically, subside. (The adage that "vengeance is a dish best served cold" disputes what is typical.)

But imagine that I immediately learn that the event never happened: Jones has said nothing about me. My anger will stop, although I will experience residual ill feelings and agitation. If someone asks, "Are you angry at Jones?" my answer must be "No." Or imagine that Jones *has* spread lies about me, but I am an accomplished Stoic. I would prefer that Jones not lie about me, but I believe that the event of Jones spreading lies about me is neither part of my good nor part of my detriment. I also believe that anger is an inappropriate response to that which is neither good nor bad for me. In all probability, I will not become angry.

Emotions are better viewed as the products of judgments or a complex judgment, not a simple judgment itself. If a loved one dies, I might judge that that event is bad and that grief is an appropriate response to such a bad event. As time passes, I may still judge that the event was bad, but my grief will subside in part because I no longer judge continued grieving to be an appropriate response to a distant event.

From a Stoic vantage point, grief, for example, is "unhealthy, unmanly, unnatural and unnecessary; no one owes it to anyone, least of all to the gods; it accomplishes nothing, interferes with our doing what we should, and does nothing for the departed; it is absurd to care for the dead more than oneself; and in general, it contradicts Stoic values."[9]

My assent to or rejection of an impression, which triggers emotions such as anger and grief, reflects the inner disposition of my mind which is not identical to the inner disposition of your mind. The impression in and of itself is not enough to compel my assent or rejection. Our actions are ours in the sense that they flow from the internal condition of our minds. Yes, the state of our minds is greatly influenced by genetics, socialization, peer pressure, and the like, but those factors do not compel my dispositions to form as they do. Inner agency influences complex fated events and external causes. As does any position that accepts a strong version of fate, Stoics certainly have a problem with free will. What we take the scope and meaning of "fate" to be is crucial. However, if the distinctions between causation and compulsion, internal and external causes, and simple and complex events bear currency, Stoics may be in no worse position than contemporary advocates of soft determinism. In any event, regardless of the fragility of their theory, Stoics surely believed that human beings were responsible for their actions, and merited praise and blame in response to the quality of their deeds. If their theory cannot accommodate that conviction, modern Stoics need only adjust or dispense with their notion of fate. The Stoics' moral programs and normative categories do not depend on accepting their traditional version of fate. The tie-in to fate only solidifies a person's acceptance of everyday events because they are supposedly decreed by Zeus: loyalty to god requires acceptance of external happenings. Fate, then, is invoked to motivate human beings to embrace the inevitable. But this reinforcement is not genuinely required for the Stoic moral regimen.

The Stoic sage is an ideal: infallible, powerful, strong, free, happy, and masterful. Sages will replace desire with selection and fear with disselection: "Selection is the belief that some future thing is a [preferred] indifferent of such a sort that we should reach out for it. Disselection [rejection] is the belief that some future thing is a [non-preferred] indifferent of such a sort that we should avoid it."[10] The purging of emotion is the complex result of cognitive understanding, spiritual exercises, and the cultivation of proper habits. For Stoics, emotions flow from erroneous judgments and veridical judgments require more than grasping doctrine or poring over texts. A true sage, though, would reach the stage where he is no longer fighting emotional impulses; through proper education and training he would no longer experience wrongful emotions: "Sages are aware of their own virtue and feel joy at it; they can direct their efforts towards maintaining their virtue in the future, and thus exercise volitions; and they can take steps to avoid becoming vicious in the future, which means being cautious."[11]

By contrast, all who fall short of this exemplar are foolish, impious, and even insane. At first blush, the options are preposterous: We are either sages— perfect human beings as judged by Stoic criteria—or we are profligate fools, beyond redemption. Given that "perfect human beings" is a contradiction in terms, we are all seemingly relegated to spiritual impoverishment. The uncompromisingly bright line distinction between sages and fools rests comfortably with other Stoic tenets that refuse to recognize matters of degree: All wrongful actions are equally evil; all actions, even commonplace tasks such as brushing one's teeth, must be performed in a distinctively Stoic way; punishment for wrongdoing should be the same regardless of the nature of the transgression. While some such bromides were classified as Stoic "paradoxes," to modern readers they stand out as fatuous failures to appreciate nuance. Subtlety, then, does not shine as a Stoic virtue. Worse, why should we adopt a philosophical system that demands we attain the impossible and sneers that we are foolish and insane when we fall short?

Fortunately, savvier Stoics recognized a third class of human beings: those making progress toward the ideal sage. Still, those who seem a cut above the ordinary person remain foolish: "So even the philosophers remain slaves, impious, foolish, and mad. Indeed, none of the early Stoic philosophers appear to have presented themselves as sages, even if some of their later followers may have been tempted to venerate them as such."[12]

Stoics examined the possibilities for a fitting death. They concluded that suicide is appropriate, especially for the sage, if his life includes a majority of events and circumstances not according to nature. The Platonic Academy was generally opposed to suicide. In his *Phaedo*, Plato has Socrates argue that genuine philosophers will want to die in order to liberate their souls from the prisons of their bodies. Still suicide is a desertion of the earthly duties to which the gods have assigned us. Only if the gods levy a necessity upon a person may he permissibly end his own life (*Phaedo* 61c-62e). Necessities justifying suicide include legal requirements—one might be commanded by law, as was Socrates, to drink a poison and end his life; painful, inevitable, misfortune; and unatonable, intolerable shame are other justifications, (*Phaedo* 61c-62e; *Laws* 9.873c-e). The Peripatetics, following Aristotle, added surrendering one's life for country or friends as a justified form of suicide (NE 9.1169a19). Although compelled self-killing, aiding one's death, and martyrdom for wider causes are far from paradigm cases of suicide, the point is that suicide to escape from personal misfortunes was typically considered by classical Greek philosophers as cowardly, a mark of self-contempt, or an injustice against the state.[13]

As noted earlier, the Stoics recognized a duty of self-preservation flowing from the cradle argument. But men also have duties to their social communities. The normative weight of patriotism to country and loyalty to friends grounds permissible suicide under appropriate circumstances. Of course, whether such cases are genuinely "suicides" as contrasted with martyrdoms, self-sacrifices for higher purposes, or deaths in service to others is a concern. Deaths ordered by the state to preserve or protect society and deaths voluntarily undertaken to advance the interests of the state rarely fall neatly into the category of suicides, which are intentional, voluntary self-killings. Stoics, though, expanded the conditions of permissible suicide to include extreme cases of "pain, mutilation, and incurable disease."

> Although [moral] virtue is the only good and vice the only evil, and everything else is indifferent, there are among the indifferents positive ones [things we typically prefer] and negative ones [things we generally avoid]. . . . Life itself [like pleasure, property, and health] has value only as material for virtuous action, so that the decision to retain life or not rests . . . on the balance in life of the positive versus negative indifferents: a sufficiently adverse balance means that virtuous action, which is the aim of life, will become severely impeded or impossible.[14]

Determining how adverse one's life must have become—Must it be virtually impossible to live a virtuous life under the circumstances?—to justify suicide is tricky business. Certainly, one would expect a Stoic sage to be able to overcome almost all adverse situations and continue to ply his virtue. Allowing negative indifferents to intrude upon one's internal integrity is not the mark of a Stoic sage.

A third type of justified Stoic suicide centers on political tyranny. Stoics argued that only the wise man is free because his rationality, liberated from external constraints, directs him to virtue. The sage will exercise freedom of speech and defy torture or even death instead of performing immoral or inappropriate actions.[15] Martyrdom—accepting death as the cost of preserving one's moral virtue—resonates with basic Stoic doctrine. Celebrating one's moral and philosophical convictions unto death is more reminiscent of Socratic martyrdom for a cause than of the paradigmatic suicide victim. Should a tyranny, the ultimate power of external coercion, demand wrongful actions from a Stoic sage, then resistance up to and including death is the stock and trade of the Stoic sage.

> The same political factors that made Stoicism so appealing also led to an emphasis on dying nobly. . . . One plausible explanation of this emphasis lies in the restriction of the traditional opportunities for acquiring glory that was imposed by the autocratic system of government. The Roman nobility found it more difficult to live up to the example of their ancestors in acquiring military and civic fame, but they could still die noble and memorable deaths. Suicide had a particular advantage in this context, for it could be staged. One could make sure that one had an audience and that one said memorable things.[16]

Maybe so. But authentic Stoic sages would be less concerned with the loss of opportunities for external validation in the form of glory and honor, and more interested in the condition of their souls. The genuine Stoic motivation for sacrificing one's life in the face of tyranny is keeping faith with moral virtue: Death before dishonor.

Cato: "The Perfect Stoic"

Marcus Porcius Cato Uticensis ("Cato the Stoic" or "Cato the Younger") (95–46 BC) was a hard man. We cannot understand Cato the Stoic without first sketching the life and influence of his most illustrious ancestor. His great-grandfather and namesake was the legendary Cato the Censor ("Cato the Elder") (237–149 BC), the first in the family to hold the consulship. Renowned for upholding traditional Roman values and the privileges of the senate, Cato the Censor despised innovation. He was spawned by a plebeian agricultural family and rose up the *cursus honorum* fueled by his reputation for integrity and stern justice. Relentless and indefatigable, he ended every speech, regardless of subject, with the same fierce refrain: *Delenda est Carthago* ("Carthage must be destroyed"). Eventually Carthage was destroyed, but only after Cato had died. Cato the Censor, fearing the growing political power of the military giant who engineered the defeat of Hannibal, Publius Cornelius Scipio Africanus (236–185 BC), led accusations and charges that nudged Scipio into exile. Cato's cover was the alleged threat Scipio posed for the Roman constitution and the integrity of the republic. But Cato undoubtedly also seethed with envy at Scipio's popularity. The Censor, despite his sterling reputation, was a deeply flawed character. He treated slaves, animals, and his wife harshly; he was financially corrupt and often lined his own pockets at the expense of the common good; and was too frequently spiteful and petty when dealing with those with whom he disagreed.

Readers will recall his reaction when Rome was visited in 155 BC by the three distinguished Athenian philosophers seeking relief from taxes. Cato the Censor was never amused by rhetorical and philosophical razzle-dazzle. He had the Athenians booted out of Rome and underscored the need for young men to be thoroughly steeped in Roman military and republican traditions. The values of free speech and open inquiry chilled Cato to the marrow. Regardless, the mythology of Cato the Censor was amplified so effectively by his sycophants that he grew to symbolize Roman tradition, virtue, opposition to foreign influences, commitment to republicanism, and common-sense wisdom.

Cato the Stoic revered the legend of his great-grandfather. In numerous ways, he fashioned a similar legacy, stripped of the corruption and cruelty. To his enemies, Cato was a rigid, merciless, sanctimonious, supercilious fanatic. To his compatriots, he was a principled, incorruptible, fearless, glistening moral paragon. Both foes and friends alike understood that Marcus Porcius Cato inhabited a strictly black-and-white world. Cato greeted ambiguity less warmly than a broncobuster welcomes hemorrhoids. Persuading Cato to compromise was more difficult than convincing a penguin to play hopscotch.

Orphaned soon after his birth, Cato was raised by a maternal uncle. Far from mercurial, Cato learned slowly but surely. At an early age, he manifested the character that would become his trademark. Plutarch describes how the child was father to the man:

> He discovered an inflexible temper, unmoved by any passion, and firm in everything. He was resolute in his purposes, much beyond the strength of his age, to go through with whatever he undertook. He was rough and ungentle toward those that flattered him, and still more unyielding to those who threatened him. It was difficult to excite him to laughter.[17]

Cicero attributed the following adages to Zeno of Citium, founder of Stoicism (PM 61):

- "The sage is never influenced by favor, and never forgives someone who has done wrong."
- "No one feels pity unless he is a fool or idiot."
- "A true man is never prevailed upon or appeased."
- "Only the sage is (internally) attractive, wealthy, and regal, regardless of external appearances."
- "All misdeeds are equal: every transgression is an unspeakable crime."
- "The sage never supposes anything, never regrets anything, is never mistaken, and never changes his mind."

Cato soon discovered that this rigid version of Stoicism fit his temperament perfectly: austere, emotionally indifferent, tough-minded, drawn to rule-governed behavior, bearing a low tolerance of ambiguity . . . the boy was born a Stoic. Imagine his surprise that a distinguished philosophy had already been devised to accommodate his personality! Cato luxuriated in treating both high success and abject failure as frauds. And here was a philosophy that took Cato's natural instincts as doctrine! Giddy up!

By the age of fourteen, Cato oozed moxie and bravado. During civil strife, as numerous Roman nobles were being executed for dubious reasons by the notorious dictator Lucius Cornelius Sulla (138–78 BC), Cato asked his tutor why no one had assassinated the tyrant. His tutor answered, "Because they fear him, child, more than they hate him." Cato did not miss a beat: "Then give me a sword so that I might stab him and free my country from slavery." His tutor, stunned by the boy's anger and determination, strictly monitored Cato's activities thereafter.[18]

Cato, a virgin at the time, married Atilia, who bore him two children, one of whom, Porcia, later became the wife of Marcus Junius Brutus. Later, because of her promiscuous activities, Cato divorced Atilia and married Marcia, daughter of Lucius Marcius Philippus, a member of a Roman senatorial family.

In 72 BC, Cato volunteered for the military campaign against Spartacus. Although he displayed the discipline, courage, and wisdom that were to become his trademark, he later refused all honors and awards offered for his service. He denied that he deserved such commendations. Stoics are not seduced by baubles, flattery, or external validation. Cato assumed a military tribuneship in Macedonia where he earned a high reputation for enduring hardships willingly: "He went bareheaded in summer and winter, and travelled on foot when his contemporaries went on horseback."[19]

Upon his return to Rome, Cato was elected quaestor. He eradicated corrupt practices that had beset the running of the treasury and gained the admiration of all who were paying attention. He was elected a tribune of the plebeians and served in 63 BC, during which time he vigorously prosecuted anyone, regardless of social prominence and political connections, whom he suspected of wrongdoing. During this period, he was a major player in squashing the Catilinian conspiracy. After Caesar argued for lesser punishments than death for the conspirators before the senate, he had seemingly won the day. Cato's impassioned denunciation of the alleged evil-doers, combined with his reckless allegation that Caesar's limited defense of them demonstrated he was in league with the miscreants, turned sentiment against Caesar's position.

As a side note: These hearings provided one of the few occasions when Caesar was able to embarrass Cato. Or more precisely, when Cato's inveterate aggressiveness and accusatory stance turned against him. A messenger brought a communication to Caesar during the senate deliberations. Cato, convinced as only a true zealot could be, that the letter was from the Catilinian conspirators, demanded that the contents of the message be revealed. Caesar demurred. Cato, characteristically, refused to be placated. The communication was a graphic love note to Caesar from Servilia, Cato's half-sister. Cato fumed and fussed. Caesar grinned wryly.

Cato's apparent incorruptibility and complete indifference to the seductions that tempted most men disconcerted powerful military men such as Pompey and Caesar. Cato's relentless appeals to justice—without exceptions or special favors—won him almost boundless admiration. Cato followed one rule above all others: If Caesar was in favor of X then Cato must oppose X. Cato was the only Roman who unequivocally and consistently foresaw Caesar as a threat to the republic. Cicero had the same instincts, but he was always susceptible to Caesar's personal charm. Caesar knew which buttons to push to ingratiate himself with Cicero. He discussed literature with him, catered to Cicero's vanity, and conjured images of enduring glory. Cato had no buttons to push. Anyone who tried to curry his favor was brusquely rejected. As always, he drew a bright line in the dirt in Rome: Caesar was the force of darkness; he was Cato's enemy then, in the future, and forever.

Throughout his public life, Cato was both ridiculed and admired. He was ridiculed for his fanaticism, obstinacy, and self-righteousness; admired for his refusal to succumb to the temptations and allures that drew other Romans. In a world where even the most talented men had a price—power, money, sex, prestige—Cato's integrity was not for sale.

What most of all virtue and excellence fixed his affection was that steady and inflexible justice which is not to be wrought upon by favor or compassion. He learned also the art of speaking and debating in public, thinking that political philosophy, like a great city, should maintain for its security the military and warlike element. . . . He showed such a love of discipline, so much bravery upon occasion, and so much courage and wisdom in everything, that it appeared he was in no way inferior to the old Cato [the Censor].[20]

During Clodius's reign as tribune, he sent Cato on a mission to Cyprus. This served two functions: it removed Cato from Rome and ensured that Cyprus, a recent Roman expropriation, would be well administered. Working closely with the members of the first triumvirate, Clodius planned to exile Cicero. Cato's presence in Rome would make that more difficult. Cato, after returning from Cyprus, was elected praetor in 54 BC, but failed in his only bid for the consulship in 53 BC. Sallust comments:

Cato's enthusiasm was for restraint, honor, but especially strictness; he did not compete in riches with the rich or in factionalism with the factious, but with the committed in prowess, with the restrained in propriety, with the innocent in self-denial; he preferred to be, rather than to seem, a good man; thus, the less he sought glory, the more it attended him. (CW 54.5–54.6)

Cato also dallied in eccentricity. While serving as praetor in 54 BC, he allegedly arrived in court shoeless and sat upon the bench commando-style (without undergarments) regularly while judging capital cases involving prominent citizens.[21] Upon his return from Cyprus, Cato was approached by the fabled orator Hortensius, who sought an alliance through marriage. Cato had previously rejected a marriage alliance with Pompey, claiming he refused to morally stain his family. But Cato admired the orator. Unfortunately, no one in his household was suitable for wedlock. But few ever accused Cato of acting orthodoxically. He gave his own pregnant wife, Marcia, to Hortensius, and then remarried her, or at least took her and her children into his household, when the orator died in 50 BC. Cato, even by Roman standards, was immune to sentimentality within marriage. Or was he? After all, he did take Marcia back . . . once she was a wealthy widow.

After Crassus died in his clumsy military campaign in Carrhae in 53 BC, Cato accepted Pompey as sole consul. In order to preserve the republic, distasteful measures seemed necessary. When civil war broke out four years later, Cato joined Pompey's forces. After all, the alternative was Caesar.

Cato assumed military command in Sicily, but did not distinguish himself. He scampered from the island when superior enemy forces arrived. At the final battle of Pharsalus, Cato served only as commander of the camp. After Caesar routed Pompey's forces, Cato escaped to Africa where he joined Metellus Scipio (100–46 BC), father-in-law of Pompey. The troops asked Cato to lead them, but he unwisely declined, citing Scipio's superior standing as an ex-consul.

Cato assumed command of Utica. Scipio was convinced that the Uticans were treacherous and seditious; he advised Cato to slay them. Cato refused and advised Scipio to avoid battle with Caesar. Scipio refused and Caesar devastated his forces at Thapsus. In contrast to his usual policy of clemency to the defeated, Caesar slaughtered Scipio's troops upon their surrender. The Uticans remained true to Cato.

When others volunteered to petition Caesar for clemency on Cato's behalf, the Stoic declined. No retreat, no surrender. Could anyone genuinely suspect that Marcus Porcius Cato would yield to Caesar's mercy? Could anyone even imagine that Cato would repudiate his entire biography by asking or accepting a favor from Gaius Julius Caesar? A favor that would obligate him throughout his life to the man he most despised? That would compel him to recognize that he owed his life to the largesse of Caesar? To accept an act of mercy that would forever elevate Caesar and demean Cato?

Instead, Cato dined with magistrates of Utica, his son, and friends, including Apollonides the Stoic and Demetrius the Peripatetic. They ate and drank wine and discussed passionately a critical Stoic paradox: Is it true that only virtuous men are free and all wicked men are slaves? Philosophy would prove crucial even at the end. The Peripatetic answered negatively. Cato, with an inappropriate vehemence, argued with stentorian bravado that the answer was "yes." His guests understood the message: Cato was going to take his own life as his final act of liberation. Everyone embraced, more warmly and tenderly than usual, and took their leave.

Cato curled up with his copy of Plato's *Phaedo*, a spectacularly evocative depiction of Socrates's last moments prior to drinking the hemlock that killed him. The topic of that dialogue was the immortality of the soul, an especially relevant subject for a man of Cato's disposition. After perusing a good portion of the book, Cato reached for his sword. No luck. His son had removed it from the room. Cato bellowed for his servants and demanded his weapon. As he waited for their return, he kept reading. Cato roared, again, for his servants. He demanded his sword, angrily smacked one of his servants in the mouth, and bemoaned the lack of cooperation from those closest to him. His son and his friends entered. High drama followed. Finally, a young boy returned the sword to Cato.

A physician dressed the hand that had struck the servant. Conversations ensued. Finally, once he was alone, Cato stabbed himself in the chest or abdomen, but not fatally. His bandaged hand limited the power of his thrust. Cato fell off his bed, knocked down an abacus, and inadvertently alerted the others. They scrambled into his room. He was awash in his own blood, with most of his intestines outside his body. The physician hurried to replace the organs and stitch the wound. However, Cato pushed away the physician, tore open the wound, and ripped out his intestines. The man Cicero had called "the perfect Stoic" died immediately. When Caesar discovered events, he remarked sadly, "Cato, I grudge you your death, as you have grudged me the preservation of your life."[22] Later, when Cicero composed his glorious eulogy of Cato, Caesar responded with his *Anti-Cato*, a wholesale hatchet job on the character of the man that spoke volumes about Caesar and virtually nothing about Cato. Even in death,

Cato had the knack of annoying and besting the most powerful person in Rome. Marcus Porcius Cato was a hard man straight to the end.

Cato understood keenly that victory was possible in martyrdom. He could more effectively oppose Caesar as a dead symbol, than as a compromised stooge beholden to the tyrant for his life. Nor could Cato live free under a tyranny that would eviscerate the political traditions of the Roman republic. Always opposed to luxury, avarice, mercy, pity, and external honors in life, Cato would exemplify in death the virtuous man who applied philosophical principles and patriotic zeal to the perils of tyranny. Cato's suicide in one stroke underscored his own Stoic freedom; spurned Caesar's tyranny; indicted the moral weakness of those, such as Cicero, Brutus, and Cassius, who had lapped up Caesar's mercy; and sealed Cato's case as a moral exemplar for future generations. Good career move, that! An impliable Roman competitor right to the end, Cato won his final victory with his last gasp. And Caesar understood that keenly.

Cato, though, was a human being. Cato once proposed that men running for the office of tribune, as a condition of their candidacy, be required to deposit a large sum of money. If that proposal had been accepted, the notion of tribunes as officers of the plebeians would have been seriously compromised. But, then, Cato was no fan of irony. When civil war loomed, a senator suggested that slaves should be freed to serve military duty. As the proposal gathered momentum in the senate, Cato, with a sharp eye fixed on protecting aristocratic property rights, argued that masters should not be deprived of their possessions.[23]

> Cato was an awkward character, surly, and relatively friendless, a workaholic by day who relaxed in all-night drinking sessions with philosophers. He was perhaps respected more than he was liked.[24]

The quest to valorize Cato as virtue personified is untrue to the record. In 59 BC, he helped secure the consulship of his son-in-law, Marcus Calpurnius Bibulus, through bribery. Granted this machination was standard fare in Rome at the time and Cato justified the act in his mind as in the best interests of the republic. But Cato otherwise harshly disparaged such appeals to expediency. Cato also drove Pompey into the arms of the first triumvirate by his inflexible opposition to Pompey's proposals, however reasonable. The creation of that political union was the beginning of the end of the republic. Ten years later, Cato supported Pompey's sole consulship, which sealed the deal. Cato also swallowed Clodius's bait and headed to Cyprus when he was needed more in Rome. Moreover, Cato acted in self-interest when he opposed Cicero's plan to invalidate enactments during Clodius's reign: Cato feared the invalidation of his own administrative maneuvers in Cyprus. Also, Cato acted inconsistently in refusing Cicero's petition for recognition after a minor military victory given that Cato had supported a similar application made by Bibulus. Finally, Cato's utter refusal to bend, his systematic obstruction to progressive reform, and his dogmatic worship of the mythical past of Rome facilitated the political result he most feared: the end of the republic.

In this vein, J. P. V. D. Balsdon remarks:

> Cato was impolitic . . . he was self-centered and conceited . . . he was high-
> principled to the point of absurdity in 52 when he declined to propose the elec-
> tion of Pompey as sole consul, but was happy to second the proposal when it
> was made by his son-in-law Bibulus; he was mean and disingenuous . . . he was
> not without responsibility for one of the most crooked financial transactions of
> the period (his nephew Brutus' loan to the Salaminians of Cyprus); in his fam-
> ily and married life one is tempted to wonder whether he had any human feel-
> ings at all; and as Cicero showed so amusingly in the *Pro Murena*, he was an
> outsize prig.[25]

Cicero's *Pro Murena* is his defense of Lucius Licinius Murena, who was accused by Cato and others of bribery during his successful campaign for a consulship in 62 BC. When Cicero delivered the speech he was nearing the end of
his own term as consul. In *Pro Murena*—which played a major role in winning
an acquittal for the apparently guilty defendant—Cicero painted a portrait of
Cato that was at once flattering and revealing.

> Nature herself has made you a great and elevated human being, fashioned for
> integrity, seriousness, self-control, greatness of character, fairness, and for
> every virtue. And yet she has added to all that a philosophy [unpliable Stoi-
> cism] which is neither moderate nor mild but, it seems to me, rather more harsh
> and inflexible than either reality or human nature can tolerate. . . . The wise
> man does feel pity; there are distinct classes of misdeeds which merit different
> punishments; a man of consistent principles does have room for forgiveness;
> the wise man himself often supposes something which he does not know for
> certain, he is angry once in a while, but yet can be prevailed upon and ap-
> peased; he does occasionally alter what he has said if that is the better course,
> and he does sometimes change his mind. (PM 60, 63)

However, Cato's victory in martyrdom trumps all of the peccadilloes that can be
accumulated against him. His death symbolized the final breath of republican
liberty; it demonstrated the insoluble marriage of philosophical principle to iron
will; it manifested Cato's willingness to die rather than bend his knee to Caesar's beneficence; and underscored the Stoic's refusal to accept tyranny over
death. A free man perishes but once, Cato taught, and an honorable death amplifies the value of the life that it terminates.

In Dante Alighieri's *The Divine Comedy*, Cato is depicted as the guardian of
the seaward approach to the island of purgatory (PU 1.31–1.39). First staged in
1713, Joseph Addison's play, *Cato*, cemented the Stoic's reputation as a republican martyr. A major success, the play was a favorite among American revolu-
tionaries such as George Washington, and served to inspire the famous slogans
attributed to Patrick Henry and Nathan Hale. Henry's "Give me liberty or give
me death" derives from Cato's "But chains or conquest, liberty or death" in Addison's play (*Cato* II.IV.80); while Hale's "I regret that I have but one life to
give for my country" flows from Cato's "What pity it is that we can die but once

to serve our country!" (*Cato* IV.IV.81–82) Washington was fond of quoting one of Cato's favorite sentiments, "When vice prevails, and impious men bear sway, the post of honor is a private station."[26] Today, a libertarian think tank in the United States that has existed over thirty years calls itself "The Cato Institute." The hard-nosed Roman remains a symbol of the free individual in conflict with governmental authority. In sum, Cato has come to symbolize "preserving republican virtue, tradition, and precedent; for respecting established institutions and the Senate in particular; and for his unwavering adherence to principle."[27] For better or worse, Marcus Porcius Cato, "the perfect Stoic," lived up to his philosophical principles as well as any person in history.

Stoicism Evaluated

The Stoic's happiness quotient is unsuccessful. It fails to distinguish the satisfaction of worthy from unworthy desires. If hundreds of our unworthy but relatively few of our worthy desires are satisfied we will still be unhappy regardless of a high average on the happiness quotient. If we correct this problem by stipulating that only worthy desires are candidates for the quotient, other difficulties appear. The happiness quotient would still fail to distinguish the intensity of our desires: We want some things much more than we want other things. Even if most of our weaker desires are fulfilled, we will be unsatisfied if some of our stronger desires remain unsatisfied. The happiness quotient also does not distinguish between needs and wants. If most of our wants are satisfied but a few of our needs are unfilled, we will have a high score on the quotient but an unhappy life. The happiness quotient also makes no mention of how our desires are satisfied. If our desires are satisfied through simulated instead of real accomplishments a worthy happiness cannot result.

Let us brush these objections aside. I will now play my trump criticism: Even if all of our desires are satisfied and we achieve a perfect score on the happiness quotient, we will still be unhappy. This is true even if we stipulate that all our satisfied desires are worthy. We would still be unhappy because our life would be inhuman. We would have nothing further to strive for, no unsatisfied projects to address, no future toward which to aspire. We would be a saturated sponge of desire. Unless we could quickly devise new desires, immediately driving our happiness quotient down, boredom and anomie would result. Accordingly, the happiness quotient requires considerable refinement.

The broader critique of Stoicism is by now a cliché. While Stoicism can bring consolation to those struggling under harsh conditions, its expectations are too low for general use. The expansive richness and creativity of human experience are sacrificed on the altar of accommodation. Although it does not insist on passivity, Stoicism inclines in that direction.

Can we, should we, be indifferent to poverty, disease, natural disasters, suffering, and evil in the universe? Imagine going home today for lunch. Under the first scenario, you are met by a loved one, engage in a wonderful social interaction (fill in your own details, make them as wonderful as you can), and return to work with maximum fulfillment. Under the second scenario, you discover your loved one has been brutally murdered (fill in your own details, make them as gruesome and upsetting as you can). How can a person be unaffected by these two scenarios? If someone were indifferent to the horrifying slaying of a loved one, would we not stigmatize that person as psychologically impaired? To be indifferent under such circumstances is to relinquish what we value most.

Stoics would agree that we would prefer the wonderful scenario to the gruesome murder, but insist that the satisfaction of our preferences does not define our good. Why, though, would we prefer one scenario over another? The simplest answer: Because we take the preferred scenario to be better or to be good, because we value one scenario over another. Stoics have a heavy burden that goes unaddressed: To account for why we prefer X over Y without referring to our values. Some preferences have their genesis in mere personal tastes or whims. Other preferences exist only because a value judgment, a labeling, has occurred. The Stoic bow to common sense, which acknowledges that we do prefer some events over others, is purchased at a stiff price: A spectacularly unpersuasive view of the relationship between preferences and goods. We prefer the loving lunch to the brutal murder because we judge, accurately, that the loving lunch is a good while the brutal murder is monumental evil.

Stoics, though, have a response. They are not *antecedently* indifferent to the two scenarios: Stoics prefer a loving lunch to a brutal murder. However, they are *posteriorly* indifferent to what in fact occurs: once the brutal murder takes place they do not regard it as an evil or even relevant to their good. In that vein, the sage prefers a tasty meal to starvation. But, unlike the non-sage, he is neither pleased when he consumes a meal nor is he disappointed if no food is available. Regardless of the outcome of his preferences he feels the same: a sense of indifference because he understands that whether he eats or not is irrelevant to his human good. Only the condition of his soul, his virtue, constitutes his good and that is not influenced by his diet.

But why would the sage prefer a scrumptious dinner to starvation if he did not, in some sense, recognize the value of eating? Does not even the sage, deep down, admit that nourishment is good and starvation is bad? Not exactly. The sage, says the Stoic, is merely following nature. To prefer starvation to nourishment or disease to health or injury to physical well-being is unnatural. But following nature is a Stoic creed. Does that not concede that preferred indifferents, as the natural way, are part of the human good? The distinction between the *descriptively* natural and the *normatively* natural may help. As a matter of fact, as a function of their biology, human beings will prefer some states of affairs, such as health, to their opposites, such as disease. But from the normatively natural perspective the satisfaction of those preferences is irrelevant to the human good. Our well-being as rational, virtuous beings is unaffected by preferred indifferents. Accordingly, we should treat the outcomes of pursuing our preferences with indifference. The only value indifferents have is that of selecting or disselecting them in accord with our biological, or descriptively natural, preferences.

Stoics must insist that we have reasons to pursue preferred indifferents but those reasons do not include the fact that preferred indifferents are good things. Stoics would concede that two widely disparate types of value exist: the value of attaining preferred indifferents and the value of attaining virtue. Only the second type of value is linked to human good and is conducive to human fulfillment.

> A life of virtue exactly consists in a life in which agents exercise their rationality in the pursuit of indifferents. It is exactly by choosing wisely and avoiding bravely, by selecting temperately and distributing justly, that a life which in some sense is taken up with and given over to indifferents can nevertheless at the same time be a life directed towards the end of virtue.[28]

Although I have spoken only of preferred (for example, health) and non-preferred (for example, disease) indifferents, a third category of thoroughly neutral indifferents exists (for example, whether I have an odd or an even number of nostril hairs). Pursuing preferred indifferents too avidly runs the risk of conferring too much value upon them, of courting frustration when we fail to attain them, and of unwittingly nurturing strong emotions. The marriage of preferred indifferents to strong effort virtually ensures the destruction of genuinely Stoic aspirations. Fervently desiring certain externalities but refusing to be disappointed when we fail to attain them courts a type of schizophrenia. Although Stoics can, technically speaking, strive vigorously to attain preferred indifferents, their doing so jeopardizes their refusal to view these externalities as genuine goods. They seem to be claiming that preferred indifferents are worth choosing and pursuing, but also that whether we succeed in our efforts to obtain them does not matter. If so, then why choose and pursue such externalities? Other than celebrating moral virtue, Stoic theory seems to provide no genuine guidance on what to choose and what to reject.

How, then, are wisdom and virtue connected to things that really do not matter? The outcomes of our strivings for preferred indifferents are irrelevant to our good, say the Stoics. Why, then, are the strivings themselves of any consequence? Is it not better to spend our time and efforts on the cognitive understanding, spiritual exercises, and cultivation of proper habits that lead to the purging of wrongful emotions than to squander our concern on the pursuit of indifferents?

One might argue, as Peripatetics did, that a measure of good health and material goods are preconditions of leading the virtuous life or of living at all. To attain the good of virtue one must be alive and capable of undergoing the prescribed Stoic regimen; that requires some concern for health, food, drink, and the like, not just as preferred indifferents but as requirements for the good life; what is a requirement for the good life is at least derivatively or instrumentally good; thus, the reason virtue is connected to exercising rationality in the pursuit of indifferents is that attaining some so-called indifferents is required for virtue to blossom. However, this line of reasoning is not available to Stoics.

Suppose Jane slashes Joe with a finely honed stiletto. Louise, a medical doctor, cares for the wound. According to Stoicism, neither action advances or frustrates Joe's good. Jane inflicts a non-preferred indifferent, physical injury, upon Joe; Louise confers a preferred indifferent, restoration of health. From the standpoint of the human good, the two actions are equally irrelevant. Circumscribing the human good to only the internal dispositions of the soul toward moral virtue and then defining moral virtue only in terms of distinguishing what is fully under our control from everything else shrinks the moral universe.

Stoics can experience and cultivate genuine emotions, but their proper scope is limited and uninspiring. Feeling joy in awareness of one's own virtue is legitimate because the judgment that underlies the emotion is rational and sound: I have attained virtue; that is the only true good; my internal condition is harmonious; joy is an appropriate response to a good, internal event. However, such joy may be appropriate only for the sage, should such a paradigm exist. The rest of us are imperfect fools and madmen. (Is it appropriate to feel joy when one makes moral progress? Or would joy hinder continued moral growth?) If a person loses her moral virtue, if she backslides, some emotion—Caution? Wishing for redemption?—might be appropriate because a genuine good is in jeopardy. Still, for a Stoic what is done is done. Maybe regret and remorse are misplaced as they are emotions directed to the past. An emotion that looks to the future with resolve and rehabilitation, though, might well be permitted.

Still, the Stoics were wrong. Grieving, sorrow, and suffering are not vices. Human beings are by nature valuing creatures. We cannot be stonily indifferent and retain our humanity. To value something is to make it an object of concern. We cannot coherently value everything. We partially construct who we are through what we value. If we remain indifferent to the loss of what we value we call into question the intensity of our commitment, we hedge our bet. Because our evaluations, convictions, and actions define our lives, we cannot be indifferent to our defeats, disappointments, and losses. We stake our being on and experience life most directly through our values. Grief, sorrow, and suffering are appropriate responses to the tragedies of life. The Stoics were correct in thinking that sorrow and suffering are too often exaggerated, that they can impinge on a worthwhile life, that we can obsess inappropriately on our losses. However, to remain indifferent to everything not fully under our control is unwarranted. We should not cry over spilled milk. We should cry over spilled blood.

Outlooks, such as Stoicism, that appeal to fate have trouble accounting for robust action. If I aspire to change the world I am focusing on things outside my control and trying to alter fate. I have judged the status quo deficient and taken steps to change it. If that aspiration and the results attendant to my actions are themselves fated then my judgments about external events—how I evaluated the state of the world prior to my actions—are not under my control. I was fated to a negative view of the world and the motivation to try to change it. Rendering my freedom and control over my own judgments and actions, the pervasive direction of the World-Soul, and vigorous social action compatible is no simple choice.

Even if we eliminate the presence of the World-Soul and natural law, are my judgments and attitudes about events totally within my control? They are probably more in my control than most social and natural conditions in the world. But many influences, my socialization in a broad sense, contribute to my outlook. That my conscious judgments and evaluations arise fully from my freedom is far from obvious.

The presence of natural laws that are both descriptive and prescriptive complicates matters. Following the natural law, which binds all human beings in all places at all times, is reasonable, proper, and enhances prospects for happiness. According to Stoicism, such laws are antecedently external to those things within our control, but we should not be indifferent to them. We should understand and abide by them because they are good. Although outside our control, they provide the ground for our action. If so, then "good" and "evil" are more than labels that human beings wrongly attach to events. Events and actions that violate the prescriptions of natural law are evil as such. To regard such events and actions indifferently would itself not be in accord with natural law. Again, we see that fundamental Stoical doctrines do not coalesce easily.

Friedrich Nietzsche ridiculed the Stoics' advice to "live according to nature" as either mendacious or self-deceptive. Nature not only fails to send human beings unambiguous messages, nature is utterly indifferent to the human condition. Instead, philosophers look to nature and impose their own images and psychological yearnings upon it. They then use the supposed message from nature to justify their own projections in a classically vacuous, circular exercise.

> "According to nature" you want to *live?* O you noble Stoics, what deceptive words these are! Imagine a being like nature, wasteful beyond measure, indifferent beyond measure, without purposes and consideration, without mercy and justice, fertile and desolate and uncertain at the same time; imagine indifference itself as a power—how *could* you live according to this indifference? Living— is that not precisely wanting to be other than this nature? Is not living— estimating, preferring, being unjust, being limited, wanting to be different? . . . Your pride wants to impose your morality, your ideal, on nature . . . you demand that she be nature "according to the Stoa," and you would like all existence to exist only after your own image—as an immense external glorification and generalization of Stoicism. . . . [Philosophy] always creates the world in its own image; it cannot do otherwise.[29]

Anticipating Rousseau, Stoics believed that human beings were naturally disposed to virtue and that we stray because of shoddy external socialization and epistemological errors. Yet they also insist that adopting Stoicism requires serious reflection and training. The Stoical life, then, will not develop on its own from our inherent natures. Perhaps we are also naturally inclined toward epistemological errors—succumbing too easily to first movements—or, as an empirical matter, almost all of us are spawned in social contexts uncongenial to Stoic living. In any event, the malleability of appeals to nature remains striking.

Stoic doctrine also has an odd notion of moral progress. For Stoics, making progress toward virtue and toward the ideal of the sage was, paradoxically, not becoming more virtuous or less evil. A person buried two feet beneath the earth is closer to the surface than another person ten feet beneath the earth, but the first person is still suffocating as much as is the second. The sage, if one actually exists, is completely virtuous. Every action he performs flows from the same virtuous disposition of the soul. None of his actions is more virtuous than others, not even those that seem beyond the domain of morality. Brushing teeth, eating food, relating to friends, saving people in distress, and all other acts are completely virtuous if performed by a sage because they all originate from the same virtuous state of his soul. Moreover, they are *equally* virtuous. Saving a drowning child at great risk to oneself is no more or less virtuous than washing one's face upon waking. Everything hinges on the state of the actor's soul. Likewise, for those falling short of the ideal of the sage—probably everyone who has ever lived—all acts they perform are equally evil. Loving one's child deeply and apparently selflessly is as evil as murdering a neighbor in cold blood. Why? Because the non-sage has a flawed soul—he or she is not perfectly virtuous—so all actions a non-sage performs are evil and equally so.[30]

> What the Stoics want to emphasize is the difference between a mental disposition that is completely incapable of error and a mental disposition that is capable of error because of its inconsistency and irrationality. The fact that a particular judgment happens to be in conformity with the truth, or a particular action is in conformity with the befitting, is less important in their eyes than the fact that it is done from the very same mental state that, in altered circumstances, would have produced a false judgment or an action contrary to the befitting.[31]

For contemporary thinkers, the extension of the doctrine is nonsense squared. Viewing the inner life of human beings in absolute terms—we are either perfectly virtuous or completely evil—is deranged. This is especially true because the sage may be only an ideal that no human being has ever actually attained. The result trivializes moral assessment: we are all completely evil because we fall short of the ideal sage; those making progress toward that ideal are still completely evil; thus, Mother Teresa and Abraham Lincoln were as morally vicious as Charles Manson and Adolph Hitler! The utter failure to admit degrees and nuances into their moral world renders much Stoic teaching absurd.

Stoicism's kernel of insight—do not dwell on misfortune, put suffering behind you, do not become intoxicated with unimportant pursuits or frivolous desires—is obscured by its demand that nothing else matters that much. Even on its own terms it fails to distinguish earned tranquility from simulated tranquility. Aristotle's keen observation that a person could be mistaken about whether he is happy bears currency. If Bob is peaceful because he has been hypnotized into thinking his life is other than what it is or because he has been drugged, then his tranquility does not translate into a worthy happiness. Instead, it is merely a simulated, unearned state of mind. Bob has been tricked into thinking his unsatisfying life is satisfying. Aristotle's intuition that happiness must in an important sense be earned, not merely induced, rings true.

In another respect, Stoicism provides a corrective to earlier views of happiness. It points out that happiness is not simply achieving a set of external conditions, not just flourishing. Happiness requires some fit between a person's expectations and results, as well as an extended internal peace. While I resist the particular expectations Stoicism urges, and question whether extended peace, however attained, is enough for everyone, Stoicism contains lessons for seekers of happiness and the good life: We often cause ourselves needless suffering by our unnecessary, self-undermining reactions to events outside our control; we bear primary responsibility for our attitudes, judgments, and evaluations; we should not whine, we should be accountable for what we can control, we should suck it up; happiness requires a reasonable fit between our expectations and results; a worthwhile happiness must include a relatively enduring, positive psychological state; whether a person is happy depends largely on that person's character; we are largely responsible for our own happiness and our internal condition.

Stoicism bested its rival Epicureanism in the Greco-Roman world because it was better suited for mass acceptance. Stoicism's egalitarianism, cosmopolitanism, monotheism, natural law, and rational universe embodied popular appeal. The reign of Stoicism as the dominant way of life ended when a new philosophy of life, Christianity, promised even more.

The Joyful Transcender

Fundamental Stoicism accepts a tragic view of life. In a world where human beings are born to suffer and die, the road to the good life is paved by the bricks of emotional indifference and the mortar of moral virtue. Stoics wisely caution us against excessive desires, trivial pursuits, self-defeating activities, and external validations. But they turn the screws of their insights too tightly. They force us to harden our hearts and coarsen our souls.

Fortunately, other philosophies of the good life are available that accept a tragic view of human life but nevertheless offer a more vigorous conception of human engagement. Showing another depiction of the good life, one that shares some Stoic assumptions but concludes with a startlingly different picture of a robustly meaningful, valuable human life, opens possibilities. Allow me to raise the curtain, beat the drums, and introduce The Joyful Transcender!

The romantic-heroic tradition of the nineteenth century furnishes the image of the joyful transcender. The themes of overcoming obstacles, engaging in epic struggles, continuously striving for new goals, pursuing novelty, and going beyond existing patterns inform the joyful transcender. Friedrich Nietzsche vivifies the tradition.[32]

Nietzsche's tragic view of life understands fully the inevitability of human suffering, the flux that is the world, and the routinized character of daily life. Yet it is in our response to tragedy that we manifest either a heroic or a herd mentality. We cannot rationalize or justify the inherent meaninglessness of our suffering. We cannot transcend our vulnerability and journey to fixed security. We are contingent, mortal beings and will remain so.

However, we are free to create ourselves: we bear no antecedent duties to external authority; we are under the yoke of no preestablished goals. Contra the Stoics, no natural moral laws command our conduct, no divine providence intrudes on our designs, and no teleological cosmos structures our will. We need not recoil squeamishly from the horrors of existence, instead, we can rejoice in a passionate life of perpetual self-overcoming. Art can validate our creativity and laughter can ease our pain and soften our pretensions.

Nietzsche embraces the criterion of power: exertion, struggle, and suffering are at the core of overcoming obstacles, and it is only through overcoming obstacles that human beings experience, truly feel, their power. Higher human types joyfully embrace the values of power, while "last men," Nietzsche's male-gendered notion of embodied banality, and utilitarian philosophers extol the values of hedonism.

The highest ambitions of last men are comfort and security. They are the extreme case of the herd mentality: habit, custom, indolence, egalitarianism, self-preservation, and muted will to power prevail. Last men embody none of the inner tensions and conflicts that spur transformative action. They take no risks, lack convictions, avoid experimentation, and seek only bland survival. Hedonistic philosophers, such as the British utilitarians, unwittingly fuel the herd mentality with their celebration of pleasure, happiness, and egalitarianism.[33]

For Nietzsche, the meaning of life is not found in reason, but in the passions: in aspects of life that are of ultimate concern, our creations, devotion to worthwhile causes, and commitment to projects. Our instincts and drives create our meaning. Conscious thought can obscure our creativity. The meaning of life, for Nietzsche, focuses on stylistic movement—graceful dancing, joyful creation, negotiating the processes of a world of flux with panache and vigor—instead of goal achievement. We cannot reach an ultimate goal. But we can develop through recurrent personal and institutional deconstruction, reimagination, and re-creation. Our exertion of our wills to power in the face of obstacles, with the knowledge of inherent cosmic meaninglessness, and with profound immersion in the immediacy of life, reflects and sustains our psychological health.

Personal and institutional overcomings will permit us to become who we are: radically conditional beings deeply implicated in a world of flux. By aspiring to live a life worthy of being repeated in all details infinitely, we joyously embrace life for what it is and regard it, and ourselves, as part of a grand aesthetic epic. Whether self-mastery and self-perfection are the sole focus of the will to power, they are the prime concerns of Nietzsche's work. Neither state idolatry nor discredited supernatural images can provide human beings enduring consolations for their unresolvable existential crises. Instead, a new image of human beings is necessary.

Nietzsche's desiderata for higher human types includes the ability to marginalize but not eliminate negative and destructive impulses within oneself, and to transfigure them into joyous affirmation of all aspects of life; to understand and celebrate the radical contingency, finitude, and fragility of ourselves, our institutions, and the cosmos itself; to regard life itself as fully and merely natural, as embodying no transcendent meaning or value; to harbor little or no resentment toward others or toward the human condition; to confront the world in immediacy and with a sense of vital connection; to refuse to avert our gaze from a tragic world-view and, instead, to find value not in eventual happiness, as conceived by academic philosophers, but in the activities and processes themselves; to refuse to supplicate oneself before great people of the past but, instead, to accept their implicit challenge to go beyond them; to give style to our character by transforming our conflicting internal passions into a disciplined yet dynamic unity; to facilitate high culture by sustaining a favorable environment for the rise of great individuals; to strive for excellence through self-overcoming that honors the recurrent flux of the cosmos by refusing to accept a "finished" self as constitutive of personal identity; and to recognize the repetitive dimension to human existence: release from the tasks described is found only in death.

Given the human condition, high energy is more important than a final, fixed goal. The mantra of "challenge, struggle, overcoming, and growth," animating and transfiguring perpetual internal conflict, replaces prayers for redemption to supernatural powers. Nietzsche promotes the individualism of the highest human types while understanding that values are initially established by peoples. Human beings create the value they embody by living experimentally and by nurturing an environment that propagates great people and high culture. Existence and the world are justified as aesthetic phenomenon in that the highest artistic creations are great human beings themselves.

Nietzsche understands that greatness necessarily involves suffering and the overcoming of grave obstacles. He evaluates peoples, individuals, and cultures by their ability to transform suffering and tragedy to spiritual advantage. We cannot eliminate suffering, but we can use it creatively. Suffering and resistance can stimulate and nourish the will to power. By changing our attitude toward suffering from pity to affirmation, we open ourselves to greatness. For Nietzsche, joy and strength trump the happiness of the herd.

Nietzsche's new image of human beings is not projected for or achievable by all. His vision is an explicitly aristocratic ideal that is pitched only to the few capable of approximating it. Greatness and genius are fragile and vulnerable: they bring about their own destruction but arise stronger than ever. The thrust of Nietzsche's thought is that we can formulate entirely new modes of evaluation that correspond to new, higher forms of life. The value of humanity is established by its highest exemplars and their creations. The higher human forms are extremely fragile and rare: self-control, mastery of inclinations, resisting obstacles, experimentation, and forging a unified character require recurrent destruction, reimagination, and re-creation of the self.

We can never transcend our conditionality and the lack of inherent meaning in the world of Becoming but at least a few of us can loosen the limits of contingency, experience fully the multiplicity of our spirits, forge a coherent unity from our internal conflicts, and learn to overcome ourselves and our institutions: theoretical insight can be turned to practical advantage.

The *übermensch* (overman) is Nietzsche's male-gendered symbol of human beings overcoming themselves to superior forms. Nietzsche does not give us a definite description, but the overman represents a superhuman exemplar that has not yet or rarely existed.[34] The overman would be joyous, in control of his instinctual will to power, able to forge an admirable unity and style out of his inherent multiplicity, severe with himself, in control of his desires, a sublimator and refiner of cruelty, an unrepentant bearer of great suffering, a pursuer of "truth" who is aware of the essential unity of truth and illusion, a creator and imposer of values and meaning, who experiences his existence as self-justifying. The overman will remain faithful to this earth and not defer gratification in hopes of transcendent salvation in another world, he will possess great health and be able to experience the multiple passions he embodies, he eschews the easy path of last men, he understands the value he creates is what he embodies, he celebrates a justified self-love, he is free from resentment and revenge, he wastes no time in self-pity, he is grateful for the entirety of his life, he understands and maintains a clear distance between himself and the herd, and he exemplifies the rank order of life. The overman "shall be the meaning of the earth" in that the overman endows life with value and redeems the species's inherently meaningless tragic existence. In sum, the overman is a higher mode of being that approximates the human aspiration for transcendent greatness.

The overman embodies the virtues of the active nihilist. He relishes recurrent deconstruction, reimagination, and re-creation. The notion of overman, as symbolic, dynamic, indeterminate, provides an ideal toward which to strive. The overman symbolizes a refashioning of our sensibilities and aspiration in service of an enhanced life. The overman points a direction rather than specifies a goal. Nietzsche warns readers not to view the overman as an evolutionary necessity or as an idealistic type of higher man.

But why is self-overcoming anything more than a symptom of discontent, insecurity, and desperation? Is it only the wearing of different masks, the playing of different roles, and the strained thespianism of those lacking a sense of self? For Nietzsche, human beings are not limited to one best kind of life. We must all discharge the burden of forging our own life. Nietzsche denies the presence of a substantive self lingering beneath appearances. We are our "masks." He thinks higher types should aspire to be the most interesting series of masks they can create. To accept a particular mask or role as definitive of who you are during a lifetime is to truncate artificially the multiplicity we embody and to accept the life-denying, illusory world of being. To live beyond yourself in self-creation is to forge a complex, subtle character that is worthy of "strutting its hour upon the stage" many times, even eternally.

The slogan *amor fati* ("love of fate" and "love of life") captures Nietzsche's highest value, a maximally positive attitude toward life. We should be drawn to life so powerfully that we celebrate life in all its dimensions, suffering, and joys alike. We should not seek to edit out tragedy or revise the past. For Nietzsche suffering does not have an antecedent negative value. The value of suffering or joy or any state in between is mostly up to us.[35] Influenced by aesthetic values, he advises us to evaluate our lives in their entireties. To edit out the pain from our life is to want to be a different person, which betrays a lack of love for our life and life generally. To desire to live our life as it has been, time and time again, is the psychological test. If we had full knowledge of our lives, only the robust will pass this test. The inner power that either attracts us or repels us from life is a person's measure. The greater the attractive power, the greater the person who embodies it. As his highest basic value, Nietzsche's *amor fati* is not derived from more basic reasons or rational argument. Those who are most strongly attracted to our world, the only world for Nietzsche, will find it most valuable.

Nietzsche insists values are created by valuing beings. However, feeling, judging, or wanting something to be valuable are neither necessary nor sufficient for that something to be valuable. Our subjective responses are not the source or cause of value. For Nietzsche power is the objective measure and source of value. The highest power is the life-affirming power that draws us to life. The inner power that attracts or repels is the ground for positive and negative value. Ends that increase the individual's overall power are of higher value than goals whose achievement decreases that power. The inner power itself that draws a person to the goal defines positive value. Nietzsche denies mind-independent value, but does not succumb to a purely subjectivist account.

Other values are values only if they nurture a maximally positive attitude toward life. Art, knowledge, morality, perhaps religion are values insofar as they increase the power that moves us to affirm life. They also add products of creative activity that can serve as foci of life. Our pursuit of these instrumental values and the products they create both show and sustain a maximally positive attitude toward life. This highest value is a precondition of meaning in life, a meaning which the instrumental values provide.

Nietzsche's attitude of *amor fati* is not achieved through rational argument. Instead, it focuses on the rapture of being alive. *Amor fati* is an experience animated by faith, not cognitive discovery. *Amor fati* demands active response. First, at least, human beings have the freedom to order their interior life, their responses, to the thought of leading a life worthy of being repeated in every detail over and over again. Nietzsche's notion of eternal recurrence embodies this theme. While lower types adopt passive nihilism—and supplicate themselves compliantly before the indifference of the cosmos—higher types will embrace the entirety of life and view the lack of inherent cosmic meaning and infinite redemption as liberation from external authority. Even the Stoics recognized that nature could not control some things: our attitudes toward events in the world. Second, unlike the Stoics, Nietzsche glorifies the passions as robust manifestations of the will to power. To become who you are, to self-overcome, and to destroy, reimagine, and re-create require an active nihilism that elevates the present into a fated eternity. Third, higher types will recognize that passive nihilism or fatalism rests on the life-denying illusion that the "individual" is separate from the world.

But what is power? Primarily, power consists of activities of extending influence, dominating an environment, self-overcoming, and mastery. The activities themselves are the goal, not some further condition that results after the activities are finished. Increasing the vitality with which life forms are drawn to their goals is an increase of power and thus value. The unconditional glorification and love of life itself, *amor fati*, expresses the greatest power and is thus Nietzsche's highest value.

Nietzsche's talk of eternity, willing the world, self-overcoming, and transcendence bears the fragrance of secular redemption: religion for those who have lost their theological faith but retained their need. Furthermore, a suspicious "this is the best of all possible worlds" aura surrounds his call to affirm and love the world in all its dimensions. How can I, or anyone else, affirm, even love, the horrors of slavery, genocide, the subjugation of women, and intractable racial and ethnic strife?

How can we love everything in life? Much in the universe is alien to human life. To love ourselves and everything else is either a phony platitude, not intended to be taken literally but said only for its tranquilizing effects on listeners, or inconsistent, because our interests and the interests of other life forms are incompatible. You might argue that everything is at least a candidate for love, but that is a platitude squared, as uninteresting as saying "I love everyone." Such "love" is no love at all. Love discriminates; it recognizes unique relationships, perceived special qualities. Love takes time, effort, knowledge of the other, and a network of shared activities that preclude universality. No human being can truly "love everyone." Even someone so sensitive and giving who might love everyone, even the most despicable among us, would have the time to establish the prerequisites of love with only a few. Perhaps God can love everyone, but God has infinite knowledge, is beyond time, and is all-good. Likewise, to say that everything is a candidate for love means only that nothing is ruled out as a possible love-object from the outset. So what? Prior to knowing other people, few of us hate them as a starting point. A person who says, "My default position is to hate everything, although I might change my mind on a few things or people if they prove their worth," is deeply disturbed.

For Nietzsche, when we take responsibility for ourselves, by constructing a life worthy of being repeated infinitely and by becoming who we are, we are also willing and creating the world. Given Nietzsche's conviction that the world lacks inherent meaning, purpose, and order, we must become as gods: imposing order on chaos, creating meaning. This gigantic responsibility, along with the necessity of willing the return of the ugly, petty, and small, and directly facing cosmic meaninglessness, creates the "great weight" that lies upon our actions. The choices of active versus passive nihilism are transformed into human alternatives: to be finite gods or to self-annihilate. Because these alternatives form a unity (as do all opposites) the choices are not as clear-cut as I have been imagining them.

The texture and shadings of Nietzschean transcendence, eternality, and world creation are much different from religious versions. The focus is on this world, the premises are cosmic meaninglessness and a tragic view of life, the eternality is recurrent flux, and the transcendence is the process of destruction, reimagination, and re-creation. In sum, Nietzschean redemption is nothing more than a response to the lack of religious redemption, a message of affirmation to nudge away the nihilistic moment: there are no cosmic congratulations, but higher human types, who embody the proper attitudes, do not need any.

Nietzsche understands suffering and the horrors. But given the unity of opposites and the interrelatedness of events and things in the world, we cannot edit life to fit our preconceptions. To affirm life is to affirm the entirety of the cosmos. We must accept the sour with the sweet.

The Stoics insisted: The past is unalterable, the ways we might respond to the past are numerous. Nietzsche argues that by creating an interesting, valuable self and by advancing culture now, we can elevate the past in the only available way: we can use the materials of the past to affirm life. Remember, we cannot view our lives or the history of the world as a series of discrete moments that can be judged independently of one another. Adopting *amor fati* does not compel us to isolate and remember fondly the atrocities of the past; instead, we underscore the tragic nature of life but nevertheless joyfully embrace this world.

Part of this quest is self-overcoming, which is not fueled by discontent or negativity. Instead, self-overcoming is part of and not distinct from the self. It does not presuppose a fixed, substantial self, but rather recognizes the self's participation in the world of becoming. To affirm *amor fati* is not to renege on self-overcoming but to demand it. Once we understand and embrace this world, passive nihilism and abject fatalism cease to be viable options.

Consider, though, three outlooks or attitudes on life. First, *general exuberance*: affirming the idea of life, recognizing fully the human condition, acknowledging mortality and inherent cosmic meaninglessness, but choosing vibrancy over despair. Second, *specific exuberance*: affirming my particular life as a whole, but still harboring desires to edit out certain events that seem now to have been wrong, unnecessarily hurtful to others or self, without redeeming value, or prudentially disastrous. Third, Nietzsche's *love of fate*: to affirm and to be grateful for every aspect, part, and moment of my particular life, to want to be who I am and all the moments connected thereto eternally, and to want nothing more deeply.

Critics could argue that Nietzsche's choice creates problems. To love each part of my life equally is to dull the instincts of evaluation Nietzsche otherwise prizes. To want to be who I am eternally reneges on the commitment for recurrent self-overcoming. To love the world and self unconditionally is to demand *agape*: unwavering love that creates value in its object through the act of loving. *Agape* exists independently of the merits or demerits of the beloved, it overcomes all obstacles and endures all threats. Mistaken perceptions of value, defects in love's object, or the ingratitude of the beloved cannot erode the unshakeable certitude of the lover. But *agape* generates troubling paradoxes: If the beloved's properties are irrelevant, then whether a person is truly the object of love is unclear. For stripped of all constitutive, individuating attributes, what remains of personhood other than an abstraction called "humanity"? *Agape*, if wrongly amplified, offers much consolation but little growth. It is the love exhibited by innocents, gods, or maybe parents.

To rest affirmation of *amor fati* on feelings of gratitude for being alive is misguided. Lacking an antecedent notion of what, if anything, is genetically and culturally due to us from parents, formative environment, and the world, we can in every case fantasize about what we might have been and be resentful of being short-changed and deprived, rather than grateful for who and what we are. If preoccupied by the gap between our real and fantasized selves, we are likely to blame the imagined discrepancy on others or the human condition itself. My point is that no matter who we are we can always imagine a better life than the one we enjoy. If Nietzscheans claim that to imagine a better, or even different, life is to imagine a different person they may tacitly embrace a notion of substantive self. Unless we cling strangely to the unreasonable doctrine that all events equally constitute who I am, it is possible to affirm who I am and the world while desiring to edit out some past events.

The larger point is that general and specific exuberance can be readily affirmed. Neither attitude relies on vestiges of gods, religion, or hope of transcendent salvation. Given the choice between life and death, or between life and eternal nonbeing, I choose life and I choose the world. Even without being able to edit out the worthless or destructive parts of my life and the world, I choose life and the world over nothingness. I can also choose eternally my life and the world rather than nothingness. My choice is hardly idiosyncratic; most people living in reasonably decent circumstances would agree. My choice does not distinguish me as a higher type, nor does it generate gnashing of teeth or squeals of divinity. *Amor proprio* (self-esteem) does not require "*amor fati*"!

Nietzscheans require eternal validation of everything that constitutes life and "me" and the desire for nothing more. Is this a genuinely human desire? Critics will argue that it is an unconditional yearning in the context of a thoroughly conditional world, a vacillation between circular and linear time as convenience dictates, and a dangerous rationalization of the horrors of the past.

Nietzsche's grand individualism seems dangerous. Physicians understand that insecurity, a relentless striving for achievement, chronic impatience, intense competitiveness, and deep hostility increase bodily stress and their presence is the best predictor of several diseases. These characteristics are much more likely to be embodied by people alienated from others than people intimately connected to others. The path to health, wisdom, and joy is reached by broadening one's boundaries and widening one's subjectivity. Moral of the story: our inner deconstructions, reimaginations, and re-creations must ultimately invigorate the quality of our participation in the external world. Otherwise, internal explorations are tepid exercises in abstraction and narcissism. Are Nietzschean relationships robust enough to ensure mental and physical health?

Supporters of Nietzsche admit there is a dark or tragic side to his teaching.

The world would, of course, be more cuddly if we imagine it without its past horrors and atrocities. But it would not be our world. In our world the will to power manifests itself in many ways, including cruelty and physical violence. Edit out the historical events that make us squeamish and we also eliminate the impulses that, when sublimated and refined, produce our greatest cultural achievements. Given the unity of opposites and the impossibility of a world with only refined manifestations of the will to power, you either affirm this world, with all its horrors, or you imagine another world which edits out unfavorable events. But aspiring to the latter is nothing more than secular Christianity and is just as illusory.

To love this world and ourselves, we cannot flee to fictions or utopias. Instead, we must recognize our vulnerability to the tragedies of life. This doesn't mean we take sadistic glee in cruelty and violence. Instead, we should luxuriate in the immediacy of the moment by using the legacy of the past to create something valuable and meaningful.

Robert Nozick (1938–2002) puts a contemporary spin on the image of the joyful transcender. He imagines an experience machine that can give us any experience we desire.[36] Our brains could be stimulated so we would think and feel that we were winning the Nobel Prize, having dinner with our favorite celebrity, breaking Barry Bonds's home-run record, engaging in a torrid love affair with the person of our dreams, or anything else we want to experience. All the while we would be floating in a tank with electrodes attached to our brains. We could, if we wished, plug into the machine for life and program our entire life's experiences. Or we could program some time out of the tank every two years or so to select the experiences for the next period of our lives. While in the tank we will not know we are there. We will think it is all actually happening. Assuming all other logistics could be resolved (for example, a team to monitor the tank, ways to fulfill our nutrition needs, required medical care, arranging the blissful death that must eventually come), would we choose to enter the tank for an extended period?

In an age of developing virtual realities, Nozick's thought experiment is less bizarre than might first seem. He argues that we would reject the experience machine for at least three reasons. First, doing things is more important to us than merely having the sensations of doing them. More matters to us than merely how our lives feel from within. Second, we want to become a certain type of person, not simply float in a tank as a bland receptacle of sensations. Third, the experience machine limits us to an artificial reality which prevents actual contact with any deeper reality. The experience machine lives our lives for us instead of helping us live our own lives. However sophisticated we imagine the machine, its major function is to remove us from reality and prevent us from making any difference in the world.

Our rejection of an experience machine that encloses us within a framework of just our own experiences suggests that connecting with things and values beyond our individual experiences is crucial. Nozick takes meaning in life to involve transcending our limits. The narrow and more restrictive the limits of a life, the less meaningful it is. The more intensely people are involved and the more they transcend their limits, the more meaningful their lives are. For inherently limited human beings, finding meaning requires connecting with something that is itself meaningful or valuable. To avoid infinite regress, the chain that grounds meaning must end with something that is either meaningful or valuable in itself, or Unlimited. Thus to inquire about the meaning of a life is to ask how it is connected to other things.

For Nozick, then, meaning is relational, it concerns our connection with external value or other relational meaning, and it involves exceeding our limits, going beyond our own value. Human beings have limited transcendence: as we go beyond our limits to connect with a wider context of value, that value is itself limited. Thus our lives yield limited, finite meaning. Only if an Unlimited or Absolute exists to ground infinite meaning could our lives be otherwise.

Nozick understands keenly that processes can have value and can provide contexts in which meaning flows. The rhythms of the process—ordering diverse material, introducing new material and disaggregating the old, ordering anew, and disrupting the new order by new material—form a continuing cycle combining meaning and value.

Nozick takes meaning to involve transcending our limits and connecting to external meaning and value. Nietzsche talks about going beyond ourselves, self-overcoming, and negotiating the processes of a world of flux with panache and vigor, rather than seeking a final goal. Nietzsche insists on giving style to one's character and creating order out of multiple, conflicting impulses. Joyous transcenders glorify the process of human life: lacking final, reachable goals, only robust development through recurrent personal and institutional deconstruction, reimagination, and re-creation.

The romantic notion of deconstruction, reimagination, and re-creation stirs our fantasies and ennobles our spirits. But the advice to fashion a sequence of serial selves can foster lack of definition and a hunger for authenticity. The context-smashing self risks a robust sense of identity at the altar of expanded consciousness. Perhaps forging a unity out of multiplicity and self-mastery softens the possible excesses of the notion, but the dangers remain. If we are nothing more than a series of selves, we may not be anything.

Accordingly, we must question the point of the process of the joyful transcender. Is relentless striving merely a sign of discontentment? Is the joyful transcender a chameleon who changes color because of an inadequate sense of self? Is the forced activity merely a way to forget the pain of human life? Is there any difference between the joyful transcender and the greedy materialist who is never satisfied and who accumulates more and more wealth as an end in itself?

Perhaps not. First, the process of the joyful transcender is committed to progress. The process is not viewed as a pendulum which swings back and forth, occupying the same space repeatedly. The joyful transcender, if successful, develops and creates. Whether viewed as Nietzsche's self-overcoming to a higher human form or Nozick's connection with more meaning and value, the joyful transcender does not occupy the same space repeatedly. Second, the process of joyful transcender does not seek a final termination of the original goal and does not implicitly embrace permanence as a high value. Third, the joyful transcender finds deep meaning and value in the process itself as activity, creation, and continuing development flow. Finally, the attitude of the joyful transcender toward life is enthusiastically positive.

While I doubt that the image of the joyful transcender captures the entire deep truth about human personality and that it shows the only way to a meaningful life, it highlights important insights. Human beings are not static creatures. We flourish through ongoing creative development. The image of joyful transcender, heroic and romantic, is appealing.

Still, taken to an extreme, it invites charges that it is adolescent and fatuous. The image of the joyful transcender attracts us because it speaks to our sense of adventure, our individualism, our need to experience intensely. But we are much more than joyful transcenders. Even Nietzsche recognizes this. Our sense of community, our needs for peace and respite, and our yearning for narrative structure are also part of human personality. We need to be distinct individuals, but if this impulse is exaggerated we become isolated and alienated. We need to be intimately connected to others, but if this yearning is unchallenged we become suffocated and overly dependent. The trick is to achieve the best measure of each impulse. Neither Romanticism nor Stoicism is sufficient. Each image speaks to only part of the human condition. We need to transcend joyfully but we also need internal unity and integrated identities.

Joyful transcenders live intensely, joyfully, with great expectations although they understand human limitations. Joyful transcenders luxuriate in the immediacy of life, immerse themselves in flow experiences, and value the process of life for its own sake. They aspire to go beyond their past and current self-understandings to more glorious conceptions. However, they should also acknowledge and relish their interdependence with others and appreciate how self-identity is linked to social contexts. You will die, I will die, and the stars will fade away. But in between our births and our deaths, we can construct robustly meaningful and valuable lives.

Notes

1. Raymond Angelo Belliotti, *Happiness is Overrated* (Lanham, MD: Rowman & Littlefield, 2004), 28–37.

2. Richard McKeon, "Introduction to the Philosophy of Cicero," in Marcus Tullius Cicero, *Selected Works*, trans. by Hubert M. Poteat (Chicago: University of Chicago Press, 1950), 48–49.

3. John Sellars, *Stoicism* (Berkeley, CA: University of California Press, 2006), 91–98.

4. Ibid., 99–101.

5. Ibid., 104.

6. Ibid., 64–70.

7. Ibid., 69

8. Ibid., 71.

9. Stephen A. White, "Cicero and the Therapists," in J. G. F. Powell, *Cicero: The Philosopher* (Oxford: Clarendon Press, 1999), 239.

10. Tad Brennan, *The Stoic Life* (Oxford: The Clarendon Press, 2005), 99.

11. Ibid., 98.

12. Sellars, *Stoicism*, 38.

13. Miriam Griffith, "Philosophy, Cato, and Roman Suicide: I," *Greece & Rome* 33 (1986): 71.

14. Ibid., 73–74.

15. Ibid., 74.

16. Miriam Griffith, "Philosophy, Cato, and Roman Suicide: II," *Greece & Rome* 33 (1986): 197–98.

17. Plutarch, *The Lives of Noble Grecians and Romans*, vol. II, trans. by John Dryden, ed. and rev. by Arthur Hugh Clough (New York: The Modern Library, 1979), 270

18. Ibid., 272.

19. Philip Matyszak, *Chronicle of the Roman Republic* (London: Thames & Hudson, Ltd., 2003), 194.

20. Plutarch, *The Lives*, 272–73, 274.

21. Ibid., 298.

22. Ibid., 316.

23. Michael Parenti, *The Assassination of Julius Caesar* (New York: The New Press, 2003), 142–43.

24. Greg Woolf, *Et, tu, Brute?* (London: Profile Books, Ltd., 2006), 139–40.

25. J. P. V. D. Balsdon, "Cicero the Man," in T. A. Dorey, ed., *Cicero* (New York: Basic Books, 1965), 183–84.

26. Forrest McDonald, "Foreword," in Christine Dunn Henderson and Mark E. Yellin, eds., *Cato: A Tragedy* (Indianapolis, IN: Liberty Fund, Inc.), viii.

27. Christine Dunn Henderson and Mark E. Yellin, "Introduction," in ibid., xviii.

28. Brennan, *Stoic Life*, 144

29. Friedrich Nietzsche, *Beyond Good and Evil*, trans. by Walter Kaufmann (New York: Vintage Books, 1966), sec. 9.

30. Brennan, *Stoic Life*, 35–37.

31. Ibid., 171–72.

32. Raymond Angelo Belliotti, *What is the Meaning of Human Life?* (Amsterdam: Rodopi, 2001), 34–49, 65–71.

33. Friedrich Nietzsche, *Thus Spoke Zarathustra*, trans. by Walter Kaufmann in *The Portable Nietzsche* (New York: Viking Press, 1954), "Zarathustra's Prologue," sec. 5. See, generally, *Beyond Good and Evil*, trans. by Walter Kaufmann (New York: Vintage Books, 1966); *On the Genealogy of Morals*, trans. by Walter Kaufmann and R. J. Hollingdale (New York: Vintage Books, 1967); *The Gay Science*, trans. by Walter Kaufmann (New York: Random House, 1967); *The Birth of Tragedy*, trans. by Walter Kaufmann (New York: Random House, 1967).

34. Nietzsche, *Thus Spoke Zarathustra*, "Zarathustra's Prologue," sec. 3–44; "On Priests."

35. Nietzsche, *Thus Spoke Zarathustra*, "On the Thousand and One Goals."

36. Robert Nozick, *Philosophical Explanations* (Cambridge, MA: Harvard University Press, 1981), 571–619.

Texts and Their Abbreviations

All references are to Book numbers and/or sections, not page numbers, unless otherwise stated.
For example:

Cato IV.IV.81 =	*Cato: A Tragedy,* Act 4, Scene 4, line 81.
CW 54.4 =	*Catiline's War*, section 54, line or paragraph 4.
DS 1.28.2–3 =	*The Discourses*, Book 1, chapter 28, lines 2–3.
Laws 9.873c =	*The Laws*, Book 9, 873c (Stephanus pagination).
NE 9.1169a19 =	*Nicomachean Ethics*, Book 9, section 1169a, line 19.
Phaedo 61c =	*Phaedo*, 61c (Stephanus pagination)
PM 60 =	*Pro Murena,* paragraph 60.
PU 1.31 =	*Purgatorio*, Canto 1, line 31.

I have used the following abbreviations:

Cato =	*Cato: A Tragedy* (Joseph Addison)
CW =	*Catiline's War* (Gaius Sallustius Crispus: "Sallust")
DS =	*The Discourses* (Epictetus)
Laws =	*The Laws* (Plato)
NE =	*Nicomachean Ethics* (Aristotle)
Phaedo =	*Phaedo* (Plato)
PM =	*Pro Murena* (Cicero)
PU =	*Purgatorio* (Dante Alighieri)

Chapter Three
Epicureanism: Lucretius, Caesar, and Cassius

This chapter explores Epicureanism through the words and acts of Lucretius, Caesar, and Cassius. A brief history of the rise of hedonism and the bedrock beliefs of Epicurus is followed by an explanation of the poetic refinements to Epicureanism offered by Lucretius. The relationship between philosophy and political action is then discussed in the contexts of Caesar and Cassius. Finally, I take up the Epicurean challenge to explain how death can be bad for human beings even though when we are alive, death is not with us and when we are dead, we are no longer. In so doing, I also advance and defend a view of how posthumous events can harm or benefit human beings.

The Roots of Epicureanism

Hedonism is a theory that highlights the pursuit of pleasure as critical to the good life. As human beings understand keenly the joys of physical and intellectual activities that generate pleasure, hedonism begins with a huge lead over competing views. Instructing people to fill their days with more pleasure is not a tough sell.

Aristippus (435–366 BC) was one of the earliest hedonists. He observed that the future is uncertain, while our subjective sensations are immediately knowable. Subjective sensations are the criterion for practical conduct. The goal of such conduct is pleasure. Bodily pleasures are superior to mental pleasures because they are more immediate, certain, knowable, intense, and powerful. Taking no account of the quality of different pleasures, Aristippus was not a toady to abstraction and intellectual contemplation. Even friends are only instrumentally valuable: Intense concern for the other is unwise because our access to their feelings is indirect, sketchy, and fallible.

Aristippus, who lived in Cyrene, and his followers comprise the Cyrenaic version of hedonism. Having been influenced by Socrates, the Cyrenaics cautioned that wise people should avoid unrestrained excess in their pursuit of pleasure. Proper judgment is required to evaluate competing desires and pleasures. Short-term pleasure can lead to long-term pain. Despite their basic disposition to distrust appeals to the future as uncertain, indirect, and speculative, the Cyrenaics conceded that proper judgment required evaluations about the long-term effects of actions. These two inclinations coalesced restlessly. The Cyrenaics tacitly admitted that wise people were distinguished from foolish people in part on the basis of their ability to evaluate the unknown.

Cyrenaic hedonism contained the seeds of its own destruction. We cannot simply pursue physical and material pleasures. We must evaluate, probabilistically, long-term effects. However, this evaluation appeals to criteria other than quantity of bodily pleasures. The unrestrained pleasure-seeker meets the fate of Plato's tyrant: Immersed in the quicksand of ever-increasing desires, the tyrant is never content and only sporadically satisfied. Cyrenaic hedonism is insufficient and must look outside itself for guidance.

Worse, Cyrenaic hedonism failed to understand how the tragedy of life provides opportunities for meaning and value. For Cyrenaics, pain and suffering are to be avoided, not transformed into practical advantage. Given that in the world they knew, perhaps the world as it has always been, most people suffer more pain than experience enduring pleasure, Cyrenaic hedonism transmitted implicitly a pessimistic message. If pleasure is the greatest good, if a life in which pleasure predominates is inaccessible to most of us, what hope remains?

Under a follower of Aristippus, Hegesias, the dark side of Cyrenaic hedonism, which had hitherto lain dormant, emerged.

[Hegesias] held that since pleasure is the good, no life is good on balance, for pain always predominates in the long run. Therefore, the rational hedonist will kill himself. Hegesias expounded this thesis with such eloquence that the authorities found it necessary to suppress his lectures after many of his auditors had committed suicide. Hegesias himself, we are told, lived to be a very old man.[1]

Epicureanism: Hedonism Refined

Epicureanism was a more influential version of hedonism. Epicurus (341–270 BC) and Titus Lucretius Carus ("Lucretius") (95–50 BC) were the most important Epicurean philosophers.[2] Liberating human beings from fear and maximizing their prospects for happiness motivated Epicurus. Unlike the Cynics, he viewed pleasure, which defined happiness, as the greatest good. But not just any pleasure, only simple, sustainable ones. Worthy pleasures, those that define happiness, do not include the tortured trinity of wine, women or men, and song. The best pleasures preclude pain and produce a serene spirit. Epicurus's recipe for happiness was health, self-control, independence, moderation, simplicity, cheerfulness, friendship, prudence, intellectual and aesthetic values, and peace of mind. The calm, tranquil, harmonious life is the happy life. He explained why this is so by appealing to the conditions of the world, to human nature, and to the natural order.

The recipe for Epicurean acquisition was sparse: friendship is critical for self-validation and to nurture gentleness and sympathy; freedom is crucial and defined by liberation from the anxieties and imprisonments of social and political affairs; philosophical contemplation is required to ease irrational fears and to vivify pleasures of the mind; and simple food, clothing, and shelter are necessary to satisfy basic physical needs. This quartet and the means required to attain them are the only *natural and necessary* human desires.

Natural but unnecessary human desires would include sex, lavish banquets, private baths, spacious homes, special foods and drinks, and the like. Human beings should regard the satisfaction of such desires with indifference. *Unnatural and unnecessary* human desires, which are not grounded in reality, include fame, power, wealth, and the like. We should repudiate such desires. For Epicurus, the satisfaction of these two categories of desires can never bring human fulfillment; whereas the satisfaction of natural and necessary desires both guarantees and is required for human fulfillment. The greatest good is Epicurean pleasure. Moral virtue has instrumental value as a means of attaining that pleasure, but remains subordinate to the greatest good.

Friendship, honorably pursued, is taken to be a prime determinant of a life in which pleasure will consistently prevail over pain. This condition of Epicurean happiness is entirely consistent with the basic concepts of his moral system: the focus on natural and necessary desires, the notion that the pleasure resulting from the absence of pain can be varied but not increased, the superiority of mental to bodily pleasures, and above all, the importance of recollection and anticipation as factors in securing the continuing dominance of pleasure over pain.[3]

The satisfaction of natural and necessary desires, such as a drink of water when we are thirsty, relieves our pain. The satisfaction of natural and unnecessary desires, such as consuming a scrumptious meal, only varies a pleasure. The removal of pain and the fulfillment of necessary desires are more critical than varying sensual pleasure. Epicurus clearly insists that the good life does not arise from lavish meals, sexual indulgence, or luxurious adornments.[4] Profligate pleasures do not ease human fears or teach the limits of desire. They are more likely to distract us from higher callings. Still, moderate sensual pleasures accompanied by no pain may facilitate the fulfillment of natural desires, both necessary and unnecessary. However, Epicurus does vacillate between understanding pleasure as positive sensation and, at other times, as merely the serene absence of pain.

Epicurean prescriptions are few, but powerful: live kindly and sympathetically among friends; live quietly and avoid the troubles of competition and aggressiveness; live with few material possessions—you'll have less to lose and fewer responsibilities; live moderately and avoid excesses. Such imperatives may require common sense and practical wisdom to apply, but they do not demand esoteric understanding or deep intellectualism.

> [These injunctions] are what make Epicurus's teaching so immediately attractive in any world where there are great opportunities for indulgence and wealth, but where there is also insecurity with regard to possessions, skepticism with regard to gods, where vast and remote state organizations diminish personal autonomy, and where science or other factors cause us to see ourselves as in significant beings in a vast but ultimately purposeless system.[5]

Epicurus devised a powerful strategy. First, he identified the beliefs and actions that caused human beings unnecessary pain and suffering: Fear of the gods, anxiety about death and an afterlife, and the pursuit of self-defeating pleasures. Then, he reimagined and re-created a vision of human life that eliminated the main causes of human pain and suffering. Finally, he and his followers embodied and acted on this vision, and drew supporters attracted to the charismatic exemplars of the Epicurean lifestyle.

If fear of the gods is a problem then what is the solution? Epicurus might have simply denied that gods exist: No gods, no fear. This solution, though, would have been unpersuasive to a Greco-Roman world that acknowledged and paid tribute to numerous, anthropomorphic deities with carefully circumscribed spheres of influence. Moreover, Epicurus, uninformed by the masters of suspicion—Marx, Nietzsche, and Freud—whom he predated by over two millennia, was convinced that the universal belief in the gods could be explained only by their objective reality. The gods, then, existed.

Epicurus, though, rejected the common view that celestial bodies were deities. The sun, moon, and stars are inanimate, whereas gods must be animate; celestial bodies are destructible, whereas gods are immortal; and celestial bodies are insensitive, whereas gods enjoy pleasurable lives. Anticipating an enduring, theological problem, Epicurus was puzzled by the amount of evil and suffering in the world. How could such enormous, unexplainable evil persist if divine providence ruled? Epicurus concluded that divine providence was a myth, a misunderstanding of the nature of the gods. Although the gods existed, the nature of their existence differed from the prevalent understanding. Epicurus brought forth the good news that the real nature of the existence of the gods should not engender fear. The gods exist as beautiful, happy, calm, merry, and indifferent to human life. The gods, fortuitously, are Epicureans! Indeed, they serve as divine ideals for the proper human life. Accordingly, human beings should not fear the gods because the gods do not punish or reward us. Instead, we should look to the lives of the gods as exemplars toward which to strive while on earth.

Having eliminated to his satisfaction the fear of gods, Epicurus took on his next target: Fear of death and an afterlife. He observed that fear of death and anxiety over an afterlife disabled numerous human beings from full engagement in this world. Such suffering was unnecessary and grounded on philosophical errors.

Epicurus rejected mind-body dualism and belief in personal immortality. Subscribing to the atomic theory developed by the pre-Socratic philosopher, Democritus (460–370 BC), Epicurus argued that the world is eternal and composed of atoms that produce everything by their infinitely variable combinations. Each human being is composed of atoms that disperse entirely after the death of the body. No afterlife waits us.

Epicurus held that death is not an evil. He argued that death is irrelevant to us. For Epicurus, all good and evil consists in sensations: Pleasure is good; pain is evil. However, death is the end of all sensations, so death is nothing to us. We have no good reason to fear what is nothing to us.

Having eliminated to their satisfaction the fear of death and an afterlife, Epicureans took on their final target: Dissatisfaction caused by pursuit of self-defeating pleasures. Epicurus, following the Socratic-Platonic tradition, disparaged physical and material pleasures as enslaving: The more we get the more we want *ad infinitum*. We too easily become addicted to pleasures over which we have too little control and which jeopardize a well-ordered, harmonious internal condition. Such pleasures produce, at best, transitory pleasure that transforms into more enduring suffering. Epicurus, though, goes further. He disputes several of the projects that Aristotle thought necessary for *eudaemonia*. Epicurus observed that politics, marriage, family relations, and most passionate pursuits too often produced anxiety and ended badly. Avoiding pain, especially mental suffering, is even more important than pursuing pleasure. The absence of passion facilitates contentment. We must discard many of our desires or, at least, not act on them. The Epicurean program is explicitly for personal development, an egoistic hedonism grounded in withdrawal from public life.

> "Live unknown" was the Epicurean motto—excellent advice no doubt, especially in so turbulent a period. One ought to abstain not only from politics and other ways of perhaps fatally attracting attention, but from sex also: "Sexual intercourse never did anyone any good, and a man is lucky if it has not harmed him." It is better not to marry and have children, for families are constant sources of anxiety. You should not overeat or drink much, for fear of indigestion and hangover. Epicurus deemed a little bread and cheese to constitute a banquet . . . "plain living and moderately high thinking."[6]

Pain and suffering, though, are sure to greet us. If we focus on past pleasures and the transient nature of our plight, we can ease our pain. Seek moderate pleasures, avoid pain, accept misfortunes with aplomb, cast aside irrational fears, and strive for serenity. The Epicurean recipe seemed accessible and sagacious to loads of ancient Greeks and Romans seeking the good life.

Roman Panache

Lucretius must have known his contemporary Cicero, but little is known of their presumed relationship. A year after Lucretius died, Cicero wrote his brother and, among other things, commended Lucretius's talent and technique. We can remain confident that Cicero did not praise Lucretius's subscriptions to the Epicurean pleasure principle, the denial of divine providence, or conviction in human annihilation at death.

Stunningly, no other contemporary references to Lucretius appear. To conclude that Lucretius perfected the art of Epicurean disengagement from social life is reasonable. In his *De Rerum Natura*, Lucretius presented a comprehensive description of Epicurean philosophy with poetic flair: "His work is immensely creative not only in its poetic form but also in its rhetorical and emotional power and social relevance."[7] Epicurus had concentrated on producing an individualistic ethic framed in a distinctive metaphysics. He said little about political philosophy other than generally we are best advised to steer clear of its entanglements and frustrations. Epicurus viewed political associations as a series of agreements flowing from the human need for mutual protection. Justice was not founded on natural law, but on the conventions, exigencies, and expediencies of individuals embedded in communities.

Although Epicurus, following longstanding Greek tradition, made a bright-line distinction between the glories of philosophy and the intellectual poverty of poetry, Lucretius found verse to be a literary device congenial to winning converts to Epicureanism. Lucretius also refined Epicureanism in several ways. For example, he posited five stages of human development. At first, he theorized, human beings lived estranged from one another. With neither families nor agricultural skills, each person was completely self-absorbed. Next, our personalities were softened by the development of marriage, families, language, and extended bonding with neighbors. Soon thereafter, a few superior people emerged who founded cities, assumed rule, conjured property rights, and sought material accumulation. But consolidated power soon grew arrogant and kings were overthrown. A period of political nihilism ensued: mobs and individual power brokers were rampant. Finally, enough people understood that the rule of law, operated under elected administrators, was required for the tranquil life most human beings desired (DRN 5.925–5.1160).

De Rerum Natura also includes the fundamentals of Epicureanism 101: a rejection of religious superstition and its fear-inducing consequences; a contrast between Epicurean serenity and the hyper-aggressive, ultra-competitive, zero-sum game afflicting Roman politics; a parody of people who desperately hold on to life from their misguided fear of death; a critique of the alleged benefits of sexual desire; and an effusive eulogy to Epicurus as the potential rescuer of mankind if only more people would heed his counsel.

Both Cicero and Lucretius, contemporaries living in a time of political crisis, concluded that philosophy could explain and remedy Rome's social ills. Whereas Cicero located Rome's political crisis in a failure to live up to traditional Roman standards and values—Rome needed to return to founding principles and reward deserving citizens based only on the principle of proportionate equality—Lucretius indicted traditional Roman competitiveness and relentless striving as the source of the republic's political and social predicament: "The quietism that Lucretius advocated could not sit well with most members of the Roman elite. They had been raised on an ideology that placed a premium on military achievement and political renown. Lucretius's poem, however, coming at the collapse of the Roman Republic was a remarkable challenge to traditional Roman values."[8] In contrast to Stoicism, which supported some of Rome's cherished political, religious, and social traditions, Epicureanism seriously resisted several Roman fundamental beliefs:

[Epicureanism's] utilitarian ethics undermined the accepted ideal of Roman virtue and its picture of the gods as remote powerless beings existing in the perfect peace of inactivity in the regions between the worlds was inconsistent with the traditional religion of Rome. Epicureanism had no use for family sentiment or the ideal of public service; its founder advised against marriage and parent-hood, recommended abstention from politics and advised his followers to live unobtrusively. Moreover, the Epicureans cared little for literary culture and the graces of style, and they expected their adherents to acquire peace of mind by studying physics, whereas the average Roman valued style and literary culture and had little interest in the nature of the physical world.[9]

Nevertheless, Epicureanism offered three allures: The pleasure principle was congenial to many citizens for whom political and military success were long shots; the doctrines of this school seemed easier to grasp than some of the nu-anced renderings of their competitors; and Epicurean prescriptions were less demanding than austere, lofty Stoic ideals. The number of Roman disciples of Epicureanism fell off sharply, though, after the republic ended. To conclude that Epicureanism fulfilled a deep human need characteristic of the late Roman re-public is reasonable: "The strife, unrest, and self-seeking of the Roman world in the last years of the Republic led men by way of reaction to the quiet atmos-phere of the [Epicurean] Garden. The community of friends living quietly and without ambition had a special attraction against a background of civil war and restless ambition."[10]

For Lucretius, nonphilosophical political and military strivers are akin to in-significant insects, hopping from task to task without reflecting on the meaning of anything. Only wisdom, which demands conversion to Epicurean philosophy, can lead human beings to their highest fulfillment. The relentless striving seeks more and more, but realizes less and less (DRN 2.7–2.14).

> But nothing is sweeter than to live in calm and lofty precincts protected by the teachings of wise men. From them you can look down on others and see how they wander here and there, aimlessly trying to find a path through life. They compete with their abilities, they contend in noble birth, and night and day they struggle to climb to the heights of wealth and power. . . . Do you not see how nature proclaims that she demands no more than this—that pain be kept sepa-rate from the body, and that the mind, free from fear and anxiety, enjoy the sen-sation of pleasure. (DRN 2.7–2.19)

Lucretius concluded that the fear of death was the source of the Roman zero-sum contests for wealth, power, and honor. Horrified by their looming mortality, citizens desperately clung to life in the forms of economic security and the ce-lebrity of military and political victories. Although such unnatural, unnecessary pursuits could not provide enduring satisfaction—even if their goals were achieved—men were drawn to them as a puny, self-defeating defiance of their finitude (DRN 3.59–3.86). However, unnatural, unnecessary desires are built around fantasies; they cannot be satisfied or bring fulfillment.

Lucretius follows the classic Epicurean division between (a) natural, neces-sary desires whose satisfaction results from ingesting substances into the body (for example, food and drink); (b) natural, unnecessary desires whose satisfaction changes the state of the sense organs (for example, sex); and (c) unnatural, unnecessary desires whose satisfaction is chimerical because they are based on illusion (for example, love).

> For food and drink are absorbed into the body; since they can occupy specific places, this desire for water and bread is easily satisfied. But from the face and lovely complexion of a human being, nothing is given to the body to enjoy but insubstantial images; and this frail hope is often snatched away by the wind. Just as when a thirsty man seeks drink in his dreams, and no moisture is granted him to put out the fire in his body, but he pursues images of liquid and toils in vain, and thirsts even as he drinks in the midst of a rushing river, so in love Venus deludes lovers with images. (DRN 4.1091–4.1101)

Lucretius also argues against the transmigration of the soul and personal immortality. For those subscribing to transmigration theory—the view that the soul is immortal and at death passes into another body—Lucretius poses a question. If one argues that a human soul always passes into a human body, then why is an infant not as learned as an adult? If the reply is that the soul grows young in a young body, then the soul is mortal because it loses some of its former properties. The soul must be, then, corporeal. The union of soul and body brings forth human life. The belief that an immortal soul changes with its change of body is inconsistent: If the soul can change then it can also be disaggregated and perish. Composed of atoms, the human soul is destined for disaggregation. At death, the body dies and can no longer meld the soul together, so the atoms composing the soul must scatter. What comes into being with the body will pass from existence with the body. Death, in the sense of annihilation, holds no terror for us. By rejecting dualism, embracing monism, and appreciating our mortality, we eliminate the fear of punishment after death (DRN 3.323–3.369; 3.417–3.829).

Lucretius placed no stock in claims of antecedent natural law or the divinity of the universe. The constitutive elements of the universe are inappropriate havens for life and human thought. The laws of the universe emerge only after atoms randomly collide, form bodies, and develop structure. Moreover, because neither the universe as a whole nor its constitutive parts are animate, they cannot be divinities (DRN 5.110–5.145). The gods lack a conception of the world prior to its actual existence; no convincing account can be offered for the god's alleged change before and after creation; and the flaws in our world deny divine providence (DRN 2.167–2.183; 5.156–5.234). The gods exist not to impose upon or punish human beings, but to permit them to pursue pleasure, which is also the chief concern of the deities. The world is free from divine intervention. Human beings have no need to fear the gods (DRN 2.646–2.651). Human beings were led to believe in the gods because of dream visions and their inability to explain celestial activity. True piety, though, does not reside in rituals, sacrifices, and currying favor with divinities, but in peaceful contemplation of the universe (DRN 5.1169–5.1203).

The amount and intensity of evil in our world, particularly natural disasters, undermines the claim that the universe was designed by divine providence to benefit mankind (DRN 2.167–2.181; 5.195–5.234). Instead, atoms, although not truly animate, move freely and without divine agency (DRN 2.1090–2.1092; 1.1021–1.1028). As a collection of atoms, the world is transient, not immortal. Would not a benevolent deity, if one existed, ensure that his major creation was everlasting? Is not the environment of the world too antagonistic to yield evidence for a grand teleology or master creator? (DRN 5.91–5.415) Those who fear alleged divine retribution must answer troubling questions: If natural disasters, such as thunderbolts, were truly Zeus's punishment of human wrongdoers, why do so many such retributions land on desolate regions? Why do some even land on temples dedicated to Zeus himself? (DRN 6.387–6.422)

The only entities as such are atoms and the void. Time is a feature of the universe, not an independent dimension governing it. Atoms form combinations that comprise nature and the natural process; there are no controlling agents above the atoms and the void. The swerve of atoms falling allows them to stray from a perfectly downward course, contact one another, and form the requisite pacts that constitute the world. But for the swerve, atoms would fall straight through space into the void and our world would not exist. Our world, then, is developed empirically, through trial and error, and the purposeless play of atoms, not teleologically, through a grand design, master creator, or inherent design.

> Whilst a concept of what we might term "the survival of the fittest" is operative within his explanation, Lucretius works without a concept of "evolution." As a result, he assumes that species come into being in a fixed and final form, and that many species have failed to survive because they lacked qualities conducive to their survival.[11]

The order brought about by cooperating atoms is not eternal. In that vein, Roman political institutions exemplify the better instincts of the fifth stage of human social development; but they, too, shall pass and wise citizens will avoid political entanglements, if possible.

> Lucretius has no time for the pomp and empty glory of Roman political life, the ideal and goal of a Cicero. But like the "conservatives" he sees the opposition to this as motivated by no more than psychological aberration, greed, and envy ultimately grounded in the fear of death. He is concerned with the state of Rome, but the solution is a personal one: everyone should become an Epicurean. . . . The *De Rerum Natura* seems still focused upon individual salvation, how an individual Epicurean might survive in a hostile world. And the answer is the same as it has always been: stay away from politics.[12]

Although technically sex is an Epicurean natural but unnecessary desire, Lucretius is no fan. He passionately warns us against avid pursuit of sex:

> For of the most part men are blinded by passion, and assign to women excellences which are not truly theirs. And so we see those in many ways deformed

and ugly dearly loved, yes even prospering in high favor. And one man laughs at another, and urges him to appease Venus, since he is wallowing in a base passion. Yet often, poor wretch, he cannot see his own ills, far greater than the rest. . . . Nor is all this unknown to our Venuses, and that is why they are at pains to hide all behind the scenes from those whom they wish to keep fettered in love. (DRN 4.1153–4.1158; 4.1185–4.1188)

For Lucretius, most human desires are unnatural and unnecessary. Such desires are constructed on conventional beliefs that are false and often concocted by a

> religious elite to gain power over humans by making them unhappy and disgusted with the merely human in life. Central to this religious project is a teaching about death that engenders fear and loathing, along with the passionate longing for immortal life. And it was Lucretius's view that most of our other emotions—including the anger that motivates war and the erotic love that seeks personal salvation through fusion with a "goddess"—were disguised forms of this religious fear and longing.[13]

Lucretius also develops Epicurus's remarks on fearing death. Life is finite. We are not anxious or upset because we did not exist prior to our actual births, so we should not fear a comparable nonexistence after death. Put in a modern context: the year 1505 was nothing to us and conjures no anxiety in the year 2008; so, too, the year 2099, by which we will all be dead, should cause us no anxiety now. The reality of being dead—nothingness—will be no better or worse for us than the expansive period prior to our births (DRN 3.830–3.869).

> Think too how the bygone antiquity of everlasting time before our birth was nothing to us. Nature therefore holds this up to us as a mirror of the time yet to come after our death. Is there anything in this that looks appalling, anything that wears an aspect of gloom? Is it not more untroubled than any sleep? (DRN 3.971–3.977)

Moreover, Lucretius argues that much of our fear of death flows from our inability to perceive ourselves as distinct from our bodies. Because we understand that terrifying atrocities can beset *our bodies* at death, we wrongly conclude that those horrors are besetting *us*. Accordingly, we fear the condition or state of death in part because we anticipate possible harms to our corpses which we wrongly identify as harms to us.

> And so, when you see a man chafing at his lot, that after death he will either rot away with his body laid in earth, or be destroyed by flames, or the jaws of wild beasts . . . he believes he will have feeling in death . . . supposes something of himself to live on. . . . For neither does he separate himself from the corpse, nor withdraw himself enough from the outcast body, but thinks that it is he, and, as he stands watching, taints it with his own feeling. Hence he chafes that he was born mortal, and sees not that in real death there will be no second self, to live and mourn to himself his own loss, or to stand there and be pained that he lies mangled and burning. (DRN 3.870–3.886)

Lucretius's argument is simple but challenging: Human beings are untroubled by prenatal nonexistence; posthumous nonexistence ("death") is the mirror image of prenatal nonexistence; accordingly, human beings should be untroubled by their upcoming deaths. The core of the argument is that prenatal nonexistence was an indefinitely long experiential zero that held no terror for us. Death is an indefinitely long experiential zero the prospects of which should also hold no terror for us. Neither prenatal nonexistence nor death harms us; we have no persuasive reason to fear that which does not harm us; thus we have no persuasive reason to fear death.

Caesar

At least seven pieces of evidence support the conclusion that Julius Caesar embraced Epicurean philosophy. First, the Roman historian Gaius Sallustius Crispus ("Sallust") (86–35 BC) reports the following as part of Caesar's speech at the senate during the Catiline conspiracy: "But about punishment I am able to say what is the case, that amidst grief and pitifulness death constitutes, not torture, but a rest from affliction: it dissipates all the maladies of mortals, and beyond it there is no place for either worry or joy" (CW 51.20–21).

Here Caesar states clearly his conviction that after death no sensations are possible, and that death is, accordingly, not an evil. He suggests—but does not unequivocally argue—that death is annihilation; the soul perishes with the body; and no personal immortality or afterlife awaits us. Some historians, such as biographer Michael Grant, take this speech as evidence of Caesar's commitment to Epicureanism: "[Caesar] added (giving a rare glimpse of his own philosophical views) Epicurus had been right in saying that perpetual punishment—the penalty he was suggesting—is a worse punishment than death, since beyond the grave there is no life and therefore no suffering at all."[14] Other thinkers, such as Frank C. Bourne, are even more emphatic: "There can be no question that [Caesar's] famous speech, delivered when he was praetor-elect, on the treatment of the Catilinarian conspirators contained an unvarnished Epicurean view of death."[15]

Second, Caesar, as consul, military commander, and civilian, consistently rejected the superstitions, divinations, and observations associated with Roman religion. He systematically scorned omens, appeals to divine guidance, and the warnings of soothsayers. All this is consistent with Epicureanism's disdain for the ceremonies and ideological superstructure of Roman theism.[16]

Third, Caesar's fabled literary style—direct, unadorned, comprehensible, and transparent—mirrors Epicurean prescriptions on rhetoric and composition. In that vein, Caesar, unlike Cicero, was unimpressed by noble lineage and class snobbery. He was, after all, affiliated with the *populares* not the *optimates*. This, too, reflects Epicureanism's commitment to equality.[17]

Fourth, Caesar's vision was always long-range and not cast, myopically, on the moment. Also, he, as a master political tactician, understood and used the

Roman method of *amicitia* and *clientela* to near perfection. Again, such vision and tactic recalls Epicureanism's instructions to always calculate long-term and pursue friendships based on mutual assistance as the best means of attaining security.[18] Caesar's friendships were not all solely or even mainly grounded in cynical mutual advantage. As Sallust reports: "Devoted to the enterprises of his friends, [Caesar] would neglect his own and refuse nothing that was worth giving" (CW 54.4).

Fifth, Epicureanism was a popular philosophy among Caesar's soldiers and Caesar evinced Epicurean principles—clemency, self-discipline, prudence, foresight—when leading them. His military camps were stunningly austere, especially when contrasted to the extravagance surrounding those of Pompey.[19]

Sixth, Caesar, although amassing significant wealth, did not view doing so as an end in itself: "He heaped up wealth to use as a public fund with which to reward the deserving, to secure the future, or to shore up the present."[20] Epicurus would approve.

Seventh, Caesar had a distinctively fearless, Epicurean attitude toward possible assassination and death:

> [Caesar] repeated that life is not worth living if spent in constant watching and fear . . . he felt that he had lived long enough either for nature or glory . . . he insisted upon disregarding the plots around him. He would not exist in anxiety; and he held that it was not in his own interest that he should continue to live, but in that of his country; for he saw that his death would doom the state to civil strife. . . . He aroused and commanded the same devotion and loyalty in other Epicureans that he had shown to them and to many more.[21]

The gigantic obstacle to picturing Caesar as an Epicurean is, of course, his avid pursuit of military and political enterprises. But, according to Plutarch, "not even Epicurus believes that men who are eager for honor and glory should lead an inactive life; but they should fulfill their natures by engaging in politics and entering public life, on the ground that, because of their natural dispositions, they are more likely to be harmed by inactivity if they do not attain what they desire."[22] Even Lucretius, otherwise disdainful of the pursuit of military and political glory, understood the need to take up arms when required for the safety of the republic (DNR 1.41–1.43).

After perusing the evidence that Caesar was an Epicurean, a reader might conclude that, compared to Caesar, St. Francis of Assisi was a scallywag. Brushing past the one-sided, overly complimentary picture of Caesar's motives, dispositions, and actions, the evidence is far from conclusive. While Epicureanism built in a few exceptions to its doctrine cautioning against military and political entanglements, Caesar made the exceptions the rule. He did not labor in military and political vineyards only during emergencies or for a daintily circumscribed period of time or for a carefully defined purpose. Caesar was the epitome of the Roman hyper-aggressive, overly competitive, relentless striver for enduring glory. He stands in stark contrast to the cornerstone of Epicureanism: its counsel for a serene, peaceful life. Invoking Plutarch's understanding of the men-eager-for-honor-and-glory exception renders Epicureanism's call for with-drawal flaccid and indistinctive: If you are eager for political and military glo-ries then pursue them, but if you are not then seek the tranquil path. Does that reduce only to "Follow your antecedent, natural inclinations"? Such advice is hardly transformative or even helpful. If the point of Epicureanism is to *cure* the social maladies of Rome identified by Lucretius then the exception carved out by Plutarch is too broad. The real point of Epicureanism is to *resist* the allure of traditional Roman values as a first step toward inner peace, the only true path to human fulfillment. Caesar, in contrast, celebrates traditional Roman values, places a flashing neon sign around them, and plots their amplification in a non-republican political setting.

That Caesar's writing style, personal dispositions, and approach to action were akin to Epicurean prescriptions is interesting, but hardly compelling evi-dence. Such factors could merely track his antecedent, pre-philosophical inclina-tions, not automatically reveal a commitment to Epicurean doctrine. One does not have to be an Epicurean to enjoy the terse muscularity of Hemingway's prose in *The Old Man and the Sea*. One need not be an Epicurean to resist luxu-rious military camps, or to take a long-range vision, or to amass wealth only for strategic purposes, or to prudently select means to attain desired ends, or to cher-ish friendship. Recall also that among the major Greek philosophical schools considerable overlap in outlook persisted. For example, to separate Epicurean austerity from, say, Stoical asceticism is rarely simple.

Moreover, even Caesar's indifference to certain aspects of Roman religion is less striking than it may seem at first blush: "We remain without evidence of any widespread fear of divine wrath or punishment after death. Such ideas hardly occur at all in traditional Roman religion. Rome had no mythology of the life after death; the picture of the underworld with its grim figures . . . its gloomy rivers, its judges, and its punishments, came from Greece."[23]

Still, the strongest pieces of evidence for Caesar's Epicureanism are his views on religion and death. At least, his positions were compatible with Epicu-reanism; they were probably influenced by Epicureanism; and to call Caesar an Epicurean *in these respects* is reasonable. But to call Caesar an Epicurean *as such* remains a stretch. Caesar was not a man to limit himself to a set of philoso-phical doctrines that would place antecedent constraints on his possibilities for action: he would not voluntarily worship the idols of philosophy. Caesar was more likely to use philosophy strategically, as a means to help accomplish his goals, as a set of strategies to attain the enduring military and political glory with which he was obsessed. Julius Caesar was the quintessential Roman. He could never accept in whole any set of convictions that seriously challenged the privilege of place of the traditional values of military and political conquest.

Cassius

Gaius Cassius Longinus, leader of the assassination plot against Caesar, con-
verted to Epicureanism around 46 BC. Such a conversion would not be accompanied with rituals, pomp, and celebrations. Cassius in fact was not a man to
court the social whirl, curry an entourage, or hire a posse. He was, instead,
"practical . . . competent, efficient, ruthless, and deeply disinclined to suffer
fools gladly."[24]

His conversion may have been prefigured in 48 BC after the Battle of Pharsalus, when Cassius decided to withdraw "from republican struggle and to ac-
quiesce in Caesar's rule, expressing his hopes for peace and his revulsion from
civil bloodshed."[25] In 49 BC, Cassius was an elected tribune of the plebeians. As
civil war arose, he allied himself with Pompey the Great and the *optimates*.
Pompey had rescued Cassius from a trial brought by accusers who charged Cassius with extortion while he was governor of Syria. Cassius, as did Pompey, fled
Italy for Greece once Caesar crossed the Rubicon. Pompey appointed him commander of his fleet. Sailing to Sicily, Cassius attacked and destroyed much of
Caesar's navy, and continued to assault ships off the Italian coast. After Caesar
thumped Pompey at the battle of Pharsalus, Cassius embarked for Hellespont
(The Dardanelles Strait), but was overtaken en route by Caesar and forced to
surrender. Cassius submitted to Caesar's authority.

Of course, such action is consistent with Epicureanism: minimize political
involvement, accept governments that nurture relatively tranquil conditions.
Such action is also consistent with the rationalizations of a man who senses his
self-preservation depends on backing a winner. Did Cassius genuinely believe
that Caesar's rule would facilitate relatively tranquil conditions?

In any case, that Cassius subscribed to Epicureanism from at least 46 BC
until he died in 42 BC is clear. Cassius argued to Cicero that people have difficulty accepting the doctrine that virtue is desirable for its own sake; but the instrumental benefits of virtue, pleasure, and internal peace are easily demonstrated. Cassius insisted that Epicureans, although stressing pursuit of pleasure
as the greatest good, were genuine lovers of virtue and justice. To live according
to the Epicurean pleasure principle required living virtuously.[26] Plutarch reports
Cassius's Epicurean account of the apparition that allegedly visited Brutus prior
to the battle of Philippi in 42 BC: "Cassius behaves generally like an Epicurean
in attempting to calm Brutus by means of a materialistic explanation in accordance with the Epicurean belief that learning the physical causes of natural phenomena would free men from fear; he also ends his speech with an allusion to
Epicurus, which states that the gods do not intervene in human affairs."[27] Plutarch also notes Cassius's purported appeal to the statue of Pompey, in contrast
to his Epicurean principles, just prior to the assassination of Caesar.[28]

Cassius's early political and military involvements need not be justified philosophically. After all, they transpired prior to his conversion to Epicureanism.
His leadership role in Caesar's assassination, though, cries out for explanation.

One possibility is that Cassius's participation in the assassination flows from a subtlety in Roman Epicureanism. Although a basic Epicurean adage insisted that "tyrants by all their violence cannot destroy the internal happiness of the wise man,"[29] Lucretius's account of human development in civil society sounds a different note. The death of kings was required for the improvement of human society (DRN 5.1136–5.1143). Only after greedy monarchs were slain, could the rule of law, relative social equality, and the wisdom of elected magistrates prevail (DRN 5.1145–5.1155).

> The only other Epicurean theory of political development . . . does not distinguish a period of kings from a period of Republican magistrates. . . . To Lucretius, magistracies and laws, not kings are able to ensure durable peace . . . the whole of Lucretius is a vigorous invitation to work and fight for high ideals. An atmosphere of magnanimous enthusiasm . . . is the legacy of Lucretius to the men of 44 BC.[30]

Presumably, Cassius and his fellow henchmen, animated by Lucretius's verse, were thus able to square their treachery with Epicureanism. The death of Caesar was simply another case of Lucretius's general principle: Whack the king, save civil society. Maybe. But this explanation reeks of after-the-fact rationalization. We lack evidence that Cassius or any other conspirator pored assiduously over Lucretius's poem for guidance and justification. Brutus, presumably, invoked the name of Cicero, not Lucretius, as the symbol of republican liberty once the deed had been consummated. Moreover, even in Lucretius's poem, can we be sure that *Epicureans* were or should be the slayers of kings? Would not a true Epicurean believer maintain his internal happiness in the face of tyranny?

A second explanation of Cassius's participation is more straightforwardly Epicurean, but unconvincing. Strictly from a personal standpoint, Cassius might have reasoned that, regardless of the effects on others, *his* internal peace could not abide the tyranny of Caesar. Sure, a few Epicurean sages might be able to cope with Caesar's excesses and continue to nurture their tranquility and pursuit of pleasure, but not Cassius. His inner peace and serenity were more likely to flow from his role in the death of Caesar, the restoration of the republic, and the ensuing withdrawal he could then make from public service. Thus, for Cassius, political involvement in this discrete case would bring less inner turmoil than abstention.

This explanation is consistent with much basic Epicurean doctrine—Cassius would court political entanglement only in an emergency situation for a limited time and for a specific purpose—but its calculations are wildly and implausibly optimistic. Does inner peace typically dog the steps of assassins? Even if the republic was miraculously restored, would not some Caesarian loyalists remain and plot revenge against Caesar's killers? In what sense could Cassius realize inner peace after such a publicly violent deed?

A third explanation of Cassius's participation more plausibly joins assassination and Epicureanism. Plutarch reports that Brutus, a dedicated follower of The Eclectic Academy that purported to revive the Platonic Academy, quizzed several of his friends on their philosophical convictions prior to deciding whom he would include in the conspiracy. For example, he asked the Epicurean, Statilius, whether it was wise for a man to bring troubles and danger upon himself in service of other people who were evil or foolish.[31] Statilius replied that doing so was not the mark of a wise man with appropriate discretion. Unsurprisingly, Brutus did not invite Statilius to join his cause.

On his behalf, Statilius's answer echoes a familiar Epicurean refrain: personal tranquility trumps political and social entanglements. Brutus's question, though, was not placed in the context of how such involvement would advance, if at all, the interests of the individual agent. Instead, assuming the evil or foolish people in play were the citizens of Rome who had allowed political events to spiral out of control, Brutus "raises an excellent moral issue for Epicureans, who do take risks 'for the sake of friendship,' and might well ask whether that could ever be extended to the support of their fellow citizens."[32]

Brutus's inquiry was not merely rhetorical. He was not quizzing Statilius to determine if his friend knew the correct answer written in the Epicurean catechism. Brutus took the issue to be a legitimate debate within Epicureanism: To what extent, if any, does the Epicurean duty to friends extend to fellow citizens, most of whom are merely strangers or acquaintances? Although everyone understood that under exceptional circumstances the Epicurean abstention from politics rule was waivable, no thick doctrine accompanied that tenet. Brutus's question, not phrased as a conflict only within the individual interests of the moral agent, invites Epicureans to reexamine their duties, if any, to others:

> [Brutus's question] implies that the wise were supposed by some contemporary Epicureans, perhaps including Cassius, to be on occasion driven by an overriding sense of obligation to their non-philosophical fellow-citizens . . . for Cassius to accept the existence of a sense of social obligation to which the sage must on occasion yield need not entail any rejection of hedonism. . . . Nothing . . . would have prevented Cassius from holding *moral satisfaction* to be a sufficiently great pleasure to counterbalance the pain brought on by *political anxieties*.[33] (Emphasis added)

This provides a plausible Epicurean justification for Cassius's participation in the conspiracy. Whether Cassius seriously appealed to such a line of reasoning is contestable. True, if Brutus posed the question to Statilius, is it not reasonable to suppose he discussed it with his closer associate and brother-in-law, Cassius? But whether a philosophical thinker could give an answer different from Statilius's and remain a staunch Epicurean is another matter. Accepting dangers and risks for friends is one thing; extending that duty to "evil or foolish" strangers and acquaintances is quite another. Unless the duty to strangers and acquaintances is tightly circumscribed, it threatens to obliterate the core of Epicureanism's rule against social and political entanglement. Remember, Epicureanism is almost entirely a philosophy of personal fulfillment, not a clarion call to social action. In fairness, though, perhaps an exception to the Epicurean rule against social and political entanglements can be fashioned along the lines of the justification for political assassinations offered in chapter 1. The lingering issue would be whether Epicureanism would then begin the fall down the slippery slope of major social involvement. If so, most of its distinctiveness would evaporate. Recall, also, that much of the appeal of Epicureanism to Romans centered on the thinness of its moral demands and its prescription to withdraw from the competitive, aggressive life. Any expansion of the Epicurean duties to friends jeopardizes that appeal.

A fourth explanation of Cassius's participation in the assassination is the simplest and most persuasive: Passed over by Caesar for important military commands and political posts, obligated to him for his clemency after the battle of Pharsalus, and humiliated by Caesar's boundless success, Cassius acted from mixed motives. He did harbor republican aspirations, but he also seethed with personal ambition and hatred of Caesar: Cassius was a "stern man of violent temper, and the unparalleled despotism [of Caesar] which took ever clearer shape become too much for his pride."[34] Instead of trying to ground Cassius's actions in strict application of Epicurean doctrine, interpreters might be better served by examining his character. Here may have been a case where philosophical dogma is ignored for personal reasons. No surprise, that. Even fervent religious believers cast aside their doctrines of faith at certain times for specific purposes. (How many Roman Catholics strictly comply with the Church's teachings on birth control?) Accordingly, Cassius's masterminding of the events of the Ides of March may have had nothing to do with his general acceptance of Epicureanism: "Clearly philosophical adherence was for Cassius . . . and most other Roman Epicureans of the upper classes, an aspect of culture and not of politics. When political action is crucial, philosophical adherence is not seriously considered as an important guide in such activity."[35]

Divine Providence and Social Disengagement

I will now examine each part of the Epicurean strategy in turn. First, consider Epicurus's depiction of the gods. That universal belief in deities does not imply such deities exist is clear. Freudian, Marxist, Nietzschean, as well as numerous other explanations for the nearly universal belief in deities are available. But if gods do exist in the Epicurean fashion, their indifference to human life may not be consoling. Belief in divine providence, at least, provides human beings opportunities to earn the gods' favor. If the gods' responses correlate to our actions—if they respond to us in accord with our deserts—we have control over our fate. At least we have a fate. If the gods are indifferent to us and serve only as Epicurean exemplars, we lose hope not just fear. If the gods act providentially but capriciously, sometimes returning evil for our good deeds, Epicurus's point is sharper. But another alternative was available to him: Gods who act toward human beings only in accord with retributive justice, perhaps tempered by mercy. Such gods model behavior appropriate for all of us and permit us to retain our hope.

The problem, though, for Epicurus is not merely one of strategy. The amount and nature of evil in the world precludes divine providence, but Epicurus was not an atheist. His belief in gods indifferent to human affairs was in good faith. The success of Epicureanism as a way of life—it ran a distant second to Stoicism as the dominant philosophy in the Greco-Roman world for four centuries—suggests that belief in nonprovidential gods was a reasonable possibility in Epicurus's historical context. Robust commitment to atheism was less possible. The power of monotheistic Judeo-Christianity would emerge later, co-opt some features of Epicureanism and Stoicism, and marginalize much of those philosophies.

Epicureanism astutely reminds us that pursuing self-defeating pleasures causes unnecessary human pain and suffering. But egotistic hedonism amplifies the point grotesquely. The kernel of truth—that physical and material pleasures, if taken to extremes, are self-defeating, and, even at their best, cannot be the sole, or even the main, source of happiness—is distorted into an admonishment against a host of interpersonal relations: sex, marriage, politics, engagement in civic life. The Epicureans observe accurately that interpersonal relations entangle and often bring mental suffering. They conclude unsoundly that the solution is avoidance. The Epicureans embody muted aspirations: fly beneath the radar, simplify your life, seek serenity, anesthetize yourself from pain, minimize your needs, resist your passions, avoid turbulence, and moderate the vicissitudes of life.

We all can benefit from a dose of this advice. But like all medicines, if we consume too much we will aggravate our illness. If we take Epicureanism too seriously we dehumanize ourselves. Throughout history, writers have argued persuasively that existential tension is at the heart of human experience: our yearning for intimate connection with others and the recognition that others are necessary for our identity and freedom coalesces uneasily with the fear and anxiety we experience as others approach. We simultaneously long for emotional attachment yet are horrified that our individuality may evaporate once we achieve it. This disharmony may never be fully reconciled; we find ourselves instead making uneasy compromises and adjustments as we oscillate along an existential continuum whose polar extremes are radical individuality and thorough immersion in community. This existential tension replicates itself at numerous levels: the individual confronts family, the family confronts village, villages confront wider society, and society confronts the state.

When we meet others at institutional levels, the stakes rise in some respects. Our need to retain individual freedom and resist coercion intensifies when our relations are impersonal, where we experience less direct control over our destiny, and when entrenched bureaucracies seem ready and able to usurp our autonomy. Circumscribed by socioeconomic reality, the relentless socializing of the established order, and the inherent inertia of the masses, our sense of possibility resists extinction and thereby honors the human craving for transcendence. Moreover, individuals confront several different, often conflicting communities. They face the intimate aspirations of family; the often conflicting ultimatums of ethnicity, gender, and race; the stirring, history-laden, patriotic implorations of country; and the more distant claims of the international order. The individual-community continuum expands in several dimensions. In fact, only in the simplest cases is it ever merely one-dimensional. As such, contexts such as family, ethnicity, gender, and politics multiply the tensions, exhilarations, fears, and hopes invariably embodied by the continuum.[36]

My general objection to Epicureanism is that it fails to capture the subtlety of the antinomies generated by the individual-community continuum. Epicureans deny our existential condition by trying to extinguish our need for robust community. Even friendship is reduced to instrumental value as its main Epicurean justification is benefit to the self, not the other person. Although it was a powerful philosophy in its historical setting, contemporary thinkers might well conclude that Epicurean austerity needs a measure of nineteenth-century romanticism for completion. Anesthetizing ourselves from social pain also prevents us from experiencing our greatest joys and triumphs. By denying the human need for transcendence, our quest to reimagine and re-create our selves and our contexts, the Epicurean version of egoistic hedonism severs us from paramount sources of human meaning and value: family, civic participation, grand social projects. Critics can cogently argue that steadfast devotion to Epicureanism offers much consolation but little growth. Accordingly, Epicureanism encourages human beings to settle for small enterprises and to be satisfied with mundane engagements. The romantic impulses toward robust context-smashing, self-transcendence, vigorous social engagement, and large-scale adventures wither away.

Although best viewed as an interesting historical artifact, Epicureanism reinforces crucial elements of ancient wisdom: Worthwhile happiness focuses on a person's internal condition; physical and material pleasures are often self-defeating, especially if taken to extremes; suffering caused by speculation about or anticipation of the unknown is unnecessary; to pursue happy, meaningful, valuable lives we must confront and come to terms with our mortality; happiness results from distinguishing worthwhile from unworthy desires and acting only on the former; and deists must provide persuasive explanations for the amount and nature of evil in the world. We must all confront and come to terms with such evil.

Epicureanism attracted idealistic, refined people of a world ruled by militaristic, competitive strongmen. Although Epicurus's version of egoistic hedonism is severe, moderate versions, congenial to upper class Romans, arose that softened his prescriptions for withdrawal from public life and social interactions. Epicurus's fundamental notion, that happiness is pleasure could be taken in numerous directions. Our contemporary idea of Epicureans—those pursuing gustatory, sensual, and material pleasures—is one distorted example.

Critique of the Epicurean View of Death

Lurking quietly but closely behind all human lives is the shadow of the Grim

Reaper, the Duke of Doomsday, the Terrible Terminator, the Master of Disaster: Death. Human beings search for meaning in life with full knowledge of our mortality. What relevance, if any, is an inevitable death to the meaning of our lives?

Some human beings take comfort in a belief in personal immortality. Energized, typically by theistic faith, they view earthly life as a preparation for an eternally blissful afterlife. Under this view, death is often seen as a separation of a self-subsistent soul from the body. Others deny the dualism—the separation of immaterial soul from material body—in the immortality thesis and take death to be the cessation of all experience, the irrevocable termination of consciousness. The denial of dualism and immortality can lead to personal despair and suffocating doubt about the meaning and value of life. What can it all matter if in a few years our lives will be coldly, cruelly, and efficiently snuffed out by an unfeeling cosmos to which no appeal for mercy is possible?

Epicurus and Lucretius rejected dualism yet maintained that death is not an evil. They argued that death is irrelevant to us. For Epicureans, all good and evil consists in sensations, death is the end of all sensations, so death is nothing to us. Death, reasoned Epicurus, must be nothing to us because death is not with us while we are living and when it arrives we no longer exist. Therefore, death does not concern either the living or the dead, because for the living death is not, and the dead are no more. For Epicurus, death is the cessation of all experiences, and at death a human decomposes and no sensations can persist because there is no physical object to sense anything.

> Become accustomed to the belief that death is nothing to us. For all good and evil consists in sensation, but death is deprivation of sensations. . . . So death, the most terrifying of ills, is nothing to us, since so long as we exist, death is not with us; but when death comes, then we do not exist. It does not then concern either the living or the dead, since for the former it is not, and the latter are no more.[37]

The Epicurean view of death is unpersuasive, but annoyingly challenging. Both Epicurus and Lucretius accept a hedonistic assumption: the sensations of pleasure and pain define what is good and bad for us. This assumption is unacceptable. We are sometimes harmed by events because they violate our rights or transgress against our just entitlements. But such events—that do not cause us pain or suffering—do not necessarily hurt us if we are unaware of them. What we do not know may not hurt us, but it can still harm us. For example, if someone tells malicious lies about me to a third party behind my back, the lies may harm my reputation but I may never discover the betrayal. I am harmed because my interest in maintaining my deserved, high reputation is transgressed upon, but I am not hurt by the lies because I am unaware of them and thus I am not pained by them. The hedonistic assumption, then, defines good and bad too narrowly. Even if death does not hurt us from an Epicurean perspective, it may well harm us. Death often harms because it deprives us of the ongoing good that was our life.

The following counterexample to the hedonistic assumption has been around a long time: Your neighbor is an incorrigible Peeping Tom who gains much pleasure from monitoring the nightly activities of others. One weekend while you are away, he enters your home and installs monitoring devices in your bedroom. He is so proficient that you never learn of his act. You suffer no painful sensations or unpleasant states of consciousness because you are unaware that your bedroom has been bugged. You continue to act as you had prior to your neighbor's misdeed. Meanwhile, your neighbor gains great pleasure from listening to and watching your nightly activities. Despite the fact you suffer no unpleasant sensations, your neighbor has perpetrated an evil and a wrong against you. Your right to privacy has been invaded, although you are unaware of the transgression. You have been harmed, your rights have been violated, even though you have not been hurt because you are unaware of the harm, and have not suffered unpleasant states of consciousness from the violation.

Imagine that a police officer discovers the Peeping Tom and begins to take the miscreant into custody. The Peeping Tom objects: "Look here, officer. If you arrest me, you will have to inform my neighbors. My neighbors will then be very upset and suffer greatly because they will now know that I have been monitoring their activities for the past five years. The net effect will be great pain for them, pain for me because I face prosecution, no apparent joy for anyone. But if you let me go, I will stop my activities, and the net effect will be great pleasure for me as I really enjoyed watching them at night, no pain for them as they will continue to be unaware of what I did. You have a moral obligation on hedonist grounds to let me go." Alternate speech, if the perpetrator is feeling lucky: "But if you let me go, I will continue my activities, and the net effect will be even more pleasure for me, no pain for them, and the overall pleasure to pain ratio will increase dramatically. You have a moral obligation to let me go."

The Peeping Tom will be unsuccessful even if the calculation of net effects is correct. The example demonstrates brightly that the hedonistic assumption is unpersuasive. We can be wronged and victimized even though we suffer neither painful sensations nor unpleasant states of consciousness as a result of that wrong.

Consider another case: A mature, intelligent woman enjoys a reasonably meaningful and valuable life. Her Epicurean pleasure over pain calculus is significantly positive. She then suffers a horrible car accident. She goes immediately into shock and experiences little, if any, pain. The good news is that she survives and should live a normal life span. The bad news is that her mental capabilities are and will remain those of a seven-year-old child. However, from an Epicurean standpoint, additional good news ensues: She has heightened capability for pleasure and is desensitized to pain, and wins friends easily. Her Epicurean pleasure over pain calculus is and will remain throughout her life overwhelmingly positive. Would we judge her accident a benefit? Obviously not, but an Epicurean may have to. If this is true, so much the worse for Epicureanism. The woman does not and cannot experience her new lifestyle as harm to her; on the contrary, she luxuriates in amplified pleasure. Yet she has clearly been harmed by the accident and she would have agreed if a similar hypothetical had been posed to her prior to the auto crash.

By evaluating good and evil, and harm and benefit only by experienced sensations, Epicureans wildly miss the mark. A person may be harmed even though she does not experience negative (painful) sensations; and she may be harmed even though her balance of pleasure over pain has increased. Moreover, she is not automatically harmed simply because she experiences negative sensations. The expression "no pain, no gain" bears currency. Confronting daunting obstacles, challenging struggles, and arduous tasks are painful activities but nevertheless crucial for positive self-transformation. Such transformation cannot accurately or automatically be measured by increased overall pleasure.

Granted, Epicurus did stress mental over physical pleasure and the post-accident woman has child-like friendships; but if these tenets were merely prudent means to increasing a person's overall balance of pleasure over pain, then it remains arguable that the post-accident woman is better off if evaluated only by hedonic criteria. Accordingly, the Epicurean pleasure principle cannot capture the entire truth about morality. Good cannot simply be identified with pleasant sensations, evil with painful sensations. Thus, we cannot conclude that death is nothing to us because it is the end of all sensations.

This also demonstrates why the pleasure principle is more widely flawed. By evaluating right and wrong only in terms of individual or collective pleasure and pain, we capture, at best, only part of our fixed moral judgments. At times, morality requires performing the proper act despite the fact that our or the collective pleasure is not served. Moreover, heroic deeds are such because they sacrifice individual pleasure for wider, moral purposes.

The Problem of the Missing Person

Epicureans might rejoin that even if the Peeping Tom example demonstrates that certain events that victims never experience can still harm them—in the sense of, in that case, their interests in privacy being unjustifiably transgressed—death is different. In the Peeping Tom case, extant victims *would have* experienced negative sensations had the perpetrator's actions been revealed. In the case of death, no extant victim can be harmed; that the alleged victim could have experienced negative sensations is impossible. Thus, human beings can be harmed only if they exist at the time the alleged wrong occurs.

This claim begs the question at hand. That is, the response assumes that an extant person as victim is required for a wrong to occur. But that is the very issue at stake. Moreover, Jeff McMahan offers a counterexample to the Epicurean existence requirement:

> Consider the case of a person whose life's work collapses while he is on holiday on a remote island. Suppose we agree that the fact that his life's work has come to nothing is a misfortune for him. On reflection, it seems hard to believe

that it makes a difference to the misfortune he suffers whether the collapse of his life's work occurs shortly before he is killed or shortly afterward. Yet according to the Existence Requirement, the difference in timing makes *all* the difference. If the collapse of his life's work occurs just before he dies, then, even though he never learns of it, he suffers a terrible misfortune. If, on the other hand, it occurs just after he dies, he suffers no misfortune at all. If we find this hard to believe then we may be forced to reject the Existence Requirement.[38]

Although this counterexample is not a knock-down, drag-out disproof of the existence requirement, it casts suspicion on its persuasiveness. I will later argue that human beings can be indirectly harmed by posthumous events and offer other evidence against the Epicurean existence requirement.

Why Death Can Harm

To say a person has an objective interest in X is to say that X, on balance, improves the person's well-being or opportunity for well-being. To say that a person has a subjective interest in X is to say that the person desires, wants, or seeks X. I can be subjectively interested in something—I can desire it–even though it is not in my objective interests. For example, I might be interested in drinking a quart of motor oil even though my objective interests are not thereby served. I may want to drink the oil because I do not know the results of doing so; or I may know the results but not care; or I may know and care but value other ramifications of the act more than I disfavor the negative consequences; or I may simply have strong self-destructive tendencies and desire on some level to act in ways that undermine my overall well-being.[39]

Also, something can be in my objective interests but I may not desire it. Eating cauliflower and certain types of fish may objectively advance my nutrition and health, but I may not want to consume them. I may not be aware that eating such foods nurtures health; I may know but still prefer not to consume them; I may prefer to advance other interests more than the ones at issue; or any number of other reasons.

One way in which human beings are harmed is when our objective interests are unjustifiably set back, frustrated, transgressed, or impaired. What benefits me is in my objective interests, but not all withholdings of benefits harm me. Often withholding benefits from me is justified because I lack an antecedent claim of entitlement to them. Cashing a large wager on the winner of the Kentucky Derby is in my objective interests, in the sense that it advances my well-being (Sorry, Epicureans!), but officials at Churchill Downs do not wrong or harm me if they refuse to cash my losing ticket. Everything that benefits me is in my objective interests (advances my overall well-being), but I am harmed only when my justified claim or entitlement to a benefit is wrongly thwarted. Usually, when other people decline the opportunity to advance my objective interests their rejections are morally permissible. But when they set back, frustrate, or impair my objective interests in receiving benefits to which I am entitled then they harm me. This is the force of the expression "unjustifiably set back, frustrated, transgressed, or impaired."

Instead of being nothing to us, death makes us nothing, if we reject, with Epicurus, dualism and the immortality thesis. Death renders us incapable of enjoying pleasure and suffering pain. If death is an evil it must be because it is a deprivation; it ends those aspects of our lives that are meaningful, valuable, and good. Even if the hedonistic assumption was correct, death could still be considered a detriment. If a death cuts off a life that could have enjoyed a much greater balance of pleasurable over unpleasurable sensations if it had continued, then that death could reasonably be viewed as tragic, an unfortunate deprivation, even if we restrict, as do the hedonists, good and bad only to sensations. The person would have been better off if he or she had not died.

Why Lucretius Is Incorrect

Lucretius might rejoin that the deprivation argument plays into his hands. If death is sometimes bad because it deprives us of future goods, why is not birth bad because it deprives us of the goods we might have enjoyed if born earlier?

First, we should brush aside difficult, murky metaphysical questions— Would I really be the same person had I been born in, say, 1928 instead of 1948? Is my date of birth itself a constitutive attribute of who I am?—because the answers could dismiss Lucretius's rejoinder from a hearing on the grounds that if born earlier I simply would not be "me." Next, we must hold the comparative life spans constant. If Jones were born in 1948 and died in 2000, then we cannot fairly compare Jones's life to one in which he or she was born in 1928 and died in 2000. The earlier birth would gain appeal only by increasing Jones's life by twenty years. Now we can see why Jones's birth in 1948 rather than in 1928 is not a deprivation in the way Jones's dying in 2000 rather than in 2020 is a deprivation. A life lived from 1928 to 1980 is not obviously distinguishable from a life lived from 1948 to 2000. If anything, the later birth life might seem preferable. I may fantasize about living during the glory days of the Roman republic or the golden age of Greece, but not if the cost is nonexistence during the twentieth century. Thus, dying in 2000 instead of 2020 is often a deprivation in a way that being born in 1948 instead of 1928 is not. Dying in 2000 cuts short an active life in progress, while being born in 1948 merely locates the beginning of a life-span not quantitatively different than the one that might have begun in 1928.

My understanding of the years prior to my birth is second-hand: I have learned of the past through reading, conversations with elders, movies, and the like. But once I am alive, my death severs connections with people, projects, interests, values, and commitments that define my deepest aspirations. As I imagine the future rushing forward without me, I may conjure hollowness. When I imagine the time prior to my birth I imagine a life to which I was never actually connected. As beings impelled toward the future it is natural that humans sense an asymmetry between the future-without-me and the historical-past-when-I-did-not-exist. Even within the confines of our actual lives, we value events differently depending on their relation to our pasts and futures. Remembering the experience of having a broken arm when I was fourteen is qualitatively different from being informed that my arm will be broken next week. Recalling the gruesome terrors of the holocaust is qualitatively different from learning that an equally horrifying series of events will occur within the next five years. Death sometimes deprives us of the goods linked to our greatest concern, while prenatal nonexistence deprived us only of an historical past to which we are tenuously joined.

We do not necessarily fear the "condition" of being dead, or even the process of dying, but the deprivation of goods that constitute our lives. Following Lucretius, the condition of death, if it amounts only to annihilation, may be no more horrifying that the condition of nonexistence prior to birth. So the *condition* or state of being dead—if it makes sense to speak of annihilation and nothingness as a condition—is no better or worse than the condition or state of prenatal nonexistence. Score a point for Lucretius. But, against Lucretius, the two time periods have a glaring difference: we lose nothing prior to birth, while at death we lose our lives and the goods our lives embody. The ending of our lives is much different from our never having been born. Prenatal nonexistence is followed by existence, while death is followed by nothingness, squadoosh. Prenatal nonexistence is temporary, while death is permanent nonexistence. The permanence of death and not the condition of nonexistence as such is what stirs our concern. Moreover, our fear of death is not solely or even mainly because of a failure to separate ourselves sufficiently from our dead bodies. Rack up an "L" (as in loss) for Lucretius.

Lucretius's argument gains plausibility by wrongly riveting our attention to only one relevant dimension: the hedonic implications of prenatal and postmortem nonexistence. In both cases, the net balance of pleasure over pain is zero: nonexistence implies the absence of all sensations. Lucretius unsoundly concludes that the two states of affairs must, then, be equivalent.

Also, Lucretius's argument is not as symmetrical as it first appears. Once alive, I have interests and a host of historical facts attached to them; prior to my birth that is not the case. Death precludes us from retaining, pursuing, and acquiring a host of goods we otherwise had or would have obtained by engaging in cherished projects, purposes, and interests; death also crushes the good constituting our meaningful lives by annihilating our being.

What and Why Do We Fear?

We are not frightened merely by the state of being unconscious. If we were in a temporary coma for, say, fifty years, but regained consciousness unaged and ready to enjoy a normal span of life, we would not necessarily regard the period in the coma as a terrible evil. We would mourn the loss of loved ones who had died while we were in the coma, regret having to make new friends, and be frustrated by the interruption of our projects. But the prospect of such a coma would not overwhelm us.

Nor is the process of dying our greatest fear. The horror of the process of dying can be softened by medication or even by hastening the moment of death. While usually painful and personally degrading, most of the terror of dying is that the process leads to death. If the process typically culminated in additional life and health it would not be feared to the extent it is now.

I am not claiming that the process of dying, the condition of nonexistence, and the state of being unconscious do not add to our fear of death. They do. I claim only that these factors are not the main sources of our anxiety. Certainly how we die is important to most of us. We desire a painless, honorable, respectful demise, instead of a painful, dishonorable, degrading death. But even if a painless death could be guaranteed, certain fears would remain.

Epicurus and Lucretius have mislocated the source of our anxiety. For those who reject dualism and immortality, death terrorizes us because we fear nothingness, extinction, and deprivation, not because we anticipate that death is a painful state. The ancient philosophers intended well: to alleviate our fears about our inevitable mortality and to nurture the tranquil life. However, seduced by the hedonistic assumption, they focus only on the absence of sensation and the condition of nonexistence. Even if they are correct about nonexistence being nothing to us, the Epicureans leave much unattended: the process of dying and the deprivation that death exacts.

Valuable aspects of life, such as interpersonal relationships, projects, goals, aspirations, interests, and associations, end at death. And that is why death often seems so bad. Biological survival is not paramount. We do not hope for a permanent coma, even if we are thereby kept biologically alive. A life completely lacking value and meaning would be a life not worth living to the person in that condition. Death ensures, stipulating the rejection of dualism and the immortality thesis, that we are permanently deprived of the value, meaning, and good connected to our lives. This deprivation is the main reason we fear death and regard it as an evil. Against Lucretius, nonexistence prior to birth does not deprive us, but nonexistence at death permanently deprives us.

Although death is inevitable, this does not make the deprivation of life any less evil. Inevitability means that we cannot erase death or transcend our mortality, but this need not make death any less evil. If, on every first Thursday, all human beings suffered severe stomach cramps, bled profusely from the nose, and were afflicted with double vision, would the inevitability of these ills make them less evil, painful or bad? The inevitability of death suggests that there is no point in worrying about *whether* or in fearing that we *will* die, but that is all.

Fear of untimely or premature death is especially rational: it may impel us to take greater care of our health, adopt healthier lifestyles, and thereby maximize our possibilities of avoiding what we fear. Avoiding premature death is clearly not completely under our control. But we can greatly affect the odds.

Moreover, fear of premature death might motivate us to avoid procrastinating and to engage in our projects, interests, and purposes with intensity and vigor. Obviously, concern with premature death and focus on looming mortality, as several Woody Allen movies will attest, can take obsessive, self-defeating, starkly irrational, and stunningly neurotic forms.

Living with adequate recognition of mortality, yet responding zestfully can vivify meaning in our lives and elevate death beyond meaningless termination. Mortality is our human context, not necessarily our defeat. We need not glorify death, we need not pretend we do not fear death, but we should temper the Grim Reaper's victory by living and dying meaningfully. Our impulses to generate legacies are honorable even if permanence eludes us.[40]

How Bad Is Death?

Some deaths are more tragic than others, even though the democracy of death commands we all die once. The tragedy of a death is directly proportional to the actual and potential value of the life that has been terminated. Death is not always tragic because it does not always end a meaningful and valuable life. A meaningless and valueless life is one in which invigorating activities and aspirations cannot be engaged in, nor is there a potentiality for future participation. If life itself, or a life, is not a good then its termination is not an evil. Dying is bad when continued life would be good. Dying is good when continued life would be bad.

Still, measuring and quantifying the badness of death is vexing. Neil Feit offers the following:

> When death is bad for the person who dies, it is bad for her at all and only those times during which she would have been alive, had she not then died. . . . Suppose that Paul dies prematurely in a tragic accident in the year 2010, and that he would have lived quite happily for forty more years, until the year 2050, if he had not died in the accident. In this case . . . dying in 2010 is bad for Paul until 2050, when he otherwise would have died. Paul's premature death deprives him of value from 2010 up to 2050, after which it ceases to deprive him of value.[41]

The amount of deprivation, roughly, is tallied by subtracting the bad from the good attached to a span of life and arriving at an overall value for that span. For example, if Paul would have enjoyed a balance of, say, 200 units of value had he lived from 2010 through 2050, then that is the measure of the deprivation of his death in 2010.

Feit's convictions capture well our intuitions in certain cases. If Joe dies quickly in a car crash in June and an autopsy reveals he harbored a terminal, but painless disease that but for the auto accident would have killed him in August, the deprivation differential of the value Joe was denied by the accident is relatively small. With all this information, we might well conclude that the car crash was not as horrible as first imagined. Joe would have died soon thereafter anyway. If we change the example a bit and stipulate that Joe's disease would have turned painful during July and until his August death, we may well view the car crash as an odd benefit for Joe—when compared to his future otherwise—in that the June through August period would have proved to be an overall disvalue. The Joe-would-have-died-soon-anyway conclusion resonates in such cases. Where we are comparing one *death event* to another, Feit's calculus is often persuasive.

But the calculus does not capture all of our intuitions about the badness or undesirability of death. (Nor does Feit claim it does.) First, in the hypothetical case, if dying is bad for Paul until 2050—because that is the date in the nearest possible world that Paul would otherwise have died, and during the period between 2010 and 2050 Paul would have lived, overall, a worthwhile life—we need to account for the subject of the harm. Paul is alive prior to 2010, then dead at 2010, and presumably nothing thereafter. To what subject does the forty years of harm (between 2010 and 2050) attach? Corpses and annihilated beings cannot be harmed for they are inanimate objects and nothing, respectively. How can Paul be harmed by the deprivation of his life after Paul has been annihilated?

Second, suppose Tony dies in 2000. If he had not died in 2000, he would have died of the same disease in 2005. The deprivation differential between the two deaths is fifty overall units of value. That is, had Tony survived until 2005 he would have enjoyed fifty overall units of value that were denied him because of his death in 2000. If Tony had not died in 2005, he would have perished from the same disease in 2010. The deprivation differential between the 2005 death and the 2010 is seventy-five overall units of value. That is, had Tony survived until 2010 he would have enjoyed seventy-five units of value that would have been denied him by his 2005 death. So, Tony's death in 2000 deprived him of fifty units of value and his death in 2005 would have deprived him of seventy-five units of value. On the Feit calculus, Tony's death in 2000 is not as bad—it deprives Tony of less value—than Tony's death would be in 2005. But, surely, all rational human beings would, if given the choice, select the 2005 death instead of death in 2000. The 2005 death permits five more years of productive life measured by fifty units of additional value than the 2000 death, even if the 2005 death involves more deprivation as quantified by the calculus.

The calculus, moreover, cannot fully capture the tragedy of premature death. If Mary died at twenty, but if she had not died then she would have died at twenty-one, the deprivation differential measures her loss as the overall balance of good over bad that Mary would have garnered for one year (assuming that year would have been on balance a favorable slice of life). That is why the deprivation differential must be supplemented by considerations of untimeliness: Mary's death at either twenty or twenty-one is significantly premature and adds to the badness of her death regardless of when she would have next died but for the event that took her life.

Consider two soldiers in a war, Sal and Vito. They are both killed under the same circumstances and at the same time on July 4th. Sal is twenty, Vito is fifty-five. Had they not been killed on July 4th, they would have been killed under the same circumstances and at the same time on July 5th. Judged by the deprivation differential, their deaths on July 4th were equally bad for them (assuming their lives were qualitatively equal): their loss of one day by the events on July 4th deprived them equally. Still, that more of the story must be told is obvious. Sal is only twenty, Vito only fifty-five. Both died prematurely, but Sal's death is more tragic and bad from that standpoint.

Untimely or premature death always harms those who are enjoying a meaningful life. We imagine a typical lifespan and mourn those whose lives are cut short by comparison. A twenty-, thirty-, or forty-year-old person or younger who dies is, other things being equal, denied decades of value. I'll take a typical, active lifespan to be roughly seventy-five years old. (This is only a guide. Senior citizens, please do not write me in outrage over how ninety is the new sixty.) Those who die much prior to that age, assuming they are leading and will continue to lead meaningful lives, have been deprived of their opportunity to experience the different joys of later decades. Our special expressions of sorrow at learning of such deaths—"She died before her time," "He never had a chance to see his children grow," "Only the good die young," and the like—reflect our considered judgments that special tragedy accompanies premature death.

The timing of death, then, is also a dimension of its badness and, I would argue, its deprivation. Sal, at age twenty, was cut down by the merciless scythe of the heartless Grim Reaper. Was he not deprived of decades of valuable life? Would this not be so even if he otherwise would have died at age twenty-two?

Accordingly, to insist that the deprivation differential calculus captures the entirety of the badness of death—to say that the *prematurity* of Sal's death at twenty is merely a terrible misfortune or extremely bad for Sal, but his death itself was not because he would have died the next day anyway—is unpersuasive. The deprivation differential calculus, at most, captures only the badness of a particular death event in relation to another.

I prefer to look at the prematurity of his death as another dimension of his death which adds to Sal's deprivation. Moreover, the harm of death, particularly its prematurity, begins when the living person first acquires the interest in remaining alive. As that would be almost all of his life, it follows that almost all human beings are harmed to a degree throughout their lives. Joel Feinberg argues:

If John is going to be the victim of a fatal accident on his thirtieth birthday, then he is in at least a partially harmed condition from the time (many years earlier) when he acquires any interests at all. More specifically, he is in a partially harmed condition from the time he acquires interests which themselves need more than thirty years to be fulfilled or satisfactorily advanced. But he has thirty years worth of other interests that will be advanced, promoted, and fulfilled, to his continual and repeated benefit. . . . The degree of harmfulness of a person's premature death thus depends on how premature it is, given the interests that defined his own particular good.[42]

Feinberg takes this to echo the tragic nature of life: "Almost everyone will die with some interests that will be defeated by his death. And because of the inevitability of death, all of us are, while alive, in at least a partially harmed condition in that *those* interests are."[43] In general, death will extinguish fewer and less important interests when a person dies at ninety than when someone dies at thirty. Accordingly, Tina who will die at thirty bears greater harm in that respect—is in a greater condition of harm between ages one and thirty—than Gina who will die at ninety, who is in a lesser condition of harm between the ages of one and ninety. Death defeats fewer and less important interests of Gina than of Tina. The facts of their deaths make it true that their before-death interests were going to be defeated and they were thereby harmed even though they were unaware of the date of their deaths.

But how might we quantify or measure this dimension of deprivation? The short answer is that easy solutions are not available. Perhaps it cannot be done satisfactorily. Two possibilities recommend themselves. First, we might assign a typical, average lifespan, roughly seventy-five years, as a person's antecedent due. Anyone dying prior to that age has been deprived, independently of when they would otherwise have died in the future. The lifespan assigned would, of course, be subject to societal changes, medical advances, and the like. Maybe age ninety *will* soon be the new age sixty. Second, instead of focusing on the objectivity of a given life span, we might center on the kind of interests a particular individual embraces. If Zeke had few interests that required more than fifty years to fulfill and he dies at age forty-nine, his premature death is less harmful than Ace who also dies at forty-nine but had numerous interests that required more than fifty years to fulfill. Perhaps the deprivations of the *death event* end at the point we would otherwise be incapable of living a meaningful life (which is not automatically the next closest time when we would otherwise die), although I will now argue that we can be harmed by actions occurring after we are dead.

Can Human Beings Be Harmed Posthumously?

Our awareness of death creates opportunities for meaning that would not otherwise exist. I would argue that death also creates opportunities for meaning. How we die can add post-mortem meaning to our life, even though we will not experience that meaning.

Some philosophers dispute this. Jay Rosenberg argues, for example, "There is no possibility that a person's history might extend beyond that person's death."[44] If he means only that human beings are mortal, not immortal, his words are harmless, although disputed by theists. But if he means what he literally says, that the history of a person ends with death, then he is mistaken. The idea of biographical life revolves around human life as a narrative, a story. We are a series of stories in that we understand and identify ourselves through a chain of events, choices, actions, thoughts, and relationships. Our *biographical lives*, including value and meaning connected to our death and events thereafter, extend beyond our *biological* lives. The legacy of figures such as Jesus, Lincoln, Michelangelo, Mother Teresa, Jackie Robinson, and their like, bears meaning and value that transcend their deaths. And in some cases, such as Jesus, the way one dies brightens the legacy. The narrative of human lives often continues beyond our deaths. Many humans recognize this by consciously nurturing legacies, images, creative works, children, and projects that flourish beyond their deaths. However, we are aware that are projects cannot endure forever and we pursue them in that light. Death, then, does not supervene on life; it provides a context for life.

Admittedly, for most of us, our biographical story does not continue long after our deaths. Our fantasies to the contrary notwithstanding, we are not indispensable. At most, our departure would bring deep sorrow to those closest to us. Once those few who actually knew us and were influenced by us themselves die, most of us remain, at most, represented only by uncaptioned photos in web-covered albums stored in the corner of neglected attics. Most of our deaths will not be accompanied by massive displays of anxiety and gnashing of teeth. Beyond family, friends, and close associates, others will take note of our demise, perhaps attend a service, moan, "Too bad about Old Spike," or whisper, "No great loss," and get on with the mundane rhythms of life. Still, the question of what my future death means to me now is crucial. As Nietzsche insisted, the brio with which I live each moment of my life, the spirit of *amor fati*, is paramount. The meaning of my death hinges on the quality of my life. But we cannot exude a lifelong giddiness. However, as we project toward the future we can become more aware of the processes, not merely the outcomes that constitute our lives. To make our activities more fulfilling, to focus our creative interest in the act of creation instead of only on the result, speeds us toward the Nietzschean ideal.

I now have desires about numerous events that can only occur after my death: the disposition of my estate, the care and handling of my corpse, my reputation after death, among others. Such desires can only be fulfilled or transgressed after my death.[45] I have a stake in such matters but I cannot know now how they will be affected by posthumous events. My biographical life seems to transcend my biological life.

Can human beings be harmed posthumously, even though we stipulate that death is annihilation? I will now examine four arguments that capture many of our moral intuitions and that answer that question negatively: the argument from cognitive awareness, the transference argument, the argument from offense, and the argument from sentiment.

The argument from cognitive awareness states that suffering negative sensations is a necessary condition for having one's interests harmed; the dead lack the capability for experiencing sensations; therefore, the dead cannot be harmed. If successful, this argument would show that the wrongness of, say, necrophilia cannot be derived from the moral status of corpses. However, the argument is not successful. As illustrated by the Peeping Tom case, this argument confuses *being* wronged with *knowing* that one has been wronged. A person's interests can be violated, yet she may be unaware that her interests have been violated and thus suffer no negative sensations. Should she discover the violation, the negative sensations, the hurt, she would then experience do not *constitute* the harm, but instead they result from the victim's *recognition* that she has been harmed. Even if the victim had never learned of her transgressor's acts, her interests would have been harmed by those acts: neither suffering pain because of another's act nor becoming aware of that act is a necessary condition of having one's interests harmed by that act. Accordingly, the argument from cognitive awareness fails because it cannot be claimed persuasively that the dead cannot be harmed because they cannot know that others have acted against their previously expressed desires or because the dead do not experience negative sensations in response to the noxious acts of others.

The general moral principle reflecting our moral intuitions in this matter: It is morally wrong to contravene the objective interests or subjective desires of human beings unless complying with those interests or desires would violate weightier moral obligations, or unless the treatment required to comply with those interests or desires is supererogatory (above or beyond the call of moral duty), or unless the human beings at issue lack a justified entitlement to the benefits at stake.

Some interests of human beings can only be fulfilled or frustrated after they die. For example, a person's interests concerning the discharge of her will, the treatment of her corpse, the maintenance of her reputation after she is dead, and the future well-being of her loved ones can be affected only after she dies. So not only do human beings have interests that are fulfillable after they are dead, but they have interests that are *only* fulfillable after they are dead.

A critic might rejoin that the only interest we genuinely have in such matters is that it is important for us while living to think our desires in these things will be respected after we die. As long as we think that others will not malign our reputations, or mutilate our corpse, or discharge wrongly our will, then our interests are satisfied. Such a view confuses (a) a person's *thinking* her interests will be fulfilled after she dies and (b) her interests *being* fulfilled after she dies. Our interests and desires are not fulfilled merely by our thinking that they are. Only if the objects of our interests and desires are realized are these interests and desires satisfied. Our interests in not being slandered after we die, not having our corpse mutilated, and the like are not fulfilled by our thinking that such acts will not occur, but by those acts not occurring. If, on the contrary, our interests and desires were truly reducible to our thinking they were fulfilled then they could be satisfied by the manipulations of an able hypnotist.

The *transference argument* states that the interests and rights of a person are transferred to relatives and survivors upon that person's death; any transgression of those interests and rights is a violation against the interests of those relatives and survivors; therefore, the dead cannot be harmed because they have no interests. If successful, this argument locates the wrongness, if any, of necrophilia in the way that act violates the interests of the living. The claim that it is wrong to perform sex acts on a corpse or slander the dead, or violate wills because harm results to the dead person's surviving relatives does have an intuitive appeal. A will typically benefits a dead person's relatives or designated survivors and transgressions of the terms of that will often directly harm the interests of the living. Moreover, these living humans typically do take umbrage if the dead person is maligned, slandered, or used sexually.

However, the transference argument is not successful. What if a dead person has no surviving relatives? Or what if these surviving relatives do not care if the dead person is maligned or his corpse mutilated? Or what if the surviving relatives, themselves, are the ones who do the maligning or mutilating? Would we truly conclude that no wrong has taken place? All this suggests that it is not merely our aversion to insulting the heirs and relatives of the dead that accounts for our thinking that certain acts performed by the living against the dead are morally wrong. At best, the transference argument provides only a partial explanation of the wrongness of the acts at issue.

Suppose someone wrote a book falsely claiming that Rocky Marciano, former heavyweight boxing champion, gained the title only because his fights were fixed or because he illegally coated his hands with gauze soaked in plaster of Paris to increase his punching power. Suppose this scoundrel also slandered Rocky's reputation in other, more personal, areas as well. Surely we would conclude that this reprobate was morally wrong. We would think this, not merely because Rocky's surviving relatives would be insulted. If Rocky's surviving relatives were themselves the slanderers, we would think they were morally wrong. Accordingly, that certain acts performed by the living against the dead are morally wrong cannot be fully accounted for by our aversion to insulting the heirs of the dead.

Consider a case of gift-giving. If I wanted to give a gift to Mary, but Jane intervened and unjustifiably prevented the transaction by seizing the gift for herself, not only have Mary's interests been transgressed—she did not receive the intended gift—but also my interests have been frustrated: I had not merely desired to relinquish my hold on the gift, but had specifically identified the person to whom my entitlement to the gift was to be transferred. The same analysis holds for cases where the stipulations of a dead person's will are ignored: not only are her surviving heirs wronged, but the author of the will is wronged in some sense.

The argument from offense states that acts are wrong (at least sometimes) because people are offended by them; the dead cannot be offended; but certain acts toward the dead are wrong; therefore, these acts are wrong because they offend the living. If successful, this argument pinpoints the wrongness of acts such as necrophilia in the offense taken by wide segments of the living, and not narrowly in the offense taken by or interests harmed of the dead person's heirs and survivors. It is true that necrophilia and the needless degradation of corpses offend most of us. Stories about the shameless manner in which morbid medical students treat corpses or tales about the erotic preferences of certain sexual deviates are clearly likely to be offensive to those of us with a more refined sense of the appropriate. Thus, there is a kernel of truth in the argument from offense.

But are such actions wrong because we are offended, or are we offended because the actions are wrong? The offense we take at learning about such acts may partially constitute our collective recognition that the acts are independently wrong. Part of the explanation for our response may involve our firm conviction that necrophiliacs and those who mistreat corpses perform actions that violate what the person would have desired (or did desire) to happen to her body after her death. Would you want your corpse used by necrophiliacs? Would you want your corpse ridiculed by disrespectful, sophomoric medical students? Would you want your reputation unjustifiably demeaned after your death? At best, the argument from offense captures one of the reasons why necrophilia is typically morally wrong: the unjustified offense it brings to the living. Surely, actions such as necrophilia typically result in unjustified offense. But this need not always be the case, especially where a necrophiliac's actions remain hidden from the public. It is more likely that the argument from offense points us in another direction, on a quest to unmask the deeper reasons why necrophilia and other actions related to the dead are wrong and why the act offends the living so thoroughly.

One of the reasons we honor death-bed promises, normally take care when handling and displaying dead bodies, and avoid maliciously defaming the reputations of the dead is that we feel compelled to respect the wishes in these matters of those now dead. The living recognize the justified interests that human beings have in such matters. The offense we take at certain atrocities performed against the dead is a *recognition* that such acts are morally wrong, not the *reason* that the acts are wrong.

Those who insist that it makes sense to talk about affecting the interests of those now dead can point to the granting of posthumous awards. Does not the issuing of such honors suggest that the living do assume that the dead can be rewarded? However, critics advance *the argument from sentiment* which states that the living have deep emotional attachments to the dead; the living often present posthumous citations to the dead; the dead cannot be aware of such awards; if the dead cannot be aware of the awards, then they cannot benefit from them; therefore, posthumous citations are awarded because of sentiment only. If successful, this argument would block another avenue sometimes taken by those who claim we can be indirectly harmed by posthumous events.

Again, this argument embodies an element of truth. Many gestures toward the dead are merely sentimental. Those who try to converse with their dead spouse, or communicate with famous dead people by means of spiritualists, or who burn sacrificial offerings, may well be labeled sentimental or superstitious. But not all actions toward the dead fall so easily into these categories.

Suppose that various rules and conditions which specify who shall receive certain prizes or honors are set forth. A person who satisfies these qualifying conditions earns an entitlement to the award at issue unless an overriding consideration invalidates the claim in some legitimate fashion. Assume, upon fulfilling the qualifying conditions for the award, the person, overwhelmed by her achievement, suffers a massive heart attack and dies. Does this mean that no award should be issued? Does this mean that if an award is issued it is merely a sentimental gesture? I think not. If an award is not issued under such circumstances, in the absence of overriding considerations, an injustice takes place—a denial of the entitled person's due. That person would be wronged by failing to receive the award to which she is entitled.

One need not claim personally an award, or even be able to claim it, to be in fact entitled to it. In the absence of other overriding considerations, only the person's explicit denial of her claim to it can justify the withholding of the award. In the instant case the dead person has issued no such denial.

Of course, if a couple were entitled to a trip to Paris because they won this prize in a sanctioned lottery, but they died prior to embarking on the journey, we need not place them in caskets and carry them around Paris. Corpses do not have the ability to benefit from such treatment and this is the sort of overriding consideration that permits us to withhold justifiably the prize. However, human beings do have the ability to benefit from not being slandered posthumously and from receiving numerous posthumous awards: human beings have an interest in a good reputation *as such*. Regardless of whether our heirs and survivors appreciate what we did, we want to be remembered in light of what we accomplished and the kind of person we were. Indeed, we deserve such recognition based on our past performances and works.

Our desire, while living, to be remembered fondly is not necessarily an irrational fancy built on a desperate hope for personal immortality. Instead, this desire can be viewed as a demand that the imperatives of justice be acknowledged in dealing with us even after we are dead. Under this view, many things done to the dead are immoral because they violate the demands of justice.

Accordingly, not all posthumous awards are merely sentimental gestures. They are often requirements of justice: to withhold such an award would often be a denial of what is owed, or due, another as a matter of entitlement. The mere failure to be sentimental is not an injustice; but the denial of what is owed another, even if she cannot personally claim what is due her, is often an injustice. It is not obvious that we can transgress morality by being unsentimental. It is clear that we violate morality when we are unjust. Even after we die certain things can happen to our corpses, our reputations, and our estate. Some of these things are morally wrong not because they are offensive or a discomfort to our surviving heirs, but because they violate two constitutive principles of justice: desert and entitlement.

I have examined four arguments that try to locate the moral intuitions we share about treatment of the dead. These arguments intend to make coherent our considered judgments that certain actions involving the dead are wrong with the proposition that the dead lack moral status. But the four arguments, at best, capture only partial truths. I have tried to show that they cannot account fully, either jointly or severally, for our considered moral judgments about the treatment of the dead. Thus, the possibility that we can be indirectly harmed by posthumous events retains vitality.

Biographical Lives

I have accepted throughout the Epicurean annihilation thesis: at death we are no more; personal immortality does not await us. But each of us does persist after death to some extent. We leave a certain legacy to those who follow us and, depending on the kind of life we lead, we shall be remembered, if at all, as heroic or despicable or, most probably, as somewhere in between those extremes. Much of our behavior while alive is motivated by a desire to leave a positive legacy to those who survive our death. Few of us will achieve the monumental status of Socrates, Christ, or DaVinci, but we surely would rather be remembered in such a way instead of, say, as a Benedict Arnold, Charles Manson, or Bluebeard. Regardless of whether our heirs appreciate what we did, we want to be remembered in light of what we accomplished and the kind of person we were. We *deserve* this recognition based on our past performances and deeds.

Is our desire to be remembered irrational? Surely if annihilation is our destiny we shall never be able to experience pleasant sensations or even be aware of the fond remembrances that others may have of us; but many of us still want to be remembered fondly even after conceding all this. And this desire may be grounded in the principle of desert. One deserves to be remembered in accord with her past deeds. Our desire to be fondly remembered may reflect our conviction that a principle of justice should be applied properly when survivors evaluate the life we led.

Even after we die, certain things can happen to our corpses, our reputations, and certain of our desires and interests. Some of these things are morally wrong because they violate two paramount principles of justice: desert and entitlement. We have a justified interest that the imperatives of justice be acknowledged in dealing with us even after we are dead. Ignoring death bed promises, mutilating corpses, wrongly distributing the proceeds of wills, maliciously slandering the reputations of the dead, and like outrages are immoral because they violate the demands of justice.

Revisiting the Problem of the Missing Person

Possessing interests is a necessary condition for embodying moral status, and posthumous harms are possible only if they set back, frustrate, or infringe upon human interests. However, my earlier dissection of the four arguments against my position has at least one troubling, perhaps question-begging, feature: my analysis often assumes rather than establishes that existing human interests can be fulfilled or thwarted by posthumous events.

A grave metaphysical problem lurks: interests cannot be free-floating; they must attach to an interest-bearing entity. To what interest-bearing entity do the alleged interests of the dead attach? Moreover, there is a serious temporal problem: that I have *now* certain desires, wants, and interests regarding matters such as the disposition of my will, my surviving reputation, and the treatment of my corpse does not establish that *after* I am dead I retain those interests. After all, there is presumably no "I" that persists after death; there is only my soon-to-be-rotting corpse. Thus, we return to our original questions: How can mere corpses, which apparently lack all the prerequisites for interests, have interests predicated of them? How can the dead have moral status if they are not interest-bearing entities?

Joel Feinberg and George Pitcher[46] have provided by far the best and most innovative answers to such questions and I will borrow freely from their insights. One's biographical life, the narrative that constitutes one's entire story, is lengthier than one's biological life, the chronology of events between one's birth and death. That human beings typically have objects of interests that transcend the subjective experiences that constitute their biological lives is clear.

> We can think of some of a person's interests as surviving his death, just as some of the debts and claims of his estate do, and that in virtue of the defeat of these interests, either by death or by subsequent events, we can think of the person who was, as harmed. . . . He is of course at this moment dead, but that does not prevent us from referring now, in the present tense, to his interests, if they are still capable of being blocked or fulfilled. . . . The final tally book on a person's life is not closed until some time after his death.[47]

That certain of our interests survive our deaths has a seductive appeal, but there remains a paramount issue: How do such interests survive and to what interest-bearing entity do they attach? Strictly speaking, talk of surviving interests is only metaphorical. Once we are dead, all our interests expire. The dead are not genuinely harmed by posthumous events because they lack all interests. If not the dead, then who is harmed by posthumous events?

Feinberg, following Pitcher, says the following:

> Interests harmed by events that occur at or after the moment a person's non-existence commences are interests of the living person who no longer is with us, not the interests of the decaying body he left behind. . . . All antemortem persons [persons as they were at some stage of their lives] are subject not only to being described, but also to being wronged after their deaths, by betrayals, broken promises, defamatory lies, and the like, but no "postmortem person" [a person as he is in death] can be wronged at all.[48]

Thus, it is not a corpse, a "postmortem person," that is harmed by necrophilia, but the antemortem person whom that corpse once partially constituted. But when is the antemortem person harmed? How can an act occurring after a person has died harm the person at an earlier time when the person was living? How can an act at T+1 (some postmortem moment) cause harm to the antemortem person at T (some moment of the person's biological life)?

> The antemortem person was harmed in being the subject of interests that were going to be defeated whether he knew it or not [at T and before]. It does not become "retroactively true" that as the subject of doomed interests he is in a

harmed state; rather it was true all along. . . . Exactly when did the harmed state
of the antemortem person, for which the posthumous event is "responsible,"
begin? . . . "at the point, well before his death," when the person had invested
so much in some postdated outcome that it became one of his interests.[49]

The time when the wrongful postmortem event occurs does not mark the first
time the antemortem person is harmed; the postmortem event does not at that
point physically cause harm to the antemortem person. Neither backward causation nor retroactive harm comes into play. When the scurrilous slanderer ma-
ligns Rocky Marciano almost forty years after his death, he does not at that moment physically cause harm to the living Rocky two-score years earlier. Instead,
the wrongful posthumous event makes it apparent that the antemortem Rocky
was harmed all along: It becomes clear to us that Rocky was in a harmed state
prior to his death in that his interest in a deservedly honorable reputation as a
prize fighter was going to be set back even though Rocky would never become
aware of the slander.

Hence the antemortem person is in a harmed state prior to death. It is not at
T+1, the postmortem moment at which the act affecting the person's interests
occurs, that the antemortem person is directly harmed. Instead, T+1 marks the
moment when "it becomes apparent to us for the first time that it was true all
long—that from the time [the antemortem person] invested enough in his cause
to make it one of his interests, he was playing a losing game."[50]

By the same token, death extinguishes the interests of the antemortem person. The missing person problem evaporates if we understand the subject of the
harm of death to be the antemortem person whose interests—including that of
continuing to live while still capable of pursuing cherished projects and purposes—have been annihilated. Again, our biographical lives extend beyond our
biological lives: the spheres of our benefits and harms, contra Epicureanism, are
larger than the totality of our subjective experiences.

The Feinberg-Pitcher account is refreshing and seductive. Lingering doubts
may accompany its seeming fatalism and clever finesse of the temporal sequence problem, but it explains powerfully our numerous moral intuitions about
posthumous awards, death bed promises, postmortem defamations, and the like.
Moreover, it clarifies how death itself harms human interests. Under this account, necrophilia does not harm a corpse because corpses have no interests;
instead, it can harm the relevant antemortem person.

But if the interest-bearer of posthumous harms is the antemortem person,
does that suggest that the interest-bearer was harmed *prior* to his dying? Yes.
Reconsider my example of a scoundrel who maliciously slanders the reputation
of Rocky Marciano in 2008. He wrongs the antemortem Rocky by falsely allegedly that Rocky cheated his way to fame as a knockout puncher. He fraudulently
charges that when Rocky was alive he coated his hands with plaster of Paris to
illegally increase his punching power. The liar's wrongful allegations harm the
antemortem Rocky; they are not directed at the postmortem corpse that now
represents Rocky for no corpse can compete as a prize fighter or as anything

else. Thus, the postmortem Rocky is not harmed. The antemortem person, whose interests are extinguished and whose being is annihilated, is the subject of the harm of slander and of death itself.

Who is harmed? The antemortem person is harmed. What is the harm? That varies with the events at issue. If Rocky Marciano is posthumously slandered and his reputation is diminished then the harm is an injustice, a violation of Rocky's interests in or right to a reputation in accord with his actions. If the terms of my will are intentionally ignored after I die then the harm is a violation of my right to dispose of my property. Although in the cases mentioned, neither Rocky nor I would suffer pain as the result of the posthumous transgressions we would nevertheless be harmed in that our interests while living in having a deserved reputation and a properly executed will, respectively, after we died were wrongfully set back. When is the harm incurred? From the times at which Rocky's interests as a prize fighter and my interests in disposing of my property after death emerged.

Neither Rocky's nor my intrinsic properties (essential natures) change as a result of the posthumous harms. Only existing entities embody intrinsic properties and only existing entities can undergo changes in their intrinsic properties. But both Rocky and I would undergo relational changes, transformations in our relationship to something else. That "Machiavelli was discussed in Belliotti's political philosophy class in 2008" does not change Machiavelli's intrinsic properties—Machiavelli, long dead, has not changed as a person—but Machiavelli does gain in 2008 a relationship property that he lacked in 2007.[51] We can accumulate relational properties after our deaths, but not intrinsic properties. However, wrongful posthumous events do set back antemortem interests. Thus, they are not merely metaphorical harms.

Steven Luper argues:

> Posthumous events need not change our intrinsic properties in order to contribute to the status of our well-being. They can be truth-making conditions for propositions which hold while we are alive. Facts about the future can be against our present interests; when they are, our welfare is lower than it might have been. The fact that tomorrow we shall lack various goods, which is made true today by events that will not occur until tomorrow, may be against our present interest in having those goods tomorrow, so that our well-being today is lower than it might have been."[52]

The *wrongful event* of posthumous slander and the *harmful event* of death occur when the lie and extinction, respectively, take place. But Rocky's *being harmed* can happen earlier: He was going to die in a plane crash in 1969 although the antemortem Rocky did not know it prior to the accident; and if my hypothetical case was true, he was going to be slandered maliciously in 2008 and he was thus the subject of an interest (in a good reputation) that was going to be marred decades before the wrongful event occurred. Although Rocky adds only relational, not intrinsic, properties in 2008 through posthumous events, those events adversely affect the actual interests of the antemortem Rocky.

Events that occur in the future may advance or impair our interests now. Rocky Marciano died in 1969, but malicious slander in 2008 is bad for Rocky *while he was alive*. Slander in 2008 has no *causal* effect on Rocky in, say, 1968; it did not alter Rocky's basic constitution in 1968. The fact that in 2008 Rocky would lose his immaculate reputation as a prize fighter is against his interests in 1968. In fact, the malicious slander is against his interests, and therefore harms him, from the time Rocky had invested enough into the project of prize fighting that his reputation as a professional brawler *became* one of his interests (surely by 1952 when he became heavyweight champion, probably by 1949 when he began fighting serious contenders for the title, perhaps in 1947 when he began his professional career).

The fact that in 2008 slander would harm Rocky's reputation does not come into fruition—it does not become true—until 2008; nevertheless the slander in 2008 sets back Rocky's interest, prior to his death, in having a reputation commensurate with his actions even beyond his death. Given it was in Rocky's interest in 1968 to maintain his deserved reputation as a fighter, then the slander in 2008 harms that interest, even if Rocky was incapable then (because he was unaware of future events) and in 2008 (because he is dead) of registering the effect on his well-being. The occurrence of the slander in 2008 makes it true that prior to Rocky's death, perhaps from 1947–1969, Rocky was harmed in that the slander in 2008 was going to occur. If no slander had happened, the antemortem Rocky would not have been harmed in this respect.

Following Pitcher and Feinberg, direct harms are detriments or bad states of affairs, while indirect harms are the events bringing about direct harms. Posthumous events are indirect harms in that they are the events that bring about direct harms. Rocky Marciano being slandered in 2008 was an indirect harm which brought about the direct harm that his interest in a deserved reputation set was back. That his interest while living in having the reputation he deserved even after death was set back is the direct harm. He incurred this direct harm when it was true of him that his interests in an enduring, deserved reputation would be set back.

Posthumous events indirectly harm us by bringing about truths that affect our interests. Rocky being slandered in 2008 makes it true that his interest in the reputation he deserves is set back. He is directly harmed at all and only those times when the living Rocky had an interest in having a deserved reputation forever. While Rocky was alive his overall well-being was lowered by posthumous slander, which made certain things true that adversely affected his interests. Posthumous events, then, indirectly harm us when they occur, but directly harm us when they set back our interests. We can be directly harmed only if we exist, but need not exist to be indirectly harmed. Direct harms, as noted previously, need not be negative experiences or result in negative sensations.

Suppose Rocky was a huge fan of John Adams, Patrick Henry, powdered wigs, high-minded rhetoric, tea, fireworks, and muskets. He yearned in 1968 to view all the special events he imagined would accompany the American Bicentennial in 1976. To participate in the spectacle of the American Bicentennial in

1976, then, became one of Rocky's interests at least by 1968. Prior to 1969, if anyone asserted that Rocky's interest in the American Bicentennial was going to be squashed, she would be speculating. At and after the plane crash of 1969, the assertion would be warranted. Prior to 1969, whether Rocky would participate in the American Bicentennial, when he would die, and whether his death would be an overall harm to him were not evident. At and after August 31, 1969, all such questions were answered. The facts were set. The *claims* that Rocky's death would harm him and his interest in 1968 in celebrating the American Bicentennial was going to be squashed are accurately levied only at and after August 31, 1969.

Had someone *predicted* in 1968 that Rocky would die prior to the American Bicentennial that portend would have been an open question until August 31, 1969. That Rocky was harmed throughout his life by the plane crash in 1969; that Rocky was harmed from 1947 by the malicious slander; that Rocky was harmed from 1968–1969 by a premature death that thwarted his interest in celebrating the American Bicentennial are truths that become apparent only at and after August 31, 1969.

If skeptics scoff at the peculiarity of a plane crash harming Rocky over forty-five years prior to killing him, the view I am urging will distinguish between the *harm event* of Rocky's death, which takes place on August 31, 1969, and Rocky's *being harmed* by death, which occurs from the time Rocky had an interest in remaining alive. By the same token, the harm event of slander takes place in 2008, but Rocky's being harmed by slander begins in 1947; the harm event thwarting Rocky's interest in celebrating the American Bicentennial occurs on August 31, 1969, but Rocky's being harmed by not fulfilling that interest begins in 1968.[53]

Luper captures this idea well:

> Surely it is in my interests *now* for [the central project of my life] to be brought to a successful conclusion in the *future*. Suppose that only I can complete it, but I die prematurely. My dying ensures that it is true of me that my project will not be brought to fruition, and I am harmed *all the while* I have an interest in finishing my project, for during this time my welfare is lower than it would have been had I succeeded at my project. . . . [If my son, after my death, destroys my work which would otherwise have been completed by someone else] my son's action, a posthumous event, has harmed me. Thus, death and posthumous events may harm us *when we are alive*, in that our well-being may be lower than it might have been partly because of these events.[54] (Emphasis added)

That harm can occur prior to the event that occasions it seems zany at first glance. But such events harden truths that affect our interests: The slander of Rocky Marciano in 2008 makes it true that Rocky's reputation as a professional fighter is marred. Rocky is harmed by the slander at all and only those times when having a deservedly fine reputation as a boxer was one of Rocky's interests. Again, that period was probably 1947–1969. The problem of the missing person evaporates under this analysis because posthumous harms damage the interests only of living persons. By the same token, the plane crash on August 31, 1969, harmed Rocky at the time it occurred and Rocky died, and when its occurrence obliterated or thwarted interests, thereby lowering Rocky's well-being (for example, by extinguishing Rocky's prospects of celebrating the American Bicentennial in 1976).

A deprivation harm is a denial of a good that a person would otherwise have possessed. A deprivation benefit is a bestowal of a good or the ending of an evil that a person would otherwise not have incurred. Death deprives us when it cuts short a life that would otherwise be an overall good. Death can be seen as a benefit when it mercifully terminates a life that would otherwise be an overall detriment. In either case, though, the deprived or benefited entity is the antemortem person. We receive the harm or good connected with death while we are alive. The death of a person at a certain time is a deprivation for that person while alive if and only if that person's life would have been an overall good after that time had the person not died. The death of a person at a certain time is a benefit for that person while alive if and only if that person's life would have been an overall detriment after that time had the person not died. However, the dead, lacking all interests, cannot incur deprivation harms. This is the kernel of truth in the Epicurean position: "From the fact that deprivation harms (or benefits) cannot be incurred while we are dead, a further consequence follows: posthumous events cannot be responsible for deprivation harms or (benefits) incurred after we are dead."[55]

Death both destroys the good that is our life, by extinguishing our consciousness and terminating the meaning and value of our existence, and prevents us from acquiring new meaning and value that we would otherwise have pursued. Although posthumous events directly harm us only when truths they bring about adversely affect our interests while we are alive, death can directly harm us twice. First, death directly harms us when it occurs and extinguishes the good that is our life. Second, like certain posthumous events, death directly harms us when truths it brings about adversely affect our interests while we are alive. For example, if I had died prior to completing this book, my death would have brought about the truth that "Belliotti will never finish his book on Roman philosophy," a truth that would have set back the interest I possessed while alive that this work be completed.

Feit argues that "Lincoln's death was bad for him from the time when it took place until the time at which he would have died (given that there is such a time) had he not died when he did."[56] Although Abe is not harmed in 2008 by his death—he would never have lived to that date—he was presumably harmed for an unspecified period *after* April 15, 1865, the date of his assassination. Thus, under this account, death harmed Abe even after he no longer existed. Feit would seem to have a missing person problem in that under his view Abe was harmed after he no longer had interests that might be set back. Perhaps he could appeal to relational properties or relational harms as the solution, but these minimize instead of highlight the harms of death and posthumous events. Adding relational properties or incurring relational harms do not change the essential natures of people—they do not affect their intrinsic properties—nor do they set back actual interests. Indeed, relational harms are such only in a metaphorical sense.

One downside of my analysis is evident. Suppose that had Rocky lived past August 31, 1969, he would have developed tons of new, exciting interests; he would have lived a glorious life, then died in his sleep in, say, 2000. The analysis I am urging, unlike Feit's calculus, seemingly cannot conclude that Rocky was harmed because he was deprived of thirty-one years of fulfilling life or because his interests from September 1, 1969, to 2000 were never allowed to come to fruition. Unless Rocky *already* had developed an interest during his lifetime, under this analysis the death event and posthumous harm theory do not come into play. Accordingly, Rocky is not harmed with respect to those interests he *would have developed* and the wonderful life *he would have enjoyed* from September 1, 1969, to 2000.

Perhaps this matter is resolved by underscoring Rocky's general interest in continuing to live as long as his existence was an overall good for him. Rocky would develop this general interest at a very early age and it could account for the general deprivation harms connected with his death in 1969. As for the *specific* interests that Rocky would have developed from 1969 to 2000, I can refer to the dimension of premature death. To die prematurely always harms the victim (unless it can be shown that living a typical life span would have been an overall detriment to her). Assuming a baseline of, say, seventy-five years of meaningful life, we must factor in the timing of the death in our overall assessment of its harm to the victim. That Rocky died one day prior to his forty-seventh birthday adds to the deprivation he suffered at death because we assume that three or so added decades would have proved an overall benefit to him. We assume Rocky had vibrant interests in 1969 and would have pursued them and developed new ones for decades thereafter. If someone objects strongly to the arbitrariness of using seventy-five years as a benchmark, this analysis is compatible with a broader reading of "premature." We might conclude that a death is premature, regardless of the age of the victim, at any point at which the victim had or would have developed, had she not perished, the vibrant interests, projects, and purposes that constitute a meaningful life. Perhaps assuming that all human beings, other things being equal, have an interest in not dying prematurely (defined either narrowly by a specific age or broadly as sketched above) is also reasonable.

All the major positions on the timing of the harms of death and posthumous events remain problematic. The view I am urging struggles mightily to gingerly finesse the problem of backward causation. Other positions underscore the missing person problem by insisting that entities without interests can be harmed; or tacitly accept that free floating interests, unattached to living human beings, persist after death; or imply that we are harmed eternally; or that the harms take place at no particular time at all.[57] The richness of the topic has generated some of the best philosophy composed over the past three decades.

Epicurus and Lucretius, we must salute you! Some of the brightest human minds, laboring over a score of centuries, still have not conclusively solved the riddle on death first posed by the Epicureans.

Notes

1. Wallace I. Matson, *A New History of Philosophy*, vol. 1 (New York: Harcourt Brace Jovanovich, Inc., 1987), 167.
2. Epicurus, "Letter to Menoeceus," in *The Stoic and Epicurean Philosophers*, ed. Whitney J. Oates, trans. C. Bailey (New York: The Modern Library, 1940), 31: Lucretius, "On the Nature of Things," in *The Stoic and Epicurean Philosophers*, ed. Whitney J. Oates, trans. C. Bailey (New York: The Modern Library, 1940), 131.
3. A. A. Long, *From Epicurus to Epictetus* (Oxford: The Clarendon Press, 2006), 192–93.
4. Ibid., 178–79.
5. John Gaskin, *The Epicurean Philosophers* (London: The Everyman Library, 1995), xli-xlii.
6. Matson, A New History of Philosophy, 166.
7. A. A. Long, "Roman Philosophy," in *The Cambridge Companion to Greek and Roman Philosophy*, ed. David Sedley (Cambridge: Cambridge University Press, 2003), 195.
8. Ibid., 196.
9. M. L. Clarke, *The Roman Mind* (New York: W.W. Norton & Company, 1968), 20.
10. Ibid., 23–24.
11. Duncan Kennedy, "Making a Text of the Universe," in *Lucretius*, ed. Monica R. Gale (Oxford: Oxford University Press, 2007), 392.
12. D. P. Fowler, "Lucretius and Politics," in *Philosophia Togata: Essays on Philosophy and Roman Society*, ed. M. Griffith and J. Barnes (Oxford: The Clarendon Press, 1989), 149, 150.
13. Martha Nussbaum, *Love's Knowledge* (New York: Oxford University Press, 1990), 306.
14. Michael Grant, *Julius Caesar* (New York: Barnes & Noble, 1969), 23.
15. Frank C. Bourne, "Caesar the Epicurean," *The Classical World* 70 (1977): 421.
16. Ibid., 421–22.
17. Ibid., 422–23.
18. Ibid., 423–24.
19. Ibid., 425–26, 429.
20. Plutarch quoted in ibid., 427–28.
21. Ibid., 431–32.
22. Plutarch quoted in ibid., 421.
23. Clarke, *Roman Mind*, 23.
24. Philip Matyszak, *Chronicle of the Roman Republic* (London: Thames & Hudson, Ltd., 2003), 210.
25. David Sedley, "The Ethics of Brutus and Cassius," *The Journal of Roman Studies* 87 (1997): 41.
26. Clarke, *Roman Mind*, 21.

27. Catherine J. Castner, *Prosopography of Roman Epicureans* (New York: Peter Lang, 1988), 30.

28. Plutarch, *The Lives of Noble Grecians and Romans*, vol. II, trans. by John Dryden, ed. and rev. by Arthur Hugh Clough (New York: The Modern Library, 1979), 597.

29. Arnaldo Momigliano, "Epicureans in Revolt," *The Journal of Roman Studies* 31 (1941): 156.

30. Ibid., 157.

31. Plutarch, *The Lives*, 579.

32. Sedley, "The Ethics," 45.

33. Ibid., 46–47.

34. Grant, *Caesar*, 156.

35. Castner, *Prosopography*, 31.

36. Raymond Angelo Belliotti, *Seeking Identity* (Lawrence, KS: University Press of Kansas, 1995), 157–58, 176–78.

37. Epicurus, "Letter to Menoeceus," 31.

38. Jeff McMahan, "Death and the Value of Life," in *The Metaphysics of Death*, ed. John Martin Fischer (Stanford, CA: Stanford University Press, 1993), 240–41.

39. Raymond Angelo Belliotti, "Do Dead Human Beings Have Rights?" *Personalist* 60 (1979): 201–10.

40. Raymond Angelo Belliotti, *What is the Meaning of Human Life?* (Amsterdam: Rodopi, 2001), 135–56.

41. Neil Feit, "The Time of Death's Misfortune," *Nous* 36 (2002): 360, 369.

42. Joel Feinberg, *Harm to Others* (New York: Oxford University Press, 1984), 92–93.

43. Ibid., 93.

44. Jay Rosenberg, *Thinking Clearly about Death* (Englewood Cliffs, NJ: Prentice-Hall, Inc., 1983), 96.

45. Belliotti, *Dead Human Beings*, 203.

46. Feinberg, *Harm to Others*, 83–95; George Pitcher, "The Misfortunes of the Dead," *American Philosophical Quarterly* 21 (1984): 183–88.

47. Feinberg, Harm to Others, 83.

48. Ibid., 89–90.

49. Ibid., 91–92.

50. Ibid., 91.

51. Steven Luper, "Mortal Harm," *The Philosophical Quarterly* 57 (2007): 243; David Hillel-Ruben, "A Puzzle About Posthumous Predication," *The Philosophical Review* 97 (1988): 211–36.

52. Luper, "Mortal Harm," 248.

53. Julian Lamont, "A Solution to the Puzzle of When Death Harms Its Victims," *Australasian Journal of Philosophy* 76 (1998): 204–5; Jack Li, *Can Death Be a Harm to the Person Who Dies?* (Dordrecht: Kluwer Academic Publishers, 2002), 96.

54. Luper, "Mortal Harm," 248–49.

55. Ibid., 246.

56. Feit, "Death's Misfortune," 367.

57. See, for example, Fred Feldman, *Confrontations with the Reaper* (New York: Oxford University Press, 1992) ("eternalism"); Thomas Nagel, *Mortal Questions* (Cambridge: Cambridge University Press, 1979) ("indefinitism"); Felt, "Death's Misfortune"; Ben Bradley, "When Is Death Bad for the One Who Dies," *Nous* 38 (2004): 1–28; Lamont, "A Solution to the Puzzle"; Li, *Can Death Be a Harm?*; See, generally, John Martin Fischer, ed., *The Metaphysics of Death* (Stanford: Stanford University Press, 1993);

Charles Tandy, ed., *Death and Anti-Death*, vol. 1 (Palo Alto, CA: Ria University Press, 2003).

Texts and Their Abbreviations

All references are to Book numbers and/or sections, not page numbers, unless otherwise stated.

For example:

CW 54.4 =   *Catiline's War*, section 54, line or paragraph 4.
DRN 3.830 =   *De Rerum Natura*, Book 3, line 830.

I have used the following abbreviations:

CW =   *Catiline's War* (Gaius Sallustius Crispus: "Sallust")
DRN =   *De Rerum Natura* (Lucretius)

Chapter Four
The Ides of March

This chapter takes a close look at the events of the Ides of March. The assassination of Caesar marks the intersection of politics and philosophy. The major players rationalized and justified their plot by appeal to philosophical doctrine; they selected some of their fellow travelers only after examining the answers candidates offered to philosophical questions; and their motives were partially fueled by adherence to the doctrines of particular philosophical schools. After probing the lives and thoughts of Caesar, Brutus, and Cassius, I apply the analysis of assassination developed in chapter 1 to draw conclusions about the murder of Caesar. The fundamental question of this chapter, then, is whether the assassination of Julius Caesar was morally permissible or, perhaps, even morally required.

Gaius Julius Caesar: The Ultimate Roman

As a young man, Julius Caesar was captured by pirates. Although not in a strong taunting position, he purportedly swore to his captors that he would track them down and crucify them once he was freed from their clutches. After being ransomed, Caesar fulfilled his oath. This tale better captures the character of Caesar than does any battlefield account of his destruction of the Gauls, any story of political maneuvering with Pompey and Crassus, or any rendition of his numerous stirring speeches.

Either the legend of Caesar's insolence in the face of his pirate captors is true or it is false. If true, we enjoy the vision of a relentless warrior, confident even when seemingly confronting hopeless odds and a resolute enemy. If false, we chuckle at the shameless self-promotion of a youth turning desperate adversity into practical, political advantage. In either case, Caesar did hunt and slay the offending pirates. You do not tug on Superman's cape, you do not spit into the wind, and you surely do not accost, threaten, or falsely confine Gaius Julius Caesar.

In a world where a small, gifted class of men smoldered with *ambizione*, Caesar was aflame. He served as aedile at the age of thirty-five and two years later wangled the post of *Pontifex Maximus,* probably through bribery. A year later, he became praetor. After serving as governor of Spain, he formed a political triumvirate with the wealthy Crassus and the great general, Pompey. Because of his intransigence and political extremism, Cato the Stoic was an unwitting collaborator in the formation of the first triumvirate. By his unwavering opposition to even reasonable reforms, Cato managed to bring together three natural rivals.

In 62 BC, Pompey was still in the east with his troops during the Catilinian rebellion. A tribune, undoubtedly prompted by Pompey, proposed that Pompey be recalled with his army to restore order in Italy. Passage of the bill would have permitted Pompey to return to Italy legally under arms. Cato vetoed the bill, physically confronted its proposer, and disorder ensued. This act, along with his role in thwarting the Catilinian conspiracy, cemented Cato's influential role in the senate. Pompey returned to Rome as a military hero, but only as a private citizen. When Cato soon thereafter filibustered against Pompey's bill to ratify his eastern arrangements and provide land for his military veterans, he and his fellow *optimates* were becoming too much to bear. Caesar was returning from Spain and wanted to celebrate a military triumph and stand for a consulship in 59 BC. The *optimates*, led by Cato, blocked both requests. Generals anticipating a triumph were expected to wait with their armies outside the city until called. Nominees for a consulship were required to declare their candidacy in person. Unable to occupy two places at once, Caesar could either enjoy his triumph and forego his candidacy, or pursue the consulship and surrender his triumph. Stewing at Cato's inflexibility, Caesar, never impressed by appeals to tradition, chose to run for consul. The effect of these and other hard line maneuvers by Cato and his political cronies was to drive Caesar, Pompey, and Crassus together. The senate and Caesar could not act harmoniously. As a result, three men obsessed with their *dignitas*, who were natural foes, became surprising allies, united in their common opposition to Cato's rigidity. His older, more experienced partners assumed they could use Caesar for their own purposes then discard him when convenient. They were dialing a radically wrong number.

While passing through a poor Alpine village on his way to Spain in 61 BC, Caesar's companions jokingly asked whether there were electoral battles or feuds among great men in this jerkwater town. Caesar earnestly replied, "I would rather be the first man among these barbarians, than the second man in Rome."[1] Never has a more telling self-analysis been recorded. The Ultimate Roman, an avaricious consumer of military and political honor, and enduring glory, would not assume a subordinate role for anybody.

With the help of the triumvirate, he was elected as a consul in 59 BC. He proved to be a gifted politician who was able to enact the triumvirate's political program despite strong opposition in the senate. Caesar called a meeting of the senate and proposed a land bill favoring Pompey's veterans. The bill was reasonable and in line with past Roman practice. Cato, of course, rose in opposition. After a few hours of Cato's harangue, Caesar ordered him arrested, a right he possessed as consul. Other senators rallied in Cato's support. Caesar, convinced that working with Cato was impossible, bypassed the senate for the rest of the year. He appealed, instead, to the tribal assembly and the plebeian council, bodies to which consuls had the right to propose legislation. For the rest of his term, Caesar did not summon the senate again. This maneuver gravely transgressed tradition. Numerous bills favoring the interest of Caesar, Pompey, and Crassus were passed. Caesar's co-consul, Marcus Calpurnius Bibulus, Cato's son-in-law, was bullied and reduced to withdrawing to his home for most of the year. Bibulus had tried to block numerous governmental actions under the theory that the auspices or omens were unfavorable. Caesar considered such appeals to be nonsense on stilts. The prerogatives of tradition and the privileges of the senate were rapidly dissolving. Caesar had defined political strategy for the *populares:* circumvent the aristocratic senate and go straight to the people, not primarily as an exercise in democracy, but as a technique for effecting one's will.

After his term as consul expired, Caesar launched a ten-year campaign in Gaul. He served as his own military propagandist, composing *The Conquest of Gaul* in a lean, crisp rhetorical style. Critics in the senate objected that the Gallic war was conducted more to satisfy Caesar's boundless quest for glory and riches than for definable Roman purposes. This was Caesar's launching pad for his major aspiration: to become absolute ruler of the Roman republic. With added wealth, military reputation, and a loyal, expanding army, Caesar laid the foundations to attain that goal. He proved during the Gallic campaigns that he was Rome's greatest general.

> The hallmarks of Caesar's military style were great daring and speed. He had the mixed fortune of encountering repeated sizable rebellions against Roman authority, which, again and again, he successfully suppressed, often at unfavorable odds, by moving in quickly and exploiting the element of surprise. The glory of successive victories, his ability to rally the troops through battlefield rhetoric, and his willingness to share in their labors and deprivations, made more impressive by his own somewhat fragile physical constitution, endeared him to his men and inspired in them an intense personal loyalty.[2]

In truth, Caesar's Gallic campaign was brutal, nasty, and long. He extended war on the flimsiest rationales, treated his enemies harshly, and lusted after victories with deranged avidity. Caesar also proved he was a peerless general in attaining those military successes. In the Gallic campaign, Caesar had allegedly fought thirty battles, captured over eight hundred towns, and engaged three or four million enemies, of whom he captured one million and killed over a million more.[3]

> [Caesar] had the ability to change [battle plans] at short notice. This ability Caesar possessed to an extraordinary degree, and he combined it with exceptionally skillful timing of his lethal blows, that natural capacity to read the battlefield. . . . Caesar repeatedly staked everything on a single throw. This was his famous luck . . . he was instinctively a gambler who never paused to tremble at the odds but relied on his capacity to force them to his will . . . shrewdness was an element that appeared in almost everything he did . . . [he had] a startling capacity to work his will upon others.[4]

Meanwhile, his enemies in the senate, especially Cato the Stoic, always the uncompromising advocate of traditional Roman republican values, issued an ultimatum around 57 BC: Caesar must resign as pro-consul of Gaul, yield his army, and return to Rome. Upon his return, his opponents would levy charges against him, destroy him politically, and call for his exile. Pompey, Caesar's presumed ally, was less than vigorous in Caesar's support. The first triumvirate was unraveling and opportunistic senators were nibbling on the thread.

But Caesar had not ridden into Rome with hay in his hair. He acted, as always, decisively. He met Crassus and Pompey in Lucca and repaired their alliance. Caesar's command in Gaul was extended for five more years; Pompey was given a command in Spain and Libya; and Crassus, who never saw a penny he could not turn into a dollar, was given a command in Syria with the expectation that he would attack Parthia. Crassus was greedy for military success as he approached sixty, having only the suppression of the rebellion of Spartacus on his resume, a victory Pompey had marred by a late, dramatic appearance. Pompey and Crassus were also to be elected consuls in 55 BC. By 53 BC, Crassus's hunger for glory, along with his life, was extinguished in the disastrous Battle of Carrhae.

In 52 BC, street fighting between the rival gangs of Clodius and Milo devastated the city and paralyzed government. The senate appointed Pompey sole consul with a mandate to restore civil order. Employing the usual measures of violence and intimidation, Pompey's troops were successful. Pompey was now cozying up to the senate and even married Cornelia, a daughter of Quintus Caecilius Metellus Scipio (100–46 BC), one of Caesar's greatest enemies. Pompey had been married to Caesar's daughter, Julia, who died in childbirth in 54 BC.

As Pompey and the senate explored common ground, the demands for Caesar's recall from Gaul and for his prosecution for his excesses as consul in 59 BC and for his alleged war crimes thereafter grew increasingly acrimonious. The senate was regaining its pluck. Pompey was reluctant to join either side of the controversy. He was Caesar's ally, but senators were catering to his vanity and lauding him as the defender of traditional Roman values. Caesar, meanwhile, was prepared to return from his conquest of Gaul and slide right back into another term as consul. Negotiations between the two factions broke down. Caesar, in late 50 BC, proposed that he and Pompey should both disarm. The senate overwhelmingly endorsed the proposal. Only twenty-two out of almost four hundred voters dissented. Unsurprisingly, Cato, never one to give Caesar even an inch, led the opposition by exploiting a false rumor that Caesar had already crossed the Alps and was marching on Rome. Cato and the *optimates* implored Pompey not to disarm.

From Caesar's vantage point to return to Rome without troops while Pompey was armed was to rush into the throes of disaster. To return to Rome with troops would trigger a civil war. He was Gaius Julius Caesar. His *dignitas* required he could not back down and skulk timidly from the pages of history. Having failed in his attempts to negotiate his way out of the impasse, on January 10, 49 BC, Caesar, proclaiming "the die is cast" or "throw the dice high," with his army crossed the Rubicon River, the boundary of his province, and marched on Rome. Civil war ensued.

Pompey led the forces of Caesar's senate enemies. Caesar marched through Italy into Rome, meeting weak resistance. Although badly outnumbered, Caesar's characteristic speed, decisiveness, and bravery won the day. Pompey fled

Rome, allowing Caesar to march through Italy to Rome. During the siege at Dyrrhachium, on the eastern Asiatic shore, Caesar's supply lines were weak and he might have lost the war but for Pompey's refusal to follow up his advantage. Caesar remarked that, "The victory today had been on the enemies' side if they had had a general who knew how to gain it."[5] At the battle of Pharsalus in 48 BC, Caesar's forces, although numbering less than half of Pompey's forces, routed Pompey's army. At the first sign of adversity, Pompey left the battlefield and retreated to his camp. His troops, unsurprisingly, grew irresolute. Caesar showed mercy at the end of the battle, insisting on no unnecessary killings or reprisals. As always, Caesar's utter confidence in himself—the quality that made him "one of the greatest of fighting [in contrast to strategic] generals of the Classical age"[6]—had won the day. He remarked dryly, "This is the way they would have it; they brought me to this necessity."[7] Following Pompey to Egypt, he installed Cleopatra, who bore him a son, as queen.

After campaigns in Africa, Asia, and Spain, Caesar had eliminated all serious senate opposition. In 46 BC, at the Battle of Thapsus he thrashed the forces commanded by Cato and Quintus Caecillius Metellus Scipio. He continued to Cato's camp in Utica where he discovered that the Stoic had committed suicide. After a meandering series of campaigns in Asia, he defeated remaining Pompeians in Spain. Caesar had achieved his ultimate goal: he was absolute master of Rome. In 45 BC, he celebrated a four-day triumph for his numerous military victories, including a quick destruction of the king of Pontus memorialized by his unforgettable dispatch: *"Veni, Vidi, Vici"* ("I came, I saw, I conquered). No one ever accused Caesar of lacking style or ego.

The historian Sallust outlined Caesar's projected policies in an epistle which summarized his conversations with the conqueror:

> [Sallust] exposed the general lines of Caesar's policy: clemency for the defeated, curbs on the adventurers among his own partisans, avoidance of radical reforms, restraint of profligacy and political corruption and the inauguration of an imperial rather than a city-state approach to problems. In proclaiming the utter dependence of the commonwealth upon the actions and statesmanship of a single man, [Sallust] . . . was expressing a general belief of a population weary of civil war and of domestic dissensions and seeing no faction or other leadership capable of establishing lasting peace, achieving reconstruction and instituting belated, essential reforms.[8]

Caesar refused to order purges or proscriptions. By 44 BC, Caesar was declared Dictator for Life. He dressed in the fashion of the ancient Roman kings, but rejected that title. Caesar did not embark on any radical reforms, content, instead, to enjoy the trappings of power and privilege while reigning pragmatically.

Caesar extended Roman citizenship to include many of the provinces; he crafted a compromise between debtors and creditors; tried to reduce unemployment; settled numerous military veterans outside Italy; reduced inflation; moderated the grain supply problem; established a public library; and reformed the calendar. He also increased the size of the senate from six hundred to nine hundred, while doubling the ranks of quaestors and praetors. He filled the posts with men congenial to his interests, many of whom were foreign equestrians, centurions, soldiers, scribes, and even a few sons of freed slaves. He consulted the senate only as a formality, as his position of dictator entitled him to fill offices by nomination not election. Caesar, moreover, organized public entertainments, outlined a plan to prevent the Tiber river from flooding the city, and instituted new traffic and road maintenance regulations; he decreed that at least one-third of the labor force of large landowners be freeman instead of slaves; he replenished the state treasury with confiscations from defeated enemies; he imposed limits on interest rates charged by lenders; he granted the Jewish population the right to practice its religion; and he granted citizenship to all foreign medical personnel and teachers practicing in Rome. Such reforms—most of which were incremental changes and marginal adjustments—eased the worst burdens of the downtrodden while not significantly depriving the wealthy. While all such measures were autocratically imposed, although endorsed by the tribal assembly, their intent was not oppression. Caesar, upon becoming consul, acted to publicly post the proceedings of the senate and assembly daily.[9]

Caesar was not a thoroughly committed egalitarian, but he did soften the worst abuses inflicted on the most destitute. He had strong populist roots that were more than simply a cover for tyranny. His relations with the *optimates* had been thoroughly adversarial. The privileges and political influence—and thus the collective *dignitas*—of the aristocracy were severely compromised. The Roman masses, under Caesar, enjoyed measurable gains, although they lost the right to elect certain public officials.

The *optimates* in the senate, including Cicero, were repulsed by Caesar's social reforms, construction projects, and administrative vision: "They aspired to a restoration of the old leadership of the Senate with its rivalries, intrigues, corruption, social and political myopia and proclivity to violent repression of opponents."[10]

However, the senate lavished Caesar with every available honor, and then it invented new awards. Some members favored this approach as a strategy to undermine Caesar; others did so because they were thoroughly cowed by Caesar's power; and some out of good faith admiration for the dictator. For his part, Caesar had never confronted or conjured an honor after which he did not lust. The senate gave him, among other kudos, the right to sit on a golden throne; to wear the purple vestments of a triumphing general at all times; to brandish the title "Father of his Country." It renamed a month of the year in his honor. Early in 44 BC, Caesar's profile graced Roman coinage, an unprecedented occurrence for a living person. Finally, the senate authorized a temple for worship of Caesar as a god. Delicious irony, that, given Caesar's lifelong casual attitude toward religion.

Cicero, although vacillating more rapidly than a pendulum in his alternating praise and caution about Caesar, was firm in distancing himself from the dictator's Epicurean view of divinity and human mortality. Cicero was always prepared to use religion as an instrument to preserve property rights and forestall social reform. Caesar had never placed stock in divine providence or the master design of the universe. He was trying to understand and mold a world in flux: progress and re-creation, not reversion to a sentimentalized past or validation of entrenched privilege, were the order of the day. For Caesar, that death meant annihilation suggested we should live intensely and maximize our capabilities while on the planet.[11]

On February 15, 44 BC, at the religious feast of the *Lupercalia*, Caesar's chief bobo, Marc Antony, then a consul, offered him a *diadem* (crown). Caesar smugly ensconced on a golden throne while bedecked in purple robes, refused the gesture. The crowd, on cue, roared appreciatively. Antony made a second overture. Caesar gushed a dramatic response, "My name is Caesar, not Rex."[12] (This was a play on words: Rex was also a Roman surname.) The crowd, again, cried out in relief. This dog-and-pony show was probably designed by Caesar and Antony to elicit the reaction of the Roman people to his official elevation as a monarch. At least, this is how most savvy bystanders interpreted the theatrical performance.

The republic was still officially in place, but only in form not substance. Caesar had absolute power for life. As ever, he was not infatuated with tradition, the ways of the old Roman fathers, or the prerogatives of the senate. Unquestionably, as long as Caesar lived, the republic would suffocate. Worse, Caesar had squired Cleopatra and their infant son, Caesarion, to Rome in 46 BC. Could the balding, womanizing, epileptic be laying the foundation for a hereditary monarchy?

> Caesar did not know, or did not care, how deeply people felt for the traditional politics of the Republic. To him, they were a sham. He said so, and was also reported as observing that people must take his word as law. His personal magic and charm, his tactful courtesy and amusing high spirits were still sometimes in evidence, but rather more fitfully than hitherto. The hand was of iron.[13]

A circle of treachery was closing in on Caesar. He was widely viewed among the nobility as the tyrant who had slain the republic and eviscerated traditional Roman values. He had lavished mercy on many former enemies who now plotted vengeance. Proud men do not easily accept the largesse of a victor who through clemency underscores his superiority. He was also the inexorable target of lesser men who seethed with jealousy and envy. Even nobles who were not ex-Pompeians chafed under Caesar's authority,

Always restless and in search of new conquests, Caesar strategized a war against Parthia. Prior to his embarking, a conspiracy, led by Marcus Junius Brutus, Cassius Longinus, Decimus Junius Brutus (85–43 BC), Gaius Trebonius, and a host of others, was hatched. Brutus and Cassius were praetors, Decimus was consul designee for 42 BC, and Trebonius had been consul in 45 BC. They seriously considered extending their project beyond Caesar to kill Antony and possibly other major players loyal to the dictator in perpetuity. However, Brutus argued forcefully against any larger enterprise. Presenting the assassination only as a defense of the republic was crucial. Any larger action might suggest that the conspirators were seeking their own gain or lusting after political power akin to that held by their victims. No, Brutus insisted, only Caesar should be slaughtered. This was the first of several major errors in judgment plaguing the conspirators.

The plan was not a closely guarded secret. Several foreboding omens and soothsayer's predictions abounded. However, Caesar had always spurned the superstitions of Roman religion, unless temporarily subscribing to them held political or military advantage. Although his physical health was declining—stress and more frequent epileptic seizures were taking their toll—Caesar was secure in his robust invincibility and inveterate good fortune. He also understood that his death would spark wholesale chaos and civil disorder. Surely any rational person, even one enamored of republican traditions, could see this clearly. Only an idiot, mad man, or self-destructive loon would even *think* of killing Caesar, much less orchestrate a serious plot: "Caesar was regarded as great for his kindness and munificence . . . [he] achieved distinction for his mercy and pity. . . . Caesar acquired glory by giving, by supporting, by forgiving . . . [in him] the wretched found their refuge . . . he would neglect his own and refused nothing that was worth giving; what he desired for himself was a great command, an army, and a new war where his prowess could shine" (CW 54.2–54.5).

Some of Caesar's associates speculated that he was either intentionally courting death or levying an implicit challenge to potential murderers in accord with the Epicurean Lucretius's injunction: "Wherefore it is more fitting to watch a man in doubt and danger, and to learn of what manner he is in adversity; for then at last a real cry is wrung from the bottom of his heart: The mask is torn off, and the truth remains behind (DRN 3.55–58).[14]

Historians dispute the precise details of events leading to and culminating with the assassination of Caesar. The prevailing view: On the night prior to the Ides of March, Calpurnia, Caesar's fourth wife, had premonitions of her husband's doom. She convinced Caesar to cancel his trip to the senate on March 15th. Besides, Caesar was ill and no pressing political business remained prior to his expedition to thrash the Parthians. The conspirators, though, conjured a sweet little artifice. Decimus went to Caesar and urged him to appear at the senate. Decimus suggested that the senate was preparing to offer Caesar a *diadem*, a kingly crown to be worn in the eastern provinces and elsewhere, but not in Italy. The ruse was well-conceived. Had Decimus claimed that the senate was going to declare Caesar a king as such, the wily dictator would have whiffed the odor of treachery. The Roman aversion to monarchs was deep and wide. But the eastern provinces were accustomed to and enamored of kings. The additional title would play well in the regions to which Caesar was planning to journey and conquer. Caesar, never one to forego a major honor on the flimsy basis of dreams and sniffles, agreed to appear: *Dignitas* always trumped superstition and the flu.

Caesar's ambition soared so high because he was conscious of his power to become the master of the Empire. He had never believed in the ideologies of the *optimates* and *populares* which he had encountered on his entry into political life. A born enemy of the *optimates*, he regarded demagogy [of the *populares*] as no more than the means to an end. On the way to power he did not meet men who could impress him. He only saw selfishness and envy, and eventually emerged from a life of continuous and bitter conflict as a cynic who assessed all relationships only according to their political value and, judging the others by himself, could not believe that their *res publica* could still be to them something other than "a mere name without body and form."[15]

Caesar assumed his seat in the senate. Trebonius detained Marc Antony in an anteroom. The assassins surrounded Caesar while making a few minor personal requests. Publius Servilius Casca struck the first blow. Undoubtedly nervous, he was a poor choice to initiate the murder. Caesar grabbed Casca's dagger and cried out in surprise and outrage. Casca screeched for help. The murderers convened on Caesar with full purpose. He struggled and battled, until he saw the sword of Brutus drawn. He covered his face with his toga, submitted to Brutus's stab in the groin, and fell. His last words may have been, "What is this? Violence against Caesar?" or they may have been directed at Brutus, "You, too, my son," or Caesar may have perished in silence. Even at the end, Caesar was utterly amazed that mere mortals would presume to attack their superior.

> The proceeds of empire were shared unevenly. This led to fierce rivalry among the aristocracy and simmering resentment among the Roman poor who doubled as her soldiery. . . . Caesar died because he failed to win, or to retain, the loyalty of that inner circle of the Roman elite, for all that he spared their lives, gave them magistracies and promised them rich provinces.[16]

The assassins slew Caesar by brutally stabbing him repeatedly, twenty-three times, at the feet of a statue of Pompey. Many of the murderers had been wounded by each other's flailing blows. The Ultimate Roman was dead. The Ides of March has never been the same.

Marcus Junius Brutus: The Conscience of the Conspiracy

Brutus felt a biological destiny to uphold Roman republican traditions. His distant ancestor, the fabled Lucius Junius Brutus (ca. 545 BC – ca. 509 BC), led a popular rebellion that drove Tarquin the Proud, an oppressive monarch, from Rome. The ancient Brutus was especially instrumental in winning the military to his cause. A republic was instituted and the power of the senate restored. Shortly thereafter, agents of Tarquin the Proud returned to Rome to discuss the return of the tyrant's personal property. They also took the opportunity to foment counter-revolution and found an unlikely audience in Brutus's wife and two sons. The young men joined the conspiracy against the republic. Happily, the traitors were exposed and brought to justice. Brutus had to choose between the rule of law and his family. He chose the rule of law and all conspirators, including his two sons, were executed under Brutus's supervision.

That ancient Brutus was of a severe and inflexible nature, like steel of too hard a temper, and having never had his character softened by study and thought, he let himself be so far transported with his rage and hatred against tyrants, that, for conspiring with them, he proceeded to the execution even of his own sons.[17]

Marcus Junius Brutus, as did all Roman youth, grew up admiring the legend of the ancient Brutus, who venerated republican values even more than the lives of his own sons. If that connection was not enough to stoke Brutus's political fires, his mother, Servilia, was a half-sister of Cato the Stoic, the relentless advocate of republican values. Moreover, in 45 BC, Brutus divorced his first wife, Claudia, and married his first cousin, Porcia, daughter of Cato. The dead Cato, then, was both Brutus's uncle and father-in-law. Also, Servilia was descended from a man, Servilius Ahala, who murdered a would-be tyrant, Spurius Maelius, with a dagger. When Brutus served as an official in charge of the Roman mint, around 54 BC, one of the coins he designed had an image of Lucius Brutus on one side and that of Servilius Ahala on the other side. To add some mystery, later historical sources suspected that Brutus was the illegitimate son of Julius Caesar, who carried on a longstanding affair with Servilia. However, this is unlikely. Caesar was about fifteen years old when Brutus was born.

Brutus's father died in the aftermath of the civil war between Marius and Sulla. The elder Brutus was a Marian who served as tribune in 83 BC. He later joined the unsuccessful rebellion of Marcus Aemilius Lepidus (120–77 BC), father of the man who would become a member of the second triumvirate. Lepidus, once a political ally of Sulla, sought to overturn the Sullian order once the dictator resigned from office. The elder Brutus was in command at Mutina, Gaul, and surrendered without battle in the face of Pompey's overwhelming forces. After surrendering to Pompey under assurances that his life would be spared, the elder Brutus was summarily executed by order of Pompey.

Brutus was well educated in philosophy, rhetoric, and oratory. He reportedly was a more effective writer than speaker. He served as a quaestor in 53 BC. Brutus's political career gained momentum when he served as an aid to Cato, during the Stoic's administration of Cyprus. Brutus allegedly became a wealthy man by lending money to the Salaminians of Cyprus at the stunning rate of 48 percent (the usual rate was 12 percent). This was a forced loan on a subject city, which violated Roman law. Brutus's contacts in the senate, happy-go-lucky *optimates* often willing to gouge the provinces for the benefit of one of their own, exempted Brutus's transaction from prosecution. To ensure compliance with his extortion, Brutus planted a representative as a cavalry officer where repayments were aggressively enforced. Five members of the Salamis city council, who resisted Brutus's scheme, perished. Coerced usury was an anathema to the traditional moral code of the Roman aristocracy and the teachings of the Greek philosophical sages. Thus flowered the political education of "the noblest Roman."

Upon his return, he married Claudia, a niece of the notorious Clodius. He then firmly positioned himself with the *optimates*. Brutus was a keen student of philosophy and adherent to the Platonic Academy and the Eclectic Academy which sought to resuscitate it.

During the Roman civil war, Brutus sided with Pompey. Although Pompey had ruthlessly and fraudulently slain his father, Brutus was tightly aligned with the *optimates* who had won Pompey to their cause. At the Battle of Pharsalus, Caesar ordered his men not to harm Brutus and to take him prisoner. After routing Pompey, Caesar was thrilled to accept Brutus's plea for mercy. Plutarch reports that Brutus tipped off Caesar that Pompey was headed for Egypt,[18] but this speculation may be false.[19]

> Brutus's motives as a collaborator [with Caesar after Pompey was defeated at Pharsalus] defy interpretation. Up to this point in his life his actions appear to have been governed by self-interest. It may be that his reputation for high-mindedness and probity derived from his somewhat un-Roman bookishness and his addiction to literature and philosophy rather than from his actual behavior. Possibly, he felt that he had done enough for his family enemy [Pompey who had executed Brutus's father] and was now within his rights to switch to Caesar.[20]

Clearly, however, Brutus insinuated himself further into Caesar's warm graces. Caesar named him governor of Cisalpine Gaul in 46 BC, even though Brutus had held no political office above that of quaestor. He proved to be an excellent administrator whose lack of avarice and resort to violence won him and Caesar great acclaim.

Caesar appointed him as senior praetor in 44 BC. Caesar even alluded to the possibility that Brutus might one day succeed him: "When some maligned Brutus to him, and advised him to beware of him, taking hold of his flesh with his hand, 'What,' [Caesar] said, 'do you think that Brutus will not wait out the time of [my] little body?' as if he thought none so fit to succeed him in his power as Brutus."[21]

As forces against Caesar converged, they looked to Brutus to spearhead the assassination plot. Caesar had often favored Brutus, probably in deference to the dictator's longstanding, intimate relationship with Servilia. Brutus must have felt strong gratitude. Each man, though, probably bore deep ambivalences about the other.[22]

Notes were placed on Brutus's praetor's chair and on the statue of his famous ancestor reminding Brutus of his destiny. He had the ancestral connections and philosophical grounding. His wife, Porcia, encouraged him to assume a leadership role in the conspiracy. Brutus joined the existing schemers and sounded out other potential fellow-travelers with a philosophical quiz: Is civil war worse than an illegal monarchy? Is it wise for a man to bring troubles and danger upon himself in service of other people who were evil or foolish?[23] Presumably, the evil or foolish people were Roman citizens who had abetted or permitted Caesar's tyranny to rise; the men who would bring trouble and danger upon themselves were the assassins; and the philosophical issue centered on moral duty. Brutus took philosophy seriously and sought to justify his deed through rational argument. Further, he wanted only those likewise committed to join his number.

The standard historical judgment of his role: "Brutus provided the ideological backbone to the conspiracy. He was famously puritanical and consciously imitated the old Roman virtues. He was motivated not by greed or ambition, but by a desire to emulate his famous ancestor and liberate Rome."[24] Reality is rarely so simple.

Gaius Cassius Longinus: Nobody's Fool

Married to a daughter of Servilia and a half-sister of Brutus, Cassius was Brutus's brother-in-law. He was fluent in Greek, had studied philosophy, and was a recent convert to Epicureanism. Cassius had distinguished himself in the otherwise military debacle in Syria. He had tried to persuade Crassus from attacking the Parthians without first securing a base. By this time as greedy for military glory as he had been in his lifelong quest for wealth, Crassus brushed aside Cassius's concerns and led his troops confidently into the battle of Carrhae. The ensuing rout was the worst Roman defeat since the Second Punic War. Cassius rallied the vestiges of the army and escaped with around five hundred cavalry. Thereafter, he governed Syria for two years, valiantly defending the borders against Parthian invasions.

Upon his return to Rome, civil war prevented Cassius from being indicted by his political enemies for extortion while in Syria. Cassius was elected tribune of the plebeians in 49 BC. He cast his lot with the *optimates* and commanded Pompey's fleet. After Pompey's defeat and his own capture by Caesar, Cassius accepted Caesar's clemency. He served as Caesar's legate in Egypt, but declined to join Caesar's fight against Cato and Metellus Scipio in Africa. Instead, he spent two years in Rome without political or military office. He examined the nuances of Epicurean philosophical doctrine and cozied up to Cicero. Caesar appointed him a praetor in 44 BC, but elevated Brutus to a more prestigious praetorship even though Caesar recognized Cassius's superior credentials for the post.

> Brutus had only the reputation of his honor and virtue to oppose to the many and gallant actions performed by Cassius against the Parthians. But Caesar, having heard each side, and deliberating about the matter among his friends, said, "Cassius has the stronger plea, but we must let Brutus be first praetor." So another praetorship was given to Cassius; the gaining of which could not so much oblige him, as he was incensed for the loss of the other.[25]

Although Cassius was also promised the governorship of Syria at the expiration of his term, he was not a man to suffer slights gladly. He already resented his obligation to Caesar for sparing his life; he loathed his own willingness to recognize Caesar's superiority by accepting dishonor instead of death; and soothed his weakened *dignitas* with fantasies of revenge. Cassius knew that Caesar did not trust him and that his own political fortunes were thereby limited. The charade played by Caesar and Marc Antony at the *Lupercalia* deepened his resolve. He began gathering confederates, most of whom insisted that Brutus assume a leadership role. These were not common thugs or professional hit men. The conspirators would number among the most respected *optimates* in Rome. They yearned for legitimacy and Brutus, with his high reputation for moral rectitude and a profoundly philosophical temperament, exuded the *gravitas* required to justify tyrannicide.

Cassius began his recruitment campaign. Playing upon Brutus's presumed hereditary destiny and his visceral aversion to tyranny, Cassius strummed a beguiling tune of political liberation. Brutus pondered the alternatives, filtered them through the complexities of Platonic doctrine, consulted with others, and committed to the cause. He recruited others, but only after subjecting potential confederates of unknown motivation to the philosophical quiz noted earlier.

The standard historical judgment of the role of Cassius: He was the manipulative, "lean and hungry" dynamo who orchestrated the plot. Whereas Brutus is typically portrayed as a philosophically principled enemy of tyranny who loved Caesar but despised his rule, Cassius is pictured as a fierce warrior who detested Caesar and who fumed with designs of vendetta. Whereas Brutus embodied pure motivations and entered the project with a heavy heart, Cassius boiled with envy and resentment, and initiated the conspiracy with a heavy hand. Cassius yearned to slay Antony along with Caesar, but the noble Brutus prevailed, insisting that any carnage beyond slaying the dictator would contaminate the moral message of the deed.

Even Plutarch understood reality is not so neatly sorted. He noted that Cassius, even in his youth, despised tyranny. When a son of the notorious dictator Lucius Cornelius Sulla boasted of his father's power, Cassius smacked him in the head several times. When guardians of the assaulted lad sought to press charges against Cassius, Pompey the Great intervened. He brought both boys together, seeking an amicable resolution. Cassius, though, sneered at the other boy, "Say it again, so I can hit you again."[26] Gaius Cassius Longinus, even as a boy, was nobody's fool.

The Aftermath

Was not the deed too great for the assassins? Must they not now amplify to seem worthy of the deed? Brutus turned avuncularly to the senate, assuring its members that all would be well and outlining the reasons for the murder. But the senators were not prepared for a lecture. At times such as this, panic is eminently reasonable. They flew out of the senate house. The conspirators waving their bloody weapons and proclaiming *libertas* strode triumphantly down the street. So tone deaf were they to the temper of common folks that they genuinely expected the masses to rise up and greet them as republican heroes. The news spread through the city. At the forum, a crowd gathered to hear how all Romans would benefit from the slaying of the tyrant. The assassins, their cronies, and armed gladiators convened at the Capitol where they offered sacrifices. Meanwhile, Marcus Aemilius Lepidus (90–13 BC), consul in 46 BC and Caesar's Master of the Horse (in effect, second-in-command to Caesar), rushed to the Forum and rallied a crowd against the assassins' treachery. Caesar's legions, hordes of plebeians, and enemies of the aristocracy united in common cause. While the conspirators understood keenly the Roman aversion to kings and tyrants, they wildly misunderstood that Caesar was not universally taken to be of that ilk. The plotters' conviction that upon Caesar's death all right-thinking Romans would celebrate in paroxysms of republican glee was exposed as delusion.

On March 17th, Marc Antony addressed the senate. He proposed that all of Caesar's reforms be ratified, the lives of the assassins be spared, and that Caesar's body not be further defiled and tossed in the Tiber as was originally designed. Caesar, instead, would receive a public funeral in the forum, an honor reserved for the greatest Romans. Cicero, never a fan of economic redistribution, privately seethed that Caesar's reforms had solidified. But he publicly joined Antony as a peacemaker. Caesar's army and the threat of popular uprisings demanded concessions. Moreover, ratifying Caesar's acts ensured that numerous senators would retain praetorships, consulships, and provinces allotted them by Caesar.

Caesar's body was presented at the Forum. Antony eulogized Caesar and reminded the masses of his greatness. The burly militarist rose to the challenge and attained his finest moment. Antony then played his trump. He read Caesar's will. The ultimate Roman, vilified as a tyrant by his murderers, bequeathed every Roman adult man a generous sum of money and assigned his gardens by the Tiber River for public use. Antony laid out the garment in which Caesar was slain, displaying the sites of the twenty-three blows. The crowd, roused to a fury, put Caesar's corpse on a pyre and set it on fire. Civil disorder was widespread. Unorganized groups sought out the assassins' homes in retaliation. The armed forces of the *optimates* struggled mightily to repel the numerous disturbances. Within several weeks, the murderers of Caesar finally recognized that the Roman republic was not about to be restored by acclamation. The Roman masses understood that the assassins had fought for the freedom of the senate, not for liberty as such. Brutus, Cassius, and other confederates skulked out of town. Cleopatra returned to Egypt with Caesar's illegitimate son, Caesarion.

As Caesar had predicted, his death sparked a civil war. The *optimates* were unwilling to expend enough of their fortunes to raise an army powerful enough to squash the Caesarians. Arriving on the scene was Gaius Octavius Thurinus (63 BC–AD 14), the great-nephew whom Julius Caesar adopted by terms of his will. Caesar did not name as his heir his former Master of the Horse, Marc Antony, whom he recognized as a fine soldier but often unreliable character. Nor did he anoint the noble Brutus, even though Caesar had alluded that Brutus was his likely political successor. Nor did he legitimize his son with Cleopatra. Instead, he designated the son of his niece, Atia, daughter of Caesar's sister, Julia. In 46 BC, Atia had permitted Octavius to join Caesar in Spain, where he planned to fight the vestiges of Pompey's forces. Octavius, though, contracted an illness and was unable to travel. When he had recovered, he sailed to the front, but was shipwrecked. He struggled ashore with a few cohorts and traversed hostile territory to arrive at Caesar's camp. His great-uncle recognized moxie when it passed his way. During their time together, Julius Caesar became convinced that young Octavius embodied potential for greatness. Caesar's eye for measuring men and their talents was never so keen.

Upon his adoption in 44 BC, he was known as Gaius Julius Caesar Octavianus or Octavian. Having been greatly influenced by Cicero, he first allied himself with the *optimates* against Antony.

> In view of Octavian's youth and inexperience, Antony at first did not view him as a threat. But it soon became clear that Octavian was succeeding in his attempt to displace Antony as leader of Caesar's friends and supporters, especially among the city populace and the veterans. When asked by Octavian to release Caesar's money, Antony found various reasons not to, and Octavian then won tremendous popularity by selling off his own property in order to pay the bequest of 300 sesterces to each citizen.[27]

Meanwhile, the senate had eased the retreat of Cassius and Brutus, appointing them governors of the minor provinces of Crete and Cyrene. Antony, sensing a loss of momentum in his battle with Octavian, left with an army for Cisalpine Gaul. Inconveniently, Decimus Brutus, one of the conspirators against Caesar, was already in position as governor. Antony, never one to allow formalities to intrude on personal desires, lay siege to Mutina, where Decimus was located.

Cicero, sensing an opportunity to eliminate his nemesis, implored the senate to invite Octavian and his huge assembly of troops to confront Antony. Octavian was pleased to accept. In 43 BC, not yet twenty years old, Octavian defeated Antony's forces at Mutina. Antony escaped to the west and joined Lepidus.

Octavian had carefully nurtured Caesar's veterans, trading unabashedly on his name and his aura as Caesar's chosen one. The senate granted him the rank of senator. But Octavian was not born to be one of several hundred loquacious politicians. He marched on Rome with eight legions, suggested strongly that the senate recognize him as Caesar's son, and appoint him consul.

Octavian, with the cooperation of the senate, ensured that all of Caesar's assassins were formally outlawed and condemned. Lepidus brokered reconciliation between Octavian and Antony. The following year, Octavian formally joined forces with Antony and Lepidus to form the second triumvirate. Octavian and Antony decided to raise twenty legions each to pursue Caesar's killers. To raise funds necessary to support their design to avenge Caesar's death, the members of the new triumvirate followed the reliable but horrifying methods of proscriptions and plunder of eighteen Italian cities. To solidify their stations, they instituted a law granting them autocratic powers for five years. The most famous person exterminated in the proscriptions was Cicero, who had miscalculated Octavian's intrigues and Antony's resilience.

Early in 42 BC, the senate officially deified Caesar and renamed the month of his birth in his honor. As a manufactured "son of a god," Octavian's prestige blossomed. Later that year, he and Antony moved eastward to join battle against Brutus and Cassius. Lepidus remained in Rome to monitor activities. At the battle of Philippi, Antony and Octavian defeated the forces of Brutus and Crassus, both of whom committed suicide.

> In the first battle, Brutus wiped out three of Octavian's legions and captured his camp, while the troops under Cassius' command were so decisively routed by Antony that he committed suicide. The second battle may also have begun well for Brutus, but in the end his entire front broke, and he too killed himself. It is really his death which marks the end of the Republican cause.[28]

Antony's military skills were crucial in both battles and he was duly honored. Octavian's efforts were undistinguished and he was responsible for settling the discharged veterans of the campaign in Italy. Having learned from Caesar's mistake and being temperamentally unsuited for reconciliation, the members of the second triumvirate conferred no mercy upon the defeated. Proscriptions and revenge killings were the order of the day.

However, by 36 BC, the alliance that was the triumvirate had crumbled. Lepidus was placed under house arrest for allegedly collaborating with a son of Pompey and claiming Sicily. By 31 BC, Octavian had defeated Antony in a sea battle at Actium and ruled supreme for the next forty-five years. The grand Roman republic, as both an abstract rallying point for aristocratic privilege and as the legacy of the founding fathers, was dead. Resurrection was not in the offing. Over the next four hundred years, no substantial effort was generated to restore the republic. Every Roman emperor brandished exponentially more political power than had Julius Caesar.[29]

Was the Assassination of Julius Caesar Morally Justified?

The debate over the morality of the assassination of Caesar has raged for over 2,050 years. During that period, few new relevant historical facts have been unearthed. Yet for centuries, countless great thinkers have pored over the evidence and arrived at radically conflicting conclusions often expressed in dogmatic, intemperate language. The events of the Ides of March have inspired grand literature, compelling cinema, effusive poetry, and rigorous philosophy.

That a purely objective, neutral assessment of the assassination is possible is unlikely. Evaluation of the evidence must always be filtered through the prism of the fears and hopes of the judge. This is especially so when the available sources provide conflicting accounts of aspects of the events and the historians who subsequently retell those accounts are often (subconsciously) affected by their social position. In eras where kingly excesses pose felt dangers, we can expect Caesar to receive limited appreciation. In periods where special sensitivities to the fate of the oppressed predominate, we anticipate that the privileges and understandings of the *optimates* will be less warmly received. We may be frustrated by the impossibility of not projecting our contemporary social meanings and values upon people who predated us by over two thousand years. Yet to strive to reflect only the social meanings and values prevalent in 44 BC seems redundant: To think as Brutus and Cassius, or as Caesar, is only to repeat their visions and deeds.

To a significant extent, an assessment of Caesar's death screams volumes about the evaluator. Is Cicero correct that private property is inviolable and all confiscations, including taxes, are outright theft? Contemporary libertarians would applaud, although even they include a principle to rectify accumulations wrought by force, fraud, and coercion. Contemporary centrists and liberals would hiss; they would emphasize the communal nature of any polity and endorse some version of progressive taxation. Socialists and Marxists might well echo Engels's conviction that "Cicero was the most contemptible scoundrel in history."[30] Accordingly, that the morality of the events of the Ides of March continues to be hotly contested is a function of the controversies inherent in political philosophy, the limited historical record, the biased accounts of historians throughout the ages, and the inevitable infusion of evaluators' own cherished principles. No algorithm exists that might churn out a pure, incontestable right answer to the question, "Was Caesar's murder morally justified?"

However, this fact should not cause anxiety. The same may be said of virtually every paramount question nipping at our curiosity. Part of the human condition is to confront profound issues and enduring questions that resist final resolution. Errors arise when answers to such questions present themselves as more than they are; when tentative, situated, highly subjective solutions take themselves to be final, fixed determinations.

Here are a few examples of prominent thinkers who have carefully reviewed the events surrounding Caesar's murder. In his *Divine Comedy*, Dante Alighieri (1265–1321) places Brutus and Cassius in the lowest rung of hell, where their torsos are munched on eternally by two of Satan's mouths (IN 34.61–69). The third mouth is devoted to chewing on Judas Iscariot, betrayer of Christ. Dante places Caesar among the virtuous pagans. Dante's evaluation typified the approach in medieval writings. Later, with the growing influence of Plutarch and Shakespeare, and a rethinking of regicide, Brutus was no longer viewed as an ungrateful traitor who had betrayed his benefactor. He became the noble Roman who abrogated personal allegiance and risked everything for honor and country.[31] But even Plutarch, who was generally favorably disposed to Brutus, understood that monarchy was the inevitable development in Rome and that Caesar was a relatively mild autocrat when compared to historical tyrants and those of his day.[32]

One the most important political and cultural leaders of Renaissance Florence, Coluccio Salutati (1331–1406), in his *De Tyranno*, echoed Dante's conclusion. Caesar was not a tyrant because the defective way he rose to power was cleansed by the people's acceptance of his rule and by his reasonable reforms. Salutati insists that Caesar's assailants, "not lawfully, but by abuse of law, laid accursed hands upon the father of their country. [They] sinned against the state in the most serious and damnable way possible by kindling the rage and fury of civil war in a peaceful community."[33]

Not everyone agreed with Dante and Salutati.

> Caesar evoked the full spectrum of Renaissance opinion and so did his assassination. Salutati, for example, praised Caesar as "the father of his country and benignant ruler of the world" and justified Dante's consignment of the traitors Brutus and Cassius to the lowest circle of hell. Suarez, however, condemned Caesar as a usurper of sovereign power "through violence and tyranny," lauded the assassination, and seconded Cicero's praise of Brutus and Cassius's courage. The medieval John of Salisbury and the late Renaissance John Milton, like many others, took a position between the extremes: both recognized that Caesar unlawfully assumed power and in so doing acted the part of a tyrant; but both expressed regret about the assassination, respecting Caesar's virtues and showing ambivalence toward Brutus and Cassius.[34]

Thomas Gordon (1692–1750), a Scot, published, along with John Trenchard (1662–1723), *The Independent Whig*, a weekly periodical. From 1720 to 1723, Trenchard and Gordon, wrote a series of 144 essays entitled *Cato's Letters*, excoriating the corruption and the lack of values within the British political system, and warning against tyranny. Gordon championed Brutus as "perhaps the most amiable character, the most accomplished man, that ever the world saw." He gushed that Brutus was "animated by a most sublime and glorious spirit of value and liberty," while Caesar was "one of the greatest robbers and murderers that ever lived."[35] Eighteenth-century America and France, both engaged in casting off monarchies, also looked to Brutus for inspiration. The past two centuries continued the debate with Brutus depicted as everything from the eternal paradigm of patriot and freedom-fighter to a feckless romantic whose self-absorption brought calamity upon his people; and Caesar portrayed as everything from the symbol of progressive democracy to an avaricious power-monger obsessed with his own glory at all costs.

Fools often rush in where wiser people have already trod. Accordingly, I will now assess the assassination of Caesar using the framework developed in chapter 1.

Assassination Is Morally Justified If and Only If the Following Conditions Pertain:

1. The Tyrant Has Evilly and Systematically Transgressed against the Common Good

Caesar, too, embodied an ancestral destiny. His uncle by marriage was the fabled Gaius Marius (157–86 BC), honored general and seven-time consul, leader of the *populares* in their battle against the tyrannical Lucius Cornelius Sulla. Caesar's first father-in-law was Lucius Cornelius Cinna, Marius's loyal ally and a four-time consul. Although from a patrician family, Julius Caesar, cast his allegiance with the *populares* and he, too, responded to the siren call of family history. During Sulla's reign of terror in 82 BC, the eighteen-year-old Caesar was a prime candidate for the tyrant's fondest weapon, proscription.

The office of dictator in the Roman republic was typically limited to the duration of time required to remedy a crisis, at most six months. Sulla held the position for almost three years prior to resigning, but was granted the extraordinary powers of dictator indefinitely. The senate's willingness to do this marks for some commentators the beginning of the unraveling of the republic.[36]

Sulla, uncharacteristically flexible, offered Caesar a deal: If Caesar would join his number, his life would be spared; to seal the deal, Caesar would divorce his wife and marry someone chosen by Sulla. Caesar saw this as an offer he could refuse. He declined to toss aside his wife, Cornelia Cinna, who would bear him his only legitimate child, Julia. Sulla was persuaded not to whack so young an opponent. The tyrant was satisfied, instead, to confiscate Cornelia's dowry and Caesar's inheritance. Sulla noted that anyone who "did not see more than one Marius" in Caesar knew little.[37] Caesar was forced to leave Rome.

If Caesar was merely crusading for political advancement by any means necessary, Sulla offered an attractive opportunity. But the young Caesar never hesitated in declining that invitation even though doing so put him at serious risk. Anyone viewing Caesar's alliance with the *populares* as merely a cynical ploy to seize personal power is either uncharitable or unaware of his background. He was viscerally repelled by the self-indulgence, infatuation with luxury, and self-satisfaction of the *optimates*: They talked a fine game, but inclined too easily to political complacency and appeals to tradition. Just as Brutus felt the pull of family legacy, Caesar was temperamentally suited to the reformist zeal of Marius and Cinna.

Evaluators must be fair. While Caesar's *dignitas* fueled his passage across the Rubicon, consider the circumstances. Caesar, feeling the hot breath of civil war on his neck, proposed mutual disarmament as a compromise with Pompey. With only twenty-two dissenting votes out of almost (count 'em) four hundred, the senate approved this reasonable measure. But Cato and his obdurate cronies, in the face of the overwhelming will of the senate, encouraged a tribune to veto the proposal. They thought they had Caesar at a severe military disadvantage and the *optimates* were ready to squeeze. The next month, in early January 49 BC, Caesar again offered the compromise through the agency of Marc Antony, then a tribune. The senators, led by the relentless *optimates,* hostilely rejected it without a hearing. They sensed weakness in Caesar and, as always, were not about to give him a centimeter. After all, they had the mighty Pompey primed to lead them to military victory. And the senate passed a *senatus consultum ultimum*—the type of ultimate decree that was typically passed only to quell mutinies or other civil disorders—which ended Caesar's command and suppressed the tribunes of the people. Antony tried to veto the measure, but the *optimates* turned ugly. Antony and his fellow tribune sprinted out of Rome.

So what was Caesar to do? Submit to the authority of Cato and his senatorial jackals? This would lead inexorably to Caesar's disgrace, humiliation, and probable death. After the Battle of Pharsalus, when Caesar viewed the routed Pompey's camp, he reportedly observed wryly that his enemies had brought the calamity upon themselves.[38] Some take this as further evidence of Caesar's arrogance, but in light of the circumstances the remark resonates with stone cold truth.

For their part, Cato and his fellow *optimates* suspected that Caesar's offers of compromise were disingenuous. When Caesar waved an olive branch, they instinctively grabbed for their wallets and assumed skullduggery was afoot. Would not Caesar hide his best troops beyond the Alps, await Pompey's disarmament, and then storm Rome to his military advantage? Would he not roll into Rome and assume full control once the naïve senate accepted his phony invitation? Perhaps. But such subterfuge would have established Caesar as a genuine tyrant, not the avuncular progressive that flattered his self-image.

Once he was in power, the senate aristocrats correctly perceived Caesar as a threat to their political prerogatives. He had squashed the authority of the senate while advancing to a limited, but discernible degree, the interests of small farmers, debtors, and urban workers. The *optimates* were convinced that such reforms came at their expense. The call for republican liberty, which resonates so sweetly in our ears today, was in the practices of the late Roman republic a euphemism for aristocratic privilege. Under cover of lofty appeals to the "common good" and "traditions of our fathers," the *optimates* and their cohorts luxuriated in class advantage.

These same "constitutionalists" [such as Cicero] swindled public lands from small farmers (in violation of the law), plundered the provinces like pirates, taxed colonized peoples into penury, imposed back-breaking rents on rural and urban tenants, lacerated debtors with usurious interest rates, expanded the use of slave labor at the expense of free labor, manipulated auspices to stymie popular decisions, resisted even the most modest reforms, bought elections, undermined courts and officeholders with endless bribery, and repeatedly suspended the constitution in order to engage in criminal acts.[39]

Show-trials, random executions, death squads, systematic torture of political opponents, abuse of human rights, strict censorship, restrictions on emigration and travel, no or sham elections of public officials, complete and unlawful power vested in one ruler, dynastic aspirations, and careful seclusion of the tyrant from citizens—these are the marks of tyranny.[40] Philosophy recognizes rulers who are tyrannical in how they attained power and those who are tyrannical in how they wield power, and those who are defective in both respects. Was Caesar a tyrant? Or do we entertain that notion because he was slain in the name of liberty?

Salutati argued that although Caesar's title to rule was defective, as its source was unconstitutional violence, his administration brought order and stability to Rome. Events had conspired against continued republican government: The rule of one man was inevitable, even Cicero acknowledged that in his more reflective moments. The senate and the people lavished numerous and continual honors upon Caesar, underscoring both their explicit and implicit acceptance of his authority. More strikingly, the precise people who conspired against and murdered Caesar were happily disposed to accept his favors: Junius Brutus, Cassius, Decimus Brutus, and most of the other assassins had petitioned for and had received clemency after military defeat or significant political office or public honors without worry that their benefits were tainted by the soiled hands of tyranny. Decimus gained the rule of Cisalpine Gaul; Gaius Trebonius was assigned Asia; Tillius Cimber was assigned Bithynia; Marcus Brutus and Cassius were appointed senior and junior praetors, respectively. Conspirators all, they gobbled up their privileged positions without even a murmur of protest about the authority of their benefactor.

Also, after the assassination, all of Caesar's decrees and every future plan he had committed to writing were confirmed by the senate. If Caesar was so manifestly a tyrant would such an endorsement follow his death? Would so much public mourning have accompanied his passing? Would the conspirators have encountered so much resistance after their supposedly liberating deed?[41]

> What did [Cicero] find lacking in the perpetual dictatorship of Caesar which the conquered could ask for? Was it not a protection to the defeated and a bridle upon the victors? His dictatorship ruined no one, but on the contrary preserved the lives and the fortunes of many. It was a protection to the timid, a restraint upon the cruel, safety for all and a glory to the chief. The public welfare increased daily, and already the conquerors and the conquered were being set upon an equal level of honor and service.[42]

Salutati's description of Caesar's administration is overly sanguine and one-sided, but he makes some reasonable points. Yes, Caesar came to power without constitutional warrant: He defeated Pompey's forces and seized political command. Contrary to Salutati's conclusion, whatever honors and offices the senate conferred upon him were tainted by the implicit threat of force and Caesar's expansion of the senate with loyalists. Upon his military triumph, Caesar, in theory, might have had himself declared dictator for six months, restored social order, then relinquished all political power. But he was convinced that the former political arrangements—which rested so tediously upon sentimental appeals to tradition, delusions that strong senatorial power benefited everyone, and manipulations of religious superstitions—had exhausted themselves. Caesar would have also undoubtedly believed that social order in Rome could not have been restored within six months. The senate was feckless and self-serving; the masses spewed forth a gaggle of conflicting claims and counter-claims; and the relatively small middle-class was preoccupied with commerce. In his mind, Caesar was merely fulfilling his destiny. True, this was conveniently self-validating, but not unreasonable.

Yes, Caesar also wielded power in a few respects reminiscent of tyranny: he appointed numerous public officials; elections were either skirted or *pro forma*; and he controlled political power in Rome. But he avoided the worst abuses that characterize tyrannies. The masses of Romans were somewhat better off economically under Caesar, although they lost the genuine right to vote for most public officials. The aristocracy in Rome was somewhat worse off economically under Caesar, but still prospered. They were, though, significantly worse off politically as Caesar eviscerated the privileges of the senate. The small middle class was somewhat better off economically under Caesar, but had greater opportunity to attain public office even though elections were limited. At his death, Caesar's generosity to citizens was manifest and contrasted starkly to the avarice that most unadulterated tyrants embodied. Can we imagine Josef Stalin or Idi Amin, upon death, dispersing a large part of their fortunes to all their citizens equally? Would villains of their stature have ever shown mercy to vanquished foes in a civil war? Would they have ever eschewed proscriptions and purges for the sake of reconciliation?

> Caesar's purpose seems to have been not to destroy republican liberty but to mobilize sufficient popular power to break the stranglehold of the senatorial aristocracy, reducing it to an advisory and administrative body. He himself claimed his intent to be the people's champion rather than their master.[43]

Moreover, Caesar felt no need to isolate himself from the people; he was not the typical tyrant, surrounded by bodyguards and justifiably suspicious and fearful of the treacheries of the masses. He was easier to murder because his precautions were faint. Caesar had not tried to instill monolithic thinking through repression; he had rejected terror as a political bludgeon; he had extended mercy to countless military opponents; he refused to cower in the wake of gossip, rumor, and speculation; and he neither used informers nor tracked down alleged subversives.[44]

In the classical philosophies of Plato, Aristotle, and Polybius, monarchy—in contrast to tyranny—was classified as one of the good political structures. Even Cicero, following his philosophical ancestors, accepted this designation. None of the theorists mentioned thought monarchy was the best form of government with the exception of Plato: In the theoretically possible, but practically impossible, situation where one person is overwhelmingly superior to all others in moral virtue and philosophical insight then that person should rule supremely.

Caesar had seized power unconstitutionally. To call him a tyrant in arrival is fair. To call him a tyrant in political practice is contestable. In terms of truncating or limiting the elections of public officials, in claiming full political power, and in governing with the form but not substance of law, he begins with the common indicia of all tyrants. But in light of the counter-indicators sketched above, he falls far short of the paradigm. Whether his actions, on balance, deflated the common good is also highly disputable. A strong case can be made that the alleged common good that pre-existed Caesar benefited only (or stunningly disproportionately) the aristocrats. Caesar's reforms benefited in substance more people than did the pre-existing "common good," although some political rights of all people withered away under Caesar.

2. The Assassination Will Advance the Common Good

The conspirators, stunningly naïve, were convinced that the death of Caesar would automatically resuscitate the Roman republic. They considered, but rejected, the possibility of including Antony and other high-level Caesarians in their design. They did nothing to pacify Caesar's troops or lay a foundation for mollifying the common people. They had gathered no armed forces about them. They gave no consideration to the possibility Caesar would name an heir.

The assassins were so tone deaf to social reality that they never considered the prospect that the political liberties of the Roman *aristocracy* did not define liberty *as such*. They did not *reject* the view that middle class, poor, and disenfranchised people might embody interests other than their own; they never even *entertained* the possibility. The freedom of Roman nobles to compete for public office, honors, and enduring glory *constituted* traditional republican liberty.

> The plotters were well aware that under Caesar's autocracy their opportunities for financial gain and political power would vanish, and the prestige of the Senate would be obliterated by further dilutions. . . . Blinded by their arrogance and corrupted by avarice, they overlooked the causes of the struggle, and persuaded themselves that were Caesar removed, the republican machinery would at once begin to function.[45]

The Roman aristocracy had hijacked the common good: What was good for the *optimates* and their fellow travelers was good for Rome. This theft was not contrived cynically and self-consciously. Instead, three ideological dimensions converged to design the result. First, the romance of civil socialization: the grand parables and heroic epics of how brave Romans and founding fathers had resisted kingly oppression both internal and external in forging centuries of world supremacy. Second, isolation from the core of Roman life: the aristocracy willingly profited from slave labor and poorly paid free labor, but had little or no understanding of the legitimate grievances less fortunate people embodied. Third, the universalizing of their own class interests as the common good of the entire polity: the aristocracy deluded itself that the privileges and prerogatives its members enjoyed were the natural outcome of the rule of law neutrally applied.

> The Roman nobility reacted fiercely when their interests were infringed upon, especially their untrammeled "right" to accumulate as much wealth as possible at the public's expense. If not their only concern, accumulation was a major preoccupation. In a word, the nobles were less devoted to traditional, procedures and laws than to the class privileges those procedures and laws were designed to protect.[46]

Accordingly, the reason that the assassins did not more carefully plan the aftermath of Caesar's death was that they were sincerely convinced that all right-thinking Romans desired precisely what motivated them. The conspirators harbored a good faith, but deluded, belief that once their deed was understood to be spawned from lofty aspirations, the Roman citizenry would plead to join their cause. No plan to reestablish the republic was necessary because no serious opposition would be encountered. After all, the machinery of the republic was already in place. Caesar had not destroyed the republican structure; he had merely ransacked its substance.

> [The conspirators] spoke of liberty and meant plunder, and with boundless arrogance they assumed that the populace would not merely accept but even welcome the restoration of the oligarchic city state, under whose constitution and military power a coterie of aristocratic pirates had pillaged a helpless empire. . . Balking at any modification in the traditional city-state institutions, the Old Guard had shown themselves myopic in policy, corrupt in private and public affairs and quick to violence in face of any challenge to their hegemony . . . the praters of piety, of patriotism and of ancestral virtues were prepared to pull down the world if their outmoded privileges were not restored.[47]

Whether the beneficial changes to state practices, policies, institutions, or laws that the assassins sought would in fact have facilitated the common good is highly disputable. A return to the old ways—which was the critical goal of the conspirators—would not have served equally the interests of all citizens. The failure of the conspirators to grasp this, even dimly, invites the accusation that they were culpable for their political insensitivity to social reality.

> Republican Rome was in most respects quite unlike the modern states we inhabit. It was a violent, under-policed, volatile world with little social justice and few restraints on the whims of the rich. . . . No group in Rome was more committed to the rule of law than the propertied classes, whose interests law largely served. . . . *Libertas* for Roman aristocrats meant freedom to fulfill their political ambitions, under the laws but without being subjected to anyone else's power. . . . Freedom, that is, to compete for honors.[48]

If Brutus represented the best of the conspirators then that is faint consolation. He was an unlikely restorer of republican liberty. Brutus aspired only to a return to a sentimentalized past: "He would not have abused his position if victorious, but more was needed than to remove the new tyrants and to let the old machinery of government get moving again. And nothing in Brutus's career suggests that he could have done, or would have wished to do, anything more than this."[49]

3. Assassination Is a Last Resort

Critics can always imagine further actions that might have been explored prior to assassinating a government leader. The opposition might have asked for a conference with Caesar, presented him a list of grievances, implored him to arrive at an accommodation with the *optimates* in the senate, and negotiated in the spirit of reasonable compromise. They did not. Perhaps they were correct in not bothering. Caesar was embarking on his Parthian campaign a few days after the Ides of March. Time was short. If he was successful in teaching the slayers of Crassus, and the dispensers of the worse defeat on Rome since Hannibal, a military lesson his standing would only be enhanced. His political power would be amplified and any motivation to negotiate would be deflated. Postponement of the plot would increase the chances of exposure, decrease the possibilities for success, and permit Caesar's political position to thicken.

What is more interesting is examining Caesar's own actions prior to his assassination. Why the dog-and-pony show at the *Lupercalia*? The conventional view is that Caesar was testing the waters for his official ascension to kingship. Why, though, would Caesar, whose great strength was his acute insight into the character of people and the times, have not understood the transparency of the drama? No one with an IQ over twenty-eight was going to conclude that Caesar's refusal of the *diadem* signaled his aversion to the very thought of monarchy. Most people, certainly the *optimates* and even some favorably disposed to Caesar, would be deeply offended by the act. These were, after all, Romans who grew up on the heroic tales of plucky citizens killing tyrants, defending the republic, and celebrating traditional values. They might well be able to stomach a dictator, even one self-appointed for life, but a king?

Minority interpretations suggest that Antony might have pulled the stunt on his own. Perhaps he wanted to flatter Caesar and enhance his standing with the ruler. Perhaps, more invidiously, he wanted to undermine Caesar by anticipating the precise reaction that ensued. Either view is possible, but unlikely. In either case, Antony was risking much and had relatively little to gain. At worst, Antony would incur Caesar's wrath and marginalize himself; at best, Antony would diminish Caesar before the crowd. But how would Antony be thereby benefited? Would Roman citizens rise up, destroy Caesar, and replace him with Antony? Chances are slim to none and slim just had a stroke.

Why was Caesar lured into the senate on the Ides of March by Decimus Brutus's ploy? Granted, Decimus conjured a clever twist: The senate was about to confer a *diadem* on Caesar, but to be worn only outside Italy. But why would Caesar so wildly misread the temper of the times? He was a man whose stock-in-trade was discerning and exploiting opportunity; he avoided snares as assiduously as the wiliest fox; yet he was suckered by an amateur grifter. Was Caesar losing his edge? Did he subconsciously desire death? Was the crown of power becoming too burdensome?

In fairness, I must note that Decimus Brutus was held in such high esteem by Caesar that he was named second heir, behind only Octavian, in the dictator's will. Placement ahead of Antony, Junius Brutus, and Caesarion in Caesar's affections suggests that Decimus had earned enormous confidence. Maybe the answer to the riddle is simple: Caesar trusted Decimus above all others in Rome at the time and was lured to the senate by the one person capable of lulling him into a sense of false security. Perhaps this was simply an uncharacteristically shrewd move by the conspirators.

Still, other odd behavior begs for explanation. Caesar gleefully accepted honor after honor, many of which had never been bestowed on a living Roman.

Contrary to Salutati's whitewashed descriptions, the senate lavished these en-
comia not in grateful recognition of Caesar's deeds, but because it feared his
power and sought to curry favor. Also, if Caesar did not reject or moderate the
senate's offerings then the greatest fears of anti-Caesarians would be confirmed.
The great military leader and savvy politician fell straight into the trap. Except
for Antony's offer of a *diadem* at the *Lupercalia*, Caesar lapped up every drop
of external validation as greedily as a confined feline offered its first bowl of
milk in a week.

Caesar's triumphs were accompanied by troubling spectacles in which the
calamitous deaths of prominent Roman victims, including Cato, were graphi-
cally displayed; hundreds of lions were hunted to death in the Circus Maximus;
gladiators fought in groups and as individuals; a great naval battle was staged;
two armies, composed of war captives and condemned criminals, fought each
other to the death: "This horrifying and wanton display of power exceeded anything yet seen in Rome, and it revealed a side of Caesar's character which did
him little credit. It unmasked his arrogance and his dominance, and . . . the people sensed it and were frightened."[50]

And, then, there was Cleopatra. Having engaged in unnecessary, distracting
warfare on her behalf in the east prior to the complete pacification of Pompey's
army, Caesar brought her to Rome, along with her infant son, Caesarion. He
arranged for their domicile in a mansion beyond the Tiber River. That Caesar
dallied with a mistress was not news; he had, after all, engaged in countless
trysts during his career. But Cleopatra was a foreign queen against whom the
public took umbrage. Rumors of Caesar's kingly and, perhaps, dynastic ambitions swirled.[51]

Caesar also dispensed with bodyguards. Perhaps he was seduced by the
senate's unbridled enthusiasm in ingratiating itself with the supreme power.
Perhaps he took the senate's unending bestowals of honors for genuine affection. In fact, part of the senate was playing to Caesar's boundless lust for glory
as a way to nurture the public's hatred of him; another part of the senate included a host of craven toadies. In any event, Caesar grew confident that the
senators and equestrians would protect him. No bodyguards were needed. How
could such an otherwise acutely perceptive strategist make such a grave miscalculation?

[When a confidant] had urged him to recall his bodyguard, [Caesar] had set the
suggestion aside, presumably because the members of the Senate had sworn to
protect him, and his *dignitas* forbade that he should either doubt their loyalty,
or quake before their treachery. It was an irrational decision, an act of pride and
not of reason.[52]

Other annoying incidents add to the puzzle. At a festival, an anonymous trickster
placed a *diadem* on a statue of Caesar. Two tribunes had it removed. Caesar
scolded them and booted them out of office. Maybe he was offended that the
suggestion he should be king was so rudely received; or maybe he yearned for

the honor of publicly refusing the *diadem* one more time. In either case, Caesar rendered a sorry performance. Moreover, on one occasion when senators arrived to confer honors upon Caesar at the temple of Venus, he refused to rise to greet them. Remaining seated under such circumstances was understood as an insult to the senators' collective *dignitas*. Caesar offered only a lame excuse for his failure to adhere to tradition: He was suffering from diarrhea and suspected any quick movements might prove embarrassing. The underlying subtext was well understood by the senators.

Such incidents dripped with gratuitous disdain of public opinion and brazen indifference to common courtesy; they oozed arrogance. Why did Caesar, who held all the substance of monarchic rule, act against his own self-interest and arouse political antagonism for no evident reason? Was he so over-confident that he was convinced nothing he could do would rebound against him? Was he racked with guilt at the violence of his career and did he seek, subconsciously, to undermine his own position? Did he sense that he was near the end of life and was he desperately grasping for every possible final indicia of glory? Was his self-destructive impulse the logical extension of his exaggerated quest for *dignitas* and his extravagant self-esteem? Were his worst characteristics merely the amplified reflections of his best attributes, the ones that had greased his way to pre-eminence?

In any event, a priest in charge of the Sibylline Books, a collection of oracular utterances consulted at momentous crises through the history of Rome, announced that the Books declared that the Parthians could be conquered only by a king. This was taken to mean either that the senate should confer that title upon Caesar prior to his military expedition to the east or that Caesar's anticipated military victory over the Parthians would prove to everyone that he was destined for the throne.[53] The conspirators understood that they must act prior to March 18, 44 BC, the scheduled departure of Caesar. Accordingly, in light of all the circumstances, I conclude that the assassination did not violate the requirement that from a practical standpoint the murder must be a last resort.

4. Assassination Produces the Greatest Balance of Good over Evil

That the changes sought by the assassins were benefits is disputable. Yes, the aristocratic senators would have gained much politically and even more economically. That other social classes would have gained much is doubtful: perhaps some political rights. But how effective had those rights been in securing members of those social classes a reasonable chance to flourish? The aristocrats had purloined the common good. The changes brought by an assassination followed by the resurrection of the republic in substance would have understood the common good, as ever, in strictly aristocratic terms.

Moreover, even if I grant—contrary to fact—that the changes sought by the assassins were unambiguous benefits to everyone, they did not have a high probability of occurring. The republic was not going to rise spontaneously from

Caesar's ashes and that was foreseeable in 44 BC, at least by those not blinded by their class interests, romantic dreams of redemption, or personal vendetta.

In fairness, no other beneficial modifications that could be achieved in a reasonable length of time were apparent. Caesar was bound for the east. If he trounced the Parthians resoundingly, whispers of kingship would spread. That Caesar, from such a staggering position of strength, would have agreed to modifications in his managerial style is impossible to accept.

If we stipulate—in accordance with the perspective of the conspirators— that the changes they sought would amplify the common good, that they had a high probability of being realized, and that no other less drastic measure would achieve beneficial reform then the assassination has an initial chance to fulfill this criterion of the analysis. But nagging questions about whether the common, in contrast to the aristocratic, good would have been enhanced and about the probability of success remain.

Even if the assassination had foreseeable, probable prospects of serving the common good, would the good achieved have outweighed the evil incurred by murder? Favonius the Stoic, upon being questioned by Brutus, argued that civil war was worse than the most illegal monarchy: the end of the civil war between Pompey and Caesar was purchased at the cost of Caesar's dictatorship.[54] Whether Favonius anticipated that the death of Caesar would produce *another* civil war is unclear. In any case, Favonius flunked the philosophical test required of recruits to the assassination plot.

That the conspirators wildly miscalculated the aftermath of their deed is indisputable and has been chronicled above. But were they culpable for their errors? Was their good faith, but stunningly inaccurate, belief that the republic would rise again excusable?

The Roman Stoic philosopher, Lucius Annaeus Seneca (4 BC–AD 65), would later offer a measured critique of Brutus:

> Another [mistake of Brutus's] was to hope for freedom when the rewards of power, and of subservience to power, were so great. He was wrong too in thinking that the old constitution could be restored when the old moral standards were lost, or that the rule of law could be established when he had seen so many men fighting to decide not whether they would be slaves but which master they would serve. Finally, he must have forgotten the lesson of both human nature and of history if he thought that after Caesar's death others would not appear with the same aims as his.[55]

The death of a relatively mild autocrat often results in a worse state of affairs. Caesar had predicted that civil war would follow his untimely death. Cicero may have also sensed the possibility. That Cicero was excluded by the conspirators from their intrigue was no accident. Brutus, himself, with unintended irony would later write a letter criticizing Cicero to their mutual friend, Atticus: "If the price of crushing Antony is the acceptance of another in Antony's place and if the man who destroys evil is found encouraging another [evil] likely to have stronger foundations, and deeper roots, if we allow it. So that it is now doubtful whether those actions of his show fear of what constitutes despotism or only of a particular despot" (Ltr. 146: 6/15/43 BC).

The assassins' self-absorbed identification of their class interests with the common good as such; their estrangement from and ignorance of the concerns of less fortunate classes; their failure to set in motion a plan to facilitate a transition to republicanism in substance; and their disregard of the predictable reactions of Caesarian loyalists were then and are now morally culpable.

> The great conflicts of the late Republic resulted from divergences of interests and sentiment between the senatorial nobility at large on one hand, and (at various times) the Italian allies, the Equites, the urban plebs, and the peasantry on the other; it was also because the senate had failed to win the hearts of the mass of the rural population that the soldiery, mainly recruited from that population, displayed so little loyalty to the government.[56]

The result was thirteen years of renewed civil war that devastated the Roman world, doomed the republic, and ushered in centuries of emperors. The conspirators had failed to address the most daunting obstacle blocking political change, the problem of the transition: How does a revolution or assassination, if successful, then nurture the political structure its instigators prize? Caesar's murderers dim-wittingly concluded that their aspirations reflected the hopes of all right-thinking Romans and no blueprint for political transition was required. No, the republic in full form and substance would arise spontaneously or through an invisible hand instructed by the general will. An atrocious case of wishful thinking, that.

Accordingly, the view that the assassination produced a positive balance of good over evil is unpersuasive. Overall, the death of Caesar resulted in thirteen years of devastating civil war, served as the obituary for the Roman republic, and inaugurated the reign of centuries of emperors. Caesar, Antony, Cleopatra, Cicero, all of the conspirators, and countless others perished. The assassins' goal of restoring the republic was squashed.

> The human cost of that thirteen-year detour from one monarchy [Caesar's] to another [Octavian's] was staggering: aristocrats were hunted down and slaughtered, Roman soldiers clashed with Roman soldiers in bloody battles, allies were drawn in on both sides, provincial cities and neighboring kingdoms were casually despoiled and destroyed.[57]

From the divergent perspectives of all the main players—with the exception of Octavian—the assassination did not produce a balance of good over evil. On the contrary, the murder of Caesar produced a balance of evil over good. We have no need to conjure and assess other available actions in order to conclude that Caesar's assassination fails this requirement of the analysis. Unless one argues that the net evil produced by the assassination was less than the net evil that would have been created by all alternative actions—that the assassination caused the least evil among a host of worse options—that conclusion is inexorable. The argument required to unsettle it would be wildly speculative, abstract, and question-begging.

5. The Assassination Must Flow from Morally Acceptable Motives

Plutarch offered the conventional view of the motives of the two primary conspirators, Cassius and Brutus.

> Men generally reckoned Cassius a very expert soldier, but of a harsh and angry nature, and one that desired to command rather by fear than love. . . . But Brutus, for his virtue, was esteemed by the people, beloved by his friends, admired by the best men, and hated not by his enemies themselves. For he was a man of singularly gentle nature, of a great spirit, insensible of the passions of anger or pleasure or covetousness; steady and inflexible to maintain his purpose for what he thought was right and honest. And that which gained him the greatest affection and reputation was the entire faith in his intentions.[58]

The tidy picture of Brutus as single-minded, noble, firm in purpose, and incorruptible in spirit is unworthy of belief. He was an avaricious money-lender, even by Roman standards. He fought on the side of Pompey, the man who dishonorably murdered his father. Upon defeat, he implored the victor, Caesar, for forgiveness. After Caesar had granted clemency and rewarded Brutus with desirable political posts to the chagrin of better qualified applicants, he plotted against and assassinated his benefactor. He positioned himself as a contemplative philosopher, but was spurred to political action. He celebrated peace but commanded an army. He was the symbol of republican constitutionality, but assumed extraordinary political powers while in the east. He left Italy in the aftermath of Caesar's assassination to avoid civil war, yet rose to command a sizable army that fought against his fellow-citizens.[59]

Undoubtedly, Brutus was moved by a sense of ancestral destiny and a sincere love of Roman tradition and republican government.

> Aristocratic Romans had long been brought up to regard it as their duty to kill tyrants, and Brutus' ancestry, temperament, and studies in Greek history, which abounded in glorious tyrant-slayers, all combined to make him see that this was a sacred duty, and a duty peculiarly and urgently incumbent upon himself.[60]

Moreover, Brutus was trained in philosophy. He wrote several treatises on moral virtue, patience, and duty. As a champion of the Platonic Academy, he understood well the theoretical and practical justifications of slaying tyrants when necessary to redeem citizens. For Brutus,

> notions like "safety" and "exile" are determined by situation, not location. Is he in danger and exile [after the assassination when he fled Rome]? No. His own "safety," properly understood, *began*, rather than ended, when he formed the conspiracy against Caesar. Likewise, wherever he may be, he cannot be in exile

so long as he does not rate enslavement and vilification, the worst evils he can suffer.[61]

Brutus turned to the Platonic Academy for both justification and solace: Possessing and exercising virtue defines human happiness. Moral virtue was necessary and sufficient for happiness, although the supremely happy life required a measure of luck and external goods. Nurturing virtue, though, under a tyranny is problematic. Brutus understood that freedom is not merely a personal, but a political issue. Plato insisted that just men need a just state, and vice versa. The connection between the social good and personal flourishing resounded in the Platonic Academy. Tyrants upset social equilibrium: They pandered to, then oppressed the masses; their endless desires were uninformed by moral virtue; and they failed to educate citizens properly. Accordingly, Brutus had two choices: He could isolate himself from social life and immerse himself in philosophical contemplation, or he could continue to act politically. The former seems more of an Epicurean or even Stoic resolution. Only the latter offers robust possibilities for enhancing the well-being of fellow citizens, a duty Brutus felt keenly. To act politically under such circumstances required tyrannicide, an act that would destroy the power that was suffocating the possibilities for virtue among citizens. The Platonic tradition, which carefully categorized types of government and advocated tyrannicide in appropriate situations, dovetailed with the heroic actions of Brutus's esteemed ancestors, Lucius Junius Brutus and Servilius Ahala.[62]

That "the doctrines of the dogmatic [philosophical] sects were too complex to provide definite directives on particular occasions [but] they provided the moral vocabulary for weighing alternatives and justifying decisions"[63] is a reasonable position. But where, as here, the doctrines of the Platonic Academy lean so strongly in the direction of ancestral destiny and Roman tradition, that they played a significant role in Brutus's motivations for acting is also reasonable.

Accordingly, the popular view of Brutus as The Noble Roman, who risked everything for principle and patriotism has a sound basis in his sense of ancestral destiny and commitment to Platonic philosophy. But that view tells only part of the story.

Brutus was neither Goody-Two-Shoes nor Braveheart. Brutus had first disapproved of his Uncle Cato's suicide at Utica. The Platonic Academy generally opposed suicide as an unmanly and unvirtuous yielding to the forces of adversity. Only the gods or rightful authority such as law could appropriately command the taking of one's own life. But contrast the iron-willed, often unreasonable Cato to the big-talking, often pusillanimous Brutus. When Cato was confronted by the prospect of petitioning for or receiving Caesar's clemency he took his life rather than bend his knee in supplication to his adversary. A genuine man of principle, Cato, for better or worse, understood brightly who he was and for what he stood. History has celebrated Cato and his principles lavishly, although probably more than a complete picture of the man and his actions merits. When Brutus was on the losing military side, he pleaded for Caesar's clemency immediately and warmly accepted honorable political offices thereafter. Whereas Cato chose death before dishonor, Brutus selected privilege over principle.

Prior to the battles of Philippi, Brutus changed his mind about suicide. He told Cassius that if he lost the military campaign he would praise Fortune for allowing him to give his life for his country and thereby endure in liberty and glory.[64] His change of heart might be taken as adjusting his principles to necessity or as a newfound steeling of his republican spirit.

Brutus's initial repudiation of Cato's suicide, though, might have flowed partially from guilt. He was not then prepared to die for the republican cause. Perhaps he needed to rationalize his own convenient willingness to reconcile with Caesar by damning Cato. To conclude that the spirit of Cato cast a menacing shadow upon Brutus's later actions, as an assassin and initiator of suicide, is reasonable.

Brutus may also have harbored resentment against Caesar for the dictator's longstanding adulterous love affair with Servilia, Brutus's mother. That Servilia was one of Caesar's most cherished lovers was well known in Rome. Servilia's yearning for Caesar was well-documented. Despite numerous reports of their mutual affection, that tension existed between Caesar and Brutus is clear. That Caesar did not name Brutus as an heir in his will speaks loudly.

Moreover, the granting of clemency is a multi-edged weapon. Caesar's mercy to vanquished Roman foes was a miscalculation squared. While it flowed from mixed motives—Caesar enjoyed the superior position that granting mercy entailed, but he also understood that reconciliation was preferable to proscriptions and wholesale slaughters—it was destined to fail. If Caesar expected gratitude or the turning of temporary enemies to enduring friends, he was dialing a radically wrong number. Powerful men who must petition for or otherwise be granted mercy do not forget the stain on their honor. And these were Romans for goodness sake! Honor, reputation, glory, and competitive advantage defined the noble Roman. They might accept the clemency of a victor as a strategy for survival or even in the spirit of good faith pacification, but their repressed resentment would fester and boil over at a later date. What they would not do is accept in perpetuity the diminished status that defeat had conferred. Coupled with Caesar's populist reforms, which further nipped at their privileges, the Roman aristocrats would not remain under Caesar's thumb forever. Brutus resented his own capitulation to Caesar's largesse and Caesar's implicit assertion of superiority.

I must note, again, Brutus's jackbooted deeds as a usurer in Cyprus. We could well dub contemporary loan sharks Brutuses instead of Shylocks, without doing any violence to history or literature. Brutus, despite the lofty philosophical pretensions, retained a clear eye on his class prerogatives.

Caesar, who knew [Brutus] well, once said that "whatever Brutus wants, he wants it badly." A Freudian psychoanalyst might identify Brutus as an anal personality—self-disciplined, parsimonious, obstinate, hard-driving, guilt-ridden, and aggressive. Such a syndrome can be a positive factor in a politician or businessman.[65]

While in the east, Brutus minted coins in 43 and 42 BC, some of which bear Brutus's own image on one side, a dagger and cap of liberty on the other side, with the inscription "Ides of March." Delicious irony: One of the alleged outrages committed during Caesar's dictatorship was the appearance of his image on minted coins. Roman tradition forbade using representations of living people on currency.

> [Brutus provides] a spectacle of the self-righteous, opinionated, humorless, intellectually limited do-gooder in public life . . . "one of those admirable, highminded people who happen to be always wrong;" with the very noblest intentions and the greatest self-esteem, he manages to wreak havoc.[66]

Accordingly, the praiseworthy motives fueling Brutus's participation in the conspiracy coalesce uneasily with his guilt over Cato's honorable end in contrast to his own petition for mercy, his resentment of Caesar's superiority and dalliances with Brutus's mother, and his class interests.

> Marcus Brutus [is] hailed as acting only from upright motives. Brutus could not hide his distaste for Caesar's reforms, showing little sympathy for destitute petitioners and much concern for the brimming purses of the rich, especially his own. He was a leading conspirator in the assassination of a great popular leader, who had pardoned him and treated him well.[67]

History has been less kind to Cassius than to Brutus. That Cassius despised Caesar is uncontested. What Brutus found distasteful, Cassius loathed. He resented the inferior position that accepting Caesar's mercy had engendered; he despised Caesar for appointing Brutus first praetor after acknowledging Cassius's superior credentials; he suspected that Caesar had an adulterous affair with his wife, Tertia; and he bristled at Caesar's high-handed expropriation of lions that Cassius had earmarked for public games. Moreover, Cassius was a tougher, more aggressive, more overtly prideful man than was Brutus. He treasured his *dignitas* as profoundly as did Caesar himself.

> An irascible man, he did not easily forget a grudge and fell out for a time with Brutus when the latter won a promotion [as first praetor] at his expense. His contemporaries took the view that he opposed Caesar for personal reasons rather than on principle. According to Plutarch, he was furious when, during the civil war, Caesar came across a number of lions Cassius had acquired for use at some games he was due to stage in Rome and confiscated them for his own purposes.[68]

To paint Cassius's portrait in one dimension, though, does violence to history and to truth. He, too, was an aristocratic patriot, inspired by the heroic sagas of his youth, and overflowing with pride in Roman tradition. He was forged from harder steel than Brutus, but the two men shared political vision.

The requirement that assassination is morally justified only if the motives of the perpetrators are appropriate and grounded in reality must not be upgraded to a demand that motives be pristine and uncontaminated. Maybe God can neatly compartmentalize the evilness of deeds from the evilness of the actor: Hate the evil act, but love the person who produced it. Human beings are less tidy in their assessments.

Viewed from the prism of their aristocratic mindset and Roman socialization, the main conspirators against Caesar do not clearly flunk this test. Their motives were mixed, but such is the case in all tyrannicides. Their motives were not delusional, although their expectations for a resurrected republic may well have been. Do not lose sight of the serious risk the conspirators undertook and the palpable price they eventually paid for their enterprise. Surely, the assassins acted from greater principles than merely the elimination of a politician they despised for purely personal reasons. That those who willingly petition for mercy, gleefully accumulate benefits, silently gain during an autocratic regime, then rise up to slay the tyrant when opportune are vulnerable to strong criticism is clear. Whether such actions, when joined to loftier aspirations, violate the requirement of this part of the test for morally permissible tyrannicide is unclear.

6. The Assassins Must Employ the Least Wicked Means

Other things being equal, assassins should not inflict gratuitous suffering on their political victims. Caesar's death was bloody and terrifying: twenty-three knife wounds to his torso amid enormous panic and confusion. Did his murderers minimize the evil of their method of execution?

Lacking firearms which would have rendered the deed quicker and less traumatic, the most obvious alternative to a dagger attack was poison. Poison, though, was risky. Slow to act, easy to detect, and susceptible to antidotes, it was an unreliable method of killing. Poisoning an intended victim also involved wider subterfuges which might be exposed. Death by dagger was surer and swifter where access to the target was assured. Accordingly, I cannot fairly conclude that the assassins violated this requirement of the analysis.

7. The Assassins Should Subject Their Actions to Legal Processes, If Practical

The utter chaos that immediately dogged the death of Caesar prevented thoughts of resolving the justification of his assassination through due process of law. The agreement in the senate brokered by Antony and Cicero—that included ratification of all of Caesar's decrees and appointments; a public burial for Caesar; and no official retaliation against the assassins—was reasonable and necessary. Later, when Octavian assumed political control, the assassins were formally outlawed and condemned. Accordingly, Caesar's murderers never had a genuine opportunity to submit to the due processes of law. The question whether they should have done so does not even arise.

In sum, the assassination of Gaius Julius Caesar was morally unjustified. The act did not bring about worthy consequences and this is true from the vantage points of Caesarians and republicans alike. Because of this failure the deed cannot fulfill several parts of the test for justified tyrannicide. Moreover, civil war was the actual and foreseeable result of the assassination. Accordingly, the assassins are morally culpable for their delusional conviction that the republic would arise spontaneously from the ashes of Caesar's body. Their mindless refusal to plan for political transition is morally blameworthy. They bear responsibility for much of the carnage that ensued. Dante Alighieri, though, was merciless: Consigning Brutus and Cassius to the lowest rung of hell to suffer the endless torment of having their torsos nibbled on by a ravenous Satan is pitiless and disproportionate punishment. Surely, the two main conspirators deserve a lesser retribution: To sizzle in hell's fires until Caesar, with his mercy strained, grants a reprieve.

Notes

1. Plutarch, *The Lives of Noble Grecians and Romans*, vol. II, trans. by John Dryden, ed. and rev. by Arthur Hugh Clough (New York: The Modern Library, 1979), 206.

2. Jules Gleicher, "On Plutarch's *Life of Caesar*," *Interpretation* 29 (Spring 2002): 272.

3. Michael Grant, *Julius Caesar* (New York: Barnes & Noble Books, 1969), 82.

4. Ibid., 84, 85, xi, xii.

5. Plutarch, *The Lives*, 226.

6. J. F. C. Fuller, *Julius Caesar* (New Brunswick, NJ: Da Capo Press, 1965), 324.

7. Plutarch, *The Lives*, 230.

8. Arthur D. Kahn, *The Education of Julius Caesar* (n.p.: iUniverse.com, Inc., 1986), 404.

9. Michael Parenti, *The Assassination of Julius Caesar* (New York: The New Press, 2003), 149–54; Mary T. Boatwright, Daniel J. Gargola, and Richard J. A. Talbert, *The Romans: From Village to Empire* (New York: Oxford University Press, 2004), 236–37, 254–61.

10. Kahn, *Education of Caesar*, 416.

11. Ibid., 430.

12. Boatwright, Gargola, and Talbert, *The Romans*, 264.

13. Grant, *Caesar*, 150.

14. Kahn, *Education of Caesar*, 441–42.

15. Matthias Gelzer, *Caesar* (Cambridge, MA: Harvard University Press, 1997), 333.

16. Greg Woolf, *Et, tu, Brute?* (London: Profile Books, Ltd., 2006), xiv-xv, 49.

17. Plutarch, *The Lives*, 572.

18. Ibid., 575.

19. M. L. Clarke, *The Noblest Roman* (Ithaca, NY: Cornell University Press, 1981), 21.

20. Anthony Everitt, *Cicero* (New York: Random House, 2001), 220–21.

21. Plutarch, *The Lives*, 577.

22. Clarke, *Noblest Roman*, 36.

23. Plutarch, *The Lives*, 579.

24. Philip Matyszak, *Chronicle of the Roman Republic* (London: Thames & Hudson, Ltd., 2003), 210.

25. Plutarch, *The Lives*, 576.

26. Ibid., 577–78.

27. Boatwright, Gargola, and Talbert, *The Romans*, 270.

28. Ibid., 273.

29. Parenti, *Assassination of Caesar*, 176–85, 197–99; Boatwright, Gargola, and Talbert, *The Romans*, 267–88; Plutarch, *The Lives*, 242–44, 592–608; Matyszak, *Chronicle of Roman Republic*, 211, 216–23, 233–35, Woolf, *Brute*, 11–21, 39–43, 94, 182–83.

30. Arthur D. Kahn, "Was There No Superstructure in Ancient Rome?" *Monthly Review* 41 (February 1990): 37.

31. Woolf, *Brute*, 169–70.

32. Clarke, *Noblest Roman*, 81.

33. Coluccio Salutati, "De Tyranno," in Ephraim Emerton, ed., *Humanism and Tyranny* (Cambridge, MA: Harvard University Press, 1925), 101, 110.

34. Robert S. Miola, "Julius Caesar and the Tyrannicide Debate," *Renaissance Quarterly* 38 (Summer 1985): 272.

35. Clarke, *Noblest Roman*, 98.

36. Gleicher, "*Life of Caesar*," 266.

37. Plutarch, *The Lives*, 199.

38. Ibid., 230.

39. Parenti, *Assassination of Caesar*, 193–94.

40. Woolf, *Brute*, 54.

41. Salutati, "De Tyranno," 93–105.

42. Ibid., 106.

43. Parenti, *Assassination of Caesar*, 138.

44. Kahn, *Education of Caesar*, 452.

45. Fuller, *Caesar*, 303–4.

46. Parenti, *Assassination of Caesar*, 82.

47. Kahn, *Education of Caesar*, 448, 449, 451.

48. Woolf, *Brute*, 57, 99.

49. Clarke, *Noblest Roman*, 77.

50. Fuller, *Caesar*, 285.

51. Ibid., 287.

52. Ibid., 304.

53. Ibid., 302–3.

54. Plutarch, *The Lives*, 579.

55. Clarke, *Noblest Roman*, 81–82.

56. P. A. Brunt, *The Fall of the Roman Republic* (Oxford: Clarendon Press, 1988), 386.

57. Woolf, *Brute*, 21.

58. Plutarch, *The Lives*, 591–92.

59. Clarke, *Noblest Roman*, 72.

60. Grant, *Caesar*, 157.

61. David Sedley, "The Ethics of Brutus and Cassius," *The Journal of Roman Studies* 87 (1997): 51.

62. Ibid., 53.

63. Miriam Griffin,"Philosophy, Politics, and Politicians in Rome," in Miriam Griffin and Jonathan Barnes, eds., *Philosophia Togata* I (Oxford: Clarendon Press, 1997), 36.

64. Plutarch, *The Lives*, 599.

65. Thomas W. Africa, "The Mask of an Assassin," *Journal of Interdisciplinary History* 8 (Spring 1978): 611.

66. William R. Bowden, "The Mind of Brutus," *Shakespeare Quarterly* 17 (Winter 1966), 67.

67. Parenti, *Assassination of Caesar*, 146.

68. Everitt, *Cicero*, 262.

Texts and Their Abbreviations

All references are to Book numbers and/or sections, not page numbers, unless otherwise stated.

CW 54.2 =	*Catiline's War*, section 54, line or paragraph 2.
DRN 3.55 =	*De Rerum Natura*, Book 3, line 55.
IN 34.61 =	*Inferno*, Canto 34, line 61.
Ltr 146: 6/15/43 BC =	*Letters of Cicero*, number 146, dated June 15, 43 BC.

I have used the following abbreviations:

CW =	*Catiline's War* (Gaius Sallustius Crispus: "Sallust")
DRN =	*De Rerum Natura* (Lucretius)
IN =	*Inferno* (Dante Alighieri)
Ltr =	*Letters of Cicero* (Cicero, ed. and trans. by L. P. Wilkinson)

Chapter Five
Stoicism II: Seneca, Musonius Rufus, Epictetus, and Marcus Aurelius

This chapter deepens the discussion of Stoicism by probing Roman refinements to doctrine offered by a host of influential theorists. The Roman commitment to venerate the *mores maiorum*, steeped in the tradition of military and political conquest, coalesced uneasily with some of the doctrines of Stoicism, the dominant philosophical movement at the time. Such towering figures as Seneca, Musonius Rufus, Epictetus, and Marcus Aurelius struggled diligently to balance the often conflicting demands of political activity, philosophical conviction, and personal salvation. In so doing, they attained a glowing measure of enduring glory, always a Roman preoccupation, as they solidified their status as moral exemplars in a relentlessly competitive world.

I underscore the Stoic cognitive theory of the emotions and why Stoics were convinced that deep emotional reactions were nearly always generated by epistemological errors. Finally, I offer a contemporary version of the cognitive theory of the emotions that concludes, against the Stoics, that human emotions are the ballast of a robustly meaningful, valuable life.

Lucius Annaeus Seneca: Soul Doctor

Lucius Annaeus Seneca (4 BC–AD 65) was a physician of the soul and a philosopher of adversity. The second of three sons born into a prosperous equestrian family in southern Spain, Seneca and his brothers were sent to Rome at a young age. Seneca's father was of Italian descent and flourished as a rhetorician. His mother was probably of Spanish descent.

In Rome, Seneca undertook the standard course of study for wealthy boys earmarked for careers as advocates or politicians. Well-versed in Stoic philosophy and schooled in rhetoric, Seneca was beset with poor health, especially respiratory problems, throughout his life. As a young man, he traveled to and remained in Egypt for the alleged health benefits. He returned to Rome around AD 31 and pursued a political career for just over a decade. Seneca's early attraction to vegetarianism was extinguished during the reign of Tiberius Claudius Nero ("Tiberius") (42 BC–AD 37), when abstinence from pork was taken as conversion to Judaism.[1] Seneca wrote several treatises and entered politics. He first served as quaestor, but in 39 he rendered a spectacular courtroom performance that aroused the jealousy of the notorious emperor, Gaius Julius Caesar Augustus Germanicus ("Caligula") (12–41). Caligula, whose first, second, and usually final response to frustration was violence, decided to whack Seneca. However, fortune smiled on Seneca when an influential courtier convinced the deranged ruler not to bother. After all, Seneca was so sickly that he was destined to die soon of natural causes. Ironically, Seneca lived while Caligula, reaping his just reward, was murdered within two years.

But some folks, such as Seneca, just have a knack of annoying politically powerful people. Seneca immediately drew the attention of Valeria Messalina (19–48), the third wife of the new emperor, Tiberius Claudius Caesar Augustus Germanicus ("Claudius") (10 BC–AD 54). Seneca was accused by Messalina and Claudius of adultery with Julia Livilla (18–41), one of Caligula's sisters. Both Seneca, who favored a less autocratic style of rule than that preferred by the emperors who succeeded Augustus Caesar, and Julia, who had earlier conspired unsuccessfully against her brother, were considered potential political problems. In one fell swoop, the crafty Messalina managed to get both malcontents exiled in 41. Seneca was banished to Corsica where he continued to study and write philosophy.

But all overreaching schemers meet their expected end: In 48 Messalina conspired against her husband, the plot was discovered, and she was executed. By 49, Julia Agrippina (15–59), another sister of Caligula, married Claudius, her uncle. She convinced Claudius to recall Seneca to tutor her son, Nero Claudius Caesar Augustus Germanicus ("Nero") (37–68), who was then twelve years old. Claudius sweetened the deal by offering Seneca a praetorship. Philosophy, though, was excluded from Nero's curriculum because Agrippina thought it unsuitable for a future emperor. (Is it any wonder that Nero eventually strayed from righteousness and prudence?) Rhetoric was thought by Agrippina to be the more worthy discipline.

In 54, Claudius was allegedly poisoned, probably through the agency of Agrippina. Nero, Claudius's adopted son, was named emperor over Claudius's younger biological son, Tiberius Claudius Caesar Britannicus ("Britannicus") (41–55). Seneca and praetorian prefect Sextus Afranius Burrus ("Burrus") (1–62), were Nero's senior advisors during the early years of his reign. Seneca was Nero's speech writer and counseled him on appropriate political appointments.

> A few years of successful government followed, in which Nero had comparatively little involvement, notable successes included the quelling of crises at the margins of the empire without major military operations. But it turned out that Nero had primarily used his two advisors to moderate the influence his mother had over him.[2]

In 55 Nero engineered the poisoning of Britannicus. Seneca was aware of the treachery, but decided to continue as Nero's mentor.

> [Seneca] had never been a man of rigid principle. He had agreed to give up his vegetarian fad for reasons of safety [the practice was perceived as a religious superstition or conversion that might make its adherents subject to punishment] and was not ashamed to admit it later; he had pretended serious illness to escape [Caligula's] wrath; in exile he had put his literary talent and philosophical

training at the service of adulation in an attempt to return; he had accepted recall on the condition that he would teach [Nero] when he could scarcely have
been unaware that Agrippina meant him to supplant Brittanicus. Now if he
broke with Nero and retired, he might be put to death by the Emperor. . . . Seneca preferred to go on as if nothing had happened.[3]

Four years later, Nero arranged the death of his mother, Agrippina. Seneca and
Burrus were forced to accept the treachery. Seneca composed a dishonest defense of Nero to the senate. Nero was now, regrettably, his own man. Burrus
died in 62 and Seneca's influence on Nero was waning.

One function of Seneca and Burrus was to counsel [Nero] on his personal affairs where they touched politics, and to invent and impose on the public an official version of such events. . . . Their first task was to curb the political influence of the overbearing Agrippina and to end the Claudian pattern of excessive
influence by wives and freedmen. . . . Seneca warned Nero against incestuous
relations with his Mother and, with Burrus, managed public opinion after the
clumsy matricide which they had refused to execute.[4]

The Great Fire of Rome started in the summer of 64, among stores surrounding
the Circus Maximus. The fire spread quickly through the area of wooden homes.
For six days and seven nights, Rome was savaged. Four of Rome's fourteen
districts were destroyed; seven more were damaged severely. After the great
fire, Nero plundered temples in Greece and Asia to replace burned treasures.
Seneca, taking this to be sacrilegious, asked Nero for permission to retire and
offered to return much of his wealth. Nero accepted the money, but initially refused Seneca the privilege of retiring.

Hounded by charges of embezzlement, Seneca was eventually allowed to
retire from the senate and from his role as Nero's counselor to a private life of
study and writing. In 65, the unsuccessful Pisonian conspiracy was hatched
against Nero. Gaius Calpurnius Piso, a renowned Roman statesman, intended to
have Nero assassinated and to have himself declared Emperor of Rome by the
Praetorian Guard. He enlisted the aid of several prominent senators, equestrians,
and soldiers. When the plot was exposed, Nero (probably falsely) accused Seneca of involvement and ordered him to kill himself by opening his veins. Seneca orchestrated a suicide modeled on Socrates's death as depicted in Plato's
Phaedo. But Seneca, perhaps because of age and illness, bled slowly and pain-
fully. He unsuccessfully tried to poison himself with hemlock. Finally, after
dictating final words, he jumped into a hot pool to increase the blood flow. He
eventually died from suffocation as hot steam rose from the pool. Perishing in
confusion worthy of an episode of *Monty Python*, the dignified Socratic end
Seneca so deeply desired eluded him. Nevertheless, despite a slow, tormented
death, Seneca was said to have accepted his fate with equanimity.

The Good Life

Seneca begins from the basic Stoic framework: crafting a worthy soul is the primary good for human beings; the condition of a person's soul determines whether he or she enjoys a good life; so only those factors affecting the soul are critical to the good life; virtue, which depends on knowledge of what is right and wrong, and wisdom in applying that knowledge, is, accordingly, crucial to the good life.

What human beings typically desire or fear in life are, in reality, matters of indifference. Preferred indifferents are in accord with nature—health, social prestige, material security—but external to and not required for a good life. Why? Because they do not by themselves nurture the soul. To describe a thing as a preferred indifferent does not entail that attaining it is appropriate in all circumstances. In certain situations, for example, gaining more wealth may be disadvantageous to a person's well-being. Only moral virtue is always beneficial and thus always good. In that vein, suffering, low social status, and poverty, although not preferred, do not by themselves undermine the soul. Also, the best human life cannot depend on pleasure, even when it is combined with virtue. Pleasure is not an unconditional good, even when it follows from accurately recognizing our own virtue. Although such pleasure would follow from the highest good, it is not part of that good (VB 15.1–3).

Virtue is necessary and sufficient for human happiness, which is understood as a harmonious condition of the soul, not as a predominately positive state of mind such as joy, exuberance, or pleasure. Virtue requires perfected rationality. But a completely rational mind can exist only in a rational world, one that is well-ordered. Fortunately, the universe is perfectly ordered and governed by a divine reason which influences all events occurring in the cosmos. Whether referred to as nature, god, Zeus, or fate, Stoics underscore the ideally organized system of causation that flows through time. Human beings remain free within a world ruled by divine providence. Even apparent afflictions—whether related to natural disasters, misfortune, or social outrage—are part of the divine plan. The Stoic metaphor was that of a dog leashed to an unpredictable wagon. The leash is long enough to permit freedom of movement but not long enough to allow us unlimited mobility. We may desire to go wherever we please, but we are better advised to heed the direction of the wagon lest we be pulled roughly or strangled by it.

> Whatever happens we must think happens through necessity, nor may we wish to blame Nature. It is best to acquiesce when you cannot change something for the better; to follow god without complaint, for god is the origin of everything that happens. That man is a bad soldier who follows his commander with a groan. . . . If I am unwilling, I shall follow groaning, and suffer myself to do with ill grace what I could have done happily. Fate leads on the willing, and drags the unwilling. (E 107.8–11)

Here we return to an ambiguity in Stoicism: How can all external events be indifferent to us, fated and determined, and part of a structure that is the best of all possible worlds? If Zeus, part of and acting within nature, designs the best world possible and all events within that world are part of divine providence should we not regard all worldly events as good and not merely indifferent? As intuitive as this seems, Stoics reject the bait. Even though all worldly events are part of Zeus's benevolence they remain indifferent to the human good: the proper disposition of the soul that defines moral virtue. For Stoics, the important conclusion is that external events, even those bearing enormous quantities of non-preferred indifferents, are not evil. The cosmos remains the most rational, natural structure Zeus could have conjured. The human good, though, is linked inexorably to responding wisely and virtuously to the series of indifferent external events tossed our way.[5]

> [Seneca argues] that there is nothing mundane which we should yearn for, since whenever we turn away from our dealings with the divine to consider merely human affairs we are blinded and disoriented . . . and that our ability to withstand, even accept misfortune, would be greatly enhanced by knowing that whatever happens does so [from the direction of Zeus], that being miserable about mundane events is a kind of disloyalty to god.[6]

Seneca accepts the Stoic doctrine of eternal recurrence: A great fire will bring the present universe to an end. But in due course the universe will reconfigure in precisely the same form as it sustained prior to the conflagration. The cycle of destruction and reconstruction affirms divine providence. Zeus's foreknowledge, advance planning, and benevolent will are nourished between the two stages of the cycle. Seneca observes:

> What kind of life will a wise man have if he is abandoned by his friends . . . or cast out onto a desert shore? It will be like the life of Jupiter [The Roman Zeus], at the time when the world is dissolved and the gods have been blended together into one, when nature comes to a stop for awhile; he reposes in himself given over to his thoughts. (E 9.16)

For Seneca, human beings are free to harmonize their wills with the natural order or to resist it. Acceptance and accommodation lead to the internal serenity that defines happiness, while rebellion nourishes frustration, anger, and disappointment. Stoics understand that the cosmos is not perfectly just: Some seemingly bad things will happen to good people; some seemingly good things will happen to bad people.

> Why does god allow something bad to happen to men who are good? He absolutely does not. He keeps apart from them all manner of evil . . . he guards and rescues from harm the good man himself: surely no one makes the extra demand that god should keep the good man's baggage safe as well? The good man himself spares god any concern for this: he has contempt for external things. . . . Good men lose sons. . . . They are sent into exile. . . . They are

killed. . . . Why do they suffer certain hardships? The reason is so that they may teach others to endure them; they were born to set an example. (P 6)

All such events are part of the divine plan, much of which remains mysterious to us. The crucial steps are anticipating, preparing, and planning for adversity as a method of reducing its sting. The sage will remain undaunted by death, poverty, disease, hostility from his colleagues, and other misfortunes. His will is in sync with the rhythms of the universe and he does not fall prey to the four horsemen of failure: anger, frustration, disappointment, and self-pity. The sage is rare, more of an ideal than a reality; but to the extent that we are progressing toward his image we are on the proper path.

Seneca explicitly rejects Aristotle's advice to moderate, but not eliminate, the passions. The key, for Seneca, lies in self-command. Permitting oneself to feel or pursue something is different from ordering oneself to do so.

> The question has often been put whether it is better to have moderate passions or none. Our school [Stoics] drives them out, the Peripatetics [Aristotelians] moderate them. I do not see how any moderately diseased state can be healthy or useful. . . . For though I forbid you to desire I will permit you to want, so that you can do the same things, but without fear and with a surer counsel, and so that you can better perceive the pleasures themselves. And why shouldn't they make a bigger impact on you if you give them orders rather than taking orders from them? (E 116)

In that vein, anger clouds rationality because it arrogates a special standing to itself that hinders all correction of its own judgment (I 1.17).

Seneca distinguishes emotions from non-voluntary, instinctive reactions such as tears, sexual excitement, sighs, involuntary fears and nerves, and the like (I 2.3). Instinctive reactions—first movements—are not altered by judgments, but emotions are produced and can be transformed by judgments,

> The initial disturbance of the mind inflicted by the impression of harm is no more anger than is the simple impression of harm. Anger is the subsequent impulse which doesn't just accept the impression but approves of it; it is the agitation of the mind which is pressing on for vengeance on the basis of the desire and a judgment . . . just see whether you think anything could be either pursued or avoided without the assent of the mind. (I 2.3)

Seneca echoes the traditional Stoic concern for consistency:

> What is wisdom? Always to want the same thing and to not want the same thing . . . no one can be always satisfied by the same thing unless it is right. Hence men do not know what they want, except at the very moment when they are doing the wanting. No one has resolved to want or not want for good. Their judgment varies daily and reverses itself; most people live life like a game. (E 20)

Seneca, refusing to accept the Stoic sage as merely a regulative ideal, once suggested that Cato the Stoic might have even surpassed the ideal of the sage: "For greatness that surpasses ordinary common limits does not occur frequently. But I wonder whether this same Marcus Cato . . . may not even surpass our idea" (DC 7.1). Surely, Seneca overstated the case. While Cato's death was heroic and true to Stoic principles, his everyday life hardly mirrored the Stoic prescriptions against anger, strong emotions, concern for reputation, and the like. Cato's manner of advancing his *dignitas* was unique, but we must not err on this matter. Cato was too steeped in Roman tradition to be indifferent to his individual standing, class prerogatives, and the pursuit of glory. Being uncompromising, rigid in the face of opposition, and true to one's political principles—all hallmarks of Cato's life—are not sufficient for the Stoic sage.

Seneca develops his image of the sage by extrapolating from the examples of great Romans of the past (E 120). Virtue is wholly internal: the proper disposition of the soul in reaction to external events and relationships. Seneca, in fact, identifies three stages leading to the ideal of the sage. The first class, nearest the sage, includes those who have not attained wisdom, but are approaching it. Such paragons have purged themselves of the vices flowing from the emotions, but are still susceptible to transitory moods. The second class includes those who are generally free from the greatest passions, but still occasionally relapse. The third class includes those who are free from numerous vices of the mind but still susceptible to some. For example, they may transcend lust but still fall prey to anger. Most human beings do well to reach the third class. Attaining the second class and beyond requires uncommon effort, discipline, and training (E 75.8; 75.13; 75.14).

By recognizing degrees of progress and moral improvement, Seneca softens Stoicism's hard, bright line separating the ideal sage from everyone else. He thereby offers more hope to common people who are unlikely to achieve the resoluteness of a Cato, but who have the power to advance.

Seneca, as did all Stoics, identified a person with his mind, not his body. But unlike hardcore dualists, such as Plato, the separation is normative, not metaphysical. The recommendation is that human beings should identify with their minds as the central focus of excellence and flourishing; human bodies are only instrumentally and conditionally a source of well-being. Seneca, unlike Pythagoreans and Platonists, is not arguing that the mind and body are metaphysically separate substances with the material body serving as the tomb or prison of the spiritual mind.[7]

Seneca speaks of the objective self—what contemporary existentialists call "facticity"—which is unalterable and unchosen: date of birth, gender, parentage, ethnicity, and the like. He also speaks of the subjective self—what existentialists call "transcendence"—which is alterable and chosen, at least to some extent: temperament, attitudes, convictions, preferences, and the like. The subjective self is further divided between my current understanding—what I presently am—and my normative or aspirational ideal—what I would like to be.

In the Roman world . . . with its elaborate distinctions of rank and role, the social determinants of selfhood are simultaneously objective and normative, as
the word officium [a person's office, social role, and accompanying duties] in-
dicates; for the fact that someone holds an office provides no guarantee that the
office-holder will perform appropriately.[8]

The pivotal Stoic twist is that a person's normative or aspirational ideal is never
completely hostage to his objective self or immersion in social roles. Regardless
of those contingencies, the mind is free to judge and to conform itself to nature.
Progress toward one's normative ideal is possible, to greater or lesser extents,
under any circumstances. This empowering creed vivifies human imagination
and multiplies tangible prospects. Stoicism flourished in Rome because it encouraged participation in political activity, its doctrines provided solace—
especially to those enduring hardships—and its fellowship nurtured those who
were unfavored by the prevailing power brokers.

Our emotions are not merely external disruptions that agitate the soul. Instead, they are judgments. The root of misguided passion is bad epistemology:
We wrongly assent to various impressions. Errors in judgment fuel inappropriate
emotional behavior. Unlike Plato, who posited three parts to the soul, one of
which was irrational and grounded fully in desire, Stoics conceive the soul as
unitary and only rational. The world is portrayed as a universal city, inhabited
by human beings who share a common rationality regardless of their geographic
origins. Individual citizens should participate in public life as a way of contributing to the common good.

To soften the harsh blows of life, Seneca advocated the traditional Stoic
technique of *praemeditatio*, imagining possible misfortunes prior to their occurrence. The exercise was designed to fortify the mind in advance and destroy the
ability of adversities to frustrate us because of their surprise: imagination can
serve reason.[9]

Seneca also reaffirms providence and concludes that trials and tribulations
are levied on those most loved by divinity. Suffering and pain, then, are part of a
wider scheme and facilitate human happiness if confronted creatively. Anger,
though, emerges from weakness and error. We assent to impulsive impressions
and act inappropriately. Generally, an unwarranted, overly optimistic view of
the world and of our fellow human beings triggers negative judgments that issue
in anger. Our expectations, then, are critical to our subsequent conviction that
the imperfectability of our existence merits an angry response. Moreover, the
internal qualities of human beings do not automatically correlate to their external circumstances. Also, when we subconsciously suspect we are deserving of
ridicule or disrespect we are more likely to take another person's remarks in that
vein. Seneca accepts the Stoical hard line here: the sage does not feel anger because his reason shows it to be contrary to nature.

Anger results not from an uncontrollable eruption of the passions, but from a
basic (and correctable) error of reasoning . . . anger does not belong in the category of involuntary physical movement, it can only break out on the back of

certain rationally held ideas; if we can only change the ideas, we will change our propensity to anger.[10]

Seneca, though, admits that ingratitude—the failure to return a benefit—sometimes invokes his anger. Those who know neither how to give or return benefits indulge serious human error. The sage uses reason to evaluate the extent of the benefit, the motives of the donor, and the proper demonstration of gratitude. The intentions and motives of the donor are more important than the gift itself (B 1.1; E 81.3).

Excessive grief is also unnatural and imprudent. Anticipating misfortune often lessens emotional impact when the event occurs. Extended mourning calls into question whether we grieve for the departed or wallow in self-pity. We are cured through reflection on the nature of life and death. We should remind ourselves that the good life is marked by its link with virtue, not by the length it endures. In general, we best confront adversity when we have prepared for it; we are most damaged by misfortunes we neither expect nor understand (CM 1–3).

Often overlooked, but crucial to Seneca's philosophy, is distinguishing the proper measures of freedom and necessity, of the possible and impossible. His Stoicism need not be seen as bland resignation or a call to passivity.

> It is no less unreasonable to accept something as necessary when it isn't as to rebel against something when it is. We can easily go astray by accepting the unnecessary and denying the possible, as by denying the necessary and wishing for the impossible. It is for reason to make the distinction.[11]

The Roman quest for glory challenged Stoic analysis. Cicero had sketched a normative notion of glory: it is a public act, an encomium; it is conferred as a reward for excellence; and that excellence is a heroic act performed for the common good. Most important, glory can be properly bestowed only by aristocrats, who are best able to judge the common good. Popular acclaim—the applause of the masses—is part of genuine glory only when it mirrors the judgment of the aristocrats. Glory brings friendships, political power, and immortality (TD 3.3; 1.110).[12]

As a true Stoic must, Seneca downplayed the role of military and political affairs in earning glory. The toughest, most resolute enemy was a person's own psyche. Genuine Stoic glory was earned by only the sage, the person who could consistently and infallibly distinguish the human good from the pursuits of ordinary men. Earning glory, then, was a result of understanding thoroughly and acting upon the distinction between virtue and merely preferred indifferents. The sage becomes a moral exemplar, which is the highest glory. Those who court mere popularity, who seek praise for its own sake, can hope only for counterfeit glory. Genuine glory is the deserved acclaim that follows from moral virtue, which arises only from the proper disposition of the soul (P 2–4, 6; E 95, 72, 32, 113).

For Seneca, the Stoic sage cannot be harmed and brushes off all aggressive assaults:

There is no upset in a man [a sage] who is free of mistakes, controls himself, and possesses a deep and calm tranquility. For if injury touches a man he is both moved and driven on. But the wise man lacks anger, which is aroused by the appearance of injury and he could not lack anger unless he also lacked injustice—which he knows cannot happen to him. This is the source of his dignity and his light-heartedness; this is why he is elevated with a constant joy . . . he casts aside all injuries and protects himself with endurance and strong-mindedness . . . [the sage] has achieved by long and consistent training the strength to endure and wear down all hostile attacks. (DC 9.2–5)

Wealth

The topic of wealth is sensitive in Seneca. He was one of the wealthiest men of his time. Seneca enjoyed an inheritance, made numerous successful real estate purchases, lent money at profitable interest rates, and at Brittanicus's death received much of his land holdings from Nero.

Seneca's frequent arguments on the irrelevancy of wealth to the good life opened him to strident charges of hypocrisy. He contended that only a moderate amount of wealth should be held; the acquisition of wealth through political connections, usury or extortion in the provinces, crime, or seizing legacies was morally wrong; and using wealth for luxury, fancy furniture, exquisite gardens and the like was unworthy (DC 9.2; E 4.10–11; I 3.33; BV 2.1; B 2.17; E 89.20; VB 23.1; E 76.18; B 1.9; B 3.15).

The best a sympathetic reader can do by way of resolution: Wealth is a preferred indifferent; it is not required for the good life; but the Stoic sage is not required to live in poverty; the critical question is the attitude the sage has to his wealth. Does he recognize wealth as only a preferred indifferent, the loss of which would have no discernible effect on his soul and the quality of his life? Does he understand that wealth does not define human worth? Does he appreciate that wealth often distracts a person from pursuing virtue? Does he acknowledge that today's fortune may be destroyed by tomorrow's fortuity? Could he make the transition from rich man to pauper with equanimity and hope? Does the sage use wealth to amplify his virtue?

The wise man does not think himself unworthy of chance gifts. He does not love wealth, but he prefers it. He admits it not unto his mind, but into his house. He does not reject the wealth that he has, but he knows its limits, and he wishes to make his greater means the servants of his virtue. . . . Can there be any doubt that wealth gives the wise man greater resources for manifesting his character than poverty? The only virtue in poverty is not to be bowed down and prostrated. In wealth the field is open for moderation, generosity, thoughtfulness, and action on a grand scale. (VB 21.4; 22)

Government Service

Seneca was convinced, by his own experiences and history, that the worst physical threats come from powerful political men, not nature. The sage will try not to offend the powerful and capricious. Studying and writing philosophy engenders neither hate nor envy. Some argue that Cato unwisely used Stoicism truculently and enjoyed offending both Caesar and Pompey. The Roman civil war that cost Cato his life was only a personal power struggle between two insatiable glory seekers. Cato was understood to have justified his participation as a way of sharing Rome's travails and of influencing events after victory. Seneca admired the way Cato managed the misfortunes and perils of public life, and viewed him as a great moral example. Cato neither acquiesced to the values and emotions of the followers of tyrants, nor did he compromise with tyranny. He chose, instead, death at his own hand and manner.

> Against the vices of a state in decline and collapsing from its own weight
> [Cato] stood alone. He held up the republic, as far as it could be held back by
> one man's hand alone, until, dragged off, he shared in a collapse that he had
> long held off. . . . Cato did not outlive Liberty, nor did Liberty outlive Cato.
> (DC 2.1–2)

Seneca argues that the moral quality of political regimes never matches the standards of the Stoic sage, but political participation is still worthy: the evils of political life never provide sufficient reason for withdrawal. Only the drive toward knowledge and the demands of the republic itself can provide such justification. Unlike Cato, Seneca was willing to make accommodations with those wielding political power (E 14.12–13; E 104.29–34; E 71.8; DC 1.3; TA 4.8; O 8).

In his *De Clementia (On Mercy)*, Seneca does not analyze different forms of government or conjure an ideal state. He begins and ends with what he knows: the Roman Empire. The political leader holds absolute power and rules as a king, although without that title. The practical alternatives are to enjoy security and popular favor by administering as a merciful king or to labor under the hatred of one's subjects as a pitiless tyrant. The monarchy is indispensable to Rome (C I.4). Unlike Cicero and Cato, Seneca had made his peace with holders of absolute power. Seneca, in true Stoic fashion, is implicitly recognizing that the emperor is reality and citizens should adjust their attitudes appropriately; the monarch, moreover, should rule mercifully and will be rewarded with safety, honors, and public support. The call for mercy, reminiscence of Caesar's policies, strays from the inflexible Stoicism cherished by Cato. The strict morality— "let the skies fall but justice will be done"—championed by doctrinal Stoicism is tempered by Seneca's call for clemency and concern for practical effects (C I.2; I.4; I.8; I.26; I.11; II.5). Seneca consistently celebrated mercy and disparaged cruelty. Excessive punishments, gladiatorial contests, and the slaughter of animals at public games ignited his rebuke (E 7.3; E 90.45).

Seneca's call for mercy strays from the older, inflexible Stoic doctrines favored by Cato: Make no exceptions to the law; affix the maximum penalties prescribed by law; regard indulgence, pity, and equity the unmistakable signs of weakness and emotional vulnerability. On the contrary, Seneca views mercy as rationally and strategically justified; he accepts a range of penalties for legal transgressions and argues that the least severe is often the wisest choice; and mercy is often the best mark of emotional control—abrogating full vengeance for lesser retribution in the face of strong outrage. He stresses several factors that should mitigate punishment: curability, youth, *dignitas*, glory conferred on an Emperor who pardons the treacherous, and the security of the state (C I.1; C I.2; C I.20; C II.7).

Following Plato and a host of classical thinkers, Seneca concludes that slaying a person who is evil beyond redemption is morally justified (I 1.6.3; B 8.20). Seneca, though, took Brutus to task for the assassination of Caesar. He exonerated Brutus from charges of ingratitude—the preservation of his life by Caesar was not a genuine gift because Caesar's power to do so was wrongly acquired. But Brutus should have known that Stoic doctrine celebrates rule by a just king as the best form of government. (Maybe, but Brutus was a follower of the Platonic Academy, not a Stoic. Also, Cato, the "perfect Stoic," surely did not accept that doctrine. Seneca may be foisting a Stoic conviction of his time upon an earlier age. Finally, was Caesar a "just king"?) Moreover, Brutus should have understood that historical forces and popular opinion at that time supported monarchy, not restoration of the republic (Seneca scores heavily here). For Seneca, the change from the classical Roman republic to one person rule was irrevocable once Caesar ascended to power. Peace and security were won at the cost of liberty and the rule of law (B 2.20). The character of the ruler, not the constitutional form and legal limits of the state, was critical. Caesar held absolute power but his exercise of power distinguished good from bad government. The subjects of a good ruler should remain obedient and serene as long as the ruler nurtured their welfare (C I.1, 2; C I.5, 8; C II.2).

> The deified Julius [Caesar] was killed by more friends than enemies, friends whose insatiable hopes he had not satisfied. He wanted to satisfy them (for no one used victory more generously, reserving for himself nothing but the power of giving), but how could he satisfy such excessive desires, when everyone wanted what only one could have? (I 3.30)

At other points, Seneca disparages Caesar for being an ungrateful power-monger whose recurrent clemency was not worth the cost of his choke-hold on political power. He suggests that Sulla's retirement from power after bloodshed was preferable to Caesar's continued reign (BV 16; E 71.9). Although he never changed his assessment of the events of the Ides of March, Seneca was inconsistent in his evaluation of Caesar. He did bemoan the fall of the Roman republic; he preferred the side of the optimates in the civil war; but concluded that the subsequent assassination of Caesar was ill-conceived. In any event, Seneca did not believe that the general level of moral virtue in his age was surpassed by that of the late Roman republic (E 97.8–9).

Seneca condemns foreign policy grounded in war and imperialism. Relying on Stoic doctrine, he rejects militarism as the product of anger, cruelty, greed, and ambition—all emotions that distort reason. To prevail over such mental distortions is a greater victor than military triumph. However, military action in defense of the good and opposed to the wicked is permitted (I 3.5; I 3.6; B 6.30; E 90.26; B 7.3; E 113.28). After victory in such circumstances, the exercise of clemency is pivotal (C II.7). The obedience of conquered peoples must be won through bestowing benefits, not by additional coercion (CP 12.3). He consistently embraced Stoic cosmopolitanism whereby the world community offered wider chances for the exercise of moral virtue than the narrower fatherland.

Seneca discusses the crucial life choice between political service to the Roman state and a life of *otium* (leisure) devoted to philosophical study. He considers numerous political conditions that might impel a statesman to curtail his activities and revert to a life of study: fear of defeat, avoidance of slander, moral revulsion at ambition, avoidance of danger and fear, serving fellow citizens through silent obstinacy, poor health, misfortune, outstanding aptitude for philosophy, and inclination to speak sharply and unsuitably (TA 1.10; 1.12; 3.3; 3.2; 4.3; 4.7; 5.1; 5.2; 5.5; 5.5; 6.2). Traditionally, mainstream Stoicism also held withdrawal from public life was justified in a thoroughly corrupt state (O 3.2). Seneca was not drawn to that justification, but he did argue that citizens are permitted to make an initial choice to abstain from politics under the theory that the correct choice of occupation is required for a tranquil soul.

However, once involved with politics one's removal is more delicate. Seneca insisted, though, that withdrawal should be gradual, conducted in an unprovocative fashion, and under cover of neutral reasons such as ill health or the desire to serve fellow citizens through study and teaching (T 4; O 4–5). Those politicians who retire from politics in a more ostentatious fashion risk being labeled as political dissidents. Seneca relies upon a dual citizenship theory as the ground for his argument that a modest retirement is often worthy: We are citizens of both our homeland and the community of the universe. If public service at Rome is ill-advised, the diligent citizen may still serve the wider human community through study and teaching (O 3.5). The virtuous man if restricted from worthwhile political activity in his own state should remain active on behalf of human beings in general.

> [If] he has lost the duties of a citizen [because he is forbidden to speak or it is dangerous for him to enter the Forum or other reasons]: let him perform [the duties] of a human being. Therefore with a generous spirit we have not shut ourselves inside the walls of one city, but we have sent ourselves to interact with the whole world. We have declared that the universe is our fatherland, so as to give ourselves a broader field for virtue. (TA 4.3–4)

Slavery

Seneca argues compassionately that slaves are as human as their masters. They should be treated considerately and reasonably. Masters should cultivate respect, not fear. All human beings share a common, divine origin and are endowed with reason and the potential to attain virtue. Whereas most classical thinkers, beginning with Aristotle, justified slavery based on their conviction that certain people were slaves by nature—they were biologically decreed to be slaves and nothing else—Seneca highlights the serendipity that often determines who is enslaved (E 47). However, lacking any notion of radical social transformation, Seneca did not seek the abolition of slavery. Kinder treatment of slaves was justified on prudential and moral grounds: a better-treated slave would be more productive and tractable; and better treatment brightens the slavemaster's humanity and is warranted by the slave's participation in common human nature. Seneca accepted the institution of slavery as an inevitable part of his social landscape but sought to ameliorate its evils.

> [Seneca] asks that slaves be regarded as individuals with different moral capacities, as potential friends whose relations with the master are based on love or respect rather than fear, generosity on one side being matched by loyalty on the other. The slave should find in the home, not only a master, but a society with responsibilities, honors, and a sense of community.[13]

In short, slaves should be accorded the humanity, clemency, and generosity that govern other human relationships. As the institution of slavery need not cloud the mind, even though it imprisons the labors of the body, slaves, too, can access the wisdom of Stoic self-discipline (B 3.20). Genuine slavery is not physical, but mental: the voluntary yielding to desire, pleasure, and emotional upheavals.

Slaves detract from their master's self-sufficiency; they constitute a source of wealth that makes their master's devotion to philosophy more difficult; they consume the master's time as he supervises their labors; and they may also rebel and pose a danger to their master (BV 3.2; CH 11.3; CH 12.4; E 17.3). These reasons center on the master's self-interest in pursuing the Stoic ideal way of life. When combined with Sencca's appreciation of the slave's inherent humanity they could lead to the conclusion that the institution of slavery should be abolished. Seneca, though, suggests only that the number of slaves be decreased (TA 8.8–9).

Suicide

That Seneca committed suicide is a half-truth. Had he refused to have complied with Nero's demand to kill himself he would have been executed by the emperor's henchmen. Thus, to call his death a voluntary taking of his own life is misleading. The act was voluntary only within the domain of truncated alternatives.

Mainstream Stoicism held that interminable disease, loss of limbs, relentless pain, and the like were reasonable causes for suicide. Under such circumstances the virtuous person benefited himself, his friends, and his country by taking his own life. Seneca accepts the basic doctrine and cautions against taking one's life from boredom or fear (E 24.22–25). The Stoic mantra, cited by Cato prior to his own suicide, was that only the wise, therefore virtuous, man was free. Death is generally a non-preferred indifferent, not to be feared. But, as Cato exemplified, dying nobly is preferable to living disgracefully (E 70.6). As always, reason determines whether contemplated action is advisable. At times, a virtuous person, such as Cato, celebrates and underscores his freedom by extinguishing his life. That Seneca emphasizes the moral quality of a life, not its duration, should not surprise (E 70.20).

A person's social obligations are a check on suicide contemplated from reasons of severe deprivation of the necessities of life, of intolerable suffering, or incurable disease. At times, though, social obligations—to friends or country—provide a justification for sacrificing one's life. Suicide is also justified if required to avoid being forced to say or do disgraceful things that would destroy one's *dignitas*.[14] One should be willing to die rather than act wrongly.

> One of the Stoic paradoxes pronounced that only the wise man is free, because he alone is in control of his actions. He has the power of [self-determination and autonomy] because he cannot be swayed by his passions or compelled or impeded by threats so as to do anything that is not in accordance with virtue.[15]

Romans were always keenly aware of the importance of role models for moral training. They celebrated and emulated both historical and contemporary exemplars.

> The chief reason for their continuing value is moral success. The trouble with the average human being is that he believes that what he cannot do is impossible for everyone. The exemplary figure—whose function is clearly taken over by the saints of the Church—is living proof that the virtuous life is possible . . . a figure drawn from history is more credible than a myth. . . . Drawn from the past which was common to all Romans the exemplary figure was hallowed by national tradition. Reference to him or her made common ground between the moralist and his audience.[16]

In that vein, Seneca's suicide can be interpreted as a last grasp for glory and immortality. Following the example of Socrates, even to the extent of having a cache of hemlock on hand, Seneca, in true Roman fashion, surpassed his exemplar. Whereas Socrates reportedly dismissed his wife, Xanthippe, prior to discussing philosophical topics such as immortality and the nature of the soul with his cronies, Seneca granted his wife's desire to share his fate. Paulina died with her husband.[17]

As a moral exemplar, Seneca offers mixed tidings. His pursuit of wealth, even if technically reconcilable with Stoic doctrine, was too avid: chasing preferred indifferents, one would suspect, should not occupy a Stoic so significantly. His political compromises, including becoming an apologist for murder, bear no honor. His ambivalences in his relationships to political power raise concerns. However, Seneca's celebration of mercy and generosity reflect a better light. His approaches to his exile and death are admirable. His stance on the treatment of slaves and against barbaric exhibitions highlights his humanity.

Whether he was a "hypocrite" is less important. Few, if any, of us live fully up to our ideals. Seneca was surely imperfect. The more important question is what in his philosophy retains vitality today. How can Seneca's words, if not his example, inspire us now?

A critic would argue that Stoics, such as Seneca, sell the human mind short. For Stoics, human fulfillment—happiness—flows from living in accordance with nature and accepting events as they unfold. By adjusting our attitudes and judgments to extant reality, we adapt to our environment and attain internal harmony. But is this not a strategy of mere coping, a mechanism of making peace with our lot in contrast to improving ourselves and the world we inherit? Are we not merely coming "to grips with forces more powerful than ourselves"[18] instead of pressing our antecedent convictions and desires? For example, Seneca has much inspiring to say about the treatment of slaves, but he refuses to advocate the abolition of the institution even though doing so appears to be the logical conclusion of his musings. No sane person would antecedently choose to be a slave, but once a person finds himself in that position Stoics advise him to readjust his thinking to accommodate his plight. By casting off the antecedent desire for freedom which is now frustrated, the slave presumably can sing in his chains. Such strategy is too much like the one employed by the fox who could not reach the grapes he so deeply desires, but concludes they must have been sour. The fox artfully but disingenuously relinquishes his desire once he understands he cannot fulfill it. Or worse: the strategy recalls the cruelly profane advice rendered by the insensitive to victims of rape: If you cannot prevent it, then relax and enjoy it.

Seneca, though, has a rejoinder. The critic's attack depends on a victim of circumstance changing his or her desires in light of immediate circumstances. Thus, the unsatisfactory external circumstances produce convictions the victims would not otherwise have held. The fox concluded the grapes were sour only because he could not snag them; his antecedent conviction was that he would enjoy eating them immensely. The slave concludes that his condition is acceptable only after it is clear he has no real alternative; his antecedent conviction was that slavery is an abomination. For Seneca, though, a good Stoic would have antecedent beliefs that require no change: Whether one is a slave or not, he is free because his mind cannot be incarcerated; whether a person makes off with grapes or is frustrated in the quest is irrelevant to his or her connection to the human good; whether a person is raped or not should not affect her happiness. All of the matters at stake—physical freedom, consumption of food, sexual dominion—are preferred indifferents only. One's outcomes on such matters are held antecedently by Stoics to be irrelevant to human happiness. A Stoic who comes out on the short end and is victimized never needs to change his or her desires in the light of those circumstances. Let the will of Zeus be done!

This response effectively trumps the criticism that Stoicism is merely a coping mechanism, but restates the problem of preferred indifferents. That all sane people prefer X to not-X suggests that X is more valuable than not-X. Yet, for Stoics, that value, whether gained or lost, is irrelevant to human happiness. Only a very different value, the incommensurate value of the life of Stoic virtue, constitutes human happiness. However, maintaining this distinction in value requires an unconvincing picture of human personality, one that sharply distinguishes between body and mind. Even if Stoics are not committed to metaphysical dualism, the doctrine that the mind and body are distinct entities, they are surely committed to psychological dualism, the doctrine that the mind and body are distinct foci of value, and only value attendant to the mind is relevant to the human good.

Gaius Musonius Rufus: The Roman Socrates

Musonius Rufus (30–100) was as flashy as an Amish farmer on Sunday morning; he was as uncompromising as Ebenezer Scrooge before he turned soft; he was as austere as Cotton Mather on a day of atonement. Compared to Rufus, Cato was a madcap profligate.

If Seneca loosened parts of Stoic doctrine to accommodate changing political reality, Rufus retightened the screws. No one—not now, not ever—accused Rufus of being a hypocrite. A purified version of Stoic doctrine was his life and few, if any, philosophers in the annals of recorded thought lived up to their ideals so thoroughly. That Rufus was called "the Roman Socrates" is no accident.

Like Socrates, Rufus left no philosophical writings. We have his *Discourses*, written by a student named Lucius, who compiled them from notes of Rufus's lectures; and we have *Fragments* compiled from several sources including a student named Pollio, Plutarch, Epictetus, and Aullus Gellius (117–180). Rufus was born to an Italian family of the equestrian order, associated closely with senatorial families, and lived a political life. He was exiled by the imperious Nero; recalled from exile by Servius Sulpicius Galba (3 BC–AD 69), during his short reign as emperor; he was at first exempted from the general ban on philosophers imposed in 71 by the emperor, Titus Flavius Vespasianus ("Vespasian") (9–79), but later exiled at a time when a host of Stoic philosophers were banished for allegedly corrupting the youth with their teachings; and recalled again by Titus Flavius Vespasianus ("Titus") (39–81), during his short reign as emperor. Throughout such times, Rufus was celebrated for his bravery and equanimity when confronting prison, exile, hard labor, and false accusations.

Nero allegedly exiled Rufus because of jealousy of his sterling reputation and fearful that Rufus's teachings might solidify opposition to Nero's eccentric command. Nero relegated Rufus to hard labor and harsh treatment.

Contemporary stories circulated about Nero's cruel treatment of Musonius in prison, where he would have died but for his rugged constitution, and of setting him to hard labor digging the canal across the isthmus at Corinth, which labor he did cheerfully while discoursing with visitors. . . . [Musonius] taught that this was the ideal occupation for a philosopher, and the ideal situation for him to teach philosophy to young people. As for hardship, the place of exile was the worst known to people at the time . . . rocky, desolate, and waterless. . . . Yet, famously, Musonius lived cheerfully in this place.[19]

Rufus was recalled to Rome by Galba after he had risen to power at the death of Nero. Galba, though, was killed in January, 69. After Aulus Vitellius Germanicus ("Vitellius") (15–69) assumed control, civil war broke out. As the forces of Vespasian clashed with the armies of Vitellius, Rufus was part of an envoy sent by Vitellius to negotiate peace. Rufus preached what he practiced. He warned against the dangers of war, extolled peace, and tossed out a few kernels of Stoic wisdom. This, a classic case of a person not tailoring his message to the audience, drew derision from the seasoned militarists. But Rufus was never one to adjust his convictions according to fashion. His policy was simple: Say it the way you know it. In any event, the peace overture failed, Vespasian triumphed and rose to the throne. At first, the new emperor, so impressed by Rufus's moxie, exempted him from the general ban against philosophers.

Musonius Rufus taught a spare, clear brand of Stoicism. His innovation was in the way he applied Stoic doctrine and in how he stripped Stoicism of its inessential concerns. Rufus reaffirmed the four cardinal virtues of courage, justice, wisdom, and prudence. The good life is the same for all of us so we all need proper instruction in the art of discerning and acquiring virtue. Thus, Rufus gains his reputation as an early feminist.

Women as well as men, [Musonius] said, have received from the gods the gift of reason, which we use in our dealings with one another and by which we judge whether a thing is good or bad, right or wrong. Likewise the female has the same senses as the male . . . the same parts of the body . . . a natural inclination toward virtue and the capacity for acquiring it. If this is true, by what reasoning would it ever be appropriate for men to search out and to consider how they may lead good lives, which is exactly the study of philosophy, but inappropriate for women? (D 3)

Females have the same basic natures as men and therefore require the same training in virtue. They must develop the four cardinal virtues and philosophical study is essential to that aim. Women, too, need to lead the good life. In all important respects—those governing the mind and its understanding of virtue, and the constitution of the soul—women are similar to men. Accordingly, Rufus insisted on the moral and legal equality of the two sexes. They should receive the same (stern) punishment for adultery, be allowed to enter the same careers, and pursue the same version of the good life. While he understood that certain tasks, such as military combat, were generally better suited for men because of differences in physical strength, he allowed that no particular task was sex-specific as such. A few women could well qualify as combatants (D 4).

Rufus did assume that most women would remain in the societal roles—wife, housekeeper, domestic care provider—that were prevalent in his day. As an especially hard-line Stoic, he preached contentment with one's position and disdain toward wealth, celebrity, and power. His rendering of sexual morality was strict and lacked nuance. In terms of content, contemporary feminists would find much to dispute in Rufus's teachings. But his framework prefigured basic feminist aspirations: no sex-specific roles as such; no double standards between the sexes in education, morality, or law; no fixed image of what a woman must aspire to except the common goals of virtue and philosophical disposition; and equal training and education based on similar biological make-up. His feminist leaning in these respects is an offshoot of Rufus's relentless and fearless pursuit of the truth. He did not *begin* with the project of elevating the prospects of women; he discovered he must *conclude* in that vein after applying his lean Stoic logic to basic observations about the shared nature of the two sexes.

Rufus pays no heed to the Stoic category of preferred indifferents. His unadorned doctrine speaks only of virtue and vice. Pleasure is not a good. All good things must be desirable; but some pleasures are undesirable; so some pleasures are not good; therefore, pleasure as such cannot be a good (D 1). When pleasure is a good it is only because it dogs virtuous action. Wealth is not a good. One day he gave a decent sum of cash to a beggar who falsely identified himself as a philosopher. When his friends protested that the beggar was a scoundrel who deserved nothing good, Musonius wryly smiled and replied, "Well, then, he deserves money" (F 50). Toil, hardship, and poverty are not evils. We sense a lack only when we expect luxury, which we should shun. Simple living nurtures a virtuous spirit while luxury (Are you listening Seneca?) corrupts (D 1, D 7, D 9, D 18, D 20). No Stoic appreciation for preferred indifferents here: luxury threatens both body and soul; it lures us to weakness, cowardice, intemperance; it inclines us toward extravagance and injustice (D 20). Death is not an evil, it marks only the natural finale of life; it is the natural debt all human beings owe and should be faced courageously and resolutely (D 4, D 17).

For Stoics, every worldly event is fated and determined to occur. Musonius Rufus puts it this way:

> Of such a character the nature of the universe was and is and will be, and it is not possible for things that come into existence to come into existence differently from the way they now do. . . . If a man resolves to focus his thoughts on these things and persuades himself willingly to accept the inevitable, he will lead a life well measured and in harmony with the universe. (F 42)

What is genuinely good is the condition of our character. Do we possess and exemplify the four virtues? Can we distinguish what is truly good from the numerous imposters? If so, exile, hard labor, physical deprivation, and the like cannot harm us. If we sense harm from any of these it is our lack of virtue and discernment that is the evil, not the hardship. Musonius Rufus's hardnosed view recalls Socrates's admonishment that "no evil can befall a good man either living or dead."

In all areas of life—food, clothing, shelter, furnishings, beverages—Musonius Rufus counseled. He disparaged any hint of extravagance, luxury, aesthetic flair, personal style, or experimentation. All such "excesses" encourage the loss of self-control, the weakening of personal resolve, and invite covetousness in others (D 19–D 21). Preferred indifferents? Bah, humbug! Musonius Rufus drew a crisp, bright line: Anything not strictly required for virtue was a threat to virtue. Cozying up to preferred indifferents was a recipe for personal corruption.

In no area of life is Musonius Rufus's austerity so keen as in sexual relations, where his convictions fall just north of those of the Shakers. Sex is morally permissible only within the institution of marriage and only for the purpose of procreation; all birth control is impermissible; pleasure-seeking, even within marriage, is wrongful. That adultery, homosexuality, prostitution, and sexual activity other than marital intercourse are illicit should go without saying. For Rufus, any variance from his sexual prescription betrays a lack of self-restraint sure to further corrupt a person's character (D 12; D 15).

The purpose of the institution of marriage is family life and the procreation of children. Spouses share everything in common and mutual devotion is critical. In choosing a marriage partner, social background, physical beauty, wealth, and the like are irrelevant. The other person, though, should be healthy, appear normal, capable of hard labor, strong enough to bear and rear children, with a soul disposed toward virtue.

> For neither wealth nor beauty nor high birth is effective in promoting partnership of interest or sympathy, nor again are they significant for producing children. But as for the body it is enough for marriage that it be healthy, of normal appearance, and capable of hard work, such as would be less exposed to the snares of temper, better adapted to perform physical labor, and not wanting in strength to beget or to bear children. With respect to character or soul one should expect that it be habituated to self-control and justice, and in a word, naturally disposed to virtue. (D 13B)

Musonius, beyond giving solid advice on selecting potential dates, was an unabashed supporter of marriage. Not only does marriage, contra some Epicureans, not impede the philosophical life, it is crucial as an educative force: marriage teaches us about social duties.

> If you will agree that man's nature most closely resembles the bee which cannot live alone (for it dies when left alone), but bends its energies to the one common task of his fellows and toils and works together with his neighbors; if this is so, and in addition you recognize that for man evil consists in injustice and cruelty and indifference to a neighbor's trouble, while virtue is brotherly love and goodness and justice and beneficence and concern for the welfare of one's neighbor . . . it would be each man's duty to take thought for his own

city, and to make of his home a rampart for its protection. But the first step toward making his home a rampart is marriage. Thus whoever destroys human
marriage destroys the home, the city, and the whole human race. (D 14)

One of Rufus's students posed a conundrum: Was he morally required to obey
his father's demand that he refrain from studying philosophy? The Stoic's answer, characteristically, was clear and firm: Human beings are not required to
obey wrongful imperatives regardless of their relationship to the issuer. To do
wrong or to refrain from doing good are evils. Zeus, the ultimate lawgiver, decrees that human beings pursue what is good; being good is equivalent to being
a philosopher; so the student is justified in disobeying his father. When the
youth protested that his father would punish and incarcerate him should he dis-
obey, Rufus assured him that he need not suffer any evil as a result. The father
could lock up the boy's body, but no one could imprison his mind. Even under
incarceration, the youth could practice philosophy and thereby connect to virtue,
the only good (D 16).

Rufus privileged the practical over the theoretical and the social above the
personal. Whereas Epicureanism was often fashioned as a way of life for the
detached individual striving for personal fulfillment in a hostile world, Rufus's
prescriptions and preferred way of life are connected to the public sphere of
politics. His overarching project is societal reformation. First, a precise rendering of the family and the nature of marriage must be understood and celebrated.
Second, the rearing and education of children must be assiduously attended to.
Third, strict societal understandings about food, dress, and sexual and social
relationships must be advanced. As always, reason and virtue illuminate the
good life (D 12–15, 18).

> Respecting society, the consequence is a "good citizen." For instance, the per-
> son who has learned to live virtuously will forgive injury (D 10); help even the
> one who apparently wronged him (F 39, 41); help his friends and his family (D
> 20); show concern for neighbors and fellow citizens (D 14); give money to
> public and private charity rather than giving it over to his own luxury (D 19);
> benefit society by acting virtuously in his public affairs, functions, offices.[20]

Rufus won unsolicited renown for his role in the prosecution of a pseudo-
philosopher, Publius Egnatius Celer. Quintus Marcius Barea Servilius Soranus
was a senator who had served with distinction as proconsul in Asia. The affection he earned from his subjects raised the hackles of Nero, who had sought a
harsher administration. Soranus was accused of conspiring with Gaius Rubellius
Plautus, who had been executed under Nero's orders, of treasonable plots
against the emperor grounded in obtaining the goodwill of Asian provincials.
Plautus was a friend and associate of Musonius Rufus. He had sought Rufus's
advice when under attack from Nero and Musonius counseled him to accept
death bravely. The key witness against Soranus was one of his pupils, Publius
Egnatius Celer. Celer, in return for significant money, gave perjured testimony
of Soranus's alleged treachery. Soranus was condemned to death in 66, and or-

dered to commit suicide. When recalled from exile by Vespasian, Rufus vigorously and successfully prosecuted Celer. Celer represented himself as a Stoic teacher, but he had betrayed Soranus for the false glitter of wealth. Rufus corrected a public injustice and was roundly cheered.

The greatest moral icons are rarely those who craft the most sophisticated philosophical arguments. Jesus, Buddha, Confucius, Muhammad, Luther, and the like were charismatic reformers who illustrated their messages with stories and myths, and whose lives inspired many. The sacred texts of most religions lack the tightly reasoned deductive arguments favored by contemporary philosophers. Rufus offered spare, accessible arguments for his conclusions. His persuasive power flowed from the simplicity of his message and from the way he lived up to his ideals. Immune to complexity, fully confident in his precepts, always prepared to exemplify his words with his actions, Musonious Rufus never fashioned his message for a particular audience. The thought of compromising his way of life or his austere doctrine to curry favor or to placate power was unfathomable. Truth and virtue are non-negotiable.

> Always consistent himself in facing life with courage, [Rufus] constantly challenged his fellow men to be brave and strong. As a noble example of the good life, Musonius would be an outstanding character in any age; against the background of spiritual poverty and moral decay of his own generation, he appears a truly heroic figure. . . . In his personal relations, he reveals kindliness and warm human sympathy . . . in dealing with wrongdoers he preaches forbearance and forgiveness. He insists that masters respect the essential human rights of their slaves. For women he claims the right to be judged by the same moral standards as men, He is one of the first to advocate contributing to the common good by devoting one's resources to charity. These are details in the larger plan which Musonius keeps ever before his hearers, namely to prepare a social order wherein men may find a "benevolent and civilized way of life."[21]

All actions of the sage are virtuous and equally so. All actions of the non-sage are evil and equally so.[22] We might be tempted to conclude that all the non-sage who aspires to sagacity needs to do is identify a role model, a person who is a sage, and emulate his actions. That, of course, will not work. First, whether anyone has ever existed who is a genuine sage is unclear. Second, even if such a paradigm can be found—perhaps Socrates or my favorite, Musonius Rufus—merely aping his actions is insufficient. The sage is characterized by certain dispositions of the soul that non-sages lack. That two people perform the same external act does not automatically entail that both embody the same internal condition. The soul of the sage and virtue are identical. The soul of the non-sage remains unvirtuous even if he emulates the sage's actions. The non-sage, lacking the proper dispositions of the soul, cannot deliberate on fresh cases nor arrive at decisions independently nor infallibly answer moral conundrums.

> The Sages can be confident that whatever action they decide on will be the virtuous action; they are infallibly virtuous in their actions. But that does not show us, or them, how they can arrive at the specifications of the virtuous action in

this situation. By knowing that the virtuous action is the one that the Sage will perform, we still have not come any closer to putting any content into the Sage's own deliberations.[23]

Musonius may well be the most challenging Stoic. His mix of nontraditionalism such as equal opportunity for women; his utter disdain for preferred indifferents—at times one wonders whether he would genuinely prefer hardships to satisfactions as hardships are a better test of Stoic mettle; and his uncompromising regimens for sex, food, clothing, and personal appearance make him the closest approximation to the Stoic sage in the history of Roman philosophy. He was a physically hard, mentally tough, relentlessly disciplined man who lived in only a black-and-white world. While his views are subject to the criticisms lodged against virtually all Stoics, to subject a hero, martyr, or saint to mundane philosophical dissection seems presumptuous. That Nature broke the mold when it spawned Musonius Rufus is false; no mold could have structured such a man.

Epictetus: Up from Slavery

Epictetus (55–135) was born a slave in Hierapolis, Phrygia (modern day Turkey) and came to be owned by Epaphroditus, a freedman and member of Nero's court probably in charge of fielding petitions. Reportedly because of his master's cruel treatment, Epictetus was lame. Epaphroditus was later executed by the emperor Titus Flavius Domitianus ("Domitian") (51–96), brother of Titus and son of Vespasian, presumably for his role in aiding Nero's suicide. While still a slave, Epictetus studied with Musonius Rufus in Rome. He eventually was granted his freedom and taught Stoicism in Rome until around 95 when Domitian exiled numerous philosophers. Epictetus moved to Nicopolis in northwestern Greece, where he lived most of the rest of his life.

Sources differ as to whether the writings of Epictetus were well known and widely distributed, or Epictetus, following the example of Musonius Rufus, did not jot down his views.[24] For Epictetus, Stoicism is the art of living well. The success of philosophy students is judged not by whether they can glibly parse Stoic texts, but on how effectively they transform their souls in accord with philosophical principles. We are all responsible for caring for our own souls. Lectures, writings, and counsel are only instruments for salutary living. The Stoics marginalized the written word in deference to practical action. While this stance underscored the practicality of their mission, it may also help explain why numerous early Stoic texts disappeared and why Stoicism as a movement evaporated quickly once Christianity gathered strength.[25]

Stoics accept that the study of philosophical doctrine is the first step toward healthy personal transformation. But Epictetus, following Musonius Rufus, insisted that spiritual exercises were required to inculcate proper habits and responses. To act immediately and consistently to events with Stoic understanding is crucial. Writing out Stoic principles, daily reflection on and evaluation of our actual responses to the events of the past day, and a regimen of meditation are examples of spiritual exercises that cultivate good habits. To merely accept Stoic doctrines cognitively is not enough. We must, by training, nurture proper actions. Knowledge, for Epictetus, requires both mastery of philosophical doctrine and spiritual exercises. After all, Stoicism celebrates practical wisdom, not merely theoretical insight.[26]

In any event, if Epictetus did write, none of his compositions survive. Much, though, is known of his teachings from the notes published by his student, Lucius Flavius Arrianus ("Arrian") (86–146). Epictetus captured the gist of Stoicism in precise, crisp adages. First, he sketches the critical distinction between those things totally within our control and all else:

> Some things are under our control, while others are not under our control. Under our control are conception, choice, desire, aversion, and in a word, everything that is our own doing; not under our control are our body, our property, reputation, office and, in a word, everything that is not our own doing. Furthermore, the things under our control are by nature free, unhindered, and unimpeded; while the things not under our control are weak, servile, subject to hindrance, and not our own . . . if it has to do with some one of the things not under your control, have ready to hand the answer, "It is nothing to me." (EN 1)

Next, he reflects ancient wisdom regarding human will, body, and proper attitude. For Epictetus freedom and slavery were literal experiences and also metaphors for the approaches people took to everyday events:

> Do not ask that events should happen as you wish; but wish them to happen as they do, and you will go on well. . . . Sickness is an impediment to the body, but not to the will unless the will consents. Lameness is an impediment to the leg, but not to the will. . . . If someone handed your body over to a passerby, you would be annoyed. Are you not ashamed that you hand over your mind to anyone around, for it to be upset and confused if the person insults you? (EN 8, 9, 28)

For Epictetus, what falls outside our own will falls within the divine plan. Human well-being depends only on virtuous character. All desires and emotions outside our full control are unnatural. Because the cosmos is governed by rational, benevolent, divine forces, everything happens for the best even though particular events will elude human understanding. Both outwardly favorable and seemingly adverse situations will test our resolve. Freedom, for Epictetus, is less a political status and more a state of mind. Even as a slave, he was free in that his mind and will were not limited by external events or contaminated by emotional reactions. We often enslave ourselves willingly by ceding our independence and permitting emotions to overwhelm our better judgment. Our emotions are not merely instinctive reactions; they can be controlled because they depend on judgments. We decide that something is worthy to pursue, an appropriate response to a situation, or a desirable course of action. If we change those judgments, we transform our emotional responses. Human beings do not experience the world in pure, unexpurgated form. Our attitudes and judgments filter our experiences and mold our responses. Because our judgments and attitudes are fully within our control, so too, are our emotions. By adjusting our antecedent mindset, we alter the filter through which we experience the world. By acknowledging our freedom, Epictetus underscores our responsibility for emotions.

Our identities are fundamentally our wills from which our freedom flows. Too often, we are unwitting collaborators in our own imprisonment. We fall sway to the dominant ideas; hold ourselves hostage to acquiring power, wealth, and honors; and depend too heavily upon the countless externalities outside our control. Most strikingly, we fail to appreciate the cornerstone of Epictetus's Stoicism: Everything outside the individual will—beyond a person's judgments and attitudes—is external to human freedom and happiness. Even such apparent goods as family, country, health, and congenial relationships are inessential for Epictetus's good life. Worse, desire and attachment to such externalities court frustration, disappointment, and even corruption. Only the perfected will and the virtue that emerges from it are crucial to human happiness. Respect of others, the proper discharge of one's social roles, and basic decency all flow from the perfected will.

Throughout the quest for the good life, the proper Stoic should not lose heart because of modest talents. Human excellence is more a function of maximizing one's gifts than attaining the ideal of the sage:

> Well, do all horses become fast? Are all dogs hunters? What then—if I lack talent, should I for that reason give up the effort? By no means. Epictetus will not be better than Socrates. But if I am no worse, that is enough for me. . . . We do not abandon any discipline out of despair of becoming the best. (DS 1.2.34–37)

Equanimity is more valuable than material possessions and the yearning to obtain them. Those who lack the desire for wealth, power, and beautiful women are superior to those who actually possess such externalities. The absence of the need for wealth, power, and beautiful women is superior to and more valuable than the actual possessions of wealth, power, and beautiful women (DS 4.9.1–5). The longing for such externalities increases the likelihood of jealously, fear of loss, evil thoughts, and wrongful actions: "Such things, taken by themselves, are quite neutral in value. [Epictetus's] point is that when *having* them is combined with *longing* for them, the outcome is tantamount to an incurable fever."[27] All human desires and emotions are true or false value judgments: "It is not things that disturb people but their judgments about things" (EN ·5). By restricting our focus to only those things fully under our control, by recognizing that they are the only authentically good and evil things, we scurry toward the path leading to the good life.

> For one person it is reasonable to hold a chamber-pot, since he only considers that, if he does not, he will be beaten and deprived of food, whereas if he does hold it, nothing harsh or painful will happen to him. . . . I will tell you that get-

ting food is preferable to being deprived of it, and being whipped is worse than not being whipped. So that if you compare your interests by these criteria, then go ahead and hold the pot. "But it would not be worthy of me." That is an additional consideration which you alone bring to the question, not me. You are the one who knows yourself, how much you are worth in your own eyes, and at what price you sell yourself. (DS 1.2.8–11)

Epictetus makes no appeal to a final judgment day or personal immortality. The punishment for those who ignore Stoic wisdom befalls them in this world: they remain "just as they are—dissatisfied, desolate, and imprisoned" (DS 1.12.21–22). For Epictetus, "fulfillment as a human being comes in an embodied state or not at all."[28] Epictetus accepts the general Stoic teaching that suicide is appropriate as a rational exit from extreme circumstances, but he cautions that suicide is inappropriate as an escape from adverse circumstances such as political tyranny or slavery: "But for now be content to remain in the place where [god] has stationed you. Short indeed is the time of your sojourn, and easy for those of your convictions. For what tyrant, thief, or court of law can daunt those who make so little of the body and its possessions? Stay, do not depart on unreasonable grounds" (DS 1.9.16–17).

> Zeus is not omnipotent. . . . He wishes nothing but good for human beings, and that is demonstrated by his giving them the potentiality to share his own rational excellences. . . . Zeus's virtue is manifested in his doing the best he reasonably can with the materials at his disposal, and doing so with the best of intentions. . . . Just as [Zeus] has done the best he can with the materials at his disposal, so individual persons can be invited to take this divine model as an authority and guide for their own lives.[29]

Epictetus, following traditional Stoic doctrine, held that human beings act from rational self-interest and from an instinct for self-preservation. He has, implicitly, a descriptive and a normative rendering of this notion. Descriptively, human beings will in fact act in ways they take to preserve their life and advance their interests. Normatively, what is critical is acting to advance one's interests and to preserve oneself as a rational being. For example, suppose a tyrant threatens to murder me if I do not carry out his morally evil order. The instinct to preserve my life as such inclines me to do his bidding. But my fulfillment as a human being, as an essentially rational entity whose good is connected to the condition of his soul, militates that I refuse to carry out the tyrant's decree. Instead of preserving my biological life as such and becoming the tyrant's instrument of evil, I am better served by preserving the integrity of my soul and forfeiting my biological life (DS 1.2; 4.1.165). Thus, my rational self-interest in the instant case is to relinquish my life, if necessary, to preserve my genuine well-being. The Stoic's understanding of the true human good must inform his notion of self-preservation and advancing his interests. An extension of this normative notion informs the Stoic's doctrine of rational suicide. At times, a person's good as a rational being is best served by his death, even at his own hand. Our merely biological life, then, is a preferred indifferent. The only authentic good is moral virtue which advances our interests as rational beings.

Human freedom is conditioned on our willingness to accept our predestined share of fate. Our futures are neither entirely open nor free from antecedent causes. Our freedom is centered on liberating ourselves from errors stemming from misuse of reason and misguided passion. Although freedom of this sort is available to everyone, its attainment is not automatic. The discipline, training, and cultivated habits required to practice Stoic philosophy constitute an arduous project.[30] The existence of apparent natural evils such as plagues, earthquakes, hurricanes, provide human beings opportunities to test and to display virtue.

> Surrendering oneself to Zeus is not a recipe for resignation or passivity. It is a metaphor for a mentality that makes the best of actual eventualities as distinct from wishing for things to be different from how they are independently of ourselves, wasting mental energy on frustration and disappointment.[31]

Epictetus accepted the Stoic notion of a unified soul with diverse functions. Evildoing stems from poor judgments about good and evil; perpetrators of evil should not be hated as their mischief flows from misguided attachment to preferred indifferents (DS 1.18.1–10).

In sum, external events of themselves are neither inherently good nor bad. Our attitudes and judgments about those events, though, are good or bad depending on whether they exercise reason well or poorly. If we judge that an external event is bad—when it is in fact indifferent to our flourishing—then the judgment, not the event, is bad. If we judge that an external event is irrelevant—when it is in fact irrelevant to our flourishing—then the judgment is good. Zeus has done the best he can for everyone given the structures available to him. Human beings are limited in their direct power to affect external events; we are responsible only for consequences flowing from our own judgments, attitudes, choices, and actions. What is outside our control need not and should not adversely influence our values or well-being.

A charitable reading of Epictetus concludes that he did not advocate the elimination of all emotions, but only those irrational passions that lead to unnecessary internal turmoil. Thus, lust, anger, jealousy, envy, anxiety, yearning for externalities, and the like are proscribed. But cheerfulness, sociability, respectfulness, kindness, and caring are permitted at least to the extent that these "good feelings" connect Stoic values to correct judgments. The objects of good feelings are moral excellence. Irrational passions, by contrast, are grounded in irrationality—valuing externalities that are merely preferred indifferents, pursuing goals not fully under the individual's control, trying to alter a past that is already set in the historical record.[32] The job of reason is to "affirm the true, reject the false, and suspend judgment about what is unclear" (DS 1.7.5).

Unlike Rufus who apparently dismissed preferred indifferents, Epictetus retains the common sense of Stoic doctrine that human beings quite naturally prefer health to disease, wealth to poverty, grand reputation to public humiliation, honor to social shame, and the like. In so doing, Epictetus rekindles the objection about how things that are naturally preferred remain indifferent to human well-being. Why are such externalities preferred? Do human beings have a natural inclination toward their own debasement (from the vantage point of Stoicism)? Moreover, the use of "natural" reenergizes the objection that Stoics vacillate between two usages of that term: (a) a biological sense—what is typical and statistically normal for human beings given their makeup, and (b) a normative sense—what facilitates the proper human *telos*. Human beings naturally prefer certain externalities in the biological sense, but doing so is not natural in the normative sense. Accordingly, the Stoic life is not natural to human beings in the biological sense. We must work hard to attain it and doing so is crucial to achieving what is natural in the normative sense, our own well-being. Although we start out by pursuing preferred indifferents naturally (in the biological sense), we also have the natural capability (in the biological sense) to achieve—through discipline, hard work, and cultivating the right habits—what is natural in the normative sense: valuing only that which is under the full control of our minds.

Epictetus's view of happiness follows the ancient Greek idea of human flourishing as an objective condition of the human soul or mind. Regardless of a person's subjective assessment of her happiness, she is happy if and only if her internal condition is harmonious and morally righteous. Just as a person's physical well-being is an objective condition of her health, her happiness is an objective condition determined by her degree of compliance with Stoic moral doctrine. The union of morality and happiness, though, incurs a cost: a person could be sad—could lack a sense of gratification, joy, exuberance, and emotional upbeatness—yet be declared "happy" under Stoic doctrine. In contrast, our contemporary understanding of happiness rests on our achieving a level of subjective satisfaction; indeed, a predominately positive state of mind defines "happiness." If such a state of mind can be attained by a less than moral life then the contemporary notion of happiness, unlike the Stoic conception, does not require high moral rectitude. Most strikingly, for Epictetus high moral rectitude is sufficient for human happiness.

With the typical Stoic affinity for bright line distinctions, Epictetus aspires to make human beings invulnerable. We can guarantee our happiness by eliminating desires and focusing only on our own judgments and attitudes. We are thereby immune from disappointments, frustrations, and anxiety. We are the complete masters of our destiny, at least insofar as we accept the prior crafting of our fate by Zeus. We will be happy, in the Stoic sense, even if tortured. We are rocks, islands; we feel no pain; we do not cry. But rising above most of our biologically natural longings we can achieve our normatively natural end. Our natural (in the normative sense) end is not hostage to our subjective determination, but is fixed by the kind of rationality that defines our identities. Somehow the biological and normative senses of "natural" reunite.

But the doctrine that only states of mind are good or bad leads to a too easy acceptance of social, political, and economic inequalities and wrongs. Dismissing matters in these domains as merely preferred indifferents trivializes human misery caused by poverty and defers too facilely to physical deprivations generated by tyrannies. The notion that human beings can be happy—in the sense of being fulfilled by attaining their human *telos*—while being tortured reduces Epictetus's doctrine to absurdity. Only if we are being tortured for a higher cause that defines our life's mission—witness the martyr, hero, or saint—can such a view be plausible. Does complying with Stoic doctrine itself constitute such a project? Is a project that teaches us to place value only on our internal states of mind sufficiently noble to fit that bill?

Epictetus's oscillation between biological and normative senses of "natural" remains problematic. Either we are naturally schizophrenic—because part of our biological nature, our capability of achieving the Stoic human *telos*, requires us to overcome the rest of our biological nature—or what is biologically natural and what is normatively natural are at odds from the start. The only apparent solution is to recall Musonius Rufus and reject preferred indifferents straightaway; but the cost is an excursion away from common sense. Surely, that human beings naturally prefer certain externalities to their opposites is clear.

Moreover, Epictetus's view of preferred indifferents calls into question our settled convictions about charitable deeds. Stoicism can be unappealingly insular and egoistic. For example, Epictetus when advising a person who was concerned about his slave's virtue, sputtered: "It is better for your servant to become vicious than for you to become unhappy" (E 12). After all, the virtue of other people may well be, at most, a preferred indifferent. Whether others are vicious or not should not affect my well-being. As for charitable contributions, consequences are unclear. On one hand, I might be generous with my material possessions because I view them as indifferents. On the other hand, I might see charitable contributions as irrelevant and possibly a hindrance to the genuine good of the disenfranchised. Perhaps recognizing health, food, and clothing as preferred indifferents would tip the scale in favor of donating to those in material need. Oddly, my willingness to donate or not to donate is motivated by my Stoic conviction that the money or things I donate are not genuine goods. So in either case the phenomenon of charitable contributions is radically altered from contemporary understandings.

We typically consider feeding the hungry, clothing the poor, providing shelter for the homeless, and the like, paradigm cases of morally praiseworthy actions. Indeed, such actions are extolled in the sacred texts of religions and endorsed equally by secular humanists. However, under Epictetus's philosophy, philanthropists have performed no significant service for the downtrodden. Donors have only satisfied the yearning for preferred indifferents, while providing no automatic benefit for the goodness of the souls of disenfranchised people. Would it have been better to have slipped starving people a treatise on Stoicism so they might learn that their well-being lies not in food but in proper judgment? Perhaps a Stoic lecture on why the content of their character, not a satisfied belly or a clothed body, is the key to happiness? If time was a factor, maybe a few kernels of Stoic wisdom: No harm can befall a starving, destitute, impoverished person unless he is an unwitting collaborator; the only evil is in misjudgments, not in physical deprivations; the yearning for preferred indifferents, including food, clothing, and shelter, is the root of all evil; difficult circumstances should be viewed as a test of character; the more one has, the more one has to lose; if a circumstance is genuinely unbearable, suicide is always a wise option? Indeed, perhaps our imaginary philanthropists, by providing the basic necessities of survival, have reinforced the yearning of the destitute for preferred indifferents and unwittingly added to their long-term misery. Would it have been better to console them by reading Stoic chapter and verse on the true sources of good and evil as they starved to death?

For Epictetus it is natural, in both the biological and normative senses, to cultivate gods and fellow human beings and receive benefits in return. We need not sacrifice our interests for the common good because contributing to the common good advances our own interests. Our concern for others grows out of our concern for self.[33]

> This is the nature of the animal: he does everything for his own sake and so, for that matter, does Zeus. . . . Zeus has so constituted the nature of the rational animal that he can attain none of his proper goods without contributing to the common interest. And so it is no longer anti-social to do everything for one's own sake. (DS 1.19.11–14)

Epictetus's position vacillates between his insistence that moral virtue is the only good and its attainment depends solely on the will of individuals (DS 1.22.13–16; DS 4.12.7–8) and his concession that "there are things of value that others can give and take away, the 'primary things in accordance with nature.'"[34] Only a Stoic zealot such as Musonius Rufus could maintain the utterly consistent position that preferred indifferents were thoroughly illusory goods. Such consistency, though, rendered that part of Rufus's philosophy fecklessly unpersuasive. Other Stoics, such as Epictetus, had to be satisfied with an element of waffling in their views on human goods.

Marcus Aurelius Antonius Augustus: The Warrior Philosopher

Marcus Aurelius (121–180) embodied the ideal of the philosopher-king. He reigned as Roman emperor from 161 until his death. Although not a stunningly original thinker, Marcus exemplified and refined Stoicism. As a ruler, Marcus Aurelius was moderate, just, and effective during troubled times. The fabled *Pax Romana* was breaking down. Marcus struggled with internal discord—aggravated by natural disasters such as famines and plagues—and external threats from Germanic tribes in the north and Parthians in the east. But Marcus persevered and improved social conditions for the disadvantaged, slaves, and criminals. He also fiercely persecuted Christians, particularly in Gaul, because he viewed them as superstitious immoralists whose values jeopardized the principles underlying Roman greatness.

Marcus was of noble birth. He served as a quaestor in 139, and as a consul in 140 and 145. The family life of Marcus Aurelius was troubled. His wife, Faustina, was rumored to be an instigator of a conspiracy against Marcus, while his son, Lucius Aurelius Commodus Antoninus ("Commodus") (161–192)—who was widely thought to be the product of Faustina's adulterous affair with a gladiator—was anxiously eyeing the throne. One school of thought is that Marcus was poisoned by a medical doctor in the employ of Commodus. Once Commodus assumed power at Marcus's death, his reign exhibited excesses of corruption, sadism, cruelty, and debauchery similar to those that devoured the terms of Nero and Caligula.

In *The Decline and Fall of the Roman Empire*, Historian Edward Gibbon described Marcus Aurelius's life:

> His life was the noblest commentary on the precepts of Zeno [founder of Stoicism]. He was severe to himself, indulgent to the imperfections of others, just and beneficent to all mankind. He regretted that Avidius Cassius, who excited a rebellion in Syria, had disappointed him, by a voluntary death, of the pleasure of converting an enemy into a friend; and he justified the sincerity of that sentiment, by moderating the zeal of the senate against the adherents of the traitor. War he detested . . . but when the necessity of a just defense called upon him to take up arms, he readily exposed his person to eight winter campaigns on the frozen banks of the Danube, the severity of which was at last fatal to the weakness of his constitution. His memory was revered by a grateful posterity, and above a century after his death, many persons preserved the image of Marcus, among those of their household gods.[35]

Romans were generally tolerant of foreign deities and religious practices. But Christianity, as viewed by Marcus Aurelius and many others, was founded on passiveness and, at most, muted allegiance to the state. These values were unsuited to the continued vitality of the Roman Empire. Conventional Roman wisdom insisted that veneration of the state was required of all good citizens. Christianity, influenced strongly by Platonism, adamantly contended that this world is a pale imitation of a higher reality. Where, as here, foreign religious practices were inconsistent with the values of Roman greatness, tolerance was misplaced. Accordingly, Gibbon's commentary to the contrary notwithstanding—Marcus Aurelius was "beneficent to all mankind"—the emperor expressed no qualms about his persecution of Christians.

Marcus Aurelius composed his *Meditations* during the time he was repelling an insurrection in the Danube. The work consists of reflections, aphorisms, and principles by which good people should live their lives. A historically influential text, probably originally intended only for his own eyes, the *Meditations* crystallize Marcus's refinement of the Stoic tradition. At the crux of Stoicism are commitments to inner harmony, and single-minded pursuit of virtue.

If we take this position firmly, expecting nothing and avoiding nothing, but instead remaining content simply that we have conducted ourselves in accordance with what we know to be right, and with truthfulness with our fellow man, then this is the path to a happy life, and there is no man or god who can prevent us from following it. (M 3.12)

Living in accord with nature requires living harmoniously with one's essence as a rational being, with nature as a whole, and living unimpeded by internal emotional turmoil. Part of the program is viewing events from a cosmic perspective, the vantage point of nature as a whole, not merely from a personal perspective. Shifting perspectives will change our focus from judging events in relation to us to seeing them from a perspective that underscores their status as indifferents. Judged from a cosmic vantage point, our everyday concerns shrink to the infinitesimal. Marcus Aurelius states it this way:

You have the power to strip off many superfluities which trouble you and are wholly in your own judgment; and you will make a large room at once for yourself by embracing in your thought the whole Universe, grasping ever-continuing Time and pondering the rapid change in the parts of each object, how brief the interval from birth to dissolution, and the time before birth a yawning gulf even as the period after dissolution equally boundless. (M 9.32)

Part of the greatness of Marcus Aurelius is that he sensed weaknesses in Stoic doctrine and tried to refine it. For example, he understood well the Stoic conviction that if one chooses not to value anything in life—other than the agency one has over his or her own judgments and attitudes—then one cannot lose anything of value. But Marcus concluded this conviction signals a retreat, even a withdrawal, from the world. He anticipated, then, a modern criticism of Stoic rectitude. For Marcus Aurelius, worldly engagement entailed that we must risk disappointment in the results of our projects and sorrow at the loss of those people whom we cherished.

He also adjusted Epictetus's division of phenomena into things fully under our control and everything else. Instead of siding with the inflexible Stoic orthodoxy that a person's will is sufficient for making morally correct choices, Marcus Aurelius concluded that the will must be helped by things not under its control. In such matters, human will "needs the help of the gods and fortune" (M 1.17). Marcus, then, ends up with three categories of phenomena: those fully under the control of a person's will, those outside the control of human will, and those partially under and partially outside the control of human will. In this third category Marcus placed matters where his will to control his emotions was aided by something not under his control. His impulse to study philosophy, his sexual restraint, his ability to be generous to those in need, his chance to live according to nature unhindered, and his opportunity to live simply yet not tarnish the gravitas of the office of emperor were some of the matters Marcus placed in the third category (M 1.17).

We might be tempted to tweak Stoic doctrine under Marcus Aurelius's advisement. Perhaps we should be concerned with something *to the extent* it is under our control. We should attend to events in proportion to how much control we have over them. Still, the doctrine is unsatisfying. A single person has little control over world peace, repercussions from natural disasters, and the prevention of major wars, yet such events are reasonable foci of our attention. Maybe we need to add a dimension: We should be concerned with something to the extent it is under our control and in proportion to its effects on the common good. This addition to Stoic doctrine would allow us to attend to major world and national events even though individuals have meager control over them. But Marcus Aurelius would still think the doctrine is insufficient. He would be correct. For example, sometimes we should invest significant emotion in events over which we have no control and which do not seriously harm the common good. The loss of people whom we cherished and the destruction of our dearest projects are two such cases. Even if those losses do not measurably detract from the common good and even if we have no control over them, sorrow is appropriate. Marcus Aurelius intuited that suffering, contrary to orthodox Stoicism, is not an evil as such. Our struggles with suffering are a crucial part of creating worthy selves.

Marcus's notion of manliness strays from the traditional Roman celebration of military and political *virtù*. Instead, he lionizes basic Stoic practices: to bear suffering and be satisfied with little; to work with one's own hands; to avoid meddling in the affairs of others; to shut one's ears to slander; to remain unruffled and thus unharmed; to fulfill social duties courageously; to overcome the weakness of irascibility; and to enjoy the ascetic life (M 1.3; 1.5; 2.5; 5.18). Although Marcus conceded that anger was less vicious than lust, he followed Stoic tradition in refusing to believe that anger could be funneled into useful purposes:

> One who loses his temper is turning away from Reason with a kind of pain and inward spasm; whereas he who offends through appetite [lust] is a victim of pleasure and is clearly more vicious in a way and more effeminate in his wrong-doing . . . an offense attended with pleasure involves greater censure than one attended with pain. (M 2.10)

Marcus denigrates the pursuit of reputation and fame because such preferred indifferents depend on the shaky judgments of people of dubious principles: "He who has a powerful desire for posthumous fame does not consider that every one of those who remember him will himself die soon; then again also they who have succeeded them, until the whole remembrance shall have been extinguished as it is transmitted through men who foolishly admire and then perish" (M 4.19). We are better served by recognizing that whatever occurs comes to be with justice: we should not decry our fate, blame the gods, or wish for things to be other than they are (M 4.10).

> The Stoics had a special reason not to seek the realization of justice in the world, for they were persuaded that it exists already; the cosmic reality is a reality with a moral essence which contains within itself perfect wisdom and per-

fect happiness. Reason told Marcus that the world was good beyond improvement, and yet it constantly appeared to him evil beyond remedy.[36]

Like many Stoics, Marcus oscillates between viewing the world as pre-destined,
fixed, necessary, and untransgressable—in which case the possibilities of voluntary moral choices and special divine providences are problematic—and picturing the world as subject to divine intervention. Add to this difficulty the theme
of this as the best of all possible worlds that the gods might have constructed
given the materials at hand (M 10.7). One is left to scratch his head and wonder
at the limited powers of divinity and the shoddy building fabric inherent in the
cosmos: "[Marcus] tends to speak in vaguely generalized terms of 'the gods' or
'Nature' or 'the Universe': the terms are virtually synonymous. There is little
sign that he thought of the traditional Olympian deities as individual entities
with the personalities they possess in myth and poetry."[37]

The possibility of cosmic meaninglessness, the lack of any inherent order
and purpose in our world, repelled Marcus Aurelius. He prefigured the existential tension of the twentieth century: Human beings have a compelling need to
understand reality in meaningful and purposive ways, but the cosmos seems
indifferent to our yearnings. Marcus responds through faith—belief, conviction,
and action in the face of radical uncertainty. Again adjusting Stoic orthodoxy
and refusing to accept cosmic meaninglessness because doing so devalued human intellect and reason, he places his faith in a type of pantheism. The divine is
the universe and all things, including human beings.

> All things are implicated with one another, and the bond is holy; and there is
> hardly anything unconnected with any other things. For things have been coor-
> dinated, and they combine to make up the same universe. For there is one uni-
> verse made up of all things, and one god who pervades all things, and one sub-
> stance, and one law, and one reason. (M 7.9)

The eternal journey of the divine is assumed to be worthy and grand, although
ineffable. Anticipating Hegel,[38] Marcus Aurelius locates the meaning of human
life in its role in advancing the divine goal. The divine, for Marcus, is not an
independent being or substance, but rather the process of glorious cosmic evolution toward more valuable ends.

> Constantly regard the universe as one living being, having one substance and
> one soul; and observe how all things have reference to one perception, the per-
> ception of this one living being; and how all things act with one movement; and
> how all things are the cooperating causes of all things which exist; observe too
> the continuous spinning of the thread and the contexture of the web. (M 4.40)

As a faith, Marcus Aurelius understood that his world view could not be independently and rationally proved. His faith, though, spawned a practical advantage: it vivified engagement with the world and nourished healthy human relations. A worthwhile human life must be purposive. The highest human purpose

is contribution to society. The most valuable human skills are scarce and make the greatest positive impact on the common good.

Marcus Aurelius, unsurprisingly, advised us to accept our mortality and view death as transmutation and not as an end. Part of our gratitude for our lives required that we perceive our deaths as necessary for the cosmic cycle. He does not champion personal immortality. Instead, our souls persist after death only to reenter the cosmos and the flow of nature.

> You have existed as a part. You shall disappear in that which produced you; or rather, you shall be received back into its seminal principle by transmutation. . . Pass then through this little space of time conformably to nature, and end your journey in content, just as an olive falls off when ripe, blessing nature who produced it, and thanking the tree on which it grew. . . . . Every part of me will be reduced by change into some part of the universe, and that again will change into another part of the universe, and so on for ever. And by consequence of such a change I too exist, and those who begot me, and so on forever in the other direction. (M 4.14; 4.48; 5.13)

Throughout his work, Marcus, reminiscent of Pythagoreans and Platonists, disparages the body, calling it a "corpse," "clay and gore," "corruption, blood, and dust" and "lifeless" (M 3.3; 4.41; 8.37; 10.33). Death releases the soul from the body and points it to its cosmic destination. He was convinced that regardless of whether we live short lives or long lives, our loss upon death is equal. Marcus Aurelius reasoned that a person cannot lose more than he or she possessed—a person must first possess something for that something to be taken away. We do not possess our future for it is yet to come and we cannot possess it until it becomes present. We do not possess our past for it is mere recollection. Although we may glean honor or dishonor from the past, we do not possess it. At any span of life, then, people possess only the present. Thus, whether we live long or short lives, we lose only the present.

> Mortal man, you have been a citizen in this great City; what does it matter to you whether for five or fifty years? For what is according to its laws is equal for every man. Why is it hard, then, if Nature who brought you in, and no despot or unjust judge, sends you out of the City—as though the master of the show, who engaged an actor, were to dismiss him from the stage? "But I have not spoken my five acts, only three." What you say is true, but in life three acts are the whole play. For He determines the perfect whole, the cause yesterday of your composition, today of your dissolution; you are the cause of neither. Leave the stage, therefore, and be reconciled, for He also who lets his servant depart is reconciled. (M 12.36)

Within this suspicious argument lay a few kernels of wisdom. We should not assume an entitlement to the future. As the cliché reminds us, tomorrow is not promised to anyone. Also, we should not hold onto the past in self-defeating ways. Savoring the past should not prevent us from engaging in the present.

On the whole, though, the argument is stunningly unpersuasive. Even if we agree that all deaths involve "only" the loss of the "present" it hardly follows that losses upon death are equal. Not all "presents" are equally valuable under Marcus Aurelius's own criteria because not all lives are equally worthwhile and purposive. Those lives that greatly energize the common good through virtuous use of scarce, positive human skills are more worthwhile than lives that do not. Even if we agree that the death of two people who exemplify those two sorts of lives involve only the loss of their respective "presents" it does not follow that the losses are equal. One loss is of a "present" that, on Marcus's own criteria, vibrates with worth and meaning, while the other loss is of a "present" that does not.

Moreover, although the future is never guaranteed, probabilities come into play. If I am twenty years old, in good health, and reasonably prudent my life expectancy—the probability of my future—is greater than if I am eighty years old, suffering from numerous diseases, and reckless to boot. To die under such circumstances at twenty is, other things being equal, a greater loss than to die at eighty.

Much the same can be said about the respective quality of different "presents" independently of their contribution to the common good. The "presents" of two lives can vary dramatically in terms of suffering and enjoyment even if their contributions to the common good are equal. Thus, the respective losses upon death may well not be equal.

Marcus Aurelius's view of the past is also incomplete. While it is true that obsessing about the past can often hinder engagement in the present, it is equally true that reflecting on the past can facilitate successful engagement in the present. The past is not irrelevant to us. Our past choices, actions, and relationships help form the people we are becoming. We do, in a sense, possess the past, or it possesses us.

His reflections on the passage of time and temporality were generally interesting but unpersuasive. For example, Marcus Aurelius rejected a common view during his time that attaining enduring fame is a worthy goal for the good life. He argued that to pursue the adulteration of future generations was just as irrational as resenting that our forebearers do not lavish honor upon us. This position is probably consistent with his focus on the "present" and it underscores the unreliability of banking on the reactions of generations yet unborn—for those responses are not fully under our control. But his reliance on a supposed symmetry between the distant past and future is misplaced.

Our distant forbearers cannot lavish anything upon us because their deaths precede our births, they have no record upon which to evaluate our lives. Such is not the case with those who immediately succeed us. While the biographies of most of us fade quite quickly from memories and history, a few human beings do achieve enduring fame or ignominy. While Marcus Aurelius is correct to point out that pursuing enduring fame is a highly speculative goal, resting that conclusion on a supposed symmetry between the distant past and future is unsound.

Stoicism and the Emotions

The Stoics advanced a version of what is now called the cognitive theory of the emotions.[39] While emotions involve feelings and sensations, they are never simply or fundamentally constituted by feelings and sensations. Instead, emotions are triggered by beliefs and judgments. I am angry at Mary because I judge that something bad has happened; Mary is responsible for the event; and my anger toward Mary is an appropriate response to what she has done. I will also probably feel upset, my blood pressure may rise, my face might redden, my voice will become louder, and my equilibrium will be tossed out of whack. But these sensations are not the emotion of anger; they typically, but not automatically, accompany the emotion, which is fundamentally constituted by beliefs and judgments. Under this view, because emotions are rational, we are responsible for our emotions and actions taken pursuant to them. My judgments can be transformed through attention to arguments, consideration of evidence, and resolve to alter self-defeating beliefs. Emotions do not merely happen to us, we are not randomly struck by thunderbolts that force emotions upon us. Accordingly, our emotions are not irrational as such. A particular emotion at a particular time may well be irrational if based on a hasty judgment grounded in scanty evidence and shaky beliefs. But, overall, our emotions serve our purposes and manifest our characters: they are intimately connected to our motives, beliefs, and intentions.

Emotions are not exactly like other judgments we arrive at. They have an amplified sense of importance, urgency, purpose, strategy, and motivation. As Sartre observed, "emotions magically transform the world" not by altering reality but by changing our perceptions of it. As a system of judgments, our emotions structure our experience. Thus, the emotion of anger is an experience of interpreting the world in this rather than that way. As the Stoics intuited, change the interpretation and you will extinguish or change the emotion. Under a cognitive view of the emotions, the human tendency to use the emotions as ways of evading responsibility for our actions—"Hey, I didn't really mean to chase you with a chain saw; I was overcome with anger at the time"—is disingenuous. I am responsible for my emotions and the actions I take pursuant to them because I am responsible for developing them, nurturing or revising them, and affirming or critically examining them. The overall story of our life choices and self-development contains chapters on various emotions.

Emotions often seem irrational because they flow from ill-grounded judgments or take place in urgent situations or advance short-term goals that conflict with long-range interests or are poor strategies for attaining our ends. Often, we do not recognize the purpose for which our judgments have been made. For emotions that have subtle, manipulative purposes—a child throws a temper tantrum to intimidate a parent into granting the malevolent urchin's desire—to explicitly acknowledge the purpose may undermine the judgment fueling the emotion. In this case, the temper tantrum depends on a sincere, self-righteous belief of having been wronged. To recognize the manipulative, self-serving purpose of the emotion would be to destroy the reality of that sense of being wronged; the child would be acting as if she had been wronged in contrast to firmly believing that she had been wronged. Unless she was a gifted thespian, she could not then attain her end. The emotion would lose its panache.

> Emotions are judgments, intentional and intelligent. Emotions therefore may be said to be rational in precisely the same sense in which all judgments may be said to be rational. They require an advanced degree of conceptual sophistication, including a conception of self and at least some ability in abstraction. They require at least minimal intelligence and a sense of self-interest, and they proceed purposefully in accordance with a sometimes complex set of rules and strategies. . . . Even the most primitive emotions, fear for one's life or love of one's mother, require intelligence, abstraction, purpose, and "logic." . . . Most emotions involve much more, strategies for the maximizations of self-interest that would shame a professional confidence man and a prereflective awareness of psychological intrigue that would impress even S. Freud.[40]

A complete rendering of the contemporary cognitive theory of the emotions requires much more. Can human beings not make the same judgments that allegedly constitute emotional judgments without being emotional? Do we not make emotional judgments that we would have preferred not to have made? Does not every emotion have distinctive neurological correlates? Does not the wide range of emotions imply that no simple cognitive theory can capture the truth about emotions as such? Do we really choose our emotions in the same way we select this rather than that entrée at a restaurant? Does not basic biological make-up affect the emotional range we are most likely to exemplify?

A satisfying defense of the cognitive theory of the emotions requires examining such questions carefully. I am firmly convinced that the cognitive theory can supply persuasive answers to some, but probably not all, of these questions. But a thorough examination of the theory would wander far beyond the purposes of this work. Accordingly, I introduce the contemporary cognitive theory of the emotions for the limited purpose of evaluating a Stoic position that prefigured it.

How our emotions influence our general outlook on life and how they affect our possibilities of leading the good life preoccupied the Stoics. Reflecting a dominant Stoic view, Seneca insisted that emotions are judgments, but they are irrational judgments. They transgress reason because the beliefs grounding the emotions are false (I 3.2–5). Take the case of anger: We believe that something bad has occurred; we believe that a certain person is responsible for that bad event; and we believe that anger is an appropriate response. For a Stoic, such as Seneca, all three beliefs are false. Events are neither good nor bad as such, only our labeling makes them so. Typically, what we judge as a bad event is what we take to be the wrongful frustration of a preferred indifferent. That is our first cognitive error: the loss of or failure to attain a preferred indifferent is neither a wrong to us nor a bad event.

Next, we hold someone responsible for what we wrongly take to be a bad event. But that person is not culpable because the event is not bad. Moreover, even if it were bad the person's action flows from ignorance, not malevolence.

The Stoics, following Socrates, contended that we all seek the good and stray from it only because we fail to understand where it lies—in the felicitous union of virtue and self-interest. Thus, our indictment of the perpetrator of the alleged wrong is doubly mistaken: It rests on the erroneous beliefs that a bad event has taken place for which moral blame should be affixed.

Finally, given that nothing bad has happened and no one is culpable for anything bad then anger is an inappropriate response to the situation. Accordingly, for Seneca, the emotion of anger is always irrational as it is grounded in completely false beliefs.

What about positive emotions? Are they always irrational? Not automatically. Some leeway exists for Stoics to extol gratitude, friendship, and even love, but we must be careful. If events are neither good nor bad then symmetry of judgment requires that we should not cultivate positive emotions in reaction to our belief that a good event has occurred. The only exception might be events that benefit our attainment of Stoic virtue. Such events would be genuine goods in that they nurture the only true Stoic good; they do not merely facilitate our obtaining preferred indifferent, they nurture Stoic virtue. So a Stoic student who has learned at the feet of a great teacher-sage such as Musonius Rufus has legitimate reason for positive emotion toward him. The imagined student would judge, correctly, that something good has occurred; that Rufus has brought that good about; and that gratitude, friendship, even love is an appropriate response. So gratitude, friendship, and love may be genuine Stoic emotions, at least insofar as they are directed toward those who helped us achieve the human good.

Would this not entail, though, that a student who has been misled as a youth by a renegade teacher away from Stoic teachings would have genuine cause for anger? Perhaps not. The charlatan instructor, remember, must have acted from ignorance not malevolence. Unless he is culpable for his ignorance, he is not morally responsible for his shoddy instruction.

The problems afflicting Stoicism and its cognitive theory of the emotions are numerous and deeply entrenched. First, the Stoic interpretations of the nature of events are stunningly unpersuasive. Under the first interpretation, with the possible exception of happenings that directly nurture or frustrate Stoic virtue, events are neither good nor bad. Mass murders and selfless philanthropies, and everything in between, do not bear any inherent evil or goodness. At most, Stoics would concede that mass murders destroy and philanthropies advance the preferred indifferents of certain people, but that is not enough to label the acts as genuinely bad or genuinely good. Only by adopting such a position can Stoics deride the so-called negative emotions as erroneous. Non-Stoics would unanimously criticize the Stoic interpretation of events as unbelievable.

Second, the Stoic belief, cadged from Socrates, that vice invariably flows from ignorance is unconvincing. From the earliest times, thinkers understood that human beings often act wrongly from weakness of the will. We know the good but do not pursue it because doing so is difficult or inconvenient. Moreover, at times we harbor self-destructive or self-undermining tendencies that lure us toward evil. At other times, we often privilege our own perceived benefit over the well-being of others. Our prisons are stocked with criminals who understood clearly what a morally right action was but skipped over in the direction of evil.

Third, if some events are evil and if their perpetrators are sometimes morally culpable for their occurrences then the question whether anger is an appropriate response is reopened. Stoics would still insist that anger lacks salutary effects: it cannot alter the past and it clouds our assessment of how to respond in the present. In this, Stoics are undoubtedly correct, at least to a point. Where anger distorts our vision and jeopardizes our judgment it is an inappropriate indulgence. But is that always the case? Cannot anger help steel our resolve and energize our motivation for righteous action?

Anger is a biologically natural emotion that often promotes human survival, a way of amassing psychological resources for salutary action. Of course, taken to an extreme, anger destroys relationships and unsettles social fabric. But systematically suppressing anger may also be harmful. Suppressed anger may cause physical illness, explode into misplaced violence, or promote the manufacture of social scapegoats. That anger is sometimes, even often, a poor strategy for attaining our ends does not mean that it always is. Even religious paragons, such as Jesus, occasionally displayed anger. Are not some outrages so profoundly destructive and unforgettably evil that they merit anger? In the same way that mourning is an appropriate response to the loss of a loved one under tragic circumstances, anger is sometimes an appropriate response to wrongdoing and injustice. If extended inappropriately, mourning can easily morph into unseemly self-pity. If widely practiced and indiscriminately nurtured, anger can quickly transform to a weapon of manipulation and mass destruction. Understanding the dangers should serve as a caution. The elimination of the so-called negative emotions, though, is ill-advised. We need to magically transform our perceptions of the world to cope with an environment otherwise largely beyond our making. Anger, sorrow, and the like are sometimes artful strategies for attaining our ends.

Conclusion

Roman life was grounded in *mores maiorum*, military supremacy, and political power. But like the Spartans before them, the Romans came to understand that tradition, domination, and conquest were not enough to promote a vibrant, enduring culture. Cautiously, the most reflective among them turned to philosophy. As predicted by the hard-line advocates of *mores maiorum*, philosophy threatened to unsettle received opinions and jeopardize univocal social understandings. But philosophy also offered several, often conflicting, paths for personal salvation in a pre-Christian world. Moreover, philosophy forced the best Romans to attend more carefully to such matters as normative justification and social obligation: might could no longer masquerade so easily as right.

The chronicle of the struggle of the noblest Romans to make sense of a universe not of their making, to find meaning and purpose beyond the brute struggle to survive, and to leave a worthwhile legacy—perhaps even to serve as moral exemplars for future generations—is only one chapter in the enduring human story. Those Romans have long ago passed away. We remain to carry on the struggle. Soon, too soon, we shall also pass from the scene, leaving our children to assume the burden. By reexamining the stories and struggles of the ancient Romans, we revitalize possibilities for meaning and significant in our own lives. This book is a modest offering in that direction.

Notes

1. Miriam T. Griffin, *Seneca: A Philosopher in Politics* (Oxford: The Clarendon Press, 1976), 40.
2. Seneca, *Dialogues and Essays*, trans. by John Davie (Oxford: Oxford University Press, 2007), x.
3. Griffin, *Seneca,* 135.
4. Miriam T. Griffith, "Imago Vitae Suae," in John G. Fitch, ed., *Seneca* (Oxford: Oxford University Press, 2008), 39–40.
5. Tad Brennan, *The Stoic Life* (Oxford: The Clarendon Press, 2005), 238–39.
6. Brad Inwood, *Reading Seneca* (Oxford: The Clarendon Press, 2008), 166–67.
7. A. A. Long, *From Epicurus to Epictetus* (Oxford: The Clarendon Press, 2006), 364–65.
8. Ibid., 367.
9. Mireille Armisen-Marchetti, "Imagination and Meditation in Seneca," in Fitch, ed., *Seneca,* 104–6, 112.
10. Alain de Botton, *The Consolations of Philosophy* (New York: Vintage Books, 2000), 82–83.
11. Ibid., 109.
12. Robert J. Newman, "*In Umbra Virtutis*: *Gloria* in the Thought of Seneca the Philosopher," in Fitch, ed., *Seneca,* 317.
13. Griffin, *Seneca,* 256.
14. Ibid., 379.
15. Ibid.
16. Roland G. Mayer, "Roman Historical *Exempla* in Seneca," in Fitch, ed., *Seneca,* 312–13.
17. Ibid., 300.
18. Inwood, *Reading Seneca,* 253.
19. J. T. Dillon, *Musonius Rufus and Education in the Good Life* (Lanham, MD: University Press of America, 2004), 6–7.
20. Ibid., 43.
21. Cora E. Lutz, *Musonius Rufus: The Roman Socrates* (New Haven, CT: Yale University Press, 1947), 24, 29–30.
22. Brennan, *Stoic Life,* 187.
23. Ibid., 189.
24. Compare, for example, A. A. Long, *Epictetus: A Stoic and Socratic Guide to Life* (Oxford: The Clarendon Press, 2002), 4, with Epictetus, *Discourses: Book I*, trans. with an intro. and commentary by Robert Dobbin (Oxford: The Clarendon Press, 1998), xx-xxiii.

25. John Sellars, *Stoicism* (Berkeley, CA: University of California Press, 2006), 28–29.

26. Ibid., 48.

27. Long, *Epictetus*, 138.

28. Epictetus, *Discourses*, commentary by Dobbin, 72.

29. Long, *Epictetus*, 172.

30. Ibid., 221.

31. Ibid., 249.

32. Ibid., 245.

33. Epictetus, *Discourses*, commentary by Dobbin, 178.

34. Ibid., 179.

35. Edward Gibbon, *The Decline and Fall of the Roman Empire*, volumes 1–3 (New York: Everyman's Library, 1993), 89–90.

36. P. A. Brunt, "Marcus Aurelius in His *Meditations*," *The Journal of Roman Studies* 64 (1974): 18.

37. Marcus Aurelius, *The Meditations*, trans. by A. S. L. Farquharson with an intro. and notes by R. B. Rutherford (Oxford: Oxford University Press, 1989), 153.

38. Georg W. F. Hegel, *The Phenomenology of Mind*, trans. J. B. Bailie (London: George Allen & Unwin, 1949); *The Philosophy of Right*, trans. T. M. Knox (Oxford: Clarendon Press, 1942). Hegel (1770–1831) argued that finite objects and beings are transitory manifestations of the Absolute, which is called at various stages and in different dimensions Mind, Reality, Reason, Idea. Unlike the Western God, Hegel's Absolute is not a transcendent reality that stands independent from the world and complete from the beginning. Instead, the Absolute develops through time, as the goal and result of an historical process. The Absolute comes to know itself through the movement of finite reality. Every concrete particular is a moment in the development of the Absolute. Thus, human beings make an historical contribution to the life of the Absolute and to Its awareness and freedom. We are necessary for the Absolute to become aware of Itself.

Unlike the Western God, the Absolute has no meaning apart from the cosmos.

39. Robert C. Solomon, *Not Passion's Slave* (New York: Oxford University Press, 2003); Cheshire Calhoun, "Cognitive Emotions," in Calhoun and Robert C. Solomon, eds., *What Is an Emotion?* (New York: Oxford University Press, 1984); Baruch Spinoza, *Ethics* (Malibu, CA: J. Simon, 1981); Martha Nussbaum, *Upheavals of Thought* (Cambridge, Cambridge University Press, 2000); Jean Paul Sartre, *The Emotions*, trans. by B. Frechtman (New York: Citadel, 1948).

40. Solomon, *Passion's Slave*, 35.

Texts and Their Abbreviations

All references are to Book numbers and/or sections, not page numbers, unless otherwise stated.

For example:

M 12.36 =   *The Meditations*, Book 12, section 36. (Marcus Aurelius).

P 6 =   *De Providentia* ("On Providence"), section 6. (Seneca).

I have used the following abbreviations:

B =	*De Beneficiis* ("On Benefits") (Seneca)
BV =	*De Brevitate Vitae* ("On the Shortness of Life") (Seneca)
C =	*De Clementia* ("On Mercy") (Seneca)
CH =	*De Consolatione ad Helviam* ("Consolation to Helvia") (Seneca)
CM =	*De Consolatione ad Marciam* ("Consolation to Marcia") (Seneca)
CP =	*De Consolatione ad Polybium* ("Consolation to Polybius") (Seneca)
D =	*The Discourses* (Musonius Rufus)
DC =	*De Constantia* ("On Firmness") (Seneca)
DS =	*The Discourses* (Epictetus)
E =	*Epistles* ("The Letters") (Seneca)
EN =	*Encheiridion* ("The Manual") (Epictetus)
F =	*The Fragments* (Musonius Rufus)
I =	*De Ira* ("On Anger") (Seneca)
M =	*The Meditations* (Marcus Aurelius)
O =	*De Otio* ("On Leisure") (Seneca)
P =	*De Providentia* ("On Providence") (Seneca)
TA =	*De Tranquilitate Animi* ("On the Tranquility of the Mind") (Seneca)
TD =	*Tusculanae Disputationes* (Cicero)
VB =	*De Vita Beata* ("On the Happy Life') (Seneca)

Appendix A
Important Dates in Roman History
(753 BC–AD 180)

BC

753	Legendary founding of Rome by Romulus and Remus.
753–509	Period of Kings
510–509	The king's son rapes a nobleman's wife, who later commits suicide. Led by Lucius Junius Brutus, rebels eject the king, Tarquinius the Proud. Roman republic is established.
500–440	Incursions of Aequi and Volsci, tribal mountain-dwellers.
494	First Secession of the Plebeians as their economic and social demands are rejected. Eventual reconciliation occurs.
449	Another Secession of the Plebeians as their demand for codification of law is rejected. Laws of Twelve Tables soon published.
396	Rome captures Etruscan city of Veii.
390	Gallic raiders defeat Rome at Battle of Allia. Gauls sack Rome.
343–341	First Samnite War ends with the renewal of Romano-Samnite Treaty.
340–338	Revolt of the Latin League.
326–304	Second Samnite War. Rome wins; its power extends deep into former Samnite territory.
298–290	Third Samnite War. Rome wins; incorporates Samnites; dominates central Italy.
295	Battle of Sentinum. Rome defeats a coalition of Samnites, Umbrians, Etruscans, and Gauls.
287	Hortensian Law: made plebiscites binding on all citizens.
280	Battle of Heraclea. Greek colony of Tarentum, pressured by Roman expansion, secures the aid of King Pyrrhus of Epirus.
279	Battle of Asculum.
275	Battle of Beneventum. Rome and Pyrrhus fight to a standstill. Pyrhus leaves Italy.
273	Establish accord with Ptolemaic Egypt.
264–241	First Punic War. Carthage and Rome struggle for control of Sicily.
262	Rome storms Agrigentum successfully.
260	Roman naval victory at Mylae.

255	Roman fleet destroyed in storm and Roman unit destroyed in Africa.
241	Battle of the Aegates Islands. Carthage surrenders. Sicily made Rome's first province.
238	Corsica and Sardinia annexed.
241–220	Carthage conquers Spain.
220	Cisalpine Gaul annexed as a province.
218–202	Second Punic War. Hannibal invades Italy.
218	Battle of Trebia. Hannibal defeats a large Roman force.
217	Battle of Lake Trasimene. Hannibal defeats a smaller Roman army.
216	Battle of Cannae. Hannibal inflicts the worst defeat ever upon Roman forces.
209	Romans defeat Carthaginian forces in Spain.
207	Battle of Metaurus River. Romans defeat and kill Hannibal's brother, Hasdrubal.
202	Battle of Zama. Under Publius Cornelius Scipio ("Africanus"), Rome lays a crushing defeat on Hannibal. Carthage surrenders. Rome levies harsh terms.
215–204	First Macedonian War ends in a negotiated peace.
200–196	Second Macedonian War. Rome wins and Macedonia is debarred from Greece and the Aegean Sea.
198	Two Roman provinces formed in Spain.
197–133	Roman wars in Spain.
192–189	Syrian War.
189	Battle of Magnesia. Under Scipio Africanus, Rome routs Syrian forces of Antiochus III.
172–168	Third Macedonian War. Rome wins decisively. Macedonian kingdom is divided into four republics.
149–146	Third Punic War.
146	Carthage is destroyed by Rome. Corinth is destroyed by Rome. Rome annexes former kingdom of Macedonia as a province.
135–133	Slave war in Sicily.
133	Tiberius Gracchus, tribune, and three hundred supporters are murdered in riot. Tiberius had championed massive land redistribution to create more small-scale farming. Violence as a weapon to settle domestic political disputes enters the Roman polity.
133	Kingdom of Pergamum is bequeathed to Rome.
129	Pergamum formed into the province of Asia.
123–121	Gaius Gracchus, brother of Tiberius, serves successive tribunships. Gaius is even more revolutionary than Tiberius. He advocates cheap grain, employment on road projects for unem-

	ployed, founding of overseas colonies for the landless, and extension of franchise to Italian allies, among other things.
121	Gaius and three thousand supporters killed in street fighting. First passage of the *senatus consultum ultimum* ("the senate's ultimate decree"), which declared martial law. Schism between the *populares*, politicians who favored using tribunes, the tribal assembly, and appeals to the masses, and the *optimates*, who preferred tradition and a strong senate.
121	Transalpine Gaul formed into a province.
111–105	Jugurthine War in Numidia. Under Gaius Marius, Rome prevails.
107	First consulship of Gaius Marius
105	Battle of Arausio. Teutones and Cimbri, migratory Germanic tribes, defeat Roman forces.
105–102	Marius serves four successive consulships. He professionalizes the army.
104–100	Second Slave War in Sicily.
102	Battle of Aquae Sextia. Teutones defeated.
101	Battle of Vercellae. Cimbri defreated.
100	Marius serves sixth consulship.
91–88	Italian Social War. Samnites and several southern Italian communities secede and declare war on Rome. Marius assumed control of Roman forces in the north, while Lucius Cornelius Sulla commanded the southern theater. Roman citizenship was soon granted to allies of Rome.
88–84	First Mithridatic War. Mithridates VI of Pontus revolted and killed all Romans and Italians—eighty thousand—in his region on a single evening.
88	Lucius Cornelius Sulla (*optimates*) marches on Rome and drives Marius (*populares*) out of the city. Sulla was now the first to march a Roman army against other Romans. Sulla then heads east to fight Mithridates.
87–83	Lucius Cornelius Cinna (*populares*) controls Rome.
87	Marius returns and with Cinna seizes Rome.
86	Marius serves seventh consulship. Marius dies.
85	Sulla signs Treaty of Dardanus with Mithridates.
83	Civil War. Sulla's second march on Rome. He wins.
83–81	Second Mithridatic War.
82–79	Sulla serves as dictator. He writes laws and organizes the state to strengthen the power of senate and weaken tribunes.
82–81	Sulla carries out proscriptions.
78	Sulla dies. Revolt of Marcus Aemlius Lepidus (*populares*) and rebel Italians is suppressed. Pompey is given military command.

77–72	Pompey defeats Quintus Sertorius, who resists Sullan commanders, in Spain.
75	Kingdom of Bithynia is bequeathed to Rome.
74–63	Third Mithridactic War.
73–71	Slave revolt of Spartacus.
71	Crassus defeats Spartacus. Pompey returns from Spain and aids suppression of slave revolt.
70	Consulships of Crassus and Pompey.
67	Gabinian Law confers *imperium infinitum* (power not limited to one province) on Pompey.
66	Pirates, in league with Mithridates, are crushed by Pompey. Manilian Law gives Pompey command against Mithridates.
63	Mithridates dies. Pompey defeats forces of Mithridates and reorganizes the east: Bithynia/Pontus, Cilicia, and Syria are formed or reshaped into provinces. Catilinian conspiracy brews in Rome. Cicero is consul. Caesar is elected *ponitifex maximus*.
62	Pompey returns to Rome ostensibly to retire.
60	Caesar, Pompey, and Crassus form First Triumvirate.
59	Caesar's first consulship.
58–49	Caesar conquers Gaul.
58	Tribunate of Clodius.
58–57	Cato makes Cyprus a province. Cicero is exiled.
56	Conference at Lucca: First Triumvirate mends differences.
55	Pompey and Crassus serve as consuls.
54	Death of Julia, Pompey's wife and Caesar's daughter, in childbirth.
53	Battle of Carrhae: Crassus killed while invading Parthia.
52	Death of Clodius. Sole consulship of Pompey.
51–50	Cicero governs Cilicia and Cyprus.
49	Caesar crosses Rubicon. Civil War begins. Pompey evacuates Italy.
49–45	Civil War between Caesar and Pompey.
48	Caesar's second consulship. Caesar defeats Pompey at Battle of Pharsalus. Pompey killed in Egypt.
48–47	Caesar in Alexandria establishes Cleopatra as ruler of Egypt and fathers a son, Caesarion, by her.
47–44	Caesar holds successive dictatorships.
47	Caesar suppresses the revolt of the province of Pontus by defeating Pharnaces II in the Battle of Zela (Turkey) (*Veni, Vidi, Vici!*).
46–44	Caesar holds successive consulships.
46	Caesar wins the Battle of Thapsus (Africa), Cato commits suicide at Utica. Caesar's dictatorship is extended. New

	"Julian" calendar is introduced. Dedication of *Forum Julium* in Rome.
45	Caesar's army defeats remaining Pompeian forces at Battle of Munda (Spain).
44	Caesar named dictator for life. One month later, he is assassinated. Octavius is adopted by terms of Caesar's will and named Octavian; siege of Mutina begins: Octavian versus Marc Antony.
43	Octavian defeats Antony, seizes Rome, and is named consul. He, Antony, and Lepidus form Second Triumvirate. They form a proscription list that leads, among other things, to the death of Cicero.
42	Battles at Philippi: Antony and Octavian defeat Brutus and Cassius. Deification of Julius Caesar.
41–40	Antony meets Cleopatra and fathers twins by her.
40	Antony and Octavian redivide their authority within the Roman world. Antony marries Octavia, sister of Octavian.
38	Octavian marries Livia.
37	Second Triumvirate is renewed.
36	But not for long. Sextus Pompey is defeated by Octavian and Lepidus. Lepidus tries unsuccessfully to eliminate Octavian. Lepidus is muscled out of the Triumvirate and is exiled.
34–31	Antony and Octavian maneuver for position.
33	Octavian's second consulship.
32	Antony divorces Octavia.
31	Octavian defeats Antony and Cleopatra at Battle of Actium.
30	Octavian captures Alexandria. Antony and Cleopatra commit suicide. Egypt becomes a Roman province.
27 BC–AD 14	Augustus (Octavian) rules as first Roman emperor.

AD

14–68	Julio-Claudian Dynasty.
14	Augustus dies.
14–37	Tiberius rules as emperor.
37–41	Gaius (Caligula) rules as emperor.
41–54	Claudius rules as emperor.
54–68	Nero rules as emperor.
59	Nero orders the murder of his mother, Agrippina.
64	Great Fire in Rome. Persecution of Christians begins.
68	Nero deposed and commits assisted suicide as his guards revolt.
68–69	Galba rules as emperor.
69	Civil War. The year of the four emperors. In succession: Galba, Otho, Vitellius, and Vespasian.

69–96	Flavian Dynasty.
69–79	Vespasian rules as emperor.
70	Jerusalem sacked. The Temple is destroyed.
73	Siege of Masada.
79–81	Titus rules as emperor.
81–96	Domitian rules as emperor.
96–98	Nerva rules as emperor (first of the "good emperors").
98–180	Antonine Dynasty.
98–117	Trajan rules as emperor.
114–117	Trajan's Eastern Wars produce three new provinces.
117–138	Hadrian rules as emperor and abandons Trajan's eastern provinces.
122	Construction of Hadrian's wall in Britain begins.
138–161	Antoninus Pius rules as emperor.
150–200	Formation of Germanic tribal confederations.
161–169	Lucius Verus rules as emperor (with Marcus Aurelius).
161–180	Marcus Aurelius rules as emperor (with Verus from 161–169, alone from 169–180).

Appendix B
Cursus Honorum and Roman Government

The *cursus honorum* is the course of honors or the political ladder that a successful Roman politician scaled as he ascended to political power.

Military Tribune. As a precondition of beginning the climb up the *cursus honorum*, aspiring Roman aristocrats served at least eight years in the military. The most ambitious nobles sought service under the greatest commanders of the day. Each legion had six military tribunes who served as commissioned officers. Twenty-four were elected every year by the Tribal Assembly. Beyond that number, more could be appointed by army commanders.

Quaestor. Fundamentally financial officers who served either the state treasury or with commanders in the field, quaestors held the most junior rank that permitted membership in the senate. Quaestors would assist the consuls in Rome and the governors in the provinces. Twenty in number by Cicero's time, two quaestors stayed in Rome to control the state treasury, while the others were assigned to the provinces to aid provincial governors.

Tribune. An office of the Roman plebeians, tribuneships did not confer senate membership nor were they, strictly speaking, within the *cursus honorum*. Patricians could not hold this office. Tribunes were not elected by the entire Roman people, but by plebeians constituting the *Concilium Plebis* (plebeian council). Tribunes could propose and veto legislation, and, under extraordinary circumstances, arrest other state officials. The powers of tribunes extended only to the city of Rome and even within the city practical considerations limited their authority: At the expiration of their one-year term of office, uppity tribunes could face stern retribution from vindictive senators.

Aedile. Officials charged with caring for the infrastructure of Rome—its public buildings, roads, bridges, aqueducts, sanitation, and the like—and with staging Rome's public games. Logistical and managerial skills were crucial for this position, which also oversaw trade, markets, and weights and measures. *Aediles* were four in number and elected annually. The two *curule aediles* (patrician and plebeian in alternate years) were elected by the Tribal Assembly, while the two plebeian aediles were elected by the Plebeian Council.

Praetor. These versatile officials could command a province, lead an army, or judge criminal cases. The *praetor peregrines* was charged with the care of foreigners in Rome, including judging legal cases. The *praetor urbanus* was charged with judging civil suits between Roman citizens. If both consuls were absent, the *praetor urbanus* served as temporary head of state. At the expiration of a praetorship, the office holder would typically serve at least one more year as a *proprietor*, a commander of an army or governor of a less significant province.

Consul. Consuls were the chief magistrates of the Roman republic. Two consuls served annually. They were legislators and generals with supreme power. One consul could veto the actions of the other consul. Consuls originally commanded Rome's major armies, but the office evolved into mainly managing civil duties within Rome. Consuls presided over the senate and the assemblies, and held wide supervisory powers over other magistrates. Religious functions, though, were controlled by *pontifex maximus* and *rex sacrorum*. Many consuls, upon the expiration of their term of office, commanded provinces as *proconsuls*.

Censors. The final office of a political career typically awarded only to the most honored politicians. Every five years, two censors were elected for an eighteen-month term. Their responsibilities were extensive: they supervised the allocation of public contracts; maintained the roll of voters; counted the number of Roman citizens; maintained the roll of senators; and could axe a senator from membership on moral or economic grounds.

Dictator. In times of military or domestic emergencies, a dictator could be appointed for a term of six months. Constitutional protections would evaporate during this period as the dictator held absolute power. Dictators were often assisted by a *Magister Equitum* ("Master of the Horse"). When the six-month term expired, constitutional government would return. This occasional, short-term office was not an official step on the *cursus honorum*.

Pontifex Maximus. The *pontifex maximus* was the high priest who filled the most important Roman religious position. The office was gradually politicized as the republic developed and was incorporated as an imperial office by Augustus. Although not an official step on the *cursus honorum*, the *ponifex maximus* discharged ritualistic functions and administered *jus divinum* (divine law).

The Senate and Legislative Assemblies

Senate. Based on tradition, prestige, and custom, the Roman senate held massive legislative authority. The senate passed decrees, which were officially only advisory, but in practice were almost always accepted by magistrates. The major focus of the senate was foreign and military policy, but it also supervised civil administration in Rome. The Constitution of Rome was almost entirely unwritten, unsystematic, and derived mainly from precedent. Accordingly, the personal prestige and social standing of aristocratic senators was critical. Because the senate contained all Romans with political and administrative experience, its advice was nearly always accepted by magistrates, and its resolutions in practice had the force of law. Only those holding the office of quaestor or a more senior magistrate were typically appointed by the Censor. Once appointed, senators retained membership for life, unless removed by a subsequent Censor on moral or economic grounds.

Tribal Assembly. A consul presided over the *Comitia Tributa,* which was composed of thirty-five tribes. The tribes were geographic subdivisions. Representatives, by majority vote, would elect *quaestors, curule aediles,* and military tribunes. The Tribal Assembly rarely passed legislation, at least up until the time Julius Caesar took control. The Tribal Assembly could meet only when summoned to do so by a magistrate or tribune. It could vote only on measures placed before it by the presiding consul.

Plebeian Council. The *Concilium Plebis* was organized on the basis of geographical tribes. It elected its own officers, tribunes, and plebeian *aediles.* This council served as a legislative body, especially after Caesar assumed control of Rome.

Appendix C
Roman Historians

The major Roman historians who chronicled, among other things, the episodes surrounding the final days of the Roman Republic and the reign of the Roman Empire did not always agree on the fine details of events. By studying their accounts, however, contemporary thinkers can piece together a reasonable version of the big picture. In addition, the works of Cicero, especially his letters, and Caesar's *Commentarii de Bello Gallico* ("Commentaries on the Gallic War") and *Commentarii de Bello Civili* ("Commentaries on the Civil War") are also helpful in reconstructing history.

Gaius Sallustius Crispus ("Sallust") (86 BC–35 BC) was born into a plebeian Sabine family in central Italy. Sallust served as a quaestor around 55 BC, which brought with it entry into the senate. He became a tribune in 52 BC, but was ousted from the senate within two years for alleged immorality. Sallust served with Caesar during the civil war against Pompey's forces. Caesar's victory earned Sallust's political rehabilitation. Sallust returned to the senate as a praetor in 46. He reportedly performed valuable, successful service in Caesar's African campaign and was soon thereafter rewarded by being named governor of Numidia. Sallust responded by plundering the province financially and generally ruling with a heavy hand. He returned to Rome in 45 facing charges of extortion. Sallust avoided conviction, possibly through Caesar's intervention, and retired from political life. He then wrote historical monographs such as *Bellum Catilinae* ("Catiline's War"), *Bellum Iugurthinum* ("The Jugurthine War"), and *Historiae* ("The Histories").

Titus Livius ("Livy") (59 BC–AD 17) was born in Patavium ("Padua"), Italy. To call Livy prolific is to greatly understate his productivity. His *Ab Urbe Condita* ("From the Founding of the City") is a *magnum opus* of 142 books covering over 770 years of Roman history. Thirty-five of these books survive, covering the origins of Rome through the Punic Wars to the wars with Macedonia and Syria.

Lucius Mestrius Plutarchus ("Plutarch") (45–120) was born to a prominent Greek family in Boeotia. Plutarch served for many years as one of the two priests at the temple of Apollo in Delphi, site of the legendary Delphic Oracle. He traveled and lectured widely in the Mediterranean world, and his writings were well known. Plutarch also served as a magistrate and as a representative on foreign missions. His most famous work is *The Parallel Lives* in which he compares and chronicles the lives of legendary Greek and Roman statesmen.

Publius (or Gaius) Cornelius Tacitus ("Tacitus") (56–120) was born to equestrian provincials in either Northern Italy or Gaul. Acclaimed as a lawyer and orator, Tacitus enjoyed a successful political career. He served as a quaestor, praetor, senator, consul, and, finally, as governor of Asia. The major works of Tacitus are *Ab Excessu Divi Augusti* ("The Annals") and *Historiae* ("The Histories"), which closely examine the reigns of the Roman Emperors Tiberius, Claudius, and Nero. The works of Tacitus span the history of the Roman Empire from the death of Augustus in 14 to the death of the emperor Domitian in 96.

Gaius Suetonius Tranquillus ("Suetonius") (71–135) was probably born in Algeria. An equestrian, Suetonius served on the staff of Pliny the Younger in Asia Minor, as a secretary of studies under the emperor Trajan, and as the Emperor's secretary under Hadrian. More of a journalist with a penchant for sensationalism than a serious historian, Suetonius's most famous work is *De Vita Caesarum* ("The Lives of the Caesars"), a biographical collection of Julius Caesar, Augustus, Tiberius, Caligula, Claudius, Nero, Galba, Otho, Vitellius, Vespasian, Titus, and Domitian.

Lucius (or Claudius) Cassius Dio Cocceianus ("Cassius Dio") (155–235) was a renowned historian and public official, whose father was a Roman senator. Born and raised at Nicaea in Bithynia, Cassius Dio served as a praetor, senator, twice as a consul, and as governor in Africa and Pannonia. After over two decades of research and writing, he published a *History of Rome*, covering over fourteen hundred years of history in eighty books. The books spanning the periods from 65 BC to 12 BC and from AD 9 to AD 54 have nearly all survived. Numerous fragments of other books remain.

Bibliography

Books

Addison, Joseph. *Cato: A Tragedy, and Selected Essays*. Edited by Christine Dunn Henderson and Mark E. Yellin; Foreword by Forrest McDonald. Indianapolis, IN: Liberty Fund, 2004.

Alighieri, Dante. *The Divine Comedy*. Translated by Allen Mandelbaum. New York: Bantam Books, 1980.

Aristotle. *Nicomachean Ethics*. Translated with an introduction by Martin Ostwald. Indianapolis, IN: Bobbs-Merrill, 1962.

Aurelius, Marcus. *The Meditations*. Translated by A. S. L. Farquharson; introduction by R. B. Rutherford. Oxford: Oxford University Press, 1989.

Belliotti, Raymond Angelo. *Good Sex*. Lawrence, KS: University Press of Kansas, 1993.

————. *Happiness is Overrated*. Lanham, MD: Rowman & Littlefield Publishers, 2004.

————. *Justifying Law*. Philadelphia: Temple University Press, 1992.

————. *Niccolò Machiavelli: The Laughing Lion and the Strutting Fox*. Lanham, MD: Lexington Books, 2009.

————. *The Philosophy of Baseball: How to Play the Game of Life*. Lewiston, NY: The Edwin Mellen Press, 2006.

————. *Seeking Identity: Individualism versus Community in an Ethnic Context*. Lawrence, KS: University Press of Kansas, 1995.

————. *Stalking Nietzsche*. Westport, CT: Greenwood Press, 1998.

————. *What is the Meaning of Human Life?* Amsterdam: Rodopi, 2001.

Boatwright, Mary T., Daniel Gagola, and Richard J. A. Talbert. *The Romans*. New York: Oxford University Press, 2004.

Brennan, Tad. *The Stoic Life*. Oxford: The Clarendon Press, 2007.

Cassius, Dio. *The History of Rome*, volumes 1–6. Middlesex: The Echo Library, 2007.

Castner, Catherine J. *Prosopography of Roman Epicureans*. New York: Peter Lang, 1988.

Cicero. *Brutus, On the Nature of the Gods, On Divination, and On Duties*. Translated by Hubert M. Poteat; introduction by Richard McKeon. Chicago: University of Chicago Press, 1950.

————. *Defense Speeches*. Translated by D. H. Berry. Oxford: Oxford University Press, 2000.

————. *Letters*. Edited and translated by L. P. Wilkinson. London: Bristol Classical Press, 1966.

————. *On Moral Ends*. Translated by Raphael Woolf; edited by Julia Annas. Cambridge: Cambridge University Press, 2001.

————. *On Obligations*. Translated with an introduction by P. G. Walsh. Oxford: Oxford University Press, 2000.

————. *Philippics*. Translated by Walter C. A. Ker. Cambridge, MA: Harvard University Press, 1938.

————. *Tusculan Disputations*. Translated by Margaret Gravier. Chicago: University of Chicago Press, 2002.

Clarke, M. L. *The Noblest Roman: Marcus Brutus and His Reputation*. Ithaca, NY: Cornell University Press, 1981.
————. *The Roman Mind*. New York: W.W. Norton & Company, 1968.
De Botton, Alain. *The Consolations of Philosophy*. New York: Vintage Books, 2000.
Dillon, J. T. *Musonius Rufus and Education in the Good Life*. Lanham, MD: University Press of America, 2004.
Dorey, T. A., editor. *Cicero*. New York: Basic Books, 1965.
Douglas, A. E. *Cicero*. Oxford: The Clarendon Press, 1968.
Emerton, Ephraim. *Humanism and Tyranny*. Cambridge, MA: Harvard University Press, 1925.
Epicetetus. *Discourses: Book 1*. Translated with an introduction by Robert Dobbin. Oxford: The Clarendon Press, 1998.
————. *Manual for Living*. Translated with an introduction by Sharon Lebell. New York: HarperCollins, 1994.
Everitt, Anthony. *Cicero*. New York: Random House, 2001.
Feinberg, Joel. *Harm to Others*. New York: Oxford University Press, 1984.
Feldman, Fred. *Confrontations with the Reaper*. New York: Oxford University Press, 1992.
Fischer, John Martin, editor. *The Metaphysics of Death*. Stanford, CA: Stanford University Press, 1993.
Fitch, John G., editor. *Seneca*. Oxford: Oxford University Press, 2008.
Forstatter, Mark. *The Spiritual Teachings of Marcus Aurelius*. New York: HarperCollins, 2000.
Fuller, J. F. C. *Julius Caesar*. New Brunswick, NJ: Da Capo Press, 1965.
Gale, Monica R., editor. *Lucretius*. Oxford: Oxford University Press, 2007.
Gaskin, John. *The Epicurean Philosophers*. Translated by C. Bailey, R. D. Hicks, and J. C. A. Gaskin. London: The Everyman Library, 1995.
Gelzer, Matthias. *Caesar: Politician and Statesman*. Cambridge, MA: Harvard University Press, 1997.
Grant, Michael. *Julius Caesar*. New York: Barnes & Noble Books, 1969.
Griffin, Miriam T. *Seneca: A Philosopher in Politics*. Oxford: The Clarendon Press, 1976.
Griffin, Miriam T., and Jonathan Barnes, editors. *Philosophia Togata I*. Oxford: The Clarendon Press, 1989.
Holland, Tom. *Rubicon*. New York: Doubleday, 2003.
Inwood, Brad. *Reading Seneca*. Oxford: The Clarendon Press, 2008.
Jaszi, Oscar, and John D. Lewis. *Against the Tyrant*. Glencoe, IL: The Free Press, 1957.
Kahn, Arthur D. *The Education of Julius Caesar*. iUniverse.com.Inc., 2000.
Lacey, W. K. *Cicero and the End of the Roman Republic*. London: Hodder and Stoughton, 1978.
Leeman, A. D. *Orationis Ratio: The Stylistic Theories and Practice of the Roman Orators, Historians and Philosophers*. Amsterdam: Adolf Hakkert Publishers, 1963.
Li, Jack. *Can Death Be a Harm to the Person Who Dies?* Dordrecht: Kluwer Academic Publishers, 2002.
Lockwood, D. P. *A Survey of Classical Roman Literature*. Chicago: University of Chicago Press, 1962.
Long, A. A. *Epictetus: A Stoic and Socratic Guide to Life*. Oxford: The Clarendon Press, 2002.
————. *From Epicurus to Epictetus*. Oxford: The Clarendon Press, 2006.

Lucretius. *De Rerum Natura*. Translated by Rolfe Humphries. Bloomington, IN: Indiana University Press, 1968.
Lutz, Cora. E. *Musonius Rufus: The Roman Socrates*. New Haven, CT: Yale University Press, 1947.
MacKendrick, Paul. *The Philosophical Books of Cicero*. New York: St. Martin's Press, 1989.
Matyszak, Philip. *Chronicle of the Roman Republic*. New York: Thames & Hudson, 2003.
Morford, Mark. *The Roman Philosophers*. New York: Routledge, 2002.
Nagel, Thomas. *Mortal Questions*. Cambridge: Cambridge University Press, 1979.
Nussbaum, Martha C. *Love's Knowledge*. New York: Oxford University Press, 1990.
Parenti, Michael. *The Assassination of Julius Caesar*. New York: The New Press, 2004.
Plutarch. *The Lives of the Noble Grecians and Romans*. Translated by John Dryden; edited and revised by Arthur Hugh Clough, volumes 1 and 2. New York: The Modern Library, 1992.
Powell, J. G. F. *Cicero The Philosopher*. Oxford: The Clarendon Press, 1999.
Radford, Robert T. *Cicero*. Amsterdam: Rodopi, 2002.
Rosenberg, Jay. *Thinking Clearly about Death* (Englewood Cliffs, NJ: Prentice-Hall, Inc., 1983).
Sallust. *Catiline's War, The Jugurthine War, Histories*. Translated with an introduction by A. J. Woodman. London: Penguin Books, 2007.
Sellars, John. *Stoicism*. Berkeley, CA: University of California Press, 2006.
Seneca. *Dialogues and Essays*. Translated by John Davie; introduction by Tobias Reinhardt. Oxford: Oxford University Press, 2007.
Solomon, Robert C. *Not Passion's Slave*. New York: Oxford University Press, 2003.
Sperling, Daniel. *Posthumous Interests: Legal and Ethical Perspectives*. Cambridge: Cambridge University Press, 2008.
Tandy, Charles, editor. *Death and Anti-Death: Volume 1*. Palo Alto, CA: Ria University Press, 2003.
Thirsrud, Harald. *Ancient Skepticism*. Berkeley, CA: University of California Press, 2009.
Wood, Neal. *Cicero's Social & Political Thought*. Berkeley, CA: University of California Press, 1988.
Woolf, Greg. *"Et tu, Brute?" The Murder of Caesar and Political Assassination*. London: Profile Books, 2006.

Articles

Africa, Thomas W. "The Mask of an Assassin: A Psychohistorical Study of M. Junius Brutus." *Journal of Interdisciplinary History* 8 (1978): 599–626.
Asmis, Elizabeth. "The Stoicism of Marcus Aurelius." *Aufstieg und Niedergang der Romischen Welt* 36 (1989): 2228–52.
Balsdon, J. P. V. D. "The Veracity of Caesar." *Greece & Rome* 4 (1957): 19–28.
Belliotti, Raymond Angelo. "Do Dead Human Beings Have Rights?" *Personalist* 60 (1979): 201–10.
Bourne, Frank C. "Caesar the Epicurean." *The Classical World* 70 (1977): 417–32.
Bowden, William R. "The Mind of Brutus." *Shakespeare Quarterly* 17 (1966): 57–67.
Bradley, Ben. "How Bad is Death?" *Canadian Journal of Philosophy* 37 (2007): 111–28.
———. "When is Death Bad for the One Who Dies?" *Nous* 38 (2004): 1–28.

Brewer, J. S. "Brutus' Crime: A Footnote to Julius Caesar." *The Review of English Studies* 3 (1952): 51–54.

Brown, David S. "Cicero's De Officiis: Ancient Ethics for (Post-) Modern Times." *Teaching Philosophy* 25 (2002): 151–59.

Brunschwig, Jacques. "The Cradle Argument in Epicureanism and Stoicism." Pp. 113–44 in *The Norms of Nature*, edited by Malcolm Schofield and Gisela Striker. Cambridge: Cambridge University Press, 1986.

Brunt, P. A. "Book Review: The Friendship of Cicero and Caesar." *The Classical Review* 14 (1964): 90–91.

———. "Marcus Aurelius in His Meditations." *The Journal of Roman Studies* 64 (1974): 1–20.

Davies, J. C. "The Originality of Cicero's Philosophical Works." *Latomus* 30 (1971): 105–19.

DeLacy, P. H. "Lucretius and the History of Epicureanism." *Transactions and Proceedings of the American Philological Association* 79 (1948): 12–23.

DeWitt, Norman W. "Notes on the History of Epicureanism." *Transactions and Proceedings of the American Philological Association* 63 (1932): 166–76.

Douglas, A. E., "Cicero the Philosopher." Pp. 135–70 in *Cicero*, edited by T. A. Dorey. New York: Basic Books, 1965.

Esquivel, Javier. "Assassination and Tyrannicide." *Critica* 11 (1979): 3–17.

Feit, Neil. "The Time of Death's Misfortune." *Nous* 36 (2002): 359–83.

Ferguson, John. "Epicureanism under the Roman Empire." *Aufstieg und Niedergang der Romischen Welt* 36 (1990): 2257–2327.

Fowler, D. P. "Lucretius and Politics." Pp. 120–50 in *Philosophia Togata I*, edited by Miriam T. Griffith and Jonathan Barnes. Oxford: The Clarendon Press, 1989.

Gleicher, Jules. "On Plutarch's Life of Caesar." *Interpretation* 29 (2002): 265–79.

Glucker, John. "Cicero's Philosophical Affiliations." Pp. 34–69 in *The Question of "Eclecticism"* edited by John M. Dillon and A. A. Long. Berkeley: University of California Press, 1988.

———. "Cicero's Philosophical Affiliations Again." *Liverpool Classical Monthly* 17 (1992): 134–38.

Griffin, Miriam T. "Philosophy, Cato, and Roman Suicide: I." *Greece & Rome* 33 (1986): 64–77.

———. "Philosophy, Cato, and Roman Suicide: II." *Greece & Rome* 33 (1986): 192–202.

———. "Philosophy, Politics, and Politicians in Rome." *Philosophia Togata I*, edited by Miriam T. Griffith and Jonathan Barnes (Oxford: The Clarendon Press, 1989): 1–37.

———. "Philosophy for Statesmen: Cicero and Seneca." *Antikes Denken* (1987): 133–50.

——— "Seneca on Cato's Politics: Epistle 14. 12–13." *Classical Quarterly* 18 (1968): 373–75.

Hendrickson, G. L. "Brutus De Virtute." *American Journal of Philology* 60 (1939): 401–13.

Inwood, Brad. "Seneca in his Philosophical Milieu." *Harvard Studies in Classical Philology* 97 (1995): 63–76.

Kahn, Arthur D. "Was There No Superstructure in Ancient Rome?" *Monthly Review* 41 (1990): 36–38.

Kleve, Knut. "The Philosophical Polemics in Lucretius." *Entretiens sur l'Antiquite Classique* 24 (1978): 39–71.

Lamont, Julian. "A Solution to the Puzzle of When Death Harms Its Victims," *Australasian Journal of Philosophy* 76 (1998): 198–212.

Li, Jack. "Commentary on Lamont's When Death Harms Its Victims." *Australasian Journal of Philosophy* 77 (1999): 349–57.

Long, A. A. "Roman Philosophy." Pp. 184–210 in *The Cambridge Companion to Greek and Roman Philosophy*, edited by David Sedley. Cambridge: Cambridge University Press, 2003.

Luper, Steven. "Mortal Harm." *The Philosophical Quarterly* 57 (2007): 239–51.

Miola, Robert S. "Julius Caesar and the Tyrannicide Debate." *Renaissance Quarterly* 38 (1985): 271–89.

Momigliano, Arnaldo. "Epicureans in Revolt." *The Journal of Roman Studies* 31 (1941): 149–57.

Palmer-Fernandez, Gabriel. "Justifying Political Assassination." *Journal of Social Philosophy* 31 (2000): 160–76.

Pelling, Christopher. "Plutarch on Caesar's Fall." Pp. 215–32 in *Plutarch and His Intellectual World*, edited by Judith Mossman. London: Duckworth & Co., 1997.

Ruben, David-Hillel. "A Puzzle About Posthumous Predication." *The Philosophical Review* 97 (1988): 211–36.

Sacharoff, Mark. "Suicide and Brutus' Philosophy in Julius Caesar." *Journal of the History of Ideas* 33 (1972): 115–22.

Schmidt, Peter L. "Cicero's Place in Roman Philosophy." *The Classical Journal* 74 (1978): 115–27.

Scott, Dominic. "Aristotle on Posthumous Fortune." *Oxford Studies in Ancient Philosophy* 18 (2000): 211–29.

Sedley, David. "The Ethics of Brutus and Cassius." *The Journal of Roman Studies* 87 (1997): 41–53.

Wiseman, T. P. "Book Review: *The Fall of the Roman Republic and Related Essays*." *The Classical Review* 40 (1990): 106–7.

Index

About the Author

Raymond Angelo Belliotti is SUNY Distinguished Teaching Professor of Philosophy at the State University of New York at Fredonia. He received his undergraduate degree from Union College in 1970, after which he was conscripted into the United States Army where he served three years in military intelligence units during the Vietnamese War. Upon his discharge, he enrolled at the University of Miami where he earned his Master of Arts degree in 1976 and Doctorate in 1977. After teaching stints at Florida International University and Virginia Commonwealth University, he entered Harvard University as a law student and teaching fellow. After receiving a Juris Doctorate from Harvard Law School, he practiced law in New York City with the firm of Barrett Smith Schapiro Simon & Armstrong. In 1984, he joined the faculty at Fredonia.

Belliotti is the author of nine other books: *Justifying Law* (1992); *Good Sex* (1993); *Seeking Identity* (1995); *Stalking Nietzsche* (1998); *What is the Meaning of Human Life?* (2001); *Happiness is Overrated* (2004); *The Philosophy of Baseball* (2006); *Watching Baseball Seeing Philosophy* (2008); and *Niccolò Machiavelli* (2009). *Good Sex* was later translated into Korean and published in Asia. *What is the Meaning of Human Life?* was nominated for the Society for Phenomenology and Existential Philosophy's Book of the Year Award. He has also published seventy articles and twenty-five reviews in the areas of ethics, jurisprudence, sexual morality, medicine, politics, education, feminism, sports, Marxism, and legal ethics. These essays have appeared in scholarly journals based in Australia, Canada, Great Britain, Italy, Mexico, South Africa, Sweden, and the United States. Belliotti has also made numerous presentations at philosophical conferences, including the Eighteenth World Congress of Philosophy in England, and has been honored as a featured lecturer on the Queen Elizabeth-2 ocean liner.

While at SUNY Fredonia he has served extensively on campus committees, as the Chairperson of the Department of Philosophy, as the Chairperson of the University Senate, and as Director of General Education. For six years he was faculty advisor to the undergraduate club, the Philosophical Society, and he has served that function for *Il Circolo Italiano*. Belliotti has been the recipient of the SUNY Chancellor's Award for Excellence in Teaching, the William T. Hagan Young Scholar/Artist Award, the Kasling Lecture Award for Excellence in Research and Scholarship, and the SUNY Foundation Research & Scholarship Recognition Award. He is also a member of the New York State *Speakers in the Humanities* Program.